STATE OF THE UNION

State of the Union

IAIN MCLEAN

and

ALISTAIR MCMILLAN

OXFORD
UNIVERSITY PRESS

OXFORD

UNIVERSITY PRESS

Great Clarendon Street, Oxford OX2 6DP

Oxford University Press is a department of the University of Oxford.
It furthers the University's objective of excellence in research, scholarship,
and education by publishing worldwide in

Oxford New York

Auckland Cape Town Dar es Salaam Hong Kong Karachi
Kuala Lumpur Madrid Melbourne Mexico City Nairobi
New Delhi Shanghai Taipei Toronto

With offices in

Argentina Austria Brazil Chile Czech Republic France Greece
Guatemala Hungary Italy Japan Poland Portugal Singapore
South Korea Switzerland Thailand Turkey Ukraine Vietnam

Oxford is a registered trade mark of Oxford University Press
in the UK and in certain other countries

Published in the United States
by Oxford University Press Inc., New York

British Library Cataloguing in Publication Data

Data available

Library of Congress Cataloging in Publication Data

Data available

Typeset by SPI Publisher Services, Pondicherry, India
Printed in Great Britain
on acid-free paper by
Biddles Ltd.
King's Lynn, Norfolk.

ISBN 0-19-925820-1   978-0-19-925820-8

1 3 5 7 9 10 8 6 4 2

PREFACE

This book arises from the Leverhulme Trust programme 'Nations and regions in the UK'. Our first debts are to the Leverhulme Trust for funding the programme; to Robert Hazell, director of the Constitution Unit, University College, London, the Programme Director; and to our programme colleagues both in the Leverhulme Trust programme and in the Economic & Social Research Council's parallel programme. Although we do not list them here, we are profoundly grateful to them. They know who they are, and they are probably thoroughly sick of late-night emails about Lord Cooper's speech in *MacCormick* v. *Lord Advocate*, Barnett consequentials and higher education, and similarly arcane subjects. We are also very grateful to the circle of civil servants, advisers, and think tanks in UK central government and the devolved administrations with whom we have discussed our ideas.

Oxford University Press have been supportive and tolerant. This has been an exciting and a time-consuming project for us, some aspects of which took on a life of their own. In particular, the Barnett formula and public finance threatened to become tales that wagged the dog. They are highly important and highly topical; and they came to take up more and more of our time over the lifetime of the Leverhulme project and beyond. But they are not the whole story of unionism. We have therefore hived off the specialist discussion of public finance, public economics, and public choice into a separate book (Iain McLean, *The Fiscal Crisis of the UK*, to be published by Palgrave in 2005). Enough remains about finance in this book, we hope, for its role in the story to be understood.

United Kingdom Unionism is dead, except in Northern Ireland. But from a period beginning around 1740 and ending in 1997, it was the ruling ideology of most leading politicians in the UK. The historical parts of the book try to recover and explain the lost ideology of Unionism; and the analytical parts examine the likely policy consequences of the death of Unionism.

Chapter 1, 'The United Kingdom as a Union State', elucidates the concept of a union state. The UK is not a unitary state because it depends on two constitutional contracts—the Acts of Union of 1707 and 1800. Therefore, UK Unionism is not like, for instance, French Jacobitism. The 1707 Acts (the plural is important—the union required Acts of both the Scottish and English Parliaments, which then were incorporated into the first Act of the Parliament of the UK) are still in force. Although most of Ireland left the

UK in 1921, the 1800 Act has profoundly affected UK politics. Northern Ireland is the relic of the 1800 Act.

But the UK is not a federal state either. Scotland and Northern Ireland do not have powers comparable to (say) an American, or even an Australian, State. Therefore UK Unionism is not like Australian anti-federalism. When there have been subordinate parliaments (Northern Ireland 1921–72 and intermittently since 1999; Scotland and Wales since 1999), the supremacy of Westminster has been asserted by statute (but can it be asserted in practice?). There is now a severe tension between the Diceyan concept of parliamentary sovereignty (for A.V. Dicey's personal and somewhat dubious role, see Chapters 4 and 5) and the reality on the ground. We introduce Brendan O'Leary's concept that Northern Ireland is a 'federacy', that is, a self-governing unit whose constitution must not be unilaterally altered by the UK government.

As England is the overwhelmingly dominant partner in the union state, English scholars, like the English population in general, have often been insensitive to these nuances. It is tempting to see England as simply the colonial oppressor of its three neighbours, getting by force the security or the economic advantage that it could not get by agreement. This picture fits Ireland reasonably well, Wales less well, and Scotland hardly at all. And even Ireland has always contained a substantial proportion of Unionists. It now contains the only remaining parties with Unionist in their titles. Unionist ideology, from 1707 to now, must be understood.

Chapters 2–5 each look at a critical moment for the Union. In 1707 and 1800, the Union expanded; in 1921 it contracted. In 1886, the Union's legitimacy was challenged and the arguments for and against Unionism articulated clearly for the first time—the key figures in this chapter being Dicey, Chamberlain, Gladstone, and Parnell. The motives and ideologies of those who wished to add or remove units, and of those who resisted change, of Unionists and anti-Unionists, at each juncture, are studied from primary and secondary sources.

Chapter 6, 'Ulster Unionism since 1921', examines how unionism has evolved in Northern Ireland since it unexpectedly and paradoxically found itself under that Home Rule which its leading politicians had raised a private army to prevent. Northern Ireland is the only part of the UK in which primordial unionism—that is, the belief that the Union is good in and for itself—survives. But even so, primordialism runs in different streams—military, religious, intellectual—whose waters scarcely mix.

Chapter 7, 'Unionism since 1961: Elite Attitudes', studies the evolution of these in all parties. On the Unionist side, it will show how some of the earlier props of Unionism fell away (interests of local economic elites; the Empire; anti-Catholicism outside Northern Ireland), while brute facts such as

Labour's dependence on its seats in Scotland and Wales became more important. Labour became a unionist party rather than a devolutionist party in the Beveridge era, when setting and maintaining national standards appeared paramount; its swing to devolution occurred in the 1960s and 1970s, most dramatically in the summer of 1974.

On the anti-Unionist side, the chapter charts the (very different) trajectories of the Scottish National Party, Plaid Cymru, and the factions of Irish nationalism, the growth of pro-devolution factions in other parties, and that of English regionalism in some (but not all) regions. 1961 is taken as the starting-point because it was the year of the West Lothian by-election in which the SNP first emerged as a credible force outside wartime. The chapter ends with the last ideologue of Unionism (Enoch Powell) and the last principled Unionist politician outside Ulster (John Major).

Chapter 8, 'Unionism since 1961: Mass Attitudes', assembles and analyses the survey information we have on this subject. This includes the survey of attitudes to the Union commissioned (and then ignored, because its findings were embarrassing) by the Kilbrandon Commission on the Constitution, 1973; private party polls in the swing year 1974; and British and Scottish Social Attitude and political surveys conducted in the 1990s and 2000s.

Chapter 9, 'Representation in a Union State', analyses what is now called the West Lothian Question (WLQ) after its persistent poser Tam Dalyell MP (formerly for West Lothian). The WLQ asks: Given partial devolution, why can an MP for a devolved territory become involved in devolved matters in England, but not in his own constituency? It has been said that 'the WLQ is not really a question: every time it is answered, Tam just waits for a bit and then asks it again'. But that merely shows what a persistently nagging question it has been since long before Tam Dalyell. In fact, it was sufficient (although not necessary) to bring down both of Gladstone's Home Rule Bills (1886 and 1893). The chapter shows how problematic are all the proposed solutions, especially when dealing with divided government where one UK-wide party controls a territory and the other controls the UK government. However, if devolution is to be stable, the governments and parties will have to live with the WLQ. New conventions for cohabitation will arise, and the UK and devolved party systems may diverge, even if party labels do not. The UK electorate treats everything except UK General Elections as second-order. This may already be changing. Canada may offer some helpful analogies.

Chapter 10, 'Public Finance in an Asymmetric Union', deals with the other chronic headache of the union state. In both the 1707 and 1800 Unions, a poor country was joined to a rich one, therefore the tax potential per head in the expanded Union declined. However, until the 1880s, governments spent money mostly on public goods, which did not raise the issue that taxes were raised in rich areas and spent in poor ones. Distributive politics of this sort began when governments started to spend money on schools and crofters—the 1870s and 1880s. The first public spending formula for the territories is due to Chancellor George Goschen in 1888. The formula that is current (although under great strain) as we write was devised by Chief Secretary Joel Barnett and his officials in 1978; Barnett himself now leads the calls for its reform (see Lords Hansard, 7 November 2001).

Chapter 11 reviews the evidence. It examines the policy implications of the weakening of Unionism. We consider the pressures on the Conservatives (historically the principled Unionist party, but whose advantage is now served by such centrifugal factors as the advantage of having PR elections in the devolved territories) and Labour (historically the party that has needed the Union for its centralist social policy, but which no longer needs Scottish and Welsh seats as much as it did).

Now we can return to our long-suffering families, to whom we give our love and our thanks.

IM
AM
Oxford, January 2005

CONTENTS

LIST OF TABLES

LIST OF FIGURES

1

The United Kingdom as a Union State

The United Kingdom is a very familiar concept, both to its inhabitants and to scholars and observers in the rest of the world. British schoolchildren do not formally have civics lessons. But everybody knows that the United Kingdom is a union of England, Wales, Scotland, and part of Ireland. The country's national flag, usually called the Union Jack, amalgamates the St George's Cross of England (an upright red cross on white) with the St Andrew's Cross of Scotland (a diagonal white cross on blue) and the St Patrick's Cross of Ireland (a diagonal red cross on white). Wales does not feature on the Union Jack because it was fully incorporated with England before the Unions with Scotland or Ireland got under way. The same symbolism appears in the Queen's Royal Standard, which is flown to mark where she is. With exquisite precision, the UK's royal website explains:

Since the Union of the Crowns in 1603, the composition of the Royal Standard has taken various forms. In today's Standard there are four quarterings—two for England (three lions passant), one for Scotland (a lion rampant) and one for Ireland (a harp). Wales is not represented in the Royal Standard, as its special position as a Principality was recognised by the creation of the Prince of Wales long before the incorporation of the quarterings for Scotland and Ireland in the Royal Arms. In Scotland a different version of the Royal Standard is used, with two Scottish quarterings instead of two English quarterings. (*http://www.royal.gov.uk/output/Page453.asp*) consulted on 16.3.04. (Not a lot of people know that last fact.)

Wales was unilaterally incorporated into England in 1536. It had never been a political unit. Eastern Wales, like eastern Ireland, had been governed by marcher lords licensed by English kings to control their western frontiers by whatever means they saw fit. But the writ of the barons of Ludlow or Montgomery never ran into northern and western Wales. Edward I conquered it and set up the massive castles at Caernarfon, Harlech, Beaumaris, and Conwy to keep the Welsh subdued. But Owain Glyndwr's revolt against English rule broke out in the early fifteenth century. Where Edward I had failed, Henry VIII, whose father had been a Welsh baron, succeeded. All institutions of separate Welshness disappeared, except the language and the culture. The Welsh language is still concentrated in the pockets of north and west Wales that Edward I found hardest to subdue.

The Union of the Crowns of Scotland and (the enlarged) England occurred in 1603, when King James VI of Scotland succeeded Queen Elizabeth (who had had his mother executed) as king of England, while retaining the throne of Scotland. To Scottish pedants, he was thereafter James VI and I. (And the present Queen should be Elizabeth II and I. When the Post Office introduced new postboxes monogrammed 'EII' to Scotland in 1952, some Scottish nationalists blew a few of them up). The parliaments of Scotland and England were joined by the Acts and Treaty of Union in 1707 to form the Government and Parliament of Great Britain. Those in turn joined the Parliament of Ireland in 1800 to form the UK, which took shape in 1801. However, this state was never popular in most of Ireland, which left after a civil war in 1921, leaving Northern Ireland to form one of the four compon-ents of the UK with England, Scotland, and Wales. This Union is the subject of this book – how and why it happened, how and why it contracted, and the ideologies of the pro- and anti-Union sides at each of the appropriate times.

But probe a little way and you find that what everyone thinks they know about the Union is decidedly fuzzy—especially in England. People in Eng-land have a lot of trouble with the nouns *England*, *Britain*, and *United Kingdom* and with the adjectives *English* and *British*. For a start, there are three nouns but only two adjectives—Tom Nairn's coinage *Ukanian* has never caught on. So, to start at Key Stage 1:

- The United Kingdom comprises England, Scotland, Wales, and Northern Ireland.
- (Great) Britain comprises England, Scotland, and Wales.
- Scotland, Wales, and Northern Ireland all have devolved governments (although the Northern Irish Assembly is suspended as we write this). England does not. The Government and Parliament of the UK double up as the Government and Parliament of England.
- The adjective 'British' should mean 'pertaining to England, Scotland, and Wales', although Northern Irish Unionists also tend to call themselves British; and the geographical expression *the British Isles* is deemed to include Ireland, the Channel Islands, and the Isle of Man.
- The adjective 'English' should only mean 'pertaining to England'.
- As there is no established adjective for 'pertaining to the United Kingdom', in this book we use 'UK' as an adjective, as in 'the UK government'.
- The adjective 'national' is profoundly ambiguous when used in the UK. For example, the Church of England and the Church of Scotland both see

themselves as national churches. When Scots church people use the phrase, the nation they mean is Scotland. When English church people use the phrase, their meaning is unclear.

If Archbishops and professors of political science[1] can muddle the distinction between England and Britain, so can everyone else, especially in England. Table 1.1 shows that people living in Scotland and Wales have a clearer sense of local identity than people living in England.

TABLE 1.1. *The Moreno question in Scotland, Wales, and England, 1992–2003*

	1992 %	1997 %	1999 %	2000 %	2001 %	2003 %	Unweighted means
Scotland:							
Scottish not British	19	23	32	37	36	31	29.7
More Scottish than British	40	38	35	31	30	34	34.7
Equally Scottish and British	33	27	22	21	24	22	24.8
More British than Scottish	3	4	3	3	3	4	3.3
British not Scottish	3	4	4	4	3	4	3.7
Other etc	1	2	3	4	4	5	3.2
Wales:							
Welsh		17	17		24	21	19.8
More Welsh		26	19		23	27	23.8
Equal		34	37		28	29	32.0
More British		10	8		11	8	9.3
British		12	14		11	9	11.5
Other etc		1	5		3	6	3.8
England:							
English not British		7	17	19	17	17	15.4
More English than British		17	15	14	13	19	15.6
Equally English and British		45	37	34	42	31	37.8
More British than English		14	11	14	9	13	12.2
British not English		9	14	12	11	10	11.2
Other etc		5	3	6	8	6	5.6

Source: National Centre for Social Research.

[1] Archbishops: see Carey 2002, where he argues that 'From the perspective of the Church of England, establishment helps to underwrite the commitment of a national church to serve the entire community and to give form and substance to some of its deepest collective needs and aspirations', citing 'national' celebrations and services of remembrance at Westminster Abbey. But the victims of the 1966 Aberfan disaster were denied a memorial service there on the grounds that 'the Welsh Church is disestablished and has no claim on Westminster Abbey' (McLean and Johnes 2000: 224); and Carey's predecessor as Archbishop of Canterbury in 1953 would not offer communion there to the Moderator of the General Assembly of the Church of Scotland during

Table 1.1 and Figure 1.1 track answers over time to the so-called Moreno question since it was first put to survey respondents in the three countries of Great Britain. The Moreno question, named after the Spanish social scientist who first proposed it, asks respondents.

Do you feel yourself to be:

• [Local identity] and not British;
• More [local identity] than British;
• Equally [local identity] and British;
• More British than [local identity]; or
• British and not [local identity]?

where [local identity] stands for Scottish, Welsh, or English as appropriate. The trends in identification are easier to track on a chart than in a table of numbers. Figure 1.1. therefore gives them as a time series, with '*x* and not *y*' grouped with 'more *x* than *y*'.

Of the three territories, Scotland is the most nationalistic. Sixty per cent or more of those living in Scotland think of themselves as either Scottish and not British, or more Scottish than British. This proportion rose slightly when the Scottish Parliament was created, but has drifted down a small (perhaps insignificant) amount. In Wales, where the question was not asked in 2000, there seems again to have been a 'devolution bounce' in feeling Welsh. Given that the Welsh only just voted for their Assembly whereas the Scots voted convincingly for theirs, it is not surprising that the 'more or wholly Welsh' line lies below the 'more or wholly Scottish' line, nor that any devolution bounce came more recently in Wales. In England, the most popular response has been 'equally English and British', although in the 2003 survey, the response 'more English than British' has overtaken it. Some see a growth of far right, xenophobic, identifications as lying behind such a change. We doubt it. The far right party, after all, calls itself the *British*, not the English, National Party. Xenophobia of the far right was indeed directed against the Scots and the Irish in past centuries, but is now directed against people of Asian and African origin.

The Moreno question has not been asked in Northern Ireland. However, the ethnic self-identification of Northern Irish people is well known. Nationalists (mainly Catholics) identify themselves as 'Irish'—they would be quite confused if they did anything else. Unionists (mainly Protestants) identify themselves as 'British' and/or 'Ulster'.

the Coronation of Queen Elizabeth II [and I]. Professors of political science: Rose's standard textbook (1989) has always been called *Politics in England*, even though Professor Rose has always been one of the foremost scholars of multinational statehood in the UK (cf. Rose 1982).

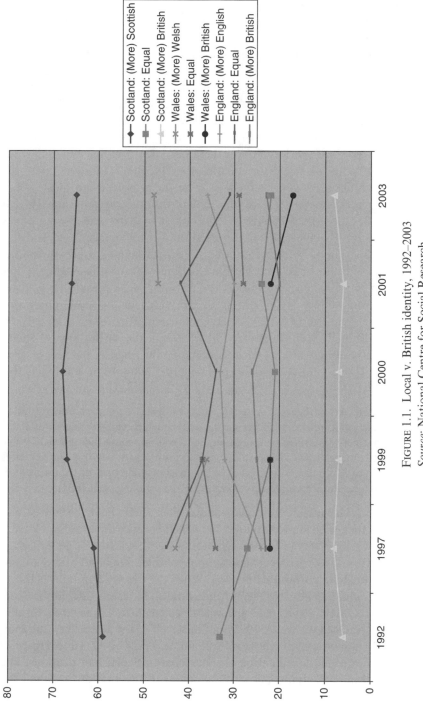

FIGURE 1.1. Local *v.* British identity, 1992–2003
Source: National Centre for Social Research.

Thus the United Kingdom is a multinational state, whose citizens feel many overlapping identities. Some of them, especially in Scotland and Northern Ireland, reject the label 'British' altogether. Other multinational or multi-ethnic democracies are mostly federal states—for example Canada and Switzerland. But the UK is not a federal state. In a federal state the Constitution fixes the powers of each order of government, and each order has sovereignty in the matters that the Constitution assigns to it. The federal government cannot interfere in state (provincial, cantonal) affairs, nor vice versa.

Nor is the UK a unitary state. The most unitary of the large democracies is France, where since the Revolution there has been a nation-building tradition. Some political scientists call this the 'Jacobin' tradition, after the ardent revolutionaries who wanted to bring the remotest and most priest-ridden village, as they saw it, into the ambit of the one and indivisible French Republic. Because the Jacobins were strongest in Paris and their enemies strongest in the provinces, Jacobin radicalism was remorselessly centralist.

There is a strain of Jacobin centralism in British politics, especially on the left. But during the French revolution, Jacobin centralism was already impossible in the UK, because there were institutions to prevent the central executive from simply giving orders to everybody in the land. There was already one treaty and two Acts of Union, and there would shortly be another. Although politicians often forget them, the institutions of union by treaty have always existed in the UK since 1707.

So if the UK is neither a federal nor a unitary state, what is it? The label 'union state' was coined by Rokkan and Urwin (1982: 11):

The union state [is] not the result of straightforward dynastic conquest. Incorporation of at least parts of its territory has been achieved through personal dynastic union, for example by treaty, marriage or inheritance. Integration is less than perfect. While administrative standardization prevails over most of the territory, the consequences of personal union entail the survival in some areas of pre-union rights and institutional infrastructures which preserve some degree of regional autonomy.

Rokkan and Urwin, a Norwegian and a Scot, may have been wistfully thinking of the union state that never happened because the Maid of Norway died in 1290 on her way to becoming queen of Scotland. But Great Britain as it evolved from 1707 fits their description perfectly. England and Scotland were dynastically incorporated in 1603. When the dynastic union was threatened by the childlessness of Queen Anne, English ministers offered the Scots a Treaty of Union. What emerged was codified in the Acts (the plural is important—see MacCormick 1998) of Union 1707. By those Acts, the integration of England and Scotland is less than perfect. The Acts and Treaty of Union guarantee the continuation of some separate Scottish institutions. The administration of Scotland was never assimilated with that of England.

The Union with Ireland was more unequal. Although the Irish Parliament voted itself out of existence in 1800 in exchange for membership of an enlarged UK, the Irish failed to achieve the terms they expected because King George III vetoed Catholic emancipation. The leaders of Catholic Ireland never regarded the Union as legitimate. As with Scotland, the administrative integration of Ireland was less than perfect. In contrast to Scotland, however, neither was its political integration. The election of a bloc of MPs from the Irish Party, beginning in 1874, meant that devolution to Ireland would be forced on to the UK political agenda as soon as the Irish party came to hold the balance of power. That first happened at the General Election of 1885. Immediately afterwards, W. E. Gladstone announced his momentous conversion to Home Rule. However, the pivotal position of the Irish Party meant that whoever governed the UK would have to consider loosening the tie with Ireland. The Government of Ireland Bills of 1893 and 1912 passed in the elected House of Commons, but failed in the unelected House of Lords, and were obstructed by the unelected Queen Victoria and King George V. Irish independence, when it came, came violently in 1921, but left behind what is now Northern Ireland in the UK. The resurgence of separatism in Scotland and Wales began in the 1960s. After a false dawn in the 1970s, all three territories[2] outside England obtained devolved governments in the late 1990s.

This tightening and loosening of the Union is the subject of this book. The UK is almost the ideal type of the union state, although the concept has been applied to other states including Spain and Canada. That it results from a union is fundamental to its 'unwritten' constitution, to its politics, religion, society, and administration. Yet that is something that English intellectuals have for three centuries found rather easy to forget.

The clearest recent exposition is in Neil MacCormick's brilliant British Academy lecture on *The English Constitution, the British State, and the Scottish Anomaly* (MacCormick 1998). He chooses his adjectives with care. The Acts and Treaty of 1707 created the British state. Does that make them fundamental legislation, unrepealable short of the dissolution of the British state? In 1707, the English Unionist propagandist, spy, and novelist Daniel Defoe thought so:

[N]othing is more plain than that the articles of the Treaty . . . cannot be touched by the Parliament of Britain; and that the moment they attempt it, they dissolve their own Constitution; so it is a Union upon no other terms, and is expressly stipulated what shall, and what shall not, be alterable by the subsequent Parliaments. And, as the Parliaments of Great Britain are founded, not upon the original right of the

---

[2] The dry term used by the Treasury when it operates their formula funding. It avoids all argument as to whether they are countries, nations, parts of nations, provinces, and so on.

people, as the separate Parliaments of England and Scotland were before, but upon the Treaty which is prior to the said Parliament, and consequently superior; so, for that reason, it cannot have power to alter its own foundation, or act against the power which formed it, since all constituted power is subordinate, and inferior to the power constituting. (Defoe 1786: 246, quoted by MacCormick 1998: xx)

The English doctrine of parliamentary sovereignty holds that Defoe was wrong. Its high priest was A. V. Dicey, Vinerian Professor of English Law at Oxford University and author of a standard textbook first published in 1885 and still in print. Dicey argued that:

Neither the Act of Union with Scotland nor the Dentists Act, 1878, has more claim than the other to be considered a supreme law. Each embodies the will of the sovereign legislative power; each can be legally altered or repealed by Parliament; neither tests the validity of the other. Should the Dentists Act, 1878, unfortunately contravene the terms of the Act of Union, the Act of Union would be *pro tanto* repealed .... The one fundamental dogma of English [sic] constitutional law is the absolute legislative sovereignty or despotism of the King in Parliament. But this dogma is incompatible with the existence of a fundamental compact, the provisions of which control every authority existing under the constitution. (Dicey 1885: 141)

Dicey assumes that the Parliament of Great Britain that began in 1707 continues the Parliament, traditions, and common law of England, not those of Scotland, and is not a fresh start. Hence 'English constitutional law'—whether the phrase is careless or careful—in the extract just quoted. If Dicey were right and Defoe wrong, then the UK would be a unitary state. In this book we aim to show that Dicey (both the man and his doctrine) is self-contradictory and therefore cannot be right. That does not mean that Defoe must be right, but it warrants our labelling the UK as a union state.

On this, political scientists, and a few Scots constitutional lawyers (canonically Smith 1957), have dissented from historians, most legal scholars, and even parliamentary draftsmen. The former insist on what MacCormick calls 'the Scottish anomaly'—viz. that the Treaty of Union was a Treaty, which preserved distinctive Scottish institutions including the notion of popular (rather than Parliamentary) sovereignty. The latter have espoused Diceyan principles as recently as in the Scotland and Wales Acts 1998, which affirm the supremacy of the United Kingdom Parliament over everything in Scotland and Wales. Diceyan lawyers point out that some clauses of the Act of Union 1707 have been repealed by the ordinary procedure of the occasional Statute Law Reform Acts. There is no entrenchment of the 1707 Act as there is of the Constitutions of the United States or of the Commonwealth of Australia. On Diceyan doctrine, therefore, the Scotland and Wales Acts 1998 are indeed as repealable as the Dentists Act 1878. Political science says differently. Devolution to Scotland was, in John Smith's sonorous phrase, 'the settled will of the Scottish people'. Devolution to Wales was a very unsettled will indeed, being agreed only at the last gasp in the last county to report in the 1997 referendum there. Yet even in Wales it will not go away. Politicians and lobbyists have adapted to it. The party that campaigned most fervently against devolution—the Conservatives—now accept it as a fait accompli even in Wales. They have gained representation in both countries that they would not otherwise have had.

This book therefore takes the side of political science and Scots constitutional law against that of Dicey and English constitutional law. It explores the implications of taking that stand. What does it mean to say that the United Kingdom is a union state, brought together by the successful treaty of 1707 and the unsuccessful Act of Union of 1800? To answer this, the succeeding chapters look at each event of Union and disunion, and at the ideology of Unionism and of resistance to the Union at each juncture. We show that the central mysteries of the Union—representation and finance—cannot be solved in a unitary state. They could be solved quite easily were the UK to become a federation. If it is to remain a union state, they will remain very tricky.

Similar but not identical issues apply in Northern Ireland to Scotland. The Government of Ireland Act 1920, which became Northern Ireland's constitution, contains in the rousingly Diceyan s.75 the assertion that 'the supreme authority of the Parliament of the United Kingdom shall remain unaffected and undiminished over all persons, matters, and things in Ireland and every part thereof'. The Northern Ireland Act 1998, which repealed the 1920 Act, nevertheless retained in s.5 (6) a statement of UK parliamentary sovereignty, which has already been asserted in two suspensions of the Northern Ireland Assembly since then.

As explained later, the persons, matters, and things in what is now the Republic of Ireland had other ideas, leading to the Treaty and creation of the Irish Free State in 1921. The 1937 constitution of the Free State, which became the Republic of Ireland in 1949, asserts a claim to sovereignty over Northern Ireland. That claim has been weakened as part of the Good Friday Agreement of 1998. A referendum in the Irish Republic overwhelmingly agreed changes to the country's constitution from irredentist to aspirational—from bald statements that Northern Ireland was part of the national territory to the aspiration that it may one day become so. The consultative institutions created in 1998 make Northern Ireland, according to O'Leary (2002), a 'federacy'. By this he means not only that each government recognizes the other's interest in Northern Ireland, but that both the UK and Irish governments have agreed that the people of Ireland, including northern Ireland, have the right to self-determination. This acknowledgement sits awkwardly with parliamentary sovereignty, as we shall revisit in the

Conclusion. In 1998 the UK and Irish governments created a set of joint bodies to discuss Northern Irish and cross-border issues. Should the majority of people in Northern Ireland express a wish to leave the UK and join the Irish Republic, the UK government (and the vast majority of the people of Great Britain) will be only too happy to see them go. Unquestionably, therefore, Northern Ireland is not part of a unitary state. It is a near-federal part of a union state.

The British Empire looms behind most of the history in this book. From the beginning, the Union and the Empire were inextricably entangled. One reason for the Scots' accession in 1707 was the failure of the Scottish Darien Company, which led some Scottish politicians to decide that a Scottish empire alongside the English empire was unachievable. The Scottish and Ulster-Scot[3] contribution to the later British empires (especially America in the eighteenth century and India in the nineteenth) bound Scots and Ulster Protestants of all classes to the Union. The upper classes could govern the empire; the lower classes could emigrate (think of Kipling's India). The connection was much weaker in Catholic Ireland. Although millions of Catholic Irish people emigrated to countries of the empire, most of them did not thank the British for the opportunity.

By 1886, the government of Ireland had become partly an imperial question. It tested how much unionism could incorporate different cultures. Could there be an Imperial Parliament as opposed to a British Parliament? How would the Irish be represented in it if they were to have local institutions as well? Any answer to this question had heavy implications for the rest of the empire, especially India.

The end of the British Empire threatened Unionism. Europe has had mixed effects. Anti-Unionists, initially uninterested or sceptical, came to see a 'Europe of the regions' as a platform. Unionists were divided. Eurosceptics tended to see Europe as a threat to the Union; Europhile Unionists saw the European internal market as an extension of the UK internal market.

But above all, the end of the empire imperilled the ideology and weakened the glue of barely articulated *popular* Unionism. From the failure of the 1745 Jacobite rebellion onwards, politicians tried to construct a popular imperial unionism, in which the people of Britain could become the soldiers (and later the traders and administrators) of the empire. Colley (1996) and other historians have traced this process—the making of Britain and of Britons— through the late eighteenth and early nineteenth centuries. The *Oxford*

---

[3] The useful American term 'Ulster-Scots' should become better known in the UK. It denotes those settlers whose ancestors had come originally from Scotland, had settled in Northern Ireland during the seventeenth-century Protestant plantations there, and whose more recent ancestors had moved on again to the eastern seaboard of the USA and the Appalachian mountains. They played a prominent role in early US politics.

English Dictionary, here reflecting its original compilation in the third quarter of the nineteenth century, is revealing. The relevant definition there of the noun 'Briton' is:

Since the union of England and Scotland: A native of Great Britain, or of the British Empire; much used in the 18th c.; now chiefly in poetic, rhetorical, or melodramatic use, and in phrases dating to the 'Rule Britannia' period, as 'to work like a Briton', 'as tough as a Briton', etc. *North Briton*: a Scotchman. *(OED* Online, s.v. 'Briton', definition A.1.c)

The defining quotations are 'Britons never will be slaves' (from *Rule Britannia*, 1740) and 'I glory in the name of Briton' (George III, 1760). The Victorian compilers, however, failed to notice, or to care, that the Scots never called themselves *North Britons*[4] (and rarely *Scotchmen*). Even in the land where Britons never would be slaves, there were local sensitivities that the English might fail to notice.

One of us (IM) is old enough to have been at school in North Britain when the map on the wall was still mostly pink; and his schoolboy stamp collection, partly inherited from his father, was restricted to the British Empire. In the 1950s the largest trading partner of the UK was Australia (population 10 million). So completely has that world vanished that the reader needs to know that it persisted until the UK's first attempt to join the European Common Market in 1961. It formed the glue of popular unionism. Now that it has gone, so has popular unionism outside Northern Ireland. The consequences of that disappearance are profound. This book attempts to say what they are.

---

[4] Except for the North British Railway—but that was originally promoted by Englishmen. The last relic of the title, the glorious Edwardian North British Station Hotel in Edinburgh, is now the Balmoral.

2

The Union of Westminster and Edinburgh Parliaments, 1707

There is nocht tua nations vndir the firmament that ar mair contrar and different fra vthirs nor is Inglismen and Scottismen, quhoubeit that thai be within ane ile and nychtbours and of ane langage. For Inglismen ar subtil and Scottismen ar humain in prosperite. Inglismen ar humil quhen thai ar subieckit be forse and violence, and Scottismen ar furius quhen thai ar violently subiekit. Inglismen ar cruel quhen thai get victorie, and Scottismen art merciful quhen thai get victorie. And to conclude, it is onpossibil that Scottismen and Inglismen can remane in concord vndir ane monarche or ane prince, because there naturis and conditions ar as indefferent as is the nature of scheip and woluis'.

(Complaynt of Scotland, from *c*.1549, Pryde 1950: 3)

The motives will be, Trade with most, Hanover with some, ease and security with others, together with a generall aversion to civill discords, intollerable poverty and . . . constant oppression.

(Earl of Roxburgh,[1] a member of the *Squadrone Volante*[2] in 1706; Whatley 1989: 153)

Statesmen or Rogues: Traditional Interpretations and a New Alternative

The history of the Union of Scotland with England and Wales of 1707 has been extensively recounted, and contentiously recast. For Diceyans it was an act of supreme statesmanship, cementing the political and geographical basis from which the British Empire could be consolidated. For Scottish nationalists it was a betrayal, rooted in corruption and the subsumation of Scottish

---

[1] Brief descriptions of the main actors are in the Appendix, 'Principal Characters'.

[2] The *Squadrone Volante* ('Flying Squadron') of members of the last Scottish Parliament switched position from an anti-English to a pro-Union stance over the life of the Scottish Parliament of 1703 to 1707. They were 'distinguished by a "presbyterian" religious tinge, and a record of commitment to principles of civil liberty and parliamentary independence' (Hayton 1996: 86). Hayton suggests that their support for union was driven by a close tactical alliance with the English Whig Junto.

interests to English[3] expansionism. In the nationalist imagery immortalized by Robert Burns, 'We're bought and sold for English gold—Such a parcel of rogues in a nation!' Namierite historians share the Scottish nationalist analysis without the poetry. Other views stress the advantage of a union as a free-trade area, and the Scots' need to recoup the losses from their disastrous Darien expedition. None of these adequately recognizes that the Treaty of Union was a true treaty from which both sides gained, but both made concessions. Union did involve a strengthening and consolidation of the parliamentary sovereignty based at Westminster, but also entrenched the Scottish Presbyterian church, and established a unified trading, financial, and military system that had advantages for the political establishments in both London and Edinburgh.

We analyse, for the first time, the flow of votes in the last Scottish Parliament to show that none of the traditional explanations of the Union are correct. The Earl of Roxburgh was a better guide than Dicey, Namier, or Burns. The key issues were trading relations; the succession of the monarchy (a politico-religious question); and the military situation.

The issue of the trading relations between Scotland and the British economy was presented at the time, and in more recent accounts, as a balance between the security of protection and the possibility of a free-trade area that would allow greater benefits for all. A weakened Scottish economy was strengthened by closer political links with the booming English trading society. The humiliation of the failed Darien venture,[4] which squandered Scottish capital and exposed the Crown's disinterest in Scottish affairs, was exchanged for a united trading empire that the Scots were able to exploit. Whilst recognizing the general effect of such arguments, our analysis is more focused on the particular benefits that the Union brought to parliamentarians in the Edinburgh and London Parliaments.

The succession of the monarchy was a focus for the opponents of the Union in Scotland, who responded to the Act of Settlement passed in Westminster in 1701—asserting the Hanoverian succession across Britain—with their own

[3] The uniting territories were England & Wales and Scotland. Therefore we prefer to refer to the Westminster, rather than the English, Parliament. However, given Wales' peripheral position in the English and Welsh state, we often refer for brevity and with little loss of accuracy to English interests.

[4] The Darien venture involved two expeditions to central America, which sought to establish a colony opening up trade from the Far East, as well as the Americas. The first expedition sailed in July 1698, with some 1,200 colonists, but was devastated by illness, and failed to establish a habitable community at 'New Edinburgh'. The settlement was abandoned in June 1699. A second expedition was dispatched before news of the failure of the first had reached Scotland, and encountered a Spanish military force that defeated the Scots. Darien was abandoned by the Scots in April 1700. For the history of the Company of Scotland and the Darien scheme see Barbour (1907); Insh (1932); Fry (2001): ch. 2; Devine (2003: ch. 2).

Act of Security, which reserved the Scottish Parliament's right to choose the monarch. This challenged the legacy of the 1603 union of the crowns under James VI and I, and the sovereignty of the British Isles. This debate exposed the complex relationship between the role of the state, the balance between monarchy and parliament, and the association of crown and religion. The battles of the seventeenth century, and the English settlement through the Glorious Revolution of 1688, had a different resonance in Scotland, where the accession of William was shorn of its episcopal association. The acceptance of William had been associated with the establishment of the Presbyterian Church, but the Glencoe massacre,[5] the Darien escapade, and the obstinacy of the London court had since undermined Scottish allegiance to the Crown.

Religious issues were vital. In the seventeenth century, Presbyterians and Catholics had attacked the Stuarts' Anglican monarchy from opposite sides. There were no Anglicans to speak of in Scotland. Therefore the Crown had to choose the lesser of two evils to be its Scottish ally. The association between the Crown and Scottish Presbyterian interests made their Jacobite[6] enemies opponents of the Union. 'Such a parcel of rogues in a nation' is a Jacobite ballad (real, or invented by Burns). Under Queen Anne, who cherished her ties to the Church of England, the issue of succession could unite Jacobites with those who sought to assert a Scottish regal line, but balked at a Catholic (i.e., Jacobite) succession. The succession provides a cross-cutting cleavage in parliamentary politics that explains much of the failure of an alternative constitutional settlement, in both the Westminster and Edinburgh Parliaments.

Roxburgh's 'ease and security' relates to military discord. The military situation at the time of Union was fraught, with a war against France. In the previous French war the Jacobites had attacked the new English regime in both Scotland and Ireland, with French support. England needed to secure its north and west frontiers, with troops based in Northumberland and Ireland poised to march. Scottish troops were diffused amongst the different armies campaigning at the time, but the possibilities of another Cromwellian

---

[5] In February 1692, on orders sanctioned by William III and his Scottish ministers, a regiment whose colonel was the Duke of Argyll massacred MacIain, the leader of the Macdonalds of Glencoe, and about thirty-eight of the clan, for MacIain's alleged refusal to take a loyalty oath to King William, which in fact he had taken, albeit late. The Macdonalds were Catholics, and the regime suspected all the highland Catholic clans of Jacobitism. The regiment had been the guests of the Macdonalds before the massacre.

[6] *Jacobite*: supporter of (the Catholic) King James (Latin *Jacobus*) II, deposed in 1689, and of his descendants James Stuart ('The Old Pretender') and Charles James Stuart ('Bonnie Prince Charlie', 'The Young Pretender'. The Jacobite Risings of 1715 and 1745 were failed attempts to restore James, the 'Old Pretender', to the throne; his son Charles came to Scotland to be the figurehead of the 1745 rebellion.

invasion of Scotland were slight. The English knew that military conquest of Scotland was expensive and dubious. Cromwell had succeeded, but Edward I and Charles I had failed. The Union offered a bulwark against a Jacobite invasion; more importantly it offered a military consolidation. When Jacobite invasions did come in 1715 and 1745, unitary military command made them easier to contain than they would have been without union.

On the other side, the leading Scottish opponent of Union, Andrew Fletcher of Saltoun, sought a system of security based on militias raised at the regional level, rather than a united army that would be at the command of the monarch. Fletcher's challenge to a unified military force was part of an alternative to an incorporating union that failed to gain support.

We go beyond Roxburgh to emphasize finance and representation. The financial weakness of the Scottish establishment opened them up to the prospect of patronage and bribery to an extent to which they were not willing to resist. The incorporating Union of 1707 allowed a consolidation of the Whig interest in the expanded state, as well as an expansion of a developing military–financial infrastructure, which tied parliamentary limitation of the Crown to a more stable form of administrative finance. This approach has two advantages: first, it explains why the Westminster Parliament was willing to promote union as a policy, second, why the Scottish legislature was happy to forfeit notional independence for a role in Westminster.

The fact that a majority of the Scottish Parliament was willing to vote itself out of existence, trading short-term patronage for a subordinate role in a London-centred system, suggests a fundamental weakness in the operation of the Scottish state in the run-up to the Union. However, one reason Westminster politicians were willing to accept an incorporating union (which had been resisted a number of times since the union of crowns in 1603) was that the expression of Scottish interests through the Edinburgh Parliament had been seen to be an effective challenge to English and Welsh interests. After the accession of King William, which had been independently endorsed by the Scottish establishment, the Edinburgh Parliament became more assertive in its right to develop its own political programmes that were not necessarily in accordance with those of the sovereign or the Westminster Parliament. This conflict between the apparent weakness of the Edinburgh Parliament and the apparent strength of its challenge to the operating constitutional framework is critical to our narrative.

Whereas the necessities of financing military and trading operations had led the London government to widen the tax base and improve its yield, the Scottish government had been hindered by economic stagnation and administrative weakness. This meant that Scottish control over revenue and patronage was limited: 'finance was the Scottish government's most glaring weakness' (Ferguson 1977: 202–3). Incorporating Union was one solution to this situation, but it was not the only one. However, there was no great support for the status quo as a viable method for the continuance of government. Whilst Andrew Fletcher developed a public policy that involved a radical reworking of constitutional and governmental relations between London and Edinburgh, his views were not embraced by the aristocratic establishment in Scotland. The failure of opponents of an incorporating union to develop a coherent alternative undermined their attempts to prevent a constitutional restructuring favoured by Queen Anne, the Westminster Parliament, and a significant body of Scottish politicians.[7] Whilst there is little doubt that popular opinion in Scotland was opposed to the Union (and English and Welsh popular opinion apparently indifferent), the attempt to mobilize on a wider basis was hindered by the concessions offered to the Presbyterian church interest.

The Union was carried out in the aftermath of the romantically conceived but disastrous Darien expedition, which was supposed to establish the basis of a Scottish Empire. This followed the Glencoe massacre of 1692 and subsequent inquiry of 1695, and undermined the faith that had been placed in the joint monarchy of King William. Relations between the parliaments in London and Edinburgh were set on collision course partly as a result of the slow arrival of the news of Marlborough's great victory at Blenheim, in 1704.[8] The Union was a solution to the ongoing debate over sovereignty, religion and the state, the role and organization of the army, and the nature of political representation. The case was argued by some of the most colourful characters of the period. Daniel Defoe was sent to Scotland as a pro-Union propagandist, and William Paterson, founder of the Bank of England and driving force behind the Darien venture, also campaigned for the Union. The anti-Union campaign in Edinburgh was led by Fletcher of Saltoun, renowned for both his political radicalism and violent temperament.

The Act of Union was, according to the doyen of Unionism, A. V. Dicey, 'one of the wisest Acts ever placed on the statute book' (Dicey [1915] 1982: lxxix). He saw the Union as the foundation of British military success, and an act of great statesmanship, its benefit shown by the failure of any move to repeal. For Dicey it was also a prime example of a conflict between a wise decision and a popular one: in England the measure received little general

---

[7] Robertson (1994: 242) outlines the two main alternatives to an incorporating union: the Jacobite option, which would see a Stuart restoration under French protection, and Fletcher's proposal of a confederal union under a limited monarchy.

[8] Godolphin advised the Queen to give her assent to the Scottish Act of Security in order to gain supply required to pay the army, which was already delayed, and seen as imperative in the light of the threat of a French invasion. Queen Anne assented to the Act on 5 August 1704, without knowing that three days earlier Marlborough had beaten the French army at Blenheim (Riley 1964: 7–8).

acclaim, and in Scotland it was greeted with widespread hostility. The Union stood, therefore, as a warning to the sensible and patriotic Englishman against a constitution that allowed the predominance of the popular over the wise (Dicey [1915] 1982: cxix). According to the economic historian, T. C. Smout, the Union was a stage in the Scottish assimilation into a wider Britain, a consequence of a trade-off between, on the one side, political stability and access to a common domestic and imperial market, and, on the other side, the loss of a sovereign Scottish Parliament (Smout 1969*a*: Ch. 9). For both Dicey and Smout, the Scottish Parliament had failed to effectively assert the powers it had secured after the Williamite succession of 1689.[9] The Union represented a sharing of sovereignty, entrenching a British national interest in a constitutional framework that promoted political stability, military strength, and economic development.

The Diceyan view of Union as an act of Statesmanship, carried through the storm of popular dissent so as to promote the British interest, has been most vehemently challenged by Ferguson (1964 and 1977). For Ferguson the Union was an inglorious 'political job', carried out under English pressure to consolidate the Hanoverian succession, and facilitated by the machinations of the Scottish political elite, lubricated by generous bribes from England. Most recent work on the passage of the Union has focussed on the reasons for the Scottish acceptance of the measure. The transformation, from the Anglophobe parliamentary sessions of 1703 and 1704 to the sweeping majorities of 1706, when the Parliament voted itself out of existence, has proved a focus of attention. Such attention is rewarded by a rich seam of personal accounts and a detailed record of voting behaviour in the Parliament. The English side of the story has received less thorough attention, partly because the passage of the Act of Union was relatively smooth, and, in any case, no roll-calls remain showing detailed voting behaviour. However, here again there is a story of a change in attitudes towards Parliamentary Union, which had been strongly opposed after the Union of the Crowns in 1603, and allowed to wither after the Cromwellian Union. How did the Act pass through Westminster with such serenity, when similar measures had previously attracted the objections of the trading interest and aroused 'a maelstrom of prejudice in which the Scots were eclectically damned as beggars, thieves and murderers' (Ferguson 1977: 102–3)?

For an explanation of the causal factors that underpinned the Act of Union we step back and look at Roxburgh's issues of trade, sovereignty,

---

[9] Dicey and Rait (1920: 72) suggest that, despite the powers asserted under the 1689 Claim of Right, 'the Scottish Parliament never won for itself the heart of the Scottish people'. This was largely attributed to the competing strength of the Kirk, which provided a forum for popular participation and civic influence. Smout (1969: 217) argues that the Scottish Parliament was unable to free itself from the influence of the Crown and London.

and military power at the time, and alternative constitutional structures proposed during the debate over an incorporating union. We conclude by examining the issues of finance and representation, and discuss their relevance to the acceptance of the abolition of the Edinburgh Parliament and the acceptance of an incorporating union.

The Scottish Parliament and the Crisis of Anglo-Scottish Relations

The fortunes and powers of the Scottish Parliament during the seventeenth century had waxed and waned in counterbalance to the strength of the monarch. At the Union of the Crowns the Parliament had little power. James VI and I commented that 'Here I sit and governe it [Scotland] with my pen, I write and it is done, and by a Clearke of the Councell I governe Scotland now, which others could not do by the sword' (Rait 1901: 101–2). From 1641 to 1650 Scotland was ruled by the Scottish Parliament, in conjunction with the National Assembly of the Presbyterian Church. Cromwell's victory saw a short-lived 'union', under which the Government of Scotland was neither ecclesiastical nor civil, but martial. The Edinburgh Parliament agreed to the union, 'once again because it was ordered to do so' (Rait 1901: 106). During this period, free trade with England was established, and feudality abolished. After the Restoration, the Parliament was again reduced to subservience, and dominance of the King and the episcopalian establishment reasserted: 'Between 1660 and 1689 the Scottish Parliament was once more the merest instrument for official sanction' (Rait 1901: 107).

The Scottish Parliament welcomed William's accession. As in England, a pact between King and Parliament extinguished the old claims of divine right. But it was a different pact. The acceptance of William and Mary in Scotland was formalized, through the Claim of Right and the Articles of Grievances, in a way that entrenched Scottish parliamentary authority (Mitchison 1983: 115–19). The Church of Scotland leader William Carstares promoted the establishment of the Scottish Convention, which met in Edinburgh in March 1689, and legitimized the accession of William to the Scottish throne (Dunlop 1967: 65–73). His influence over William eased the passage of the Act Ratifying the Confession of Faith and Settling Presbyterian Church Government, 7 June 1690. The General Assembly reaffirmed, in 1698, the independence of the Church from the state, declaring that 'Jesus Christ is the only Head and King of his Church' (see Goldie 1996: 234). In return the powers of the Parliament were strengthened by the abolition of the Lords of the Articles, the Parliamentary committee through which the Crown's executive authority had been exercised, and the removal of the estate of the bishops (Devine 2003: 50). From 1695 the Crown sought to control Parliament through a system of 'management' by which patronage was directed through a network of groups centred around powerful aristocratic politicians. However, the coherence of the Scottish administration was undermined by factional competition between the supporters of the prominent aristocratic leaders.

The last Scottish Parliament, which sat between 1703 and 1707, has been charged with first asserting Scottish autonomy, and finally and terminally betraying it. The initial confrontations with London were due to three issues that highlighted the subordination of Scottish to English politics. First, the Act of Settlement[10] passed by the Westminster Parliament in 1701 seemed to override Scottish authority over sovereignty and regal succession in Scotland. Second, the delay in calling a parliament in Edinburgh was seen as a challenge to Scottish parliamentary authority.[11] Third, the declaration of war against France in May 1702 was done without consultation with the Scottish Parliament, contravening the 1696 Act of Security (Brown 1992: 177).[12] The Scottish Parliament responded to what were seen as anti-Scottish policies that originated in London with a hostile and assertive programme, emphasizing Scottish interests over the succession, trade, and military affairs. The parliamentary session of 1703 has been lauded as the clarion call of Scottish independence, which rallied against English domination and sought an alternative to the subservience of Scottish politics to the interests of the London court. However, the same members of the Edinburgh Parliament that successfully pressed this anti-English agenda voted, within three years, to pass an Act of parliamentary union that removed all legislative power to London.

The Edinburgh Parliament was a unicameral body, with the three estates of nobles, barons (shire representatives), and burgh representatives, voting together in Parliament House.[13] Votes were held with a clerk reading out the roll of members, and each member present giving his vote individually and aloud (Ditchfield et al. 1995: 140). Key votes were recorded in the *Acts of the Parliament of Scotland*, alongside lists of voters drawn up by those present.

---

[10] This stated that, in the absence of any natural heirs of Anne, the succession should pass to Sophia, Electress of Hanover (granddaughter of James VI and I), and her issue. The measure was passed after Anne's last surviving child, the Duke of Gloucester, died in July 1700. The Act included a number of limitations on the Crown, imposed without consultation with the Scottish Parliament (see Ferguson 1977: 197–8).

[11] The existing parliament was supposed to meet within twenty days of the king's death, under the Act of Security of 1696. However, it was not recalled until ninety days after William's death, with Queensberry and the Court Party reluctant to hold elections. The irritation with this delay led to the Duke of Hamilton boycotting the 1702 session, which allowed the Court Party to press through key legislation, including measures designed to secure an incorporating Union (Ferguson 1977: 200–1).

[12] A fourth Act, the Wool Act, passed in 1704 was also 'viewed as an openly aggressive act against English trade' (Devine 2003: 52).

[13] In the 1690s the Parliament operated a system of committees, to which officers of state who were not members of the Parliament could sit (but not vote). All of the key votes running up to the Act of Union were discussed by the full Parliament (Riley 1964: 11).

This method of voting provides for a more accurate record of voting than that for the Westminster Parliament, where voting was through leaving the chamber into a lobby.[14] Three Acts passed in the 1703 parliament 'had the appearance of being militantly nationalist and anti-English' (Riley 1968: 129). *The Act for the Security of the Kingdom* (Act of Security) and *The Act anent Peace and War* asserted the right of the Scottish Parliament over the succession and declaration of war. These were part of Fletcher's campaign to impose limitations on the influence of the English court on Scottish affairs. The third Act, the *Act for Allowing the Importation of all Wines and Foreign Liquors* (the Wine Act) was seen in London as part of the Scottish assertion of independence and anti-Englishness—opening up Scottish trade to French imports—but was actually an administrative proposal pressed by the Edinburgh court in an attempt to gain some much needed revenue.[15] It was bitterly opposed by the Country Party (including Fletcher[16]), which had pushed through the previous Acts.[17] In fact, the records of votes against the Act of Security and the Wine Act show that only Sir Robert Dundas of Arniston voted against both, with 190 other MPs taking opposing sides.[18] This allows us to construct a cross section of the pro- and anti-court position in the Scottish Parliament in 1703. This can then be compared with the voting

---

[14] The roll of the Scottish Parliament dated 6 May 1703 in the Bodleian Library (see item 34; Ditchfield et al. 1995: 147) lists 305 members: 151 nobles, 87 barons, and 67 burgh members. However, the list of nobles includes 14 listed as 'minors', 6 'papists', 8 'extinct', and 16 'English', as well as 28 'absent'. Adding members active in key votes between 1703 and 1707 listed in the *Acts of the Parliament of Scotland* gives us a total list of 336 members for the Scottish Parliament. Of these, 71 (including two barons and three shire members) took no active part, leaving 265 active members.

[15] Mathieson (1905: 90) notes that the Wine Act was a measure that the Scottish government undertook 'for the sake of bringing a few thousand pounds into the Exchequer', but which 'was regarded in London with the greatest alarm'. He cites Harley's papers describing the measure 'as opening a back door to the enemies of England'.

[16] See his speeches delivered in Parliament in September 1703, reprinted in Robertson (1997: 168–71). He denounced the Act as 'a design of the blackest nature, hurtful and ignominious to the nation' (Robertson 1997: 171).

[17] Riley (1968: 148–9) argues that the 1703 session was not primarily concerned with asserting Scottish national interests and anti-English sentiments, but rather that these measures were seized upon by the opposition in order to undermine the Court Party, which was being pressed from London to ensure supply for the military campaign against the French. He suggests that the Wine Act was passed with the support of the *Squadrone Volante*, and had 'no connection with anything but the ministers' desire to have their salaries paid'. However, this does not explain why none of those recorded as supporting the Wine Act appear to have supported the Act of Security.

[18] The lists of voting records of the Scottish Parliament are given in Ditchfield et al. (1995: 147–51). Those on the Act of Security and Wine Act are listed as numbers 34 and 35. The description of the voting list on the Act for Security given in Ditchfield et al. suggests both for and against are shown—but we found only votes against in our investigation of the MS in the Bodleian Library. The record of votes on the Wine Act are in favour of the 'Protestation of the Marquess of Tweeddale and others' against the Act. A total of 106 votes are recorded on the first issue; 86 on the latter.

patterns on the Act of Union, which was passed by the same parliament in 1706,[19] allowing an analysis of vote switching over the Parliament.

The 1704 and 1705 sessions of the Edinburgh Parliament were chaotic. Lord Queensberry's administration fell, in the aftermath of false claims of a Jacobite conspiracy (the 'Scotch plot' or 'Queensberry plot'). In Edinburgh the new Commissioner, Lord Tweeddale, struggled to press for a resolution of the question of the succession with little parliamentary support (the 'New Party', which never commanded more than thirty votes (Ferguson 1977: 217)), amidst Queensberry's attempt to undermine his ministry and a continued agitation from the Country party. The London court offered a deal, whereby in return for the Scottish Parliament's acceptance of the Hanoverian succession the Parliament would gain a veto over court appointments. This addressed Fletcher's criticisms of the lack of parliamentary control over patronage. However, it did not go far enough, and instead the Parliament passed a resolve, proposed by the Duke of Hamilton: 'Not to name the Successor till we have a previous Treaty with *England* for regulating our Commerce, and other Concerns with that Nation' (listed in Boyer 1705). This measure was vague enough to unite those seeking to undermine Tweeddale, the Jacobites, and Fletcher's desire for limitations on the monarchy and a strong parliament. Riley (1978: 98) attributes the passage of this resolve, which blocked the settlement of the succession, to the defection from the court interest of Queensberry and his supporters.

In order to secure the supply necessary to support the military campaign in Europe, building up to Blenheim, the Edinburgh court was forced to concede the Act for Security, alongside an Act permitting the export of wool. Both these measures, although accepted by the Queen's advisors as necessary to secure supply, were seen as hostile to English interests, and led to a welling-up of popular anti-Scottish feeling (Ferguson 1977: 222). Retaliation from Westminster came in the form of the 'Act for the effectual securing of the Kingdom of England from the apparent dangers that might arise from

---

[19] Whereas there is information on every Scottish vote on the Act (and clauses) of the Union, there is no information on how English and Welsh MPs voted at Westminster. This is largely a consequence of the systematic collection of information contained in the *Acts of the Parliament of Scotland*, but also reflects the relatively uncontentious nature of the passage of the Act of Union through the Westminster Parliament (see Speck 1994: 114–18). The Scottish records are extensive and reliable (see the *Introduction* by Patrick Riley in Ditchfield et al. 1995: 140), although the only previous systematic analysis has been by Macinnes (1990). Macinnes provides a simple view of the cohesion of party votes over the various clauses of the Act of Union, showing the variation in support amongst party divisions during the final debate on the Act. By extending this database, it is possible to examine some further aspects of parliamentary behaviour over the period that saw a (purportively) hostile parliament vote through Union. With the help of Prof. Macinnes and Michael Moss of Glasgow University we were able to recover a partial version of the original database, which had become corrupted. This included some, but not all, of the variables collected for the original study. By adding earlier votes from the period of 1703–5 we have a view of how votes changed over the period running up to the vote on Union.

several Acts lately passed in the Parliament of Scotland', known as the Alien Act. This threatened to treat the Scots as aliens, and restrict trade in cattle, linen, and coal: a 'naked piece of economic blackmail, designed to bring the Scottish Parliament swiftly to the negotiating table' (Devine 1999: 3). The Act marked the nadir of Anglo-Scottish relations over the Parliament, and led to riots in Edinburgh and the end of Tweeddale's spell as Commissioner. It marked the end of piecemeal attempts to resolve the succession through specific concessions granted to the Scottish Parliament, and emphasized the difficulties of running a Scottish government that was acceptable in Westminster and the London court.

Up to 1705 there was no clear majority in the Scottish Parliament for a coherent programme of government. In part this was due to the prevalence of issues that were pressed by the court under pressure from the monarch and the London court. The succession of the Crown and the need to press for supply, in order to meet the demands of military campaigns on the European mainland, were seen as threatening Scottish interests. The weakness of the constitutional institutions linking London and Edinburgh were exacerbated by a Scottish party system split between Court, Country, and Jacobite/Cavalier parties. The Court interest was split by competition over patronage and places, most clearly seen in Queensberry's obstruction of any lasting settlement whilst out of office.

The volatility of the voting behaviour of MPs in the Edinburgh Parliament has ascribed by P. W. J. Riley, in one of the most detailed accounts of the approach to the Act of Union, as the outcome of a rather grubby scramble for short-term preferment. He asserts:

The union was made by men of limited vision for very short-term and comparatively petty, if not squalid, aims. In intention it had little to do with the needs of England and even less with those of Scotland, but a great deal to do with private political ambitions.... Cynicism and crackling malice are better guides than reverence to the politics of that, or perhaps of any other, time. (Riley 1978: xvi)

Riley discounts high political or ideological motivations behind the actions of those negotiating and voting on Union, but presents the passage of the Act through the Edinburgh Parliament as a series of manoeuvres for status and preferment. This approach leads Riley to dismiss any appeals to higher principles as mere disguise for pettier concerns. The anti-English programme pressed by the Scottish Parliament in 1703–4 is dismissed as a ruse to 'embarrass the court' (Riley 1978: 57); and during the discussion over the succession to Queen Anne is described in a similar way: 'The various parties to the act were obscuring their real intentions and conducting the debate in largely fictitious terms' (Riley 1978: 122). The party positions voiced in the run-up to the Union are summarily dismissed:

On neither side were the leaders saying what they meant. The opposition talked of trade and a treaty; the court claimed that the best way to achieve such aims was by limitations and settlement of the succession. The latter were making the best of the task they had been given; the former were trying to sabotage their efforts. All the rest was just talk. (Riley 1978: 94)

In this situation, argues Riley, it was a simple matter for the London court to influence negotiations in their own interest, using a combination of patronage and bribery, and he gives a detailed analysis of the financial resources used to buy votes and smooth the passage of the Act of Union through the Edinburgh Parliament.

For Robertson (1995*b*) on the other hand, this approach denies the strength of the ideological alternative presented by Andrew Fletcher of Saltoun. Fletcher presented a blueprint for a federal constitution, whereby the dominance of London would be tempered by a limited monarchy, and parliamentary and military power diffused across a number of regional centres. This country Whig perspective challenged the centralizing vision of a UK based on a Westminster Parliament controlling the regal territories. Fletcher's radical constitutional alternative, and his strong denunciation of a venal and corrupt political system,[20] threatened the traditional basis of Scottish government as fundamentally as the Union proposals. Fletcher and the Unionists agreed that the current mode of government in Scotland was unsustainable. The English discontent with the way the Scottish establishment operated was clearly focused on the challenge to the regal union, and a wish to suppress the religious controversy associated with the Jacobite challenge, alongside a more administrative concern to simplify the regulation of trading, military concerns, and taxation.

The opposition to the Union failed to present a coherent alternative to the Scottish establishment. In part, this was due to the weak leadership offered by the figurehead of the anti-Union movement, the Duke of Hamilton. Hamilton's failure to rally the anti-Unionist cause has been put down to a number of factors (see Ferguson 1977: 189–90). Hamilton 'bitterly resented' Queensberry's control of the Douglas clan, as well as Queensberry's role as leader of the Court interest; despite marriage to a wealthy English heiress, Hamilton was in constant financial difficulty;[21] and his claim to the crown of

---

[20] In Fletcher's [1698] Two Discourses Concerning the Affairs of Scotland he denounces corruption as 'the blackest of crimes', writing, 'I confess I have been often struck with astonishment, and could never make an end of admiring the folly and stupidity of some men living under some modern governments, who...suffer great numbers of those who have the legislative authority, to receive the constant bribes of places and pensions to betray them' (Robertson 1997: 35).

[21] Sir John Clerk of Penicuik records that Hamilton 'was so unlucky in his privat circumstances that he wou'd have complied with anything on a suitable encouragement' (Clerk 1892: 57).

Scotland, through descent from Mary Stuart (daughter of James II of Scotland) complicated his relations with the Jacobites and Queen Anne. These factors led to some otherwise incomprehensible decisions that undermined the anti-Union movement, notably his acquiescence in the vote that saw Queen Anne given the right to appoint the Scottish Commissioners to discuss Union.[22] He failed to support a popular rising against the Union,[23] and pleaded toothache when the time came to lead the parliamentary opposition to the passage of the Act of Union.

Whilst Andrew Fletcher provided an ideological focus with a radical constitutional alternative to the Union, his views were too radical to form a coalition across the middle ground of the Scottish establishment, and he was temperamentally unsuited to the role of parliamentary coalition building. As Robertson (1997: xvii) notes of Fletcher, 'his temper frequently let him down', and this contributed to a limited influence on the debate in 1706. He clashed with the Earl of Roxburgh in 1705 over Roxburgh's defection from the anti-Union cause, with Fletcher so incensed that he challenged Roxburgh to a duel.[24]

At the inception of the Scottish Parliament, in May 1703, Fletcher set out his opposition to a court demand for supply, arguing that first 'the house would take into consideration what acts are necessary to secure our religion, liberty, and trade' (Robertson 1997: 131). This programme involved a restructuring of the relationship with the Crown and the London court, a system of administration that had, under the union of the Crowns, subjugated Scottish interests to such an extent that 'we have from that time appeared to the rest of the world more like a conquered province, than a free independent people' (Robertson 1997: 133). As a supporter and advocate of the Act of Security and the Act anent Peace and War, Fletcher led the campaign for limitations on the English court. However, his proposals also sought to entrench the role of the Scottish Parliament over patronage and procedure, presenting a constructive programme as an alternative to an incorporating union. These measures included the entrenchment of the elected portion of the Parliament, and the right of the Parliament to select the administration and appoint government officials (see Robertson 1997:

---

[22] Scott (1992: 138–44) describes the circumstances surrounding Hamilton's decision, and the strong opposition of Andrew Fletcher to this course of action. Scott suggests that Hamilton's motive was a desire to gain the Queen's approval, and be one of the Commissioners, but describes the act as 'a treacherous and ingenious double game which finally destroyed the cause which he professed to lead' (Scott 1992: 141).

[23] As many as 7,000–8,000 fighting men had been expected to meet outside the town of Hamilton, after the approval of the Article 1 of the Act of Union, but the Duke took fright, and in the event less than fifty turned up (McNeill and MacQueen 1996: 152).

[24] The dispute was settled without violence on the sands of Leith, after Roxburgh complained of a leg injury (Scott 1992: 129).

138–9). The Edinburgh Parliament would also have control over the military and appointments to all military commissions (in Robertson 1997: 151).

The two most prominent modern historians dealing with the legacy of Andrew Fletcher, Paul H. Scott and John Robertson, have clashed over the extent to which these proposals were a viable assertion of 'the national independence of Scotland' (Scott 1992: 94), or part of a more intellectual espousal of a federal system of government 'able to realise the ancient republican ideal of freedom and self-government' (Robertson 1987: 219). For Scott (1992: 220), Fletcher 'provided the [opposition] party with intellectual inspiration and made most of the best speeches'. In this guise, Fletcher was the rhetorician who articulated the cost of Union to the interests of the Scots, only to be undermined by English bribery and aristocratic weakness. For Robertson, whilst Fletcher's opposition to the Treaty of Union was 'insuperable', there is 'no denying that he was in favour of a degree of union between Scotland and England' (Robertson 1987: 203). This view suggests that, despite Fletcher's skill as a spokesman against the incorporating union, his wider constitutional prescriptions were too radical to gain widespread popular and parliamentary support. As Ferguson (1977: 190), looking at the vacillations of the Duke of Hamilton, notes, 'When Fletcher made his astringent speeches denouncing Queensberry and his lickspittle faction he was lionised by the opposition, including its leader, but when he proposed reforms that would have reduced the powers of crown and nobility alike the applause died away and his support dwindled'. This shows how the anti-Union coalition was so disparate, containing as it did Jacobites, country Whigs, and disappointed office-seekers, that even without Hamilton's toothache and Fletcher's temper it would have disintegrated.

After the fall of the interim administrations led by Tweeddale and (in 1705) by Argyll, the court interest was consolidated, and, under the leadership of the Duke of Queensberry, was able to consolidate its support and present a united front in the votes on the Union. This may have been due to the bribery and patronage that Queensberry was able to command, but represented a greater coherence amongst the court interest than had previously been evident. It also showed that the London administration was willing to overcome their discontent with Queensberry's earlier involvement with the 'Scotch plot'. In this venture, Queensberry was supported by the Earl of Seafield, who served as a Union Commissioner in 1703 and 1706, and provided continuity over the Parliament and a devotion to the policies demanded by the Crown.

The consolidation of the court interest in Edinburgh represented by Queensberry's return as the Queen's Commissioner for the 1706 session of the Scottish Parliament coincided with a rare conjunction of English (and Welsh) regal, military, administrative, and parliamentary agreement. The prospect of an incorporating Union brought together Queen Anne,

Marlborough, Godolphin, and Harley, each of whom was persuaded to press the Unionist cause. For Queen Anne Union represented the solution to the issue of the succession; to Marlborough the removal of a potential military weakness; for Godolphin the extension of administrative control over a recalcitrant region; and for Harley the entrenchment of Whig parliamentary authority.

Negotiations over the Union were somewhat half-hearted in 1702, with the Scottish Commissioners focusing on trading concessions and the English so uninterested that the proceedings had to be frequently adjourned because they could not raise a quorum (Mathieson 1905: 77–8; Ferguson 1977: 201–2). In 1706 there was a much greater sense of purpose. The Scottish Commissioners first proposed a federal union, a suggestion that was rejected out of hand by the English Commissioners;[25] but an incorporating union having been settled on, negotiations were straightforward. The Scottish Parliament would be abolished, in return for representation within the Westminster Parliament (the extent of which was the only issue that forced a joint meeting of the negotiating teams (Speck 1994: 98)). The monarchy was to be settled on the House of Hanover, dependent on a Protestant succession. There would be freedom of trade in the new state, with certain aspects of the Scottish economy given a buffer of protectionism. The cost of taking on a share of the English (and Welsh) national debt would be addressed through the provision of compensation, which would also ameliorate the loss of trading rights given to the Company of Scotland. The issue of coordinating the passage of two separate Acts of Union through the Edinburgh and Westminster Parliaments was settled by organizing the passage through the Scottish Parliament first, to be considered in London thereafter.

Attention then shifted to Edinburgh and the voting that would turn the Treaty of Union agreed by the Commissioners into Acts of Union by both Parliaments. The Scottish Parliament opened its session on 3 October 1706, with the reading of an address from Queen Anne, which stated 'The Union has been long desired by both nations, and we shall esteem it as the greatest glory of our reign to have it now perfected' (Speck 1994: 106). The Articles were read, and the key vote on Article 1, which stated 'That the Two Kingdoms of Scotland and England, shall ... be United into One Kingdom by the Name of GREAT BRITAIN ... ', was taken on 4 November 1706. It passed, by 116 votes to 83. The Scottish court was able to carry all of the twenty-five Articles with only minor revision, and the Act of Union was

---

[25] In his memoirs, Clerk of Penicuik records that the federal scheme 'was most favoured by the people of Scotland, but all the Scots Commissioners, to a Man, considered it rediculous and impracticable' (Clerk 1892: 60). The Scottish Commissioners were also aware that the English Commissioners were unlikely to compromise on this point, being settled on an incorporating union.

ratified in Edinburgh on the 16 January 1707 by 110 votes to 69. News of this reached London on 20 January, and the Act of Union was approved by both Houses of the Westminster Parliament by 24 February, and given the assent of Queen Anne on 6 March, with effect from 1 May 1707 (Speck 1994: 106–17).

Figure 2.1 shows the flow of votes between two key votes in 1703 and the passage of the crucial Article 1 of the Act of Union in November 1706. Whilst it does not give a full picture of the transfer of votes, the picture in 1703 being based on a composite of two minority protests against successful measures, it does present the pattern of volatility over the Parliament.

The portrait of Scottish expediency described by Riley is allied to a view of party politics that was driven by a powerful Court Party that was able to harness and direct patronage and bribes, and used these methods to get the support of a key group of swing voters, known as the *Squadrone Volante*. Table 2.1 replicates Riley's allocation of party labels, set against the changing voting behaviour between 1703 and 1706 (Riley 1978: 328). Riley notes the strength of party voting across the Parliament, suggesting that 'Practically all voted their normal party line to an extent that is quite beyond coincidence' (Riley 1978: 275). However, this appears to present a rather contradictory

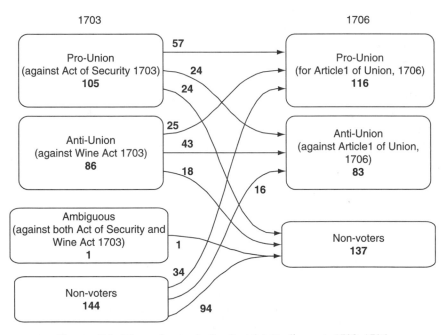

FIGURE 2.1. Flow of votes in the Scottish Parliament, 1703–1706

argument: on one side votes were effectively bought, on the other side there was a remarkable party cohesion. If the first side of the argument held, we would expect to see much greater cross-party switching to the pro-Union side, as members sought the advantages of aligning with court interest in order to gain the monetary benefits and patronage of the Union. Party cohesion, in contrast, suggests that there were real ideological differences between the parliamentary groupings. The evidence from Figures 2.1 and Table 2.1 suggests that the second argument has more strength. Table 2.2 shows that the nobles were significantly more pro-Union than the other two orders.[26] However, Riley's attribution of party labels appear to be at least partly contingent on how members of Parliament voted on the Union. Hence the strength of party voting on the Union is circularly explained by party labels attached according to voting on the Union.[27] Therefore, applying significance tests to Table 2.1, which would reveal huge 'significance', would be misleading.

TABLE 2.1. *Party identification and voting in the Scottish Parliament 1703 and 1706*

	Country /Cavalier	Court	*Squadrone*	Total	
Unionist in 1703 and 1706	3	53	1	57	
Anti-Union in 1703, pro-Union in 1706	2	3	20	25	116
No vote 1703, pro-Union 1706	1	30	3	34	
Anti-Union in 1703 and 1706	43	—	—	43	
Pro-Union in 1703, anti-Union in 1706	17	7	—	24	83
No vote 1703, anti-Union 1706	14	2	—	16	
Pro-Union 1703, no vote 1706	3	7	—	10	
Anti-Union 1703, no vote 1706	5	—	2	7	29
Other absent/abstained	6	5	1	12	
	94	107	27		228

[26] The significance test used is the probability that the association shown has arisen by chance. This is measured by the chi-square (χ^2) statistic. So, for example, the statement 'p of $\chi^2 < 0.001$' means that there is less than one chance in 1,000 that the association arises by chance.

[27] A more complex picture of party voting in the Scottish Parliament can be gained by introducing the intervening vote on the Duke of Hamilton's resolve, on which the Duke of Queensberry, then out of favour with the London court and facing a humiliating inquiry into his role in the 'Scotch plot', led a defection of his supporters from the court interest. But this vote was vaguely worded, and the circumstances of the vote are caught up in court intrigue, that it can be dismissed as 'Queensberry's harmless little ramble from the straight and narrow' (Ferguson 1964: 100).

Riley (1969) and Ferguson (1964) place much of the weight of their explanation of the Scottish switch in attitudes towards unionization on the provision of £20,000 sterling, secretly sent from London in order to cover the arrears of past and present office holders.[28] However, the list of recorded arrears and payments (shown in Appendix B of Riley 1969) suggests that, although a large proportion of this went to the swing voters of the *Squadrone Volante*, this was largely to cover expenses incurred during Tweeddale's tenure as Commissioner. Such payments are hard to distinguish from the general expenses incurred and recompensed from the Treasury during the normal practice of parliamentary management. Queensberry was recorded as receiving £12,325, but this was against recorded arrears of £26,756, and he had received a larger amount in 1705, when out of favour with the London and Edinburgh courts, in recognition of arrears incurred in his earlier tenure as Commissioner.[29] A far greater source of remuneration was through the payment of the 'Equivalent', designed to compensate for Scotland's acceptance of a national debt, discussed below.

Riley's account does expose the underlying weakness of the popular basis of the Scottish Parliament. Whilst there was widespread popular opposition to the Union amongst the Scottish population, this was apparently incidental to the voting patterns in the Edinburgh Parliament. The Scottish MPs were insulated from popular opinion by the very limited extent of electoral participation. Scottish electorates in both shire and burgh constituencies were extremely small: Midlothian, with around 100 voters, had the largest electorate, and most burghs had an electorate of twelve or fewer (Hayton 1996: 81). This ensured that the elections were easily controlled by the aristocratic interests. And in a unicameral parliament, unelected members of the nobility voted alongside the elected members.

Fletcher saw the danger that the London court would attempt to exert influence over the Parliament through the creation of new titles, which could tilt the balance within the Parliament. His proposed limitations on the Crown that included a provision 'That so many lesser barons shall be added to the parliament, as there have been noblemen created...and that in all time coming, for every nobleman that shall be created, there shall be a baron added to the parliament' (Robertson 1997: 138).

---

[28] See Speck (1994: 111–12) for an assessment of the impact of bribery on the passage of the Act of Union in Edinburgh.

[29] Macinnes (1990: 13–14) suggests:

> Although Queensberry as queen's commissioner did not have a vote, he received £12,325—the bulk of the covert funding—which he certainly deployed to pay spies and agent provocateurs to enhance the aura of menace surrounding the last parliamentary session. In all probability, he also made discretionary but unrecorded payments to wavering members of the Court and Squadrone.

Table 2.2 shows voting on Article 1 of the Act of Union, broken down by estates. Whilst a majority of each of the estates was pro-Union on the key vote, the majority amongst the nobles was much larger than that of the members representing the shires and burghs of Scotland. This is reinforced by Table 2.3, which shows the change in votes between 1703 and 1706. Table 2.3 shows that the majority for the incorporating union was significantly bolstered by the presence of twenty-two nobles, who had not recorded a position in 1703, but voted for the Union in 1706. Fletcher's concerns about the ability of the London court to influence the Scottish aristocracy appears to be supported, although the causal links may be more complex: 'That 1 in 7 Scottish nobles had English wives at the resumption of negotiations, testifies not only [to] their steady assimilation into the British ruling class, but also to their growing dependence on the English marriage market to build up disposable income' (McNeill and MacQueen 1996: 151). The fact that membership of the aristocracy was associated with a greater interest in trade, with

TABLE 2.2. *Membership of the estates and voting in the Scottish Parliament on the First Article of the Act of Union*

	Nobles	Barons/Shire	Burgh	Total
Pro-Union	46	37	33	116
Anti-Union	21	33	29	83
No vote	91	31	15	137
	158	101	77	336

p of $\chi^2 < 0.001$

TABLE 2.3 *Membership of the estates and voting in the Scottish Parliament, 1703 and 1706*

	Nobles	Barons/Shire	Burghs	Total	
Unionist in 1703 and 1706	18	16	23	57	
Anti-Union in 1703, pro-Union in 1706	6	15	4	25	116
No vote 1703, pro-Union 1706	22	6	6	34	
Anti-Union in 1703 and 1706	12	18	13	43	
Pro-Union in 1703, anti-Union in 1706	6	7	11	24	83
No vote 1703, anti-Union 1706	3	8	5	16	
Pro-Union 1703, no vote 1706	9	10	5	24	
Anti-Union 1703, no vote 1706	3	11	4	18	137
Other absent/abstained	79	10	6	95	
				336	

p of $\chi^2 < 0.001$

both England and abroad, has also been used to explain the greater propensity of the nobility to support the Union.

Distinguishing between the responsiveness of members of the three estates of the Scottish Parliament to the debate over the Act of Union is complicated by the close kinship and patronage links between the different estates, but it appears that (comparing the numbers of voters moving to a pro-Union position) the nobility was more likely to align with the Unionist cause, followed by the barons, whereas the burgh members who shifted allegiance were more likely to go to the anti-Unionist position. This may reflect a greater sensitiveness amongst the burgh members to public opinion within their constituencies.

The extent to which public opinion was directed against the Union has been gauged by the number, and complete one-sidedness, of the petitions raised in an attempt to influence the Scottish Parliament. During the debate and passage of the Act of Union through the Edinburgh Parliament, petitions were received from fifteen out of the thirty-three shires,[30] and twenty-one of the sixty-seven royal burghs (Macinnes 1990: 12). All were opposed to the incorporating union.[31] Further to this pressure, sixty-two 'exceptional and unsolicited addresses' were delivered to the Parliament, three from presbyteries, nine from towns, and fifty from parishes. 'These addresses against the union came predominantly from west-central and south-western Scotland, where local communities drew consciously on covenanting traditions of supplicating in support of religious and civil liberties' (McNeill and MacQueen 1996: 151). This glut of anti-Union activity has been taken to represent the widespread popular antipathy to the measure, as well as indicating grass-roots opposition to an incorporating union from members of the Presbyterian church.[32] However, analysis of the effect of petitions on the voting behaviour of members of the Edinburgh Parliament suggests that petitioning had little or no effect (Macinnes 1990: 13). If petitioning had affected behaviour, there would be a significant association between having a petition from one's constituency and switching vote. There is not (data not shown). Comparing the first key vote, on Article 1, with the coda to the Act, the ratification, Macinnes shows that petitioning did little to shore up the anti-Unionist vote. Macinnes suggests that 'Blatant disregard for the wishes of their constituents is the most identifiable response of shire and burgh commissioners' (Macinnes 1990: 13).

---

[30] 18 according to McNeill and MacQueen (1996: 151).

[31] Argyll suggested that the petitions were only fit to make kites of, and Mar suggested that the pro-Union campaign had left it too late, and that that few would look worse than none (Ferguson 1964: 109–10).

[32] See Young (1999: 29–37), who notes the tradition of petitioning as a tool of church and political mobilization going back to the Covenanting Movement in 1637–8 against the imposition of a Scottish Book of Common Prayer by Charles I.

Macinnes's analysis is hampered by the fact that he is comparing two very similar votes: the key vote on the Act of Union was Article 1, the vote on the ratification was a reflection of this. There was very little switching on the pro-Union side (only two members voted for Article 1 and against ratification, and one of these was a noble, so not subject to pressure from a petition). Applying Macinnes's coding to our more extensive database of votes, running from 1703 to 1707, and comparing positions in 1703 with the vote on Article 1 of the Act of Union gives the pattern shown in Table 2.4. This shows that petitions, to a large extent, did reflect voting behaviour by constituency members. Petitions were more likely to be presented in constituencies where the member consistently opposed Union, and were less prevalent in those constituencies represented by stable pro-Union members. Similarly, of the members with no recorded position in 1703, the pro-Unionists tended not to come from constituencies where petitions were raised, whereas the anti-Unionists were more likely. The glaring exception to this pattern is amongst the nineteen members, largely from the *Squadrone Volante*, who switched from anti-Union position in 1703 to a pro-Union position in 1706. Fifteen of these faced petitions raised in their constituencies, a sign that there was popular opposition to their change in voting allegiance. The fact that the simple relationship between petitions and vote is non-significant, whereas the more complex relationship shown in Table 2.4 is significant, shows that petitions reflected rather than induced voting behaviour.

Petitions may not have truly reflected public opinion. First, the existence of a petition for a burgh or shire does not comprehensively indicate that the interests of that burgh or shire were against the Union, just that there was an organized opposition within that area. Second, the complete lack of pro-Union counter-petitions suggests that this method was solely an opposition

TABLE 2.4. *Petitioning and vote-switching in the Scottish Parliament, 1703–1706*

	Petition	No petition
Unionist in 1703 and 1706	10 ⎫	29
Anti-Union in 1703, pro-Union in 1706	15 ⎬	4
No vote 1703, pro-Union 1706	2 ⎭	10
Anti-Union in 1703 and 1706	23	8
Pro-Union in 1703, anti-Union in 1706	8	10
No vote 1703, anti-Union 1706	6	7
Pro-Union 1703, no vote 1706	3	12
Anti-Union 1703, no vote 1706	8	7
Other absent/abstained	8	8
Total	83	95

p of $\chi^2 < 0.001$

strategy, rather than a genuine competition to voice public support for either side. Close examination of the relationship between voting in the Scottish Parliament and the raising of petitions shows that, in general, anti-Union MPs were more likely to come from a constituency where a petition was raised against the Union. However, it does appear that the key group of MPs who switched votes from an anti-Union position in 1703 to a pro-Union stance in 1706 did represent constituencies that raised petitions against the Union. This suggests that the relationship between petitioning and parliamentary voting was not simply one of blatant disregard. Voting amongst the shire and burgh members reflected the balance of petitioning, but petitioning was insufficient to swing the votes of a key group of parliamentarians. The basis of representation within the Scottish Parliament was weak, but not as weak as has been previously suggested.

'Trade with most ... '

The economic background of the Union has been presented as a trade-off between political independence and access to the markets of the English empire, creating 'an Anglo-Scottish common market that was the biggest customs-free zone in Europe' (Smout 1969*a*: 215). The weakness of the Scottish economy in the 1690s (the 'lean years', or 'ill years'[33]) was compounded by the expensive failure of Darien. This free-trade interpretation of the Union can be challenged from a number of positions. First, studies of the extent to which any cross-border tariffs were effective before the Union, and the extent to which common excise duties were imposed after the Union, suggest that the Union only provided a blurred distinction between trading practices.[34] Secondly, there was a shared appreciation on both sides of the border that protectionist measures could cut both ways, which meant that free trade was not necessarily seen as a positive benefit (Whatley 1989).

Yet the demand for free trade with England had been frequently raised from Scotland, and the threat of economic sanctions was used by the English as a means of putting pressure on the Scottish Parliament to accede to a Parliamentary Union, through the Aliens Act of 1705. Promoters of the Union, such as Daniel Defoe, stressed the benefits of free trade to the Scottish economy (Smout 1964: 463–4), and Andrew Fletcher noted that the prospect of greater trading benefits was 'the bait that covers the

---

[33] Whatley (2000: 1) suggests that famine in the 1690s caused the death of between ten and twenty per cent of the Scottish population.

[34] See Smout (1964: 458) for the tensions between English regulation and Scottish trade, and Saville (1996: 65–6) for an example of Scottish contravention of English laws in the trading of 'Negro's and elephants teeth'.

hook' (Whatley 2001: 57). Marlborough commented in 1706 that 'the true state of the matter was, whether Scotland should continue subject to an English Ministry without trade, or be subject to an English Parliament with trade' (Young 1999: 25). Marlborough's lofty position as favourite of the Queen and military destroyer of the French was built upon the foundations of a governmental revolution in terms of taxation and finance, and it was in this area that the main benefits of Union lay for the English state, rather than the expansion of free trade. The running of the Scottish government had been, if not a drain, then a distraction to the government in London. Pressing for a Union would offer a number of benefits, through the removal of a potential rival to the establishment of a monopolistic trading empire. It also offered new grounds for the expansion and consolidation of a more rigorous tax-raising regime.

A number of historians have attempted to link voting in the Edinburgh Parliament on the Acts of Union to the specific economic interests of Scottish members of Parliament. Riley (1978: 276) suggests that those with interests in grain production, coal, salt, and the raising of black cattle should have been in favour of the measure, with the opening of new markets, whilst wool growers would expect to suffer from continued limitations on trade. However, he concludes that there is 'no general correlation between a member's voting record and his ostensible economic interest'. Both Riley (1964: 263) and Smout (1969b: 188) note that the nobility had a particularly strong interest in the export market for Scottish goods; and that this could have explained their greater likelihood of supporting the Union (see Tables 2.2 and 2.3).[35] However, as Whatley (1989: 159) suggests, free market arguments cut both ways:

although a majority of those Scots involved in the making of the Treaty clearly grasped the opportunity of access to the English and colonial markets while it was on offer, others were equally concerned to obtain as many safeguards as possible to defend vulnerable elements of what . . . was an exceedingly fragile economy.

In particular, he points out that the Scottish salt industry, and the coal production that supported it, were both extremely vulnerable to competition.

The fact that the fifteen of the twenty-five Articles of the Act of Union concerned economic aspects has been taken to represent the importance of trade in the making of the treaty (Whatley 1989: 158). However, the Articles dealing with economic aspects can be differentiated by their relationship to

---

[35] Whatley (2001: 60) discusses the different impact of economic considerations across the three estates of the Scottish Parliament. He suggests that members of each of the estates had (or represented) significant trading interests, and such considerations offer little additional explanatory power to the support in Edinburgh for the Act of Union.

the broader trading concerns expressed in the Union negotiations: first, dealing with free trade; second, dealing with customs and duties and the extent of temporary measures protecting Scottish industry; and third, dealing with the compensation for the adoption of English and Welsh national debt. The key Article (4) dealing with the economic aspects of the Union stated, 'That all the Subjects of the United Kingdom of Great Britain shall from and after the Union have full Freedom and Intercourse of Trade and Navigation. . . .' This was accompanied by four other Articles (5, 6, 17, and 18), which set out the free-trade basis of the state, establishing a British navy, a common currency, and system of weights and measures. Nine Articles (6–14) dealt with the unified system of customs and duties, and contained a large number of concessions designed to protect Scottish trading interests, including the beer and liquor trade, salt, fishing, paper, and coal industries. Finally, Article 15 dealt with the payment of the 'Equivalent', amounting to just under £400,000, to compensate Scotland for the higher taxation and adoption of the English and Welsh national debt. This highlights the fact that the treaty of Union was not simply based on the establishment of freedom of trade, but also included a number of measures protecting supposedly vulnerable areas of the Scottish economy. It also shows that the Westminster Parliament was willing to accept significant concessions to Scottish trading interests.

The passage of the Articles of the Act of Union dealing with economic aspects through the Edinburgh Parliament highlights the different emphasis on free trade and protection. Article 4 was passed with the largest majority of any Article: securing 154 supporting votes versus 19 against. Figure 2.2 shows the pattern of voting between Article 1 and Article 4, showing the huge support for free trade within the Parliament. The passage of Article 4 was eased by a huge switch in voting behaviour amongst the opponents of Union, of whom thirty-one changed sides to support Article 4. This was despite Fletcher's attempt to make Article 4 a central element of the opposition attack on Union (Riley 1978: 288).

The huge majority for Article 4 appears to confirm that free trade was an important general principle for the passage of the Act of Union. Only nineteen members of the Parliament took a stand against it, whereas all other Articles were opposed with much greater enthusiasm. As Table 2.5 shows, the Article received support from the most consistent opponents of the Union programme.

But in 1707 free trade connoted access to markets, not removal of protection. In contrast to the smooth passage of Article 4 of the Act of Union, the Articles dealing with customs and duties (referred to as the 'explanations') were much more contentious, and led to significant amendments to the negotiated treaty, all adding elements of protection for particular aspects of Scottish trade and industry. Indeed, Article 8, dealing with the Salt Tax,

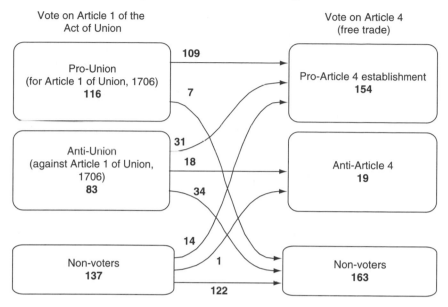

FIGURE 2.2. Voting in the Scottish Parliament on Article 1 and Article 4, 1706

TABLE 2.5. *Vote on Article 4 (free trade) and vote-switching in the Scottish Parliament, 1703–1706*

	For Article 4	Against Article 4
Unionist in 1703 and 1706	54	—
Anti-Union in 1703, pro-Union in 1706	25	—
No vote 1703, pro-Union 1706	30	—
Anti-Union in 1703 and 1706	12	13
Pro-Union in 1703, anti-Union in 1706	12	2
No vote 1703, anti-Union 1706	7	3
Pro-Union 1703, no vote 1706	6	1
Anti-Union 1703, no vote 1706	4	—
Other absent/abstained	4	—
Total	154	19

p of χ^2 not calculated because of empty cells.

involved the court's only defeat during the passage of the Act of Union (on an amendment demanding drawbacks on the export of salted beef and pork (Macinnes 1990: 17)).[36] The Scottish Parliament succeeded in adding a

---

[36] Defoe described the debate over Article 8 and the Salt Taxes as the 'Grand Affair' (Whatley 2001: 72–7).

number of amendments to the draft treaty negotiated in London (detailed in Whatley 2001), much to the consternation of Godolphin, who was worried that this could complicate the passage of the Act of Union through the Westminster Parliament (Riley 1978: 291). These amendments were accepted by the court, which 'knew where to draw the line', and was able to pass the key votes without significant numbers of defections. However, the passage of the 'explanations', and the success of the Scottish Parliament in adding protectionist measures, show the limitations of a purely free-trade explanation of the passage of the Act of Union. There was significant concern about the vulnerability of particular industries (and particular interests of Scottish members of Parliament). These were recognized in the Act of Union, which was amended to include a number of (albeit temporary) protectionist measures.

In his analysis of the causes of the passage of the Act of Union, Whatley (2001: ch. 3) has reviewed the assessments of the significance of economic factors in the passage of the Union, and notes the large number of historians who have denied that such factors were an influence. The evidence of voting on Article 4 supports Whatley's contention that, although the economic influences on the Union were multifaceted and did not all pull in the same way, economic considerations were an important reason for the passage of the Act of Union in Edinburgh.

The third element of the Act of Union involving economic factors was the payment of the 'Equivalent', ostensibly compensated for the adoption of the burden of the English and Welsh national debt. The details of this, and the way that payment would be channelled (largely to stock holders in the Company of Scotland, responsible for the Darien venture), were outlined in Article 15 of the Act of Union. We now look at the history of the Company of Scotland, and its relationship to the structure of fiscal government in the period running up to the Union.

Darien, the Company of Scotland, and the Union

In 1695–6 Edinburgh merchants launched 'The Company of Scotland trading to Africa and the Indes', incorporated under patent by an Act of the Scottish Parliament in June 1695.[37] The scheme as originally conceived was for a trading company along the lines of the English East India Company. However, in the light of a hostile reaction from the House of Commons the

---

[37] This followed the 1693 'Act for Encouraging of Forraign Trade', which granted wide privileges to any company founded to foster international trade (Devine 2003: 40).

design was changed.[38] Under the leadership of William Paterson, the focus of the Company changed, with the aim of creating a trading colony on the Isthmus of Darien (in what is now Panama). The English hostility to the Scottish Company arose from its challenge to the position of the East India Company, combined with a more general concern that the privileges conferred by the Scottish Parliament (which exempted the Company from customs duties for twenty-one years) would see trade diverted north of the border, undermining English commercial interests and revenues. The MPs and Lords in Westminster sought to quash the Scottish venture, cutting off access to the capital market in London[39] and across Northern Europe. The Board of Trade and Plantations was established in 1696 partly in response to the venture, and in 1697 it reported on the threat posed to English interests by the establishment of a successful trading colony at Darien, concluding that a rival expedition should be dispatched. The Board noted:

This work seems to us to require all possible despatch, lest the Scotch Company be there before us, which is of the utmost importance to the trade of England. (Armitage 1995: 109)[40]

The Westminster opposition was supported by King William, who felt that the Scottish Act, passed whilst he was engaged on a military campaign (the siege of Namur), undermined the joint Kingship. He sourly observed that 'I have been ill served in Scotland' (Insh 1932: 57), and is described as denouncing the project's supporters as 'raging madmen' (Devine 2003: 45). The King's wrath was further exercised when the focus of the scheme turned to Darien, which encroached upon Spanish territory, and threatened to undermine William's ally in the war against Louis XIV.

Hostility to the Company of Scotland also came from the Dutch East and West India Companies (Smout 1963: 251), and attempts to raise finance in Amsterdam and Hamburg were confounded by a combination of local interests and the communication of King William's hostility to the Company (Insh 1932: ch. 3).

Armitage (1995: 102) argues that the inception of the Company of Scotland was a justifiable attempt to assert and entrench nationhood:

---

[38] Riley (1978: 208) asserts that the Company of Scotland had never been intended to be a general trading operation, but had been conceived from the start as a colonizing venture, although this intention was hidden. He dismisses the Darien exercise as 'clever–stupid', and suggests that it was an indefensible 'attempt to establish a colony in a fever-ridden territory belonging to someone else' (Riley 1978: 210).

[39] London financiers had pledged £300,000 of the proposed start-up capital of £600,000 in 1695. Figures for the financing of the Darien venture are given in sterling, not Scottish pounds.

[40] John Locke was delegated to gather information on the Darien expedition for the Board of Trade. In 1700 the Board judged that the venture was still a danger to English interests, although in this instance the impact on relations with Spain was highlighted (Armitage 1995: 110).

for Scotland, there was the opportunity of economic modernisation and of being able to compete on an equal footing with the other nations of Europe for whom trade was now the major reason of state. There was the possibility of self-defence through prosperity, an escape from the metropolitan dominance of England, and the hope of economic growth without the attendant dangers of corruption. In sum, the Darien venture was an alternative to dependency and corruption within Britain, and to poverty and universal monarchy within Europe.

The seriousness with which the English and Spanish[41] reacted to the Darien venture showed that it was seen as a source of potential power and economic rivalry. The prohibition on capitalization of the Company in London forced the directors to focus on raising money in Scotland, and it became a great patriotic enterprise, with pledges for the revised capitalization of £400,000 reached within six months of the subscriptions opening in February 1696 (Devine 2003: 42). Andrew Fletcher wrote in 1698 that 'no Scotsman is an enemy to the African company' (Robertson 1997: 38). Fletcher's writings tied in support for the Company of Scotland to his broader schemes of limitations on monarchy, using the obstructions imposed by King William to illustrate the weakness of the Scottish interest under the existing scheme of joint monarchy.

The impact of the failure of the Darien venture on the Union negotiations and the passage of the Act through the Edinburgh Parliament in 1706–7 can be seen in both general and specific terms. As noted earlier, the Company, of Scotland highlighted the potential threat to English monopoly trading rights, most particularly associated with the East India Companies, and further highlighted the possibility that an independent Scotland could free-ride on English military expansion, undermining trade and revenue from customs and excise. For Smout (1964: 459), the disastrous Darien venture was a key element in the undermining Scottish economic confidence at the turn of the eighteenth century; for contemporaries 'it seemed . . . that Scotland was on the verge of economic collapse'. This helped swing the general debate on the trading benefits of Union towards the pro-side, whereas the economic arguments of the anti-Unionists were 'distinctly old-fashioned and more fundamentally unrealistic' (Smout 1964: 485). However, the Darien venture also became a focus for popular disenchantment with King William and the operation of joint monarchy, and a symbol of English treachery, culminating in the judicial murder of the captain and two officers of the *Worcester*—an English ship rumoured to have sunk one of the Darien vessels—that was docked at Leith in 1705.

---

[41] Devine notes that Spanish power in the Panama region was not seen as invincible. The Spanish reaction was supported by the Pope, who 'voiced his opposition at the damage to the Catholic faith that might be done in the region by these upstart Calvinist Scots' (Devine 2003: 45).

Thus Darien was an economic disaster to the Scots but also a political threat to the English. In Edinburgh the Darien venture was a humiliation, but the London court sought to assuage this by directing payments to stockholders in return for a union. In London, parliamentary union removed a potential source of rivalry to the East India company, which was subsequently free to exploit its monopolistic trading rights. The parliamentary union helped consolidate this monopolistic control of trading rights, and restricted the ability of Scottish entrepreneurs to undermine English trading interests by free-riding on the back of English military and territorial expansion.

From 1702 compensation for the losses incurred in the Darien venture, totalling £153,631—estimated to be one-quarter of Scotland's entire capital stock—were made part of the Scottish negotiations over a possible incorporating union (Riley 1978: 35, 199). This compensation was linked to the payment of the 'Equivalent', the sum of money paid to Scotland upon Union in order to assuage the burden of the English national debt, which a unitary state would have to bear.

The 'Equivalent' was calculated on the basis of English pre-Union debts,[42] but the problem remained that there was no clear way of distributing this financial largesse. A committee of the Union Commissioners agreed that there should be some transfer of funds to Scotland (and that this transfer should continue in the form of a 'rising Equivalent' as the English (and Welsh) levels of customs and taxation were applied. Whilst a great deal of consideration was given to calculating the total amount, which was agreed at £398,085 10s, the issue of who should receive it was given much less consideration. Rather than defraying past or future tax payments across the Scottish nation, it was appropriated by a number of sectional interests who were seen to have been affected by the Union; those who had lost out from the switch from Scottish to English coinage; the shareholders of the Company of Scotland; a subsidy to the Scottish woollen industry; and allowances to Commissioners who negotiated the Union. The final category shows the extent to which the 'Equivalent' was used to smooth interested parties; and further patronage was exercised in setting up a committee that was designed to spend the 'Equivalent', with suitable compensation.[43] As such, the 'Equivalent' provided a much greater source of patronage (or bribes) than

---

[42] See Riley (1964: ch. 14) for the details of the mode of calculation of the 'Equivalent'. According to Clerk of Penicuik, who was one of the Scottish Commissioners charged with supervising the process by which the 'Equivalent' was settled, calculations were made by Dr David Gregory (1661–1708), then Professor of Astronomy at Oxford, and William Paterson (Clerk 1892: 61).

[43] Appointment to the committee was seen 'as a kind of consolation prize for commissioners who had done good service during the passing of the Union'. Members were paid expenses of £920 a year (Riley 1964: 208, 214).

the amount of money that was seen as being covertly shifted to Scotland to ease the passage of the Union.

According to Riley (1964: 210–11), the payment of the 'Equivalent' was greeted as an event of great importance in Scotland:

When at last the Equivalent did arrive, carried in carts, with an escort of dragoons, demonstrations took place. Crowds collected to see it brought in and stones were thrown at the wagon drivers.

The English exchequer could not afford to pay it all in cash, so bills were issued, a situation that caused some consternation, although it helped establish the Bank of Scotland, which was charged with overseeing the exchange (Scott 1911: 268). The compensation was directed at those with the clearest claim, and so subscribers to the Company of Scotland and the Union Commissioners received first charge. For more ambiguous recipients, such as the woollen traders, the result was less satisfactory: they 'could not be paid because nobody had been named in the Act anent the Public Debts to receive it' (Riley 1964: 212). The rest of the Scottish population received nothing.[44]

The failure of the Company of Scotland created a large body amongst the Scottish establishment that had incurred a large financial loss, and whose only hope for redress lay with the English treasury. However, support for the Darien venture (financial or political) does not correlate with support or opposition for an incorporating union; two of the leading activists in the scheme took diametrically opposed views on the Union. William Paterson returned from Darien (where his wife had died) to write pro-Unionist propaganda, and he acted as an agent for the English minister Robert Harley. Andrew Fletcher, meanwhile, saw the failure of the Darien expedition (to which he had subscribed £1,000) as an illustration of the subjugation of Scottish to English trading interests, a situation that would only be worsened if the Scottish parliament were to be abolished. Similarly, the leader of the Court interest who pushed the Union through the Edinburgh Parliament, the Duke of Queensberry, had subscribed £3,000, as had a leading opponent of the Union, Lord Belhaven. The Duchess of Hamilton opened the subscription with a promise of £1,000.[45]

As Armitage (1995: 116) notes, 'It is difficult to correlate voting patterns on the Treaty of Union with support for the Company of Scotland twelve years earlier'. However, we make a tentative attempt at such a task. In his analysis of the socio-economic and geographical basis of the Company of

---

[44] Debates over the liabilities of creditors to the Scottish government before 1707 continued to 1724, and holders of 'Equivalent' debt ended up by creating a joint stock bank in the form of the Royal Bank of Scotland (Riley 1964: 229).

[45] A broader analysis of the subscription lists to the Company of Scotland is given in Jones (2001).

Scotland subscription lists W. Jones (2001: 33–4) identifies 170 subscribers (12.0 per cent of the total number, contributing 16.4 per cent of the total capital) associated with the Government,[46] including fifty-seven members of Parliament who sat between 1696 and 1700. Comparing the published list of all Darien subscribers[47] with the database of members of the Scottish Parliament of 1703–1707, there are ninety-nine members of parliament who can be (with varying degrees of certainty[48]) linked to a subscription to the Company of Scotland, contributing £62,850 (15.7 per cent) of the total.

Examination of Tables 2.6 and 2.7 suggests that, despite the strong incentives for Darien compensation and its association with direct recompense through the 'Equivalent', it does not appear to be a significant factor in the overall passage of the Act of Union in Edinburgh. Whilst the average stockholdings in the Company of Scotland were higher amongst those who favoured the Union, possession of stock does not appear to have been an indicator of voting one way or the other. Non-stockholders were more likely to vote for the Union. The relationships in Tables 2.6 and 2.7 are not significant.

TABLE 2.6. *Voting on the First Article in the Scottish Parliament compared to Darien shareholding*

| | Stockholders | | Non-stockholders | |
	votes(%)	Average stock (£)	votes (%)	Total (%)
For	44 (73%)	647.73	68 (64%)	112 (68%)
Against	16 (27%)	665.63	38 (36%)	54 (33%)
Total	60	652.50	106	166

Article 1, 4 November 1706: That the two kingdoms of England and Scotland shall upon the 1st day of May next . . . , and forever after, be united into one kingdom by the name of Great Britain. p of $\chi^2 = 0.53$, not significant.

[46] Members of Parliament, Privy Councillors, ministers of state, and high court judges.

[47] *A perfect list of the several persons residenters in Scotland, who have subscribed as adventurers in the joynt-stock of the Company of Scotland trading to Africa and the Indies.* Edinburgh, 1696. Source: Bodleian Library, Oxford, ref. (5 Delta 277 (4)). This has been checked against the list published in the Appendix to Barbour (1907).

[48] The links are made on the basis of names, titles, and geographical associations, but in many cases these do not tally precisely. There are numerous problems with such an exercise. First, spelling of names and places is imprecise, and varies across voting lists of the Acts of the Parliaments of Scotland, as well as between these and the Company of Scotland subscription lists. Second, titles may be the same, but the holders of such titles may have changed due to death and succession. Third, the places with which people were associated may have changed. Fourth, some names of Scottish MPs appear repeatedly on the subscription lists: for example there are numerous entries for Walter Scot, John Stewart, and John Murray, which cannot be linked to the MPs of the same name. Consequently, we cannot (without much further research) present this as a definitive list.

Breaking down the seventy-four members who voted on Article 1 of the Union according to their position in the 1703 session of parliament shows that thirteen members subscribing to the Darien venture switched to a pro-Union stance, but ten switched the other way. Of the Scottish members of parliament who had not registered a position in the two votes recorded in 1703, but who voted on Article 1 and had subscribed to the Darien venture, four were pro-Union, and two anti-Union.[49] It seems that the large amounts of money available in compensation for Darien subscribers included in the Union had no effect on the voting patterns in the Scottish Parliament. Riley (1978) argues that short-term gain was the incentive behind most of the voting on the Union. If this were the case, then Darien subscribers should have been much more likely to switch to a pro-Union position.[50] They were not.

The 'Equivalent' was enshrined in the Fifteenth Act of Union,[51] which sets out (in great detail: reprinted in Pryde 1950: 91–4) the method of calculation, and how it was to be disbursed. It also provides for the abolition of the Company of Scotland, in return for compensation (fully paid with 5 per cent interest). Sixty members coded as holding Darien stock voted, a slightly lower proportion of the total than voted on Article 1. However, these were more likely to approve of the measure. Looking at the flow of votes between Articles 1 and 15 shows that the pro-Unionists were solidly in favour of Article 15, and this held for both stockholders and non-stockholder.[52] Of the eight members who voted against Article 1 and for Article 15, half held Darien stock; and of the five members who did not vote on Article 1 but supported Article 15, two held Darien stock. This suggests a slight effect of self-interestedness, with Darien stockholders voting through the Article that brought them a generous compensation. However, the effect is not statistically significant; the main influence on the pattern of voting is determined by a cohesive pro-Union block, and a disintegrating anti-Union vote.[53]

---

[49] The only evidence in favour of votes being shifted to a pro-Union stance through subscription to the Company of Scotland is in the composition of the *Squadrone Volante*. Of the twenty-seven members, thirteen (48 per cent) were subscribers to the Darien venture, compared with 33 per cent of the Court party and 36 per cent of the Country party. However, the effect of the stockholding members of the *Squadrone* is balanced by cross-voting amongst the Court and Country parties.

[50] Even on the vote on Article 15, which set out the conditions for repayment of the 'Equivalent', largely to stockholders of the Company of Scotland, there was very little cross-voting amongst MPs who would directly benefit.

[51] There were three votes on possible amendments to Article 15, two voted on 7 December 1706, the third on 30 December 1706, the same day as the final vote (coded as UART15).

[52] Only one MP voted for Article 1 and against Article 15, a non-stockholder.

[53] Twenty-nine MPs voted against Article 1 and did not record a vote on Article 15; 14 of these held Darien stock. This level seems high, compared to the 3 stockholders out of 16 pro-Union MPs who did not vote on Article 15. However, this pattern of voter attrition appears more general, rather than a strategic abstention to ensure the passage of a favourable outcome. Comparing the voting patterns amongst Darien stockholders on Article 15 and Article 18 (concerning the regulation of trade and hence not impinging directly on Darien stockholders,

TABLE 2.7. *Voting on the Fifteenth Article (providing an 'Equivalent') in the Scottish Parliament compared to Darien shareholding*

	Stockholders votes (%)	Average stock (£)	Non-stockholders votes (%)	Total votes (%)
For	44 (73%)	647.73	68 (64%)	112 (68%)
Against	16 (27%)	665.63	38 (36%)	54 (33%)
Total	60	652.50	106	166

p of $\chi^2 = 0.23$, not significant.

The final recorded vote of the Scottish Parliament, on 10 March 1707,[54] concerned the payment of compensation to the Company of Scotland's shareholders, and the issue of whether it should be paid to proprietors or through a committee of appointed commissioners. The vote went in favour of a commission, by thirty votes to eleven. Twenty-nine MPs coded as having held Darien stock voted, with twenty-two in favour and seven against. There is no significant difference between the voting pattern of stockholders and that of non-stockholders (p of $\chi^2 = 0.55$). But the proportion of those voting with a direct interest to all votes cast is much higher than on any of the Articles of the Act of Union. It suggests that there is some validity to our coding of Darien stockholders.

According to McNeill and MacQueen (1996: 152), compensation for Darien was a 'powerful inducement for members of the estates not to oppose the union'. Our analysis of the relationship between the holding of Darien stock and the pattern of voting between 1703 and 1707 suggests that there was surprisingly little direct association. This goes someway towards undermining the view that special and short-term interests determined the passage of the Act of Union in Edinburgh. It still allows the strength of the general effect of the failure of the Company of Scotland and the Darien venture, in emphasizing the relative economic, political, and military weakness of the Scottish state. As Smout suggests, 'Although Darien did not "create" a Union of Parliaments, it did more than anything else to provide an atmosphere in which the relative merits of the various forms of constitutional alignment or separation would be hotly discussed' (Smout 1963: 253). Further, it had a direct effect on one key institution, the monarchy: 'The main importance of the Darien episode in the history of the Union is that it finally converted the

voted on the following day (31 December 1706), and with a similar balance of pro- and anti-votes) shows very similar patterns of voting and non-voting amongst the Darien stockholders. However, there is more vote-switching amongst Darien stockholders in favour of Article 15, compared to Article 18, which suggests that there was a small but significant element of self-interested voting.

[54] Listed in Ditchfield et al. (1995: 151) as 79; in our database coded as Darcom79.

Crown to an enthusiastic pro-Union position' (Smout 1969b: 180). As Devine (2003: 47) summarizes:

The disaster effectively served notice on the Union of the Crowns. It proved conclusively that when the vital interests of Scotland and England were in conflict, the monarch would always opt to support the position of the more powerful kingdom. This was a recipe for continuing tension and crisis.

The Darien venture had broad ramifications in the threat to King William's authority, but it also presented a threat to the monopoly trading rights of the English merchant classes. These were closely linked to the English parliamentary establishment, and caught up in the machinations over the extent of the East India Company's charter. The establishment of the Company of Scotland occurred at the time when the East India Company (seen as a Tory interest) was under attack from the Whigs. The Company of Scotland was seen to as a 'clever constitutional manoeuvre' to undermine the Tory-dominated East India Company (Lawson 1993: 54). The Whig attack on the East India Company from 1694 included a parliamentary enquiry into the Company's affairs, and combined with the establishment of the Company of Scotland, saw share prices fall from a high of £190 in 1693 to £38 in 1698 (Scott 1910: 179).

Westminster mobilized to strangle the Scottish Company, impeaching twenty-three of the directors, preventing English seamen and shipbuilders from aiding the project, and restricting the Company's access to British and European finance (Insh 1932: 58). This action comprehensively quashed the Company of Scotland's basis in the London financial and trading markets. The battle over the East India Company continued, with the Whigs forming a 'new' Company to challenge the charter of the 'old'. The 'new' East India Company offered the Crown access to cheaper finance for its military campaigns, and bolstered this with parliamentary support through the acquisition of seats in the Westminster Parliament. From 1699 to 1709 the 'old' and 'new' Companies engaged in a financial and political battle that offered support for military expansion in return for monopolistic trading rights. This debate was counter to simplistic views of free trade, being concerned with the establishment of English domination over essential foreign markets (Lawson 1993: 58–9).

The expansion of the English tax regime to Scotland was entrenched in the Acts of Union, although Brewer (1989: 22–3) notes that the entrenchment of taxation policy through the Union meant that the Scottish were particularly reluctant to accept any variation in the levels at which tax was levied. However, the Union brought Scotland within the ambit of what was becoming an established and efficient tax-gathering establishment. As Saville (1996: 5) notes, 'Scotland had a per capita tax base inferior to that of England, and the collection procedures were later found by Parliamentary inquiries to be inadequate and open to corruption'. Furthermore, it prevented the possibility of tax competition from north of the border, whereby trade and investment could be easily diverted away from England. It also restricted, although not totally ruling out, tax evasion through imports from Scotland.

The Union was crucial for absorbing the Scottish government system into an English tax and debt regime that had undergone radical transformation, what Dickson (1967) terms the 'Financial Revolution in England', which followed on the heels of the political revolution of 1688. Under the guidance of Lord Godolphin,[55] Lord Treasurer between 1703 and 1710, the tax-raising functions of the government were consolidated and allied to a system of long-term loans that reduced uncertainty over the liquidity of government and the markets. The land tax, levied at four shillings in the pound, was the 'chief pillar of direct taxation', and underwrote approximately two-thirds of the government's long-term debt (Dickson 1967: 358).[56] The figures for England and Wales show an expansion in the share of national income appropriated as taxation (calculated in constant price values) from 6.7 per cent in 1690 to 9.2 per cent in 1710 (O'Brien 1988: 3, Table 2.2).[57]

The raising of public debt was facilitated by the success of the East India Companies, which provided finance for the Exchequer, and the creation of the Bank of England in 1694. This was consolidated by the close links between these companies and parliament.[58] Interest rates on East India bonds fell from 6 per cent between 1688 and September 1705, to 5 per cent between September 1705 and September 1708 (Dickson 1967: 411, Table 67), and this was associated with a general lowering of interest rates on (English) government borrowing over the period in which the Union with Scotland was forged (Table 2.8).

In Scotland, the Bank of Scotland and the Darien Companies were unable to provide a comparable basis for a government debt.[59] The Scottish

---

[55] According to Dickson (1967: 358), 'Godolphin understood the realities of the money market, in particular the way in which the various sectors of government and credit interlocked'.

[56] Fletcher's *A Discourse of Government with relation to Militias* (1698) had argued in favour of a Scottish land tax, in order to place the government of Scotland on a firmer fiscal footing (see Robertson 1997: 41), although this was contingent on greater autonomy over how the finances raised would be spent.

[57] Scotland was not fully incorporated in the accounting system of the England and Wales government. O'Brien (1988: 3) notes that 'The collection of taxes in Scotland remained problematical for all departments concerned with the king's revenue, throughout the period 1707 1815'. In 1752 the Lord Chancellor lamented that 'some method should be taken to make Scotland pay the taxes but could any ministry hit upon that method?' (O'Brien 1988: 5).

[58] Dickson (1967: 266, Table 35) shows the peers and members of Parliament subscribing to loans or owning stock in the Bank of England and East India Companies.

[59] The Bank of Scotland was established in 1695, but was statutorily restricted in its abilities to raise government funds. The founder of the Darien Company, William Paterson, had been instrumental in establishing the Bank of England, and opposed the formation of a Bank of Scotland (Saville 1996: 32–3).

TABLE 2.8. *Government long-term borrowing (1704–1708)*

Date of royal assent to loan act	Sum raised (£)	Interest (%)
24 February 1704	1,382,976	6.6
16 January 1705	690,000	6.6
16 February 1706	2,855,762	6.4
27 March 1707	1,155,000	6.25
13 February 1708	640,000	6.25
11 March 1708	2,280,000	6.25

Source: Dickson (1967: Table 3: 60–1).

economy was, somewhat surprisingly, capable of financing the capital calls of both the Company and the Bank of Scotland, but such investment was unsustainable in the light of the lack of returns from both these issues, and by 1697 there was a credit crisis (Jones 2001: 38). Although the transformation of the credit culture in Scotland over this period has been described as providing 'the core of the financial revolution that occurred in Scotland during the eighteenth century' (Jones 2001: 39), it is probably safer to date the transformation from after 1707, when the Treaty of Union wound up the Company of Scotland on generous terms of compensation, and the Bank of Scotland was involved in the financing of the 'Equivalent' paid to smooth the economic impact of the Union.

The link between the Union and the funding of the national debt was seen as crucial by William Scott:

Riots were frequent towards the end of October 1706, and it may have been thought in London that the Jacobite faction in Scotland would take advantage of this state of feeling, and that there might be an insurrection, assisted by French troops. The reason that an invasion, in the interests of the exiled family, was dreaded was not only on account of the evils of a civil war, but because it was believed that it was the policy of the Pretender to repudiate the existing National Debt. Therefore any such rumour would have a most serious influence on the stock-market.... In January 1707, as it became known that the Union would be passed without alteration or delay by the English Parliament, prices of securities were first steady, at a low level, and then began to improve. (Scott 1911: 222–3)

Thus there was no adverse market reaction to the Union.[60] This is particularly important in the light of the thesis of North and Weingast (1989) and

---

[60] Theories of rational expectations amongst investors would suggest that they would not react directly to events, but in advance of events, depending on their perception of the effects of any likely outcome. This, as well as the multifaceted dimension of any investment decision—in which political circumstances were only one aspect—makes it difficult to directly attribute political causes to changes in stock prices at any particular time. Hence this analysis is impressionistic, rather than deterministic.

the revisions to this theory presented by Stasavage (2003). North and Wein-gast argue that the constitutional limitations imposed on the Crown as part of the Glorious Revolution of 1688 imposed a financial environment in which government was less liable to default on debt, and so enabled a system of national debt that enhanced the state's capacity to raise funds and function effectively. Stasavage refines this theory, noting that Parliamentary con-straints on the Crown were dependent on a competitive party system, and the political interplay between landowning and financial interests.

North and Weingast (1989) and Stasavage (2003) do not consider the implications of the Union with Scotland for the British state. The Scottish angle is examined more explicitly by Wells and Wills (2000), who argue that the presence of a viable Jacobite threat to the Crown would have an effect on the financial institutions that had developed alongside the government of England and Wales: 'asset prices should have fallen in the face of events that threatened the future viability of institutions established after the Revolu-tion; any events that strengthened these institutions, in contrast, should have had a positive impact on the value of financial assets' (Wells and Wills 2000: 429). Their study shows that the period of Union negotiations coincided with a strengthening stock price of both the Bank of England and the East India Company, suggesting that this period was characterized by a growing confi-dence in the constitutional environment and trading prospects for the Com-panies (Wells and Wills 2000: 430, fig. 1). An index of the London stock price index, developed by Neal (1990: 47, fig. 3.1), shows a general rise in market prices between November 1705 and 1708.

The emphasis put by Stasavage on the political composition of the Parlia-ment may shed further light on the positive reaction of the financial markets to the Union with Scotland. Stasavage shows that Tory representation within Westminster was positively associated with interest rates on debt, with Tory majorities being associated with a higher cost of borrowing. This reflected the association with the Tory party and the landed interest, who were hostile to land taxes, compared to the Whig party who were more closely linked to financial entrepreneurship, and sought a solid base of land tax and emphasized the importance of government credit (Stasavage 2003: ch. 5). Whilst the party systems in Edinburgh and Westminster were not strongly linked, the Scottish opposition to episcopalian domination meant that the Union was generally seen to favour the Whig interest. Scottish MPs elected to a united Parliament in London would be expected, on balance, to vote in the Whig interest, and hence Union was seen as consolidating the pro-finance block within the Parliament.

This section has attempted to put the history of the Company of Scotland and the passage of the Act of Union through the Edinburgh and Westminster Parliaments within the context of the development of the English fiscal state. As with the previous section, dealing with the direct influence of economic factors on the passage of the Act of Union through the Edinburgh Parliament, it does not accept that free trade was seen as an overriding benefit, but has to be seen within a more particularist interpretation of state and parliamentary interests. There were two aspects to this debate, regarding intracountry trade and the issue of wider access to international commerce. The term mercantilism was not yet invented (it was first used by the Marquis de Mirabeau in 1763 and popularized by Adam Smith (Backhouse 2002: 58)), but the idea of protectionism and national self-interest as a counter to the benefits of free trade were sufficiently established to ensure that the Union could not be presented as an economic panacea for the loss of national sovereignty. In terms of international trade, access to the burgeoning empire and the loss of protective customs barriers was more an issue of overcoming English (and Welsh) monopoly control and sharing the benefits and costs of military campaigns.

'Hanover with Some'

The unsatisfactory dual monarchy (Levack 1987) had provided the backdrop to the turbulent political history of the seventeenth century, and continued to resonate in Scotland throughout the eighteenth century. The role of King William and the issue of the succession to Queen Anne provided one of the central issues around which opponents and supporters of an incorporating Union mobilized. However, in the aftermath of the constitutional settlement of 1688, this was tied into a much broader debate about sovereignty, the powers of parliament(s), and the role of the church(es).

The 1706 session of the Scottish Parliament was opened with an address from Queen Anne stating, 'The Union has been long desired by both nations and we shall esteem it as the greatest glory of our reign to have it now perfected, being fully persuaded that it must prove the greatest happiness of our people' (Speck 1994: 106). The support for an incorporating union given by King William and Queen Anne removed any possibility of the use of the Crown veto over the Acts of Union passed by the Edinburgh and Westminster parliaments. Both monarchs had lobbied hard for such a measure, and Queen Anne attended the Westminster Parliament during the final debates on the Act of Union, in an expression of her support. However, despite the influence of the Crown over the running of the executive in London and Edinburgh, and powers of patronage through the court interest, this was subject to parliamentary control. William's desire for a parliamentary union was undone through Westminster's indifference, and Anne was forced to endure and endorse the outcomes of a hostile parliament in Edinburgh during the 1703–5 sessions.

In our analysis of the debate over 'Hanover' we focus not on the possibilities of the breaking of the dual monarchy or a Jacobite alternative (although these were certainly issues at the time), but on the religious basis of government in Britain. In London, the relationship between Nonconformists and the state shaped the domestic party political agenda both before and after union. In Scotland, the relationship between the Kirk and monarchy had drawn them into the English Civil War (otherwise known as the War of Three Kingdoms). Those Scottish politicians in favour of the Union were particularly concerned about the opposition from the Kirk (Devine 2003: 50). Devine (2003: 54) goes on to argue that 'the Kirk became the most formidable opponent of the [union] project'. However, by the time of the vote on the Articles of the Act of Union this opposition had been neutered by concessions to the leaders of the Presbyterian church, which was entrenched as the established church in Scotland.

William Carstares, the Scottish Presbyterian leader, acted as chaplain of William of Orange, and played a crucial role in establishing the Kirk in the Williamite constitutional settlement. Whilst less close to Queen Anne, Carstares was active in the promotion of the Union from his position as Principal of the University of Edinburgh, minister of Greyfriars' Church, and a prominent member of the National Assembly of the Presbyterian Church. According to the old Dictionary of National Biography:

> he used his great influence to procure the passage of the Treaty of Union, which had been a favourite project of William. It was chiefly due to him that the opposition of the presbyterian clergy was overcome. An anonymous letter, supposed to be from a member of the cabinet, declared that 'the union could never have had the consent of the Scotch parliament if you had not acted the worthy part you did'.

The central issue for Carstares was the entrenchment of the Presbyterian established church in Scotland, against the episcopal and Jacobite movements, by *An Act for the Security of the True Protestant Religion and Government of the Church*, passed alongside the Acts of Union (and incorporated with them so that it is still in force). As Carstares wrote to Harley in October 1706, 'the desire I have to see our Church secured makes me in love with the Union as the most probable means to preserve it' (Dunlop 1967: 115). Whilst this was not the unanimous view of the Presbyterian clergy, the pro-Union leaders were able to prevent outright hostility to the Union becoming an issue associated with the church (Macree 1973: 71–3). The approach of Carstares was supported and encouraged by Daniel Defoe, whose role as propagandist for the Union involved reassurance that the change in the constitution would not threaten the Presbyterian Church (Macree 1973: 65–6).[61]

---

[61] In September 1706, Defoe described his own role in Edinburgh being 'To remove the jealousies and uneasiness of people about secret designs here against the Kirk' (q. Macree 1973: 65).

The granting of *An Act for the Security of the... Church* has been described as 'a political masterstroke which removed the Kirk as the galvanizer of addresses against the union from presbyteries and local communities' (McNeill and MacQueen 1996: 152). As Young (1999: 29–37) describes, the presbytery had proved a source of organized opposition to an incorporating union, associated with various petitions raised against the measure. The establishment of the Presbyterian Church satisfied the church leadership, and removed the defence of Presbyterianism as a focus for the opposition to the Union (see Mathieson 1905: 182–8). The vote on the Act was held on 12 November 1706, in between the votes on Articles 1 and 2 of the Act of Union.[62] The Act was passed by 113 to 38, a majority larger than that of the key vote on Article 1. Figure 2.3 shows the pattern of voting.

There was a very strong association between support for Article 1 of the Act of Union and support for the *Act for the Security of the... Church*. Ninety-five members of the Edinburgh Parliament supported both measures, and no pro-Union members voted against the establishment of the Presbyterian Church. However, the opponents of the Union were more clearly

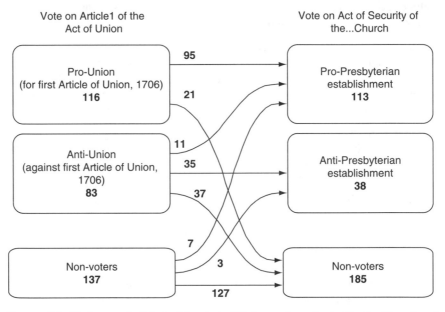

FIGURE 2.3. Voting on Article 1 of the Act of Union and on *An Act for the Security of the... Church* in the Scottish Parliament, November 1706

---

[62] According to Speck (1994: 108), the *Act for the Security of the... Church* was rushed through the Edinburgh Parliament, in response to points made by Lord Belhaven in his speech against the First Article of Union.

divided on the measure, with eleven of the eighty-three members who had voted against Article 1 voting for Presbyterian establishment. Whilst opponents of the Union made up nearly all of the thirty-eight votes against the *Act for the Security of the... Church*, more abstained on this than voted against. Whilst it is difficult to say whether these were strategic abstentions or simply due to absence from the parliament, the pattern of voting shown in Figure 2.3 suggests that the vote on church establishment divided the opposition to a greater extent than the pro-Union group.[63]

The analysis presented here emphasizes the role in which the devolution of church establishment, with the provisions made for the Presbyterian establishment alongside the Act of Union, helped remove a potential source of opposition to the incorporating union. It brought the leadership of the Kirk into sympathy with the Court party, and exposed the divisions on religious issues amongst the opponents of union in Scotland. Further to this, a similar process occurred in London, where a similar Act entrenching the Church of England was passed alongside the Act of Union at Westminster (Speck 1994: 114). Whilst there is limited evidence on voting patterns in the Westminster Parliament on this issue, it undoubtedly helped assuage Tory doubts as to the religious basis of the constitution. There was opposition from high church Tories, led by Sir John Pakington, who saw a conflict between the Queen's role as head of the Church of England and upholder of the Church of Scotland, but opposition in both the House of Lords and House of Commons was limited (Speck 1994: 114–15).[64]

The Tories had attempted to entrench Anglican dominance, pressing for restrictions on 'Occasional Conformity', by which a brief appearance (by Nonconformists and other non-desirables) in Anglican churches could qualify people for civil or military office. Two Occasional Conformity Bills were defeated in the sessions of 1702–3 and 1703–4, through Whig control of the House of Lords; the opportunist attempt to 'tack' provisions to prevent 'occasional conformity' on to the Land Tax Bill of 1704 provided a focus for the general election of 1705, and was seen as leading to Whig gains. The claim, often resonant in English politics at the time, of 'Church in Danger'

---

[63] At a more detailed level of analysis, comparing voting patterns between 1703, Article 1 of the Act of Union, and the *Act for the Security of the... Church* shows that there was very little difference in the abstention rate within those members who had been solidly pro-Union and those who had switched to a pro-union stance between 1703 and 1706. However, those who had switched from pro-to anti-union positions or had newly joined the anti-union camp were less likely to vote against the *Act for the Security of the... Church* when compared to those who had consistently opposed unionist measures from 1703. This gives some support to the argument that the issue of Presbyterian establishment cut across the anti-unionist support base.

[64] In the House of Commons the third reading of the Act of Union was passed 274 votes to 116. In the House of Lords, attempts to challenge the role of the Scottish church were defeated 55 to 19 (Speck 1994: 116).

was defused by Godolphin and Harley, and, according to Bennett (1969: 168), 'By 1707 the ecclesiastical issue had become associated with sterile factious politics, and the clergy's case seemed to be going down into the limbo of lost causes'. In part this reflected the way that the issues of succession, the role of the monarchy, and the position of the established church divided the Tory and Cavalier parties, where the interests of episcopalians, Jacobites, and supporters of the court interest were in conflict.[65] The Whigs and the Court Party in London and Edinburgh were more tolerant of Nonconformity, and an incorporating union that placed an episcopalian monarch alongside a strong parliament and devolved church establishment. This provided a solid basis for parliamentary support for the incorporating union, whilst weakening a challenge to such a measure based on religious issues.

'Ease and Security'

The Cromwellian union, imposed through conquest in 1654 after battles at Dunbar and Worcester, raised the question of whether Scotland could survive as an independent nation. The issue of military security was reinforced in 1706 by the mobilization of troops northwards. It is not clear whether this was part of a deliberate threat, designed by the London court to focus the minds of the members of the Scottish parliament on the might of the English military machine, or simply a reaction to the danger of disturbance caused by the heightened popular discontent in Scotland. Godolphin assured the Earl of Leven that forces were stationed 'to bee in a readiness in case this ferment should continue to give any farther disturbance to the publick peace' (Ferguson 1977: 256). According to McNeill and MacQueen (1996: 151), 'To underline the seriousness of their intent, the English ministry had moved troops to Berwick and northern Ireland to be held within striking distance of Edinburgh and the west of Scotland, the main areas of anticipated opposition to the union'.

The focus of English military concerns in 1706 was certainly not Scotland, but the European campaign being pursued by the Duke of Marlborough. Whilst the negotiations over the basis of an incorporating union were being thrashed out at Westminster, Marlborough was engaged in the thrashing of

---

[65] As in Scotland, where the Jacobite/Cavalier/Country party alliance was divided along lines of religious and monarchical allegiance, as well as loyalty to the court and access to patronage, the Tories in Westminster were divided when it came to the prospect of enhancing a Jacobite succession (Holmes 1967: 90–2). By contrast, the Whigs were united on the issue of succession, and found a natural conformity between this and support for the Hanoverian succession, support for Queen Anne, and the prospects for Union pressed by Godolphin and Harley: 'Without Whig initiative, wholehearted Whig cooperation, and in the final instance Whig votes it is virtually certain that the act of 1707 would never have been passed' (Holmes 1967: 85).

the French, culminating in the victory at Ramillies on 12 May. Union with Scotland may have had a military advantage in consolidating the base of the British military territory (although this was challenged in 1708, 1715, and 1745), but it also absorbed Scotland into the English model of governmental and military relations. Again, this is associated with the 'financial revolution' in England, which was closely tied in to the expansionist military commitments of the government under William, Mary, and Queen Anne. Military expenditure between 1702 and 1713 accounted for some 72 per cent of total government expenditure, and amounted to some £93,644,560, a third of which was financed by loans (O'Brien 1988: 2, Table 1; Dickson 1967: 10, Table 1). According to the English Commissioners for Union in 1702, Scotland gained from the success of the British military state:

the sayd [English Government] debts have been contracted by a long War entered into more particularly for the Preservation of England & the dominions thereunto belonging, yet that Scotland has tasted of the Benefits which have accrued to Great Brittain in general from the Opposition that has been made to the Growth and Power of France. (Dickson 1967: 8)

The relationship between the military and the government provided one of the focuses for the anti-Union campaign in Scotland. For Andrew Fletcher of Saltoun an essential part of the constraints on a potentially autocratic government was a separation between government power and the organization of the military. He was a zealous advocate of a militia consisting of all Scots capable of bearing arms, rather than a standing army:

A good militia is of such importance to a nation, that it is the chief part of the constitution of any free government. For though as to other things, the constitution be never so slight, a good militia will always preserve the publick liberty. (Fletcher (1698) in Robertson 1997: 21)

For Daniel Defoe the constitutional threat of a standing army had been sufficiently constrained by the development of Parliamentary control over the power of the king. However, Fletcher felt that only a militia-based army would counter the power of a potentially arbitrary Crown, and which, according to John Robertson, exemplified Fletcher's commitment to a civic tradition of government:

The mere principle of parliamentary consent, by which Defoe set such store, must be a thin shield against the corrupting pressures of the modern military-financial nexus: it was all too probable, indeed, that the members of parliament would themselves be corrupted, their 'sovereignty' then enhancing rather than checking government's arbitrary power. (Robertson 1985: 30)

The militia issue was partially subsumed by the importance of the war against France in the run-up to 1707. The presence of a standing army was less controversial during war—the main debate centred on how the military forces of the state should be maintained during peacetime. Appeals to Scottish martial history had become less resonant, particularly in lowland areas, whilst the English army had attracted a disproportionate number of Scottish gentlemen (Robertson 1985: 6). The European campaign also brought together Scots fighting in the Scottish, English, and Dutch armies, a common cause that would be enhanced by a more coherent organization.

Whilst, as John Robertson has described, the issue of national defence and military organization was a matter of debate through to the Scottish Enlightenment, there is little evidence that Fletcher managed to use the issue to rally opposition to the Union. The proposal presented in his pamphlet written in response to the English Standing Army Controversy of 1697–8, *A Discourse of Government with relation to Militias*, was for a system of conscription organized in one Scottish and three English camps, under joint British control (Fletcher (1698) in Robertson 1997: 25). This plan was consistent with Fletcher's wider concerns for the diffusion of power and a federal structure of government, but, as with his other constructive constitutional proposals, somewhat esoteric and hardly a rallying cause for the anti-Union movement. Whilst the role and organization of the military had been a major part of the limitations proposed by Fletcher in the parliament of 1703, they got no mention whatsoever in the Act of Union approved in 1707. The Scottish Parliament was willing to buy (or be bought) into the military system of the English state.

Fletcher's ideas about a militia took root not in Great Britain but in the USA. The 'Country Whigs', of whom he was one, argued as he did that militias preserved freedom whereas standing armies threatened it. The leaders of the American Revolution, above all Thomas Jefferson, took over Country Whig ideology wholesale as it suited their politics and their temperaments. The protection of state militias is therefore written into the US Bill of Rights in the Second Amendment, which guarantees 'the right to bear arms' to their members.

Representation and Finance

In the negotiations that took place in the cockpit in Westminster in 1706, there was only one issue that forced the Westminster and Edinburgh delegations to meet collectively: representation. England and Wales returned 513 members to the House of Commons, and Scotland was first offered 38. This was above the ratio of contributions to the British treasury, which were closer to 28:513, but below the population ratio, on which basis Scotland should have returned around 100 seats (Speck 1994: 100). The Scottish

Commissioners proposed a representation of fifty seats, and a compromise was struck at forty-five ('after a great deal of haggling' according to Ferguson (1977: 236)), alongside sixteen members of the House of Lords.[66] This settlement was entrenched in Article 22 of the Act of Union.

The passage of Article 22 was meant to be the last-ditch stand of the opponents of the incorporating Union, but was the occasion of the Duke of Hamilton's toothache (Ferguson 1977: 264–5). In the absence (or abscess?) of the figurehead of the opposition movement, the campaign failed. The importance of the Article lay not only in the general principle of Scottish representation, but in the mechanics by which the Scottish members of the Westminster Parliament would be chosen. The fact that the Westminster Parliament had decided that the passage of the Union would not be accompanied by a general election across the newly constituted state before the (English and Welsh) general election required by 1708 meant that the Scottish Parliament had to select its own method of representation in the first British parliament in Westminster.[67] This led to a period of intensive (and antagonistic) bargaining amongst members of the three estates (Riley 1978: 293) over the basis of Scottish representation. An appeal to the Scottish electorate may have led to a more representative contingent of Scottish MPs in the Westminster Parliament, but such an option was (completely understandably, in terms of party interests) rejected, and the parliament decided to choose its own delegates to Westminster on the basis of the existing parliamentary majority in Edinburgh.[68] The majoritarian system adopted meant that the court interest in Edinburgh could choose its own representatives, and the Whig interest in the Westminster Parliament was fully consolidated by the incorporation of the Scottish members.

The outcome of the procedure chosen by the Scottish Parliament in choosing its own delegates (and then representatives) to the Westminster Parliament appears to be entirely consistent with short-term political interests. The question remains, however, as to why it should accept a situation where the number of members elected from the shire and burgh constituencies

[66] Under the Cromwellian settlement Scotland had been allocated 30 seats, although the fact that Cornwall returned 44 seats undermined any great rationale for the allocation of seats according to taxation or population (see Speck 1970: 16–17).

[67] The grouping of burghs and shires was based upon the system of grouping applied under the Cromwellian Union. For the clustering of burghs and shires used, see McNeil and MacQueen (1996: 227 and 229).

[68] The Scottish Court party had agreed on the sixteen peers they hoped would be chosen for the House of Lords, including four *Squadrone* peers. This led to complaints, since apparently Queensberry had promised that all the *Squadrone* peers would be included; the Earls of Haddington and Marchmont were left out. Further, the peers from the Court party were not obliged to vote for members of the *Squadrone*. In general, Queensberry was generous in directing patronage towards the members of the *Squadrone*, in recognition of their service in passing the Union (Riley 1964: 36).

of Scotland fell from 157 to 45, and the effective representation of the nobility was reduced from 160 to 16. If, as Riley (1978) and Ferguson (1977) argue, the motives behind Scottish members of parliament voting for Union were largely determined by patronage, then surely it was an early case of (112 burgh and shire, and 144 noble) turkeys voting for Christmas (albeit with many receiving a rich stuffing). Acceptance of the incorporating union would deny a huge swathe of the Scottish political establishment from the future possibility of patronage and preferment.

The fact that so many Scottish parliamentarians were willing to remove themselves from the direct access to the patronage and influence that legislative membership gave them indicates that broader considerations were involved. We have outlined some of our conjectures as to the motivations behind the acceptance of the Act of Union in the Edinburgh Parliament, emphasizing the general and particular benefits to Scotland (and members of parliament) of the Articles regarding trade, the combination of religious and constitutional issues embodied in the issue of succession, and the fuller absorption of the Scottish state into the English military system. On top of these issues was the general viability of the Scottish system of government. As Whatley (2000: 37) notes, 'State finances . . . were in a parlous condition, with the cost of funding the civil list, the military and government being estimated to be some £14,311 sterling more than Scotland's total annual revenues of around £113,194 at the time of Union'. Membership of the Scottish executive could often involve calls on revenue that were not commensurate with the returns involved.

Conclusion: Neither Statesmen Nor Rogues

From 1690 the Scottish Parliament had developed an increasingly assertive position in relation to the Westminster Parliament and the monarch, but it had not established the fiscal or administrative basis that would support a more independent role. Under the existing constitutional system such assert- iveness brought it into conflict with the trading, military, and regal interests of the English (and to a lesser extent Welsh) state. It is not inconceivable that an alternative constitutional structure could have embraced these competing interests, but the opposition to an incorporating union was divided along ideological and pragmatic lines. As Rait (1901: 116) laments, of the Scottish Parliament:

It had entered into a new sphere, and assumed new functions. A career of usefulness seemed to lie before it. In spite of its age, its end was, in this sense, premature.

Our attempt to examine the voting behaviour of members of the Scottish par- liament suggests that personal gain, through either bribery or compensation, was less of an influence than has been previously suggested. Scottish members of parliament were willing to exchange direct involvement in a system of administrative patronage that delivered limited returns, in favour of a more powerful system of executive authority.

Although the analysis presented here suggests that economic and fiscal issues were a major influence on the passage of the Acts of Union, it does not indicate that the Union between England and Wales and Scotland was an inevitable result of such influences. Rather, the way that such interests were politicized was the key factor. Over the same period Ireland had similar trading and economic concerns, difficulties in the operation of joint monarchy, and disagreements over the relationship between a Dublin and London executive and parliament. However, the problems of assimilating the Scottish Parliament into the Westminster system and interests of the London court were much more immediate, notably as an assertive Edinburgh Parliament threatened particular English interests through the establishment of a Company of Scotland. Whilst the Company of Scotland, through the Darien venture, was a failure, it provided a focus for regal and parliamentary opposition in London to the establishment of an independent Scottish economic policy.

At the start of this chapter we grouped interpretations of the 1707 Union into:

- Diceyan (incorporating union as a supreme act of statesmanship)
- Nationalist/Namierite (a parcel of rogues in a nation were bought and sold for English gold)
- Free trading (Roxburgh's *Trade with most*)
- Uncertainty-reducing (*Hanover with some*)
- Welfare-maximizing (*a generall aversion to civill discords, intollerable poverty and... constant oppression*).

On our historical and statistical evidence, the eighteenth-century Earl was nearer the truth than twentieth-century scholars.

The Dicey view, seeing only an incorporating Union, overlooks the extent to which the Union of 1707 was a *compromise* between the Westminster and Edinburgh parliaments. The Act of Union as approved by the parliament of Scotland included a number of concessions to the trading interests of Scotland (or at least the Scottish members of parliament). More importantly, it entrenched the Presbyterian Church in Scotland. This helped neutralize opposition to the Union within Scotland, but also restricted Tory aspirations for an episcopalian settlement. The entrenchment of religious devolution under a Protestant monarch was exchanged for parliamentary union. The entrenchment of two different versions of Protestant truth, via the Scottish and English church establishment Acts that are both incorporated in the final

Act of Union, has remained a fundamental feature of the British constitution ever since. We return to it in later chapters.

As far as we know, our analysis of the flow of the vote in the last Scottish Parliament is new. Perhaps our most important finding is negative. The relationship between Darien holding and vote on Union is not statistically significant (Tables 2.6 and 2.7). That non-significance is of great substantive significance. It destroys the Namierites' central contention. Those who held Darien stock were no more prone to be bought and sold with English gold than those who did not. Likewise is the fact that the members of the Scottish Parliament were content for their numbers to be drastically reduced.

Trade was a big issue, but commentators schooled in (neo)classical economics misconstrue it. The classical view, developed by Adam Smith and David Ricardo, is that both sides of a customs union always gain from trade. Smith had seen the huge growth of the Scottish economy in his own lifetime. But it did not immediately follow the union. The negotiators of the Union thought of trade as a weapon, not as a positive-sum game. The two nations could threaten one another's trade—Scotland could threaten the East India Company, and England could counter-threaten by harassing the Darien Company or by the anti-Scottish Acts mentioned earlier. A trade treaty was a promise to put down the weapons, not a chance to gain from Ricardian comparative advantage, which was not understood in 1706.

Because so many modern commentators forget that Union was a bargain, they miss Roxburgh's last two points. Bargainers do not strike a deal unless both parties think that they will gain. Union was uncertainty-reducing and welfare-maximizing for both the English and the Scottish negotiators. For the English, reducing uncertainty about the succession meant that the northern frontier was secured and the Jacobite threat contained. Most of the voters for the Duke of Hamilton's Resolve were not Jacobites. They were shrewd bargainers, whose credible threat brought the English to the table. Though they would have preferred a federal union, the Scottish negotiators did not try very hard to get one. They were content with incorporating union on the terms they got. It took some time before Scotland's intolerable poverty was lifted, and then (from the mid-eighteenth century) it was largely due to economic forces the bargainers of 1706 did not understand.

Dicey was right that the Acts of 1707 brought fundamental change, although he and his followers have characterized it wrongly. We follow some of these changes in subsequent chapters. The Union made the Empire possible. It seemed to swallow Scottish politics up into English politics to make British politics. Actually, it never did that, but unionists have often wrongly believed that it did. That has led to some serious Unionist misperceptions from 1886 onwards, as our narrative will show.

3

Ireland's Incorporation: An 'Excusable Mistake'?

I have long suspected the Union of 1800. There was a case for doing something: but this was like Pitt's Revolutionary war, a gigantic though excusable mistake.

(W. E. Gladstone, diary for 19.9.1885)

The Irish incorporation into the UK government can be seen as part of a relentless expansionism of the English state, fuelled by imperialism and a desire to control the peripheral regions of the British Isles. However, such a view must be qualified in the light of the fact that it took nearly a century for the Scottish model of parliamentary incorporation to be transferred to the Irish situation. The Irish Parliament appealed for a Union, according to the same model as the Scottish had implemented (or had imposed), three times between 1703 and 1709, but were rebuffed by the Westminster Parliament. This raises the question of why Westminster was willing to accept the Scots, but reject Irish advances? How well does our description of the Scottish Union reflect upon the rejection of the Irish case at the same time? Further, does it shed light on the final acceptance of a more complete political union across the British Isles in 1800–1?

Both unionist and nationalist accounts of Scottish and Irish incorporation into the 'English' state or Westminster government have large amounts in common, independent from the very different contexts under which incorporation took place. The nationalist view of both events emphasizes the emasculation of national sovereignty resultant on the abolition of parliamentary authority. Undermined by bribery and corruption controlled by a coterie of politicians under the sway of the English administration and the Crown, the independence of Scotland/Ireland was relinquished, against the will of the people. The Scots sentiments of Robert Burns were echoed in the verse, attributed to an Irish judge (Bolton 1966: 51):

How did they pass the Union?
By perjury and fraud;

By slaves who sold their land for gold
As Judas sold his God.

The unionist perspective suggests a statesman-like judgement of national
interest overcoming popularist sentiment in order to consolidate the emergence of a powerful UK. Neither nationalist or unionist accounts satisfac-
torily expalin for the reasons Ireland was not considered ripe for
incorporation in 1707, when the Dublin Parliament was asking for incorporation and Westminster could have further consolidated its direct control of
the British Isles.

One major contextual factor behind the different treatment of Scotland and
Ireland at the start of the eighteenth century was the different outcomes resulting from the Williamite succession. In Scotland, as discussed in
Chapter 2, this period saw the emergence of an assertive parliamentary system
that strained the constitutional basis of a dual monarchy, and that, in turn,
exposed the difficulties of reconciling the economic, military, and political
interests of Scotland and England (and Wales). In Ireland, the Williamite
succession led to a regal constitutional settlement that was much easier to
manage from London. The military defeat of James II in Ireland led to the
establishment of the Protestant (and constitutionally Anglican) ascendancy.

The Irish Parliament and government administration was closely tied in
with the interests of the English court, and as such was much more easily
managed and manipulated. Further, some of the key influences on the
Scottish establishment—such as a desire to assert a nationalist programme
at odds with English interests, the need to maintain and develop a common
tax base and trading interest, the necessity of establishing a coherent military
basis for the state, and the issue of a general constitutional settlement—were
less pertinent in the Irish context. The Irish Parliament was weaker, and
relatively content in playing a subservient role to the London court. The
monarch was not reliant on the Dublin Parliament for control of tax revenue,
and there was no great challenge to the major trading interests of the London
stock market. There was a common interest between the Crown and the Irish
Protestant ascendancy in maintaining a military presence in the interests of
civil control and the prevention of foreign invasion, as well as a common
interest in the continued sovereignty of an English-based monarch.

However, go forward a hundred years, and the parallels between Scottish
and Irish Union are much clearer. In both cases events were precipitated by
crises over the royal succession and heightened military tension. The Scottish
Parliament's rejection of the Hanoverian succession, in response to the
insensitive attempt of Westminster to impose this across the kingdom, threatened the line of succession favoured by Queen Anne and her advisors. The
Irish reaction to the Regency crisis of 1789, when George III became too ill

to function as king, exposed similar weaknesses in London's control over the sovereignty of the realm. In both cases, crisis exposed the uncertainty that could be incurred through a system including a bifurcated legislative and executive system. They also helped focus the attention of the monarch on the possibility that independent Parliaments outside London could propose and encourage alternative routes of succession. Control over the regal line was further entangled with issues of military threat and the religious status of the countries involved. This was most evident in the French invasion of Ireland of 1798 which sought, but failed, to exploit widespread Irish dissatisfaction with the system of government. In the run-up to the Union of 1707, the French state's careful nurturing of the Jacobite line, and the association with Scottish heritage and patronage, had presented a similar danger of invasion, popular rebellion, and Catholic reassertion.

Alongside these issues of constitutional influence, Union was driven by partisan interest. In 1707 the Scots expected to join the Westminster Parliament were seen to be on the Whig side which drove through the Union. In the case of the Irish Union issues of Regency and reform meant that the government side were associated with support for Pitt, whilst the opposition was associated with Fox. The balance of power in Westminster (or expectations of how the balance of power would change) were crucial in determining attitudes to the Union.

In both the Scottish and Irish cases the combined threat to the military, religious, and royal establishment was a cause for concern in London, but it was also a source of danger to a significant element amongst the political elites of Dublin and Edinburgh. In both cases a crisis over political control of the kingdom was accompanied by fiscal difficulties, with growing parliamentary assertiveness weakened by a lack of a sufficient tax base to support any autonomous programme of government. This reflected a weakness in the representative basis of the administration in Scotland and Ireland. In the face of such issues and conflicts, parliamentary union was one option that offered political, economic, military, and constitutional consolidation.

There were four aspects of the military situation that impinged on British strategic situation in the run-up to 1800. First is the threat of invasion, and the threat that an enemy (probably French) would land in Ireland and (possibly with the threat of Irish rebels) be poised to attack the west of Britain. Second, the Irish ports provided an important strategic base, extending British naval control over shipping routes (in particular) to the Americas. Third, the army were dispersed around Ireland and used as an adjunct to the police force to cope with domestic unrest, such as that instigated by the groups of agrarian protestors such as the Whiteboys. Finally, as the international military commitments of the British increased, Ireland became an increasingly important recruiting ground for the British army. By the 1770s there was a widening acceptance that the enlistment of Catholics was a practical necessity, if not totally welcome. At the start of the eighteenth century Irishmen comprised about 5 per cent of the rank and file of the army, whilst by the start of the nineteenth century the proportion could have been as much as a third (McDowell 1979: 60–2).

This left the question of religious consolidation, which, in the Scottish case, had seen the monarch accept a devolved religious settlement, in which she would accept limitations on the scope of Anglican authority within Britain. A similar settlement was designed by the architects of the Irish Union, William Pitt (the younger) and his Irish administration, but rejected by George III. Scottish Presbyterians may have had a place in the British constitution, but the acceptance of Irish Catholics was much more contentious. The issue of Catholic emancipation was inexorably tied up with the idea of parliamentary union, but supporters and opponents of the first issue were not necessarily respectively placed in their attitudes to the second. Whilst the monarch, with his potential veto power over any legislation, was in a highly influential position, this conundrum muddied the positions of both supporters and opponents of the constitutional changes that took place in the government of Ireland at the end of the eighteenth century. This murky political situation has allowed supporters of Irish nationalism to assert and decry the influence of the Irish Parliament in passing the Union, and unionists to condemn and condone the eventual settlement.

The Crisis of Irish Representation

The constitutional settlement that had followed the military victory of William over James in Ireland in 1690, and which had established the control of a narrowly based Anglican ascendancy in Ireland, struggled to reconcile the articulation of Irish interests within a system that was representatively restricted by its narrow political and socio-economic basis. The Irish constitution in the eighteenth century was a product of the Williamite succession, in which (against King William's desire for a conciliatory settlement) the military victory in Ireland was consolidated through the entrenchment of the Protestant (Anglican) ascendancy. The Irish administration was organized on the basis of the mutual interests of the Anglican Protestants and the British government:

The Irish ascendancy could not maintain their position without the political and military shadow of England in the background: England, on the other hand, was faced with Ireland's strategic position and needed the tranquillity and loyalty of the neighbouring kingdom; a need which was emphasised by the wars of the century. (Johnston 1963: 3)

This system broke down when it could no longer respond to the military and fiscal demands faced in both Britain and Ireland. The situation was compounded by the weak administrative and representative basis of the Dublin government. The tensions that arose with British military and fiscal expansionism, compounded by confusion about how to address the issue of Catholic emancipation and tackle Presbyterian grievances, led to an uneasy coalition of Irish unionists and Pitt's government that was able to force through a legislative union in 1800.

In 1782 the British Parliament agreed to give Ireland more legislative independence than before. The establishment of 'Grattan's parliament', as it has become known, failed to break Anglican political hegemony in Ireland. Henry Grattan's hope for a more inclusive and independent legislative system, based on a gradual incorporation of the Catholic and Presbyterian middle classes, was stymied by caution amongst the Dublin political elite, a caution shared by the British administration.[1] The outcome was a legislature that had a louder voice, but no greater power or representative strength. Grattan's parliament was unable to offer a solution to the collapse of the 'Undertaker' system of government, whereby British influence was exercised by a compliant administration in Dublin, which was meant to reconcile broader British policy and Irish circumstances. Rather, it offered a modified version of this system, that Anglican interests were entrenched, but with no real mechanism for the articulation of broader Irish political demands in an administrative system that was still centred on British fiscal control and the political sovereignty of the monarchy. The crisis in Irish government caused by the American War of Independence, whose ideology found particularly strong resonance amongst the nonconformist Irish in Ulster,[2] was addressed through the concession of greater legislative autonomy, which diffused the focus of the Volunteer movement, and stability was enhanced by the control of John Beresford over the administration of the Dublin administration, based on a political grouping known as the 'friends of English government' (Johnston 1963: 72).

The impact of the American and French revolutions resonated across the Irish polity in very different ways. In Ulster, where strong connections with the Presbyterian American settlers combined with sympathy with the complaint of 'taxation without representation', initial reactions to an anti-British

---

[1] 'The parliament that bore his name was not often willing to submit itself to his guidance' (Beckett 1966: 227).

[2] Lecky (1902: 159) records Benjamin Franklin's visit to Dublin in 1771, where he found members of the Irish Parliament sympathetic to the Irish cause, and noted the possibility of exploiting shared interests. Lecky (1902: 160) notes that by 1775 'The Presbyterians of the North were fiercely American', but that this feeling was not apparent in the Irish Parliament.

agenda were positive. However, the American alliance with the French in 1778 (and the capture of a British ship by the American privateer, Paul Jones, in Belfast Lough), combined with the dispersal of British troops in Ireland, exposed fears of a French invasion: 'The Presbyterians had sympathized with the Americans, but they hated and feared the French' (Beckett 1966: 211). Meanwhile, the need for an expanded British army meant that discrimination against Catholics was a hindrance to recruitment.[3] Further, the control of the Catholic establishment had been undermined by the French revolution:

when the new regime in France began to quarrel with the Catholic Church, the prospect opened up in the British body politic, for the first time since the Reformation, that Catholicism under the British Crown might be turned into a fund of loyalty rather than potential treason. Accordingly, the years between 1791 and 1793 became, as it were, a race between the United Irishmen and the British government to capture the support of the Catholics of Ireland. The Dublin parliament found itself sidelined, even though it would have to bear any immediate consequences. It was now that the term Ascendancy was first coined—rather like the term ancien regime in France—to describe an order assumed to be on the verge of extinction. (Doyle 2000: 178)

As a result both Catholic and Presbyterian loyalties were divided, between loyalty to revolutionary principles and association with a British state that was offering resistance to French expansionism. The Irish Parliament and Dublin administration were ill-placed to exploit this state of flux, tied down by its focus on an Anglican landowning elite and the perpetuation of the status quo.

The outbreaks of Irish rebellion of 1798 reflected this complex situation of political uncertainty, based on a divergence in terms of representation, religious identity, and ideological association. The uprising, organized by the United Irishmen, had sporadic success in the southern Catholic-dominated County Wexford and in the northern Protestant-dominated County Down, but French troops landed in the western county Mayo, where a rout of the British troops at Castlebar was insufficient to gather a substantial momentum to ignite coherent opposition to British military control. The French incursion was halted at Ballinamuck, County Longford. The instigator of the invasion, Wolfe Tone, following up with a French naval force, was captured off Donegal, and then committed suicide.

The rebellion exposed the vulnerability of the Irish flank of the British Isles, in terms of both Irish insurrection and foreign invasion. For the British government, the inability of the Irish government to police Ireland effectively involved a huge cost, at a time when the campaign against the French was providing strains that required a restructuring of the British fiscal system.

---

[3] In 1774, Irish Catholics were first permitted to take an oath of allegiance to the Crown without violation of conscience (Beckett 1966: 214).

As with the Scottish case, the Irish Union was driven by an underlying fiscal crisis, exacerbated by a failure of the Irish Parliament to reconcile its own interests with those of the British military state.

'Taxation not Civilization'

Economic relations between Britain and Ireland and their impact on the passage of the Act(s) of Union has received little attention, in stark contrast to similar treatments of the Union between Scotland and England (and Wales) of 1707 (see Chapter 2).[4] This relative neglect is a reflection of the low priority that economic issues received in the drafting and passage of the Act of Union in Dublin. The Act of Union with Scotland contained numerous articles dealing with trading concessions (through the limited imposition of a common scheme of customs of tariffs and excise), and the compensation that was due to Scotland (through the 'Equivalent') on the acceptance of the English (and Welsh) national debt. The Act of Union dealing with Ireland dealt with the subject in one Article (the seventh) containing no trading concessions, and a simple division of responsibility for the United Kingdom's national debt.

The issue of free trade and the union was a focus for the pamphleteers of the late 1790s, but (as in Scotland in the run-up to 1707) there was a balance of opinions regarding the economic costs and benefits of an incorporating union. The pro-Unionists raised the prospects of huge gains in terms of investment and national prosperity that would flow from the creation of a common market with Britain: 'manifold must be the golden streams which would flow into Ireland from that source' according to a pamphlet issued in 1799 (McDowell 1943: 249). The economic strength of the Scottish economy after 1707 was used to advertise the gains that could be expected from the union. Countering such arguments, the anti-Unionists stressed the loss of economic autonomy and the likely subservience of Irish interests to the requirements of English merchants. Further to this, Ireland would become burdened with British public debt: the object of the union was 'Taxation not civilization', according to one commentator (McDowell 1943: 251).

The fact that economic issues were not a particularly contentious issue in the passage of the Union in Ireland does not necessarily mean that it was not an underlying causal factor. In Dublin, the nature of the Protestant 'ascendancy', in both its social background and constitutional establishment, meant that economic considerations were relegated to a relatively minor position in

---

[4] Neither of the two recent volumes dealing with the causes of the Union (Keogh and Whelan 2001; Brown et al. 2003) have chapters concerned with the economic background to the events.

discussion of the Irish parliamentary union. As Johnston (1963: 246) writes, 'The commercial interest in the Irish House of Commons was always extremely slender, and it is improbable that there were more than thirty members sitting in parliament during this period who were actively engaged in any type of commercial enterprise'.[5] Further, 'the far-reaching effects of the penal code had made the "ascendancy" an almost exclusively landed class, while they had encouraged Catholics and dissenters to embark on trade by making it extremely difficult for them to own land'. This meant that there was little direct representation of the trading interests in the Dublin Parliament, and accounts for the relatively low priority that economic issues were accorded in the union debates.

At the Westminster Parliament, of course, there was a much greater preponderance of MPs with trading interests, and economic issues were much more acutely politicized. Pitt argued to the House of Commons in 1799 that the Union would see an infusion of 'English capital, English manners [and] English Industry', and so engender benefits in a manner similar to that of Scotland (Bartlett 2003: 52–3). Whilst the same commercial benefits as had been offered the Scots did not pertain to the Irish situation, there were was still an imperialist agenda, although more often expressed in terms of political and military unity, as stressed by Bartlett (2003). That such arguments were expressed in terms of a 'Protestant empire' reflected the terms that were likely to appeal to the Dublin Parliament.

Developments in Anglo-Irish trading relations throughout the eighteenth century, alongside a growing fiscal crisis in the Irish administration, indicate that these provided a powerful argument in Britain for a revised constitutional settlement and an incorporating parliamentary union. The eighteenth century had seen a significant expansion in the Irish economy, accompanied by a growing level of overseas trade. However, this expansion was largely (and to an increasing extent) dependent on trade with Britain. According to Cullen (1968: 46), 'The most striking feature of Irish overseas trade in the eighteenth century is therefore the growing dependence on England'. The statistical basis for such claims is extensive and consistent. Table 3.1 shows the importance of British shipping to Irish trade, and its growing dominance. British-registered ships accounted for 64.1 per cent of total tonnage in 1700, rising to 72.9 per cent in 1800.

Tables 3.2–3.5 present a similar picture. As Irish exports and imports grew throughout the eighteenth century, the preponderance of British trade also grew. For English trade, the Irish market became increasingly important,

---

[5] In 1798 only two East India Company proprietors or stockholders were listed as Irish residents (McDowell 1979: 137). Robert Gregory, a prominent and extremely wealthy Irish nabob, sat in Westminster rather than in the Dublin Parliament. (McDowell 1979: 138)

although without the same overwhelming dominance. By the end of the century, linen exports were over half of total Irish exports to Britain (58.2 per cent of total in 1798) with butter the second most important commodity (14.2 per cent in 1798) (Cullen 1968: 50, Table 13). Linen exports from Ireland went almost exclusively to Great Britain: in 1800 92.3 per cent of

TABLE 3.1. *Tonnage of shipping invoiced in the ports of Ireland, 1700–1800*

Year	Irish-registered	British-registered	Total tonnage
1700	31,755	77,680	121,096
1730	39,997	132,343	191,637
1750	42,678	173,522	252,997
1770	64,156	310,819	401,363
1800	92,767	502,067	688,272

Source: Cullen (1968: 21, Table 1).

TABLE 3.2. *Exports from Ireland, 1700–1800*

Year ending 25 March	To Great Britain £	To all parts £	Great Britain as % of total	England as % of total
1700*	372,585	814,746	45.7	42.2
1730	430,520	992,832	43.4	42.6
1750	1,069,864	1,862,834	57.4	—
1770	2,408,839	3,159,587	76.2	—
1800	3,482,691	4,079,272	85.4	80.9

* Year ending 25 December.
Source: Cullen (1968: 45, Table 9).

TABLE 3.3. *Imports into Ireland, 1700–1800*

Year ending 25 March	From Great Britain £	From all parts £	Great Britain as % of total	England as % of total
1700*	427,603	792,473	53.9	51.5
1730	457,302	929,896	49.2	46.4
1750	920,341	1,531,654	60.1	—
1770	1,878,599	2,566,845	73.2	—
1800	4,862,626	6,183,457	78.6	73.2

* Year ending 25 December.
Source: Cullen (1968: 45, Table 10).

State of the Union

Table 3.4. *Imports into England, 1700–1800*

Year	From Ireland £	From all parts £	Ireland as % of total
1700	233,853	5,970,175	3.9
1730	294,156	7,780,020	3.8
1750	612,808	7,772,040	7.9
1771	1,214,898	12,216,938	9.9
1800	2,445,079	24,483,840	10.0

Source: Cullen (1968: 46, Table 11).

TABLE 3.5. *Exports from England, 1700–1800*

Year	To Ireland £	To all parts £	Ireland as % of total
1700	271,641	6,469,146	4.2
1730	532,699	8,548,983	6.2
1750	1,316,600	12,699,081	10.4
1771	2,125,467	14,267,655	14.9
1800	3,786,085	34,074,699	11.1

Source: Cullen (1968: 47, Table 12).

Irish linen exports were to Britain, primarily for home consumption.[6] Irish imports from Britain were much more diverse, consisting of clothing and manufactured goods, as well as commodities originating in the empire, such as sugar and tea (see Cullen 1968: 52, Table 15). Despite the removal of the restrictions contained in the Navigation Acts in 1779–80, direct trade between Ireland and the empire was limited, a reflection of the limited mercantile development of Irish commerce.

Reforms in the system of landownership instigated in the 1770s, which relaxed the penalties placed on Roman Catholics holding property as an asset, were partly designed to integrate the segmented industrial and landholding markets. Such reforms reflected Grattan's campaign to consolidate the economic and political rights of the Irish middle classes, incorporating the Catholic economic interest. This was combined with a campaign to relax trading restrictions on Irish merchants, imposed by the British Parliament. Volunteers demonstrated in Dublin on 4 November 1779, pushing a canon with the threatening slogan 'Free trade or this'. Concessions made in the light of these demands opened up British trading areas, subject to the monopoly of the East India Company, and removed many of the protectionist measures imposed on Irish trade with Britain. Beckett (1966: 218) suggests that

[6] See Cullen (1968: 60–2). Figures on linen exports from Ireland are calculated from Table 16. The linen trade was mainly based in Ulster, and reflected the growth of Belfast as an important industrial centre and trading port (see Foster 1988: 213).

Ireland thus obtained, as it were for nothing, commercial advantages for which the Scots had been obliged to surrender their independent parliament; and twenty years later, when a parliamentary union between Great Britain and Ireland was in agitation, there was no further inducement of like value for the British government to offer.

However, Grattan's parliament, established in 1782, did not resolve the fiscal crisis of the Irish state. The appointment in 1784 of John Foster to the chancellorship of the Irish exchequer consolidated Irish control over the tax and spending decisions of the Dublin administration, and his recognition of the importance of financial matters to the government of Ireland was shared by his successor, Sir John Parnell. According to Beckett (1966: 235–6) the onus of Irish fiscal affairs was also taken on by John Beresford, the first commissioner of revenue, and John Fitzgibbon, who sought to shape a new financial basis for the Irish state, taking a central role in the 'Irish Cabinet' system of administration.

Economic concessions that had been given to Ireland in the light of the American Revolution were generous but, despite Beckett's assertion quoted earlier, incomplete, and relied on the goodwill of the Westminster Parliament (as well as the policies of the newly assertive Dublin Parliament). Further, they had not addressed the fiscal weakness of the Irish government, although much of the responsibility for this had passed to the Dublin administration. In an attempt to resolve this situation, William Pitt proposed the 'Commercial propositions', seeking to make 'England and Ireland one country in effect', sharing 'equal participation of all commercial advantages and some proportion of the charge of protecting the general interest' (Lecky 1902: 437 and 436), tying economic concessions to a revenue-sharing agreement between Britain and Ireland. This involved an Irish contribution to British military expenditure (notably the navy, which was almost exclusively British and financed by the British state), in exchange for the removal of the remaining protectionist limitations on Irish trade. The 'Commercial propositions' were accepted in principle by the Irish Parliament in 1785, although the idea that the granting of free trade would constrain an Irish Parliament raised opposition, and encountered strong resistance in the Westminster Parliament. A 'Great Chamber of the Manufacturers of Great Britain' was created (under the chairmanship of Josiah Wedgwood) to oppose a policy that would, according to Lecky (1902: 445), 'make anything like free trade ruinous to English manufacturers; that the English Trader would be driven, not only out of the Irish, but even out of his own market; that the English manufacturer would be obliged in self-defence to transfer his works and capital to Ireland'. Pitt was forced to introduce a number of concessions to British trading interests, which weakened the free-trade basis of the propositions. Playing on the politics of both sides of the Irish sea, Fox stated that

'I will not barter English commerce for Irish slavery' (Beckett 1966: 239), and mobilized opposition in both Westminster and Dublin. The threat to Irish legislative independence contained in the propositions aroused the hostility of Grattan, and the weakening of the provisions for free trade reduced support amongst members of the Dublin Parliament who had previously supported the measure. Pitt was reluctantly forced to drop the legislation, worried about the effect on Irish public opinion if the measure were forced through the Dublin Parliament (Kelly 1975: 561).

The main trading concessions contained in the 'Commercial propositions' were established in 1787, through the incorporation of Ireland in the provisions of the commercial treaty with France and the Irish navigation act. As such, for Kelly (1975: 562), the controversy over the 'Commercial propositions' was a 'sterile' one: 'It is difficult to identify any substantial advantages or disadvantages that might have accrued to either country if the scheme had been put into operation in its revised form'. However, this ignores the extent to which Pitt saw the issue as an attempt to recast the financial relationship between the British and Irish governments[7] and the fact that it was British trading interests that effectively killed the measure, by forcing concessions that made it unpalatable to the Dublin legislature. The Westminster Parliament was not sufficiently exercised about the constitutional relationship to be willing to offer a greater amount of trading equality, as contained in the original proposals, whilst the Dublin Parliament was unwilling to constrain its own legislative autonomy. According to Strauss (1951: 58), for William Pitt 'the failure of the Commercial Propositions contained the germ of the Legislative Union'. In October 1785 Pitt wrote to Richard Lovell Edgeworth, the Irish author: 'An Union with Ireland with Great Britain will doubtless meet with strong opposition on your side of the water . . . [but] mature reflection may in the end convince your nation of its *equity*, and even of its *expediency*; for the fundamental principles of political and commercial connection seem to me to require an equal participation of burthens as of benefits, of expenses as of profits' (Reilly 1979: 161).

Whilst trading barriers between Britain and Ireland did continue to be removed, and the overall level of commercial activity greatly increased, the weakness of the Irish revenue system, and its unsatisfactory basis for those running the administration from both Dublin and London, continued. This situation was exacerbated by the weakness of the Irish financial system, which proved incapable (and unwilling) to fund the growing Irish national debt. The basis of the Irish revenue reflected the monarchical origins of the

---

[7] According to Dickson (1983: 42) 'The 'commercial propositions' of 1785, which would have led to a reduction and standardization in Anglo-Irish trade, might have caused, if successful, rapid changes in Irish tax policy'.

Williamite succession in Ireland (rather than parliamentary basis, as in Scotland). The Irish administration was largely funded through taxes and duties that flowed automatically to the monarch:

The Hereditary Revenue was composed of the Crown Rents, arising from confiscations during the reign of Henry VIII and following Tyrone's Rebellion; the Quit rents, from similar confiscations after the 1641 Rebellion; Hearth Money, a general tax on hearths first raised in the reign of Charles II; certain Customs and Excise duties; and finally licences for the sale of ale, beer and spirits. These formed a perpetual grant to the crown for specific purposes of government; as such they were outside the control of parliament. (Johnston 1963: 96–7)

These resources were sufficient to cover most of the administrative expenses of the Irish government up to around 1715. Costs not covered by the 'Hereditary' revenue were covered by the 'Additional', revenues raised with the assent of the Irish Parliament. Throughout the eighteenth century the importance of the 'Additional' element of the revenue increased, and the importance of the political control of the Irish Parliament increased accordingly (Johnston 1963: 97).

The war with America coincided with (and was partly responsible for) a depression in the Irish economy, and between 1763 and 1773 the national debt almost doubled, approaching a million pounds (Beckett 1966: 206). The prospect of increasing the tax revenue raised in Ireland mirrored the complaints of the anti-British revolutionaries in the USA, with a Dublin newspaper arguing, in January 1775, that 'by the same authority which the British parliament assumes to tax America, it may also and with equal justice presume to tax Ireland without the consent or concurrence of the Irish parliament' (Beckett 1966: 206). The rise of the Volunteer movement was a response to the military weakness of the Irish state, but also reflected a desire to consolidate the Irish fiscal situation in a way that would be based on a more assertive Dublin administration. Grattan hoped that the parliamentary system that was named after him would widen the popular basis of the Irish government, partly through the incorporation of the Catholic and Presbyterian middle classes. However, the legislature proved less willing to follow Grattan's reformist programme, and largely served to consolidate the political control of the 'ascendancy' and maintain the fiscal status quo.

Just as the American Revolution precipitated a political and financial crisis, so did the war with France and the threat of rebellion: 'An internal drain of cash had already developed in Ireland, where political conditions were becoming more unsettled and invasion from France appeared imminent, in the course of 1796' (Cullen 1968: 180). The national debt rose dramatically throughout the 1790s, as military and administrative costs imposed on the Dublin administration rocketed and revenues remained static (Table 3.6).[8]

The Irish Parliament maintained the national debt without any established means of government finance, relying on the sale of Government Debentures to the public. Its success in maintaining payments without default had seen interest rates fall from 8 per cent in 1715 to 4.5 per cent in 1779. However, the failure to set a balanced budged in any year after 1770, and the increased expenditure associated with the rebellion, put new pressure on the system. The Irish banking system was in no position to finance such an expansion in government debt. The Irish financial system throughout the eighteenth century was supported by 'a multitude of small and unstable private banks' (Hall 1949: 3). The Protestant ascendancy was centred largely on the landowning classes, and this was reflected in the membership and interests of the Irish Parliament. Little encouragement was given to the banking sector, a significant element of which was run by Nonconformists.[9] Attempts were made to establish a Bank of Ireland in 1695 and 1719, but failed because of the lack of

TABLE 3.6. *Irish national debt, 1794–1801*

Year ending 25 March	£
1794	2,874,267
1795	4,002,452
1796	4,477,098
1797	6,537,467
1798	10,134,675
1799	15,806,824
1800	23,100,785
1801*	28,541,157

* 9 months to 5 January.
Source: Hall (1949: 63).

[8] For an account of Irish taxation policy at the time, see Dickson (1983). The parliament had attempted to address the government deficit incurred during the American war, imposing a new malt duty in 1785, and receipts from customs and import duties and inland excise were boosted by the expansion of the Irish economy from the late 1780s. The crisis of the late 1790s, described by Dickson (1983: 47) as 'a turning point in Irish fiscal history', saw a frenzied debate on possible solutions. Leather tax and salt tax were introduced, although with little impact on the overall level of tax receipts.

[9] The Partnership Act of 1741 had limited the total capital of partnerships, preventing the development of well-capitalized banks (Hall 1949: 9). There were banking crises in 1754–5 and 1760, with only three Dublin banks surviving. The most prominent was that of La Touche and Son, established by a Huguenot who settled in Dublin in the seventeenth century.

parliamentary support, in the latter case roused by the invective of Jonathan Swift who saw it as a threat to the Anglican establishment.[10] A Bank of Ireland was finally established in 1783, with Catholics contributing some 10 per cent of the total capital (Foster 1988: 205). However, the Bank still bore the imprint of the ascendancy parliament. Catholics and Quakers were debarred from the Directorate, discrimination that was 'regarded by Irish Catholics as an extension of the penal laws, and were a source of constant embarrassment to the Bank' (Hall 1949: 41).

Whilst there were good relations between the Bank of Ireland and the government, the Bank was too small to play a major role in financing the national debt. The government made a request for £300,000 in 1796, but was refused, and only given £150,000 in 1797 (Hall 1949: 64–5). The financial pressure on the government is shown in the interest rates paid on public loans in Britain and Ireland (Table 3.7). Rates rose from 5.0 per cent in 1793 to a high of 8.2 per cent in 1798. This forced the government to turn to the London market, where rates were lower and capacity greater, and from 1798 an increasing proportion of the Irish national debt was financed this way. The fact that rates fell (in both London and Dublin) as the Union proceeded suggests that it was greeted favourably by the financial markets.

TABLE 3.7. *Public loans for Irish government, raised in Ireland and Britain, 1793–1801*

Year	Ireland Amount of loan £	Interest rate	Britain Amount of loan £	Interest rate
1793	184,615	5.0		
1793	138,462	5.0		
1794	950,446	5.55		
1795	1,469,231	5.63		
1796	590,769	5.71		
1797	300,000	8.04		
1797	369,277	7.93		
1797	461,538	7.75		
1798	184,690	8.2	1,500,000	6.34
1798	966,212	8.2		
1799	1,846,154	6.24	2,000,000	6.24
1800	2,307,692	5.77	3,000,000	5.25
1801			2,000,000	4.71

Source: Thomas 1986: Appendices 2–3, pp. 256–9

[10] According to Hall (1949: 25), 'Swift's antagonism was...largely dictated by political prejudices and personal animosities. He hated dissenting minorities, among whom he placed the Huguenots, whom he called "the French"...'.

As Johnston (1963: 97) notes, 'by the time of the Union the national finances were chaotic'. This may not have been a major concern of the Dublin Parliament, insulated from direct financial responsibility by the bifurcation of executive and legislative duties. However, it was a key consideration both in Dublin Castle and in London. At Westminster the interests of both the government party and the British commercial sector were much more closely bound into the system of representation. Whilst it is hard to pin down a direct association between the passage of the Act of Union and economic factors in Westminster, the general macroeconomic situation and the state of Irish government finances provide a rationale for a recasting of the trading and constitutional arrangements between Britain and Ireland.

We have shown that the attempts by the Scottish Parliament to establish a competing imperialist strategy did not have an apparently significant influence on the passage of the Act of Union through the Edinburgh Parliament, although we do suggest that it may have had an effect on the attitudes of the Westminster Parliament in its attempt to prevent challenges to its control over monopoly trading rights. From Dublin, there was no similar pressure on English trading interests. Whilst some Irish ports may have operated as a means of avoiding British customs and excise, there is little evidence that this was any challenge to the British imperialist trade (see Cullen 1968: ch. 8). The lack of trading concessions in the Irish Act(s) of Union implies that this was not a strong consideration of the Dublin legislature. Rather, we would argue, that the lesser influence of economic issues in the Dublin Parliament compared to that in the Edinburgh Parliament reflected differences in the constitutional situation, the representational basis of the Irish legislature, and the trading relations between the two countries.

The plan for the Union drawn up by William Pitt and Lord Grenville in 1798 was intended to be generous to the Irish, restricting exposure to the British national debt. After discussions in London, Castlereagh wrote that 'the terms are considered as highly liberal, the proportional arrangements of the expenses having completely overset the argument on which the enemies of the measure had hitherto principally relied, viz. the extension of English debt and taxation to Ireland' (McCavery 2000: 355). Although the provisions for trade and the national debt were attacked by the opponents of the Union, particularly John Foster, and the demands for some protectionist measures for manufacturing conceded, the economic basis of the union was not a source of major division.

It would appear that the concessions won for the cotton industry were the result of an initiative from Ulster manufacturers and not from politicians opposed to the Union. Again, in this debate, the opposition did not divide the House on any clause. The leaders did not even attend (McCavery 2000: 361).

Perhaps the economic provisions of the Union did not arouse the hostility of any significant political interest in Britain, as had been the case with Pitt's commercial propositions. Although protests from Yorkshire's woollen manufacturers led to a demand for amendment of the economic article in the Act of Union in the House of Commons—providing 'the only spark of excitement in England on the Union'—it was easily defeated (Bolton 1966: 201).

William Pitt had been hard-hit by the failure of his Commercial Propositions in 1785, which marked his 'most serious failure in his first two years in office', and which he had invested much emotional and intellectual effort (Ehrman 1969: 213). The Union provided a second chance to recast the public finance of the Irish state, and the constitutional restructuring of the legislative union enabled a fiscal consolidation to combat an escalating national debt in both Ireland and Britain. The trading and financial aspects of the Union did not provide a focus for opposition to Pitt's proposals, either in Ireland or in Britain. In Dublin, the landowning basis of the ascendancy and the House of Commons were not associated with any particular trading or financial interests, whilst in Westminster the extension of trading rights to Ireland did not offer a significant challenge to the trading interests of Britain. Economic links between the two countries had grown so close over the eighteenth century, and the granting of trading rights to the Irish in the 1780s, meant that these were not issues around which opponents of the Union could mobilize.

Pitt and Constitutional Reform

William Pitt the Younger was not particularly anxious to get involved with Irish political reform, which had been associated with three of his most substantial challenges as prime minister. First, his Commercial Propositions, which attempted to ally Irish legislative independence with some measure of fiscal reponsibility, had failed, as discussed previously. Second, the Irish had been associated with the Regency crisis of 1788–9, when the illness of George III threatened his position, through a Foxite alliance echoed by a majority of Grattan's parliament. The Regency crisis raised the prospect of dual monarchy. Whilst not envisionaging a constitutional split in the monarchy on the scale of the Scottish Act of Succession, Irish support for a Regent (who would have dismissed Pitt as prime minister) was an unfriendly act. By preempting the Westminster Parliament, the Irish legislature undermined Pitt's attempts to diffuse the crisis over the madness of George III. Third, his attempt to bring in the Portland Whigs into his parliamentary coalition in 1795 had been upset by the demand that Lord Fizwilliam be appointed to

Lord Lieutenant of Ireland, which led to an ill-judged attempt to enforce Catholic inclusion in the Irish government. This exposed the unwillingness of the Dublin Parliament to offer concessions to the Catholic population of Ireland.

Pitt may not have been a natural radical or political reformer, but pragmatism and administrative efficiency could reawaken the suppressed reformer shown in his earliest parliamentary performances. In one of the first efforts at indirect rule, which was to become a prominent feature of the British Empire, the Quebec Act 1774 not only permitted the French Canadians, defeated in the Seven Years War (1756–63) and incorporated in British North America, to retain their Catholic religion and legal system, but actually decreed that 'Quebec' was to extend south and west down the American river system reached by portages from the Great Lakes into the Ohio Valley. This transferred the whole of the American colonies west of the Appalachian mountains to 'Quebec'. The anglophone colonists, many of their leaders of Ulster Protestant descent, saw this as a grave provocation. If not challenged, it would prevent the land-hungry colonies from expanding into the undefined country beyond the Appalachians.

Security for both Canada and Ireland would arise within the greater encompass of a British empire, which was Protestant but not oppressive. Pitt himself was unusually secular for his era. Never in his life did he betray enthusiasm for any religion or sect. But he was sensitive to religion as a badge of allegiance. He wrote in 1792 to the Lord Lieutenant:

The idea of the present fermentation gradually bringing both [religious] parties [in Ireland] to think of a Union with this country has long been in my mind.... I believe it, though itself not easy to be accomplished, to be the only solution for other and greater difficulties.

The admission of the Catholics to the . . . suffrage could not then be dangerous. The Protestant interest—in point of power, property, and Church establishment—would be secure, because the decided majority of the supreme Legislature would necessarily be Protestant; and the great ground of argument on the part of the Catholics would be done away, as, compared with the rest of the Empire, they would become a minority. (Pitt to Earl of Westmorland, 1792, quoted by Hague 2004: 435)

Except for its failure to discriminate between the two streams of Irish Protestantism, this cannot be faulted. Giving Catholics civil rights would remove their constitutional grievance. Bringing Ireland into the Union would protect Protestant interests better than the continuation of an Irish Parliament. To achieve Union on his terms, however, Pitt needed to convince three parties: the British and Irish Parliaments, and the King. This forced him to disguise his motives: to attach Catholic emancipation to the Union would have meant that it would not have passed through the House of Lords in

Dublin, and such a measure would have struggled in Westminster. He tried to finesse it through two parliaments, but his plans to win a final hand in a united Westminster Parliament containing Irish and British members came up against the trump card of the King's veto.

The Passage of the Union

By the late 1790s Pitt was in his ascendancy, and the opportunities for the passage of a radical bill of his own design were clear. Fox and Grattan had both absented themselves from Westminster and Dublin parliaments, removing the focus for any legislative opposition. In the administration in London both Grenville and Dundas had been supporters of a legislative Union alongside Catholic emancipation.[11] The core of the Dublin Castle government—the Lord Lieutenant, Lord (Charles) Cornwallis, and chief secretary, Viscount Castlereagh (Robert Stewart), along with Edward Cooke the influential under-secretary—shared a common view of a parliamentary union accompanied by Catholic emancipation. However, both within the Dublin administration and in the parliament there were men close to the centre of government who shared a distaste for one or the other of these two aspects. Lord Clare, the leader of the House of Lords, was an ardent supporter of a legislative union but would not countenance further concessions to the Catholics, whilst John Foster, the speaker of the House of Commons, opposed the government on both counts.

At discussions of how the Union could be passed through the Dublin Parliament in 1798, Cornwallis raised the issue of whether the suppression of the Catholic issue would undermine a settlement when they comprised, with the Presbyterian population, 90 per cent of the population (Geoghegan 1999: 37). However, Lord Clare ensured that the union would be a strictly protestant (i.e., Anglican) measure. Dundas, as a Scot, could put the case for religious devolution along the lines of 1707, but there was no Irish Dundas during the debates of 1798 (Geoghegan 1999: 38–9). Irish Catholic emancipation was left open, but the decision to proceed with parliamentary Union was not challenged again.

The evidence from the debate in 1798 about whether to include Catholic emancipation along with Parliamentary Union caused ructions within the Dublin administration, with William Elliot, the under-secretary to the military department, threatening to resign his position. This is taken by

---

[11] 'He set up an informal, unofficial committee to arrange the union, and did not even confirm its existence to parliament' (Turner 2003: 144). Grenville expressed 'moderate scepticism' after the Rebellion (Geoghegan 1999: 35).

Geoghegan as signifying the extent to which Catholic emancipation was an issue that should be pushed by the Dublin administration. However, the debate also shows the consideration that was given to Lord Clare, as leader of the House of Lords in Dublin. In a bicameral parliament, he would have had a significant influence over one of the blocking options against the Union. Gaining his conformity was deemed important enough to comprom- ise one of the key elements of the inclusive ideals of the pro-Unionist faction in London and Dublin.

The Cornwallis and the Dublin administrations showed less sensitivity in dealing with John Foster, the Speaker of the House of Commons in Dublin. Foster saw his role in upholding the authority of Grattan's parliament, and was not to be persuaded to support its abolition, especially by such a 'damn silly fellow' as Cornwallis (Geoghegan 1999: 43). This suggested that the administration was less sensitive to the control of the Dublin House of Commons than to the Lords. This may indicate a recognition of the influence of the Irish Lords over the occupation of seats in the House of Commons (see Johnston-Liik 2002: 156), or pivotal role for Lord Clare in deciding the sway of aristocratic influence, but it is an interesting contrast with the unicameral Scottish Parliament, in which the influence of the Lords was incorporated with that of the Commons. Whilst the majority of the Lords were in favour of a parliamentary union, the Irish case highlights a special interest given to the leader of the Lords, who controlled a veto player in the union game.

The Irish House of Commons and the Act of Union

How could the Irish Parliament, which had gained its extended powers only in 1782, be persuaded to vote itself out of existence in 1800, having refused to in 1799? To answer this, we repeat, as far as the data permit, the analysis of vote-switching that was offered for the 1706 Scottish Parliament in Chapter 2.

The Irish House of Commons comprised 300 members, chosen from 150 two-member constituencies. There were thirty-two county constituencies and 118 borough constituencies (including the Trinity College, Dublin, university seat). The county franchise was open to freeholders worth 40s per annum (although the definition of a freeholder varied across the country (McDowell 1979: 107)). The 117 parliamentary boroughs were meant to represent urban centres, although, as in England, many of these were rotten boroughs (in Carysfort there was only one house, and Clonmines had no inhabitants: McDowell 1979: 110). According to Malcomson (1979: 138), 'The chief defect of the borough representation of Ireland was not that places of size and significance were excluded, but that far too many places were included that were of no size of significance whatsoever'. The boroughs varied in their sizes[12] and method selection of electorate,[13] which affected the extent to which returns were controlled by a patron or open to genuine electoral competition. Most borough constituencies were 'closed', that is, their electorate comprised a small group restricted in size and social composition.[14] In Belfast, a closed borough, the electorate was composed of a governing body of thirteen, always friends and relations of Lord Donegall. In Dublin, an open borough, the electorate included some three to four thousand freemen, and campaigns were vigorously contested (McDowell 1979: 115).

The franchise was widened under the Catholic Relief Act (1793) and the Election Act (1795) sought to reduce the level of corruption, but this had little impact outside the larger and more open boroughs and the thirty-two county constituencies. As Johnston (1963: 3) notes, most MPs were still chosen from corporation boroughs 'whose charters had been amended on principles of religious exclusiveness, admission of absentee burgesses and the replacement of vacancies by co-option, thus securing a continuity of interest in the corporation against which the Catholic Relief Act of 1793 was powerless'. Even in the more 'open' seats, there were large numbers of false freeholders enlisted to vote for particular candidates. As in England, election from a county seat was seen as more prestigious, the openness of the contest conferring some legitimacy on the popular support for the candidate, and the number of contests and the expense of the campaign were much greater in these seats.

Most 'closed' seats were controlled by the local aristocracy, but the government also used the purchase and control of parliamentary seats to exercise control over the legislature. The Church of Ireland controlled a number of borough returns, whose members of parliament were chosen to support the interests of the established church and the government. In 1790 Grattan protested against the government's practice of trading parliamentary seats for peerages, although his challenge was defeated in Parliament (Johnston 1963: 193–4). Reform was instigated in 1793 when the Place Act was passed. Ostensibly designed to restrict the government's ability to pack the House of

---

[12] Seventy-seven borough constituencies had electorates of less than 20; 13 between 20 and 99; 23 between 100 and 1,000; and just 4 over 1,000. For the 32 county seats the electorates estimated in 1800 varied from 600 in County Louth to 20,500 in County Cork (figures from Johnston-Liik 2002: vol. II 371–88).

[13] Johnston (1963: 159–78 and 321–8) classifies the borough constituencies into potwalloping boroughs, manor boroughs, corporation boroughs where freemen were admitted to the franchise, corporation boroughs without freemen, and (relatively 'open') county boroughs. She is able to identify a single patron for most of these seats (although sometimes the two seats were shared between patrons).

[14] Malcolmson (1979: 140) suggests that 107 out of the borough constituencies were 'closed', leaving just 10 boroughs, the university seat of Trinity College, and the 32 county constituencies 'open'.

Commons with holders of government positions, it prevented revenue officers and other officials from sitting as MPs, and forced other MPs who accepted an office of profit under the Crown to seek re-election. However, the Place Act also included a provision whereby MPs, who previously could not resign their seats, could stand down; a change that was exploited by the administration at the time of the passage of the Act of Union to remove opponents of the measure and replace them with supporters.

Parliamentary seats in Ireland were more or less openly traded, treated as the property of a patron or owner, although 'Even in the later eighteenth century there were a great many niceties and delicacies in the matter of buying and selling seats' (Malcomson 1979: 154). The price fluctuated (and varies according to different accounts) with reports of seats changing hands for between £800 and £11,000 in the 1780s (Johnston 1963: 174, 200). Johnston suggests that 'the consent of the patron accompanied by the expenditure of £2,000 to £2,500 could usually ensure a member's peaceful return for a constituency which he might never have seen and certainly need never visit' (Johnston 1963: 214). In the run-up to the Union the Dublin administration exploited the provisions of the Place Act and made use of its ability to buy seats, although, according to Malcomson (1979: 159), 'the government still balked at directly purchasing seats'. This strategy was not solely used in support of the Union, with the opposition setting up a fund to do the same—a move denounced by the government. Henry Grattan made his dramatic reintroduction to the Irish House of Commons during the Union debates after purchasing the seat of Wicklow for £2,400 (Johnston 1963: 200).

The Irish House of Lords had a membership of 247 at the time of the Act of Union, consisting of 22 spiritual and 225 temporal peers. The eighteenth century had seen an increase in the numbers of Irish peerages, which had seen the size of the House of Lords double. A number of these creations were symbolic rewards to non-Irishmen, conferred by the monarch as a reward for duty (whilst maintaining the exclusivity of the British peerage), but most were conferred on Irish landowners who had performed political service (McDowell 1979: 121–2). The Irish House of Lords was politically subservient to the House of Commons, with the focus of legislative business on the lower house. Debates were sparsely attended, and the Dublin administration rarely faced any meaningful challenge from the House of Lords, although it served as a forum where peers could raise grievances (McDowell 1979: 125–6).

According to Geoghegan (2003: 135), the most meticulous historian of the Irish Union, 'It is difficult to list precisely the names of the MPs who voted for and against the Union in 1799 and 1800'. He suggests that the published lists of supporters and opponents of the Union in the House of Commons contain significant errors. Therefore, our analysis cannot be as detailed as for the Scottish Parliament in Chapter 2. In the absence of any authoritative source for voting behaviour in the Irish House of Commons, for our analysis we have relied on the voting records provided by the *History of the Irish Parliament 1692–1800*, edited by Johnston-Liik (2002). This has the benefit of providing a single source for a variety of biographical, constituency, and voting data, although the voting tallies resulting do not exactly match the announced results of the key votes of the House of Commons.[15] Looking at members who switched votes between 1799 and 1800, the analysis from the History of the Irish Parliament data shows twelve members switching from an anti-Union vote in 1799 to a pro-Union vote in 1800,[16] but two MPs switching the other way.[17]

The overall flow of votes between 1799 and 1800, as shown by the History of the Irish Parliament data, is shown in Figure 3.1. This shows that the pro-Union vote was more solid than the anti-Union vote, and whilst the number of direct changes between pro- and anti-positions was low, the pro-Union side picked up more of the voters who, having not voted in 1799, chose to vote in 1800. The analysis is complicated by the fact that more than 300 MPs are recorded as having been members of the House of Commons over the crucial period. This is due to a large turnover in parliamentary membership, as seats were traded, with the government and the opposition battling to change the balance of the composition of the House of Commons.

The passage of the Act of the Union saw an unprecedented turbulence in the membership of the House of Commons, as the provisions of the Place Act of 1793 were used by each side to retire obstructive members and introduce more pliable voters. Keeping track of the multiple changes in constituency

---

[15] According to Geoghegan (1999: 63) the key vote in January 1799 deleting the mention of the legislative union from the King's speech was passed by 109 to 104 votes. The passage of the Union was expedited by a vote of 138 to 96 at the opening of Parliament on 15 January 1800. Figures from the History of Parliament record 117 opponents in 1799 and 110 supporters, and 98 opponents and 138 supporters in 1800. Geoghegan (2003: 177–83) provides an assessment of support/opposition for Union amongst members of the House of Commons on 22 January 1799 showing 112 opponents and 110 supporters, whilst the list in the Belfast Newsletter shows 110 opponents and 105 supporters. The Red and Black lists of supporters and opponents of the Union put the 1799 vote at 111 against and 106 for. Discrepancies may arise from the inclusion/ exclusion of tellers and the Speaker of the House (John Foster, an opponent of the Union).

[16] Bolton (1966: 187) suggests eight members switched votes on the key divisions in 1799 and 1800. Geoghegan (2003: 137) identifies twelve MPs who changed their stance; whereas the Red and Black lists provided by Barrington (1835: 188–95) suggest thirteen members who voted in 1799 and then changed sides (and another twelve who were opposed in 1799, but did not vote, then voted for the Union in 1800). The names of the switchers in our analysis do not tally with Geoghegan's: our data show William Bagwell, John Bagwell, and Thomas Whaley (whom Bolton suggests went the other way) switching; Geoghegan's data show William Gore, John Preston, and Abel Ram.

[17] William Blakeney and James Butler. This anti-government switching is missed by Geoghegan (2003: 136).

State of the Union

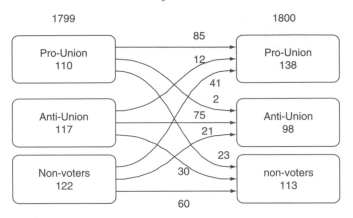

FIGURE 3.1. Flow of votes between Union votes in the
Irish House of Commons, 1799 and 1800

representation between 1799 and 1800 is a fraught task, illustrated by Geo-ghegan's (2003: 140–3) description of the 'extraordinarily complex series of manoeuvres' that took place in just two constituencies. To examine the overall effect of these changes on the Union vote in January 1800, we look at the voting behaviour of those MPs who, according to the History of the Irish Parliament, were newly elected in 1799 and 1800. This shows seventeen new MPs voting with the government, and just four voting against. However, there were forty other newly elected MPs, the majority of whom were to join the government side. This influx of pro-Unionist MPs did not take part in the key vote on the Union in January 1800, but were additional insurance for the government, and helped boost its majority to sixty by May, when the Union was waved through (Geoghegan 1999: 115). The traditional story that Pitt bought the Union by purchasing Irish MPs is not wrong, but it is far from the whole story. Analysis of the voting patterns in the House of Commons in Dublin allows (subject to reservations about the overall reliability of the data) a wider interpretation of the politics of the passage of the Act of Union.

According to Malcomson (1979: 140):

The government could have carried the Union, and in practical terms did carry the Union, through the manipulation of the borough representation under the terms of the Place Act of 1793, but this in no way diverted its attention from the open constituencies, and it was still labouring to procure popular demonstrations of support for the Union in the country long after its majority in the House was secure.

The evidence suggests that the government won its victory in 1800 through its support in the 'closed' boroughs of Ireland, winning over half its votes from members in seats with an electorate of less than twenty. Anti-Union MPs, on the other hand came from twenty-eight of the fifty-five largest constituencies. More MPs representing the county constituencies voted against the Union in 1800 (32) than supported the measure (23). Tables 3.8 and 3.9 give the best data we have been able to assemble.

There was no significant difference in voting across the four provinces of Ireland, with pro- and anti-Union votes evenly spread across each. However, the government did dominate in the county constituencies with MPs representing the largest percentage population of Catholics.

This suggests that the government, if not gaining the explicit support of the Catholic voters, had managed to prevent popular opinion amongst the Catholic population from agitating against the Union. This may not have been entirely justified. Taking a look at the members of the government majority who had voted on certain key issues in previous parliaments, the evidence suggests that the opponents of Union were more likely to have supported measures for Catholic relief in the votes of 1793 and 1795 (Table 3.10). Taken together, Table 3.9 and the section of Table 3.10 relating to the votes on Catholic relief have two important implications. First, that

TABLE 3.8. *Constituency electorate and Union vote, January 1800*

	0–19 electors	20–99 electors	100–1,000 electors	>1,000 electors	Total
Pro-Union					
1800	76	12	33	17	138
(%)	55.1	8.7	23.9	12.3	100
Anti-Union					
1800	36	8	26	28	98
(%)	36.7	8.2	26.5	28.6	100

TABLE 3.9. *% of Catholic population in county constituency and Union vote, January 1800*

	0–80% Catholic	80–90% Catholic	90+% Catholic	Total
Pro-Union				
1800	4	7	12	23
(%)	17.4	30.4	52.2	100
Anti-Union				
1800	14	11	7	32
(%)	43.7	34.4	21.9	100

the government succeeded in its attempts to stop the issue of Catholic rights and representation polarizing the political situation in such a way as to favour the opponents of Union. Secondly, it indicates that there was a core of the pro-Union support, comprising some one-third of the MPs who voted on each of the issues, within the Irish House of Commons who had been opposed to concessions directed at the Catholic population. Whilst supporting the administration's view that the two issues should be treated separately, it suggests that if the intention of Pitt and Lord Lieutenant Cornwallis to treat Union and Catholic emancipation as dual strategies for Irish constitutional reform had been made explicit, then greater opposition could have been expected.

The voting behaviour of the MPs who voted on the Union in 1800 and on the key issues of the Regency and Pitt's commercial propositions follow a weak, if understandable pattern. In both cases the balance of votes reflects a pro-administration bias, although it hardly supports any case for an underlying demand for a Union in the 1800s that can be traced through to the end of the century.

One of the changes of strategy employed by the government after the defeat of the Union measures in 1799 was to offer compensation for those borough constituencies that were to be abolished in the event of a legislative union, as the parliamentary representation of the Irish was rationalized and reduced. The original scheme planned by William Pitt and Lord

TABLE 3.10. *Voting on key issues and Union vote, January 1800*

	Against	In favour	Total
Vote on Catholic Relief, 1793 and 1795 (combined)...			
Pro-Union 1800	8	15	23
(%)	34.8	65.2	100
Anti-Union 1800	8	20	28
(%)	28.6	71.4	100
Vote on the Regency...			
Pro-Union 1800	12	27	39
(%)	30.8	69.2	100
Anti-Union 1800	6	20	26
(%)	23.1	76.9	100
Vote on Pitt's commercial propositions...			
Pro-Union 1800	11	24	35
(%)	31.4	68.6	100
Anti-Union 1800	14	15	29
(%)	48.3	51.7	100

Grenville was based on an Irish representation in the Westminster House of Commons of 150 members, but this total was reduced to 100 by the time that the proposals for the Union were announced.[18] The provision for borough compensation may have persuaded of the patrons of the borough constituencies to support the government, but evidence in terms of the shifting of the vote is limited. Of the ten members from borough constituencies recorded as having switched from the anti-Union to pro-Union positions between 1799 and 1800, six came from boroughs that were due to be abolished, and hence received compensation, and four from boroughs that were to retain their representation. Since three-quarters of the borough seats were to be abolished, this proportion is relatively low. Of the borough MPs who abstained in 1799 and then voted in 1800, the proportion voting in favour of Union from seats to be abolished (twenty-five members, out of thirty-four supporters of the Union, or 73.5%) was very similar to those from seats to be abolished voting against the Union (seventeen out of twenty-four opponents, or 70.8 per cent). This suggests that the direct effect of the offer of borough compensation was extremely marginal.

Whereas the Scottish Union involved little change in the basis of the representation, the Irish Union had different implications. The method by which seats were reallocated in the Westminster system under the Irish Act of Union changed the basis of representation towards a more popularist mode of election. The seats abolished were the rotten boroughs (all Scottish seats were basically rotten). Given that religious discrimination in the choice of electorate was removed in 1793, this gave the Catholics a certain leverage in county constituencies (although their influence could still be constrained in borough constituencies). Both Pitt and Castlereagh had begun their respective parliamentary careers at Westminster and Dublin as advocates of parliamentary reform, and whilst both were willing to moderate their radicalism in the interests of government service, one of the undercurrents of the Irish Act of Union was the removal of some of the more egregious aspects of Irish parliamentary misrepresentation. The plan for the Union focused on the size of Irish representation in a united Westminster Parliament; there was no challenge to the assumption that the greatest reduction in the number of Irish legislators would be through the abolition of the rotten boroughs.

The war with France saw a renewal of the fiscal crisis of the British state. The national debt increased by about 80 per cent between 1792 and 1798. In February 1797 the Bank of England was forced to suspend cash payments as financial confidence plummeted. Pitt responded by introducing the income tax (passed in February 1798): introducing a 10 per cent tax on all incomes in excess

---

[18] Even this figure was too large for some. Lord Sheffield thought that even eighty 'wild Irish' was too much, and worried that 'I do not think that any of our country gentlemen would venture into parliament if they were to meet 100 Paddies' (Geoghegan 2003: 130).

of £200 a year, with lower rates from £60 to £200. Income tax was seen by many contemporaries as 'too novel and inquisitorial', but it provided 28 per cent of the money raised for the war against France (against 42 per cent covered by loans: Turner 2003: 184). Its increasing importance altered the fiscal balance of the Union, as we have discussed elsewhere (McLean 2005) and return to later.

King George Says No

The Union was thus needed, in Pitt's view, for four linked reasons: to secure Britain's western frontier during the French wars; to overcome the crisis of public finance, especially in Ireland but also in Britain; to reap the gains of free trade; and to increase the legitimacy of the British state in Ireland. A group of politicians less far-sighted than him fatally damaged the last aim and caused collateral damage to the others.

Pitt dominated the Commons but not the Lords. Most of his own Cabinet were in the Lords. Some of them rejected the idea of any concessions to Catholics. They leaked Pitt's plan to its most obdurate opponent, King George III. The King had long given clear signals of his opposition to Catholic emancipation, which he described as 'beyond the decision of any Cabinet of ministers'. In September 1800, Pitt called his Lord Chancellor, Lord Loughborough, to a Cabinet meeting to discuss 'the great question on the general state of the Catholics' (both quoted in Hague 2004: 465). Loughborough was on holiday in Weymouth with the King, and promptly showed him this letter. The King exploded, in public, saying to Pitt's closest ally Henry Dundas in the hearing of the Irish Secretary Lord Camden:

What is the Question which you are all about to force upon me? What is this Catholic Emancipation . . . that you are going to throw at my Head. . . . I will tell you, that I shall look on every Man as my personal Enemy, who proposes that Question to me. . . . I hope All my Friends will not desert me. (George III's words at a levee, 28.1.1801, as recalled by Camden in 1804, quoted by Hague 2004: 468)

The King thought that concessions to Catholicism were inconsistent with the coronation oath that the 1689–1707 settlement required him to take. This royal indignation over Ireland was to be repeated by some of his successors, for instance when Queen Victoria attempted to block Gladstone from the Prime Ministership in 1892, and when George V seemed more disposed to listen to His Majesty's Opposition than to His Majesty's Government in 1912–14, and made severe difficulties about Irish Home Rule.

Pitt responded with a magnificent memorandum (quoted by Hague 2004: 470–1), as did George V's Prime Minister H. H. Asquith, equally magnificently, in the same circumstances in 1913 (Jenkins 1964: 543–9). Each prime minister pointed out that he must resign if the King maintained his attitude.

In 1913 this was sufficient to persuade the King and his advisers to back down. In 1801 it was not. The King vetoed Catholic emancipation, and Pitt resigned in February 1801. Biographies of Pitt tend to treat this resignation as mysterious. We see nothing mysterious about it. The King had made Pitt's position totally impossible. His action ensured that the Union with Ireland was illegitimate in the eyes of the majority of the Irish population from the outset. Catholic emancipation came in 1829 with great rancour, but proved inadequate to save Ireland for the Union. The King's veto in 1801 was the first great tragedy of Union. The failure of the unelected parts of the British government to accept Irish Home Rule from 1893 to 1914 was to be the second.

4

1886

What fools we were not to have accepted Gladstone's Home Rule Bill. The Empire now would not have had the Irish Free State giving us so much trouble and pulling us to pieces.

(King George V to Prime Minister Ramsay MacDonald, c.6.7.1930)[1]

The UK of Great Britain and Ireland was created in 1800, and the Union flag then took on its modern design, with crosses to represent England, Scotland, and Ireland (but not Wales). However, the Irish Union was never accepted in the way the Scottish Union was. The unravelling of the Union began seriously in 1886. This chapter opens with a survey of events between 1800 and 1886.

The British Empire

The British Union and the British Empire (never called the United Kingdom Empire) grew symbiotically in the nineteenth century. Each depended on the other. The overseas empire was already big in 1800, despite Britain's loss of the USA. On one estimate the countries of the British Empire contained 20 per cent of the world's population in 1815 (Bayly 1989: 3).

Growth of the ideological Empire lagged behind that of the physical Empire. Until after the Mutiny of 1857, India—the largest component of the Empire by far—was governed by the East India Company, a state-sponsored company, not directly by the British Crown. The government of the tropical Empire, most of whose inhabitants were not white, rarely came to public attention after the end of slavery in 1833, although that episode marks an unusual irruption of public and elite opinion into the normally private world of colonial government. Even the 'white' colonies attracted

[1] Quoted from MacDonald's diary by Rose (1983: 240). Original available in National Archives as PRO 30/69 'James Ramsay MacDonald and predecessors and successors: Papers'.

little attention most of the time. The great ideologue of Unionism, A. V. Dicey, noted that the Colonial Laws Validity Act 1865 'seems (oddly enough) to have passed through Parliament without discussion' (Dicey 1885/1982: 49). The British North America Act 1867, which remained, with later amendments, the Constitution of Canada until 1982, slid through almost as silently. It was bipartisan. It was enacted on the watch of Benjamin Disraeli, often seen as the prophet and ideologue of empire par excellence; but the six-volume biography of Disraeli by Monypenny and Buckle (1910–20: iv. 556) hardly mentions it at all.

The 1865 Act provided that any colonial law 'repugnant' to the provisions of any Act of Parliament applying to that colony 'shall, to the extent of such repugnancy, but not otherwise, be and remain absolutely void and inoperative' (s.2). The mindset of Victorian legislators towards the colonies did not advance beyond this, except in Ireland. Canada had surfaced briefly at the time of the Durham Report in 1838, which promoted the merger of Upper and Lower Canada, and again at the time of the British North America Act 1867. That Act was drafted in Canada, by federalists frightened of a resurgent USA after the end of its Civil War. Many US politicians beginning with Thomas Jefferson thought it was the manifest destiny of the USA to absorb Canada. For a fuller analysis of the Canadian Constitution, see McLean (2005).

Australia and New Zealand were further away. There was no particular reason for British politicians to pay attention to Australia in this period. It was a useful receptacle for troublemakers, and occasionally a safely remote place to try out constitutional experiments. The first scheme of proportional representation anywhere in the Empire was adopted for Adelaide City Council in 1839. New Zealand was incorporated by a dubious adventurer, Edward Gibbon Wakefield, but its constitutional founding was surer than Australia's. Where Australia was regarded as *terra nullius*—nobody's land, aboriginal Australians not being regarded as humans—New Zealand's founding charter was the Waitangi Treaty of 1840 between the representatives of Queen Victoria and Maori leaders. But the first Unionist politician to pay serious attention to Australia or New Zealand was Joseph Chamberlain, whose story belongs in the next chapter.

Imperialism *as an ideology* was not articulated till Benjamin Disraeli's periods as Conservative leader and Prime Minister from 1867 to 1880. Even then, it was not his first reaction to the Empire. In early life, although Disraeli was interested in the Middle East, he showed no particular interest in the British Empire, once notoriously calling the colonies 'a millstone round our necks'. As late as 1866 Chancellor of the Exchequer Disraeli complained to Lord Derby, the Prime Minister, 'What is the use of these colonial deadweights which we do not govern. . . . Leave the Canadians to defend themselves; . . . give up the settlements on the west coast of Africa; and we shall make a saving' (Disraeli to Derby, 17.10.1866, in Blake 1966: 455).

Imperialism's time came in the 1870s. It was not Disraeli's single-handed creation. Queen Victoria played a large part. She coveted the title of Empress of India, a desire to which Disraeli, the greatest ham actor ever to lead the UK (out-hamming even Harold Macmillan) pandered shamelessly. The results of their double act include the full incorporation of British India in the Empire; the sensationally over-the-top Durbar Room in Osborne House, Queen Victoria's residence on the Isle of Wight; and the fact that chicken tikka masala, invented by Bangladeshi restaurateurs in Britain in the 1970s, has become Britain's national dish.

Nor was imperialism confined to Tories. The left-wing Radicals Sir Charles Dilke and Joseph Chamberlain were as much imperialists as the Queen, who distrusted them so much that she tried to exclude them from Gladstone's government of 1880. The Empire provided a unifying ideology, and it offered jobs that enabled the talented and ambitious to break out of the British (especially the English) class structure. The unifying ideology was comfortably racist and xenophobic. Before modern readers rush to condemn it, remember that the past is another country; they do things differently there. Racism was universal in Victorian society at all levels, including in science. White Anglo-Saxons believed that Darwin's *Descent of Man* (1871) implied an evolutionary gradient not only among non-human animals, but among humans, with Australian aborigines at the bottom; Turks, Maori, and Irish somewhat further up; and white Anglo-Saxons at the top.[2] As to xenophobia, there is no evidence that British society was more xenophobic between 1870 and 1914 than earlier or later. But it was during that era that an Empire coloured pink appeared on the world map on the wall of every school in the country. 'We hold a vaster empire than has been', and held it, for the most part, successfully. When things went wrong, as in the (actually self-induced) death of General Gordon, whose operations in Khartoum in 1885 had been in direct defiance of his orders, politicians could blame it on the government of the day. The late Colin Matthew, the best biographer of W. E. Gladstone, reported that 'giving talks in the 1970s and 1980s on Gladstone to non-historians, I have been struck by the fact that Gladstone's part in the death of Gordon was almost always raised by a questioner' (Matthew 1999: 401).

---

[2] An interpretation that gets some support from Darwin's own private writings. 'Remember what risk the nations of Europe ran, not so many centuries ago of being overwhelmed by the Turks, and how ridiculous such an idea now is! The more civilised so-called Caucasian races have beaten the Turkish hollow in the struggle for existence' (C. Darwin to Professor W. Graham, 3.7.1881, quoted by Clark 1984: 207). That view still has resonance in the reluctance of some EU member state governments to welcome Turkey's application for membership in 2004.

Every commentator from Rudyard Kipling to Linda Colley (1996: 133–40) has noticed the role of Scots in the Victorian Empire. Kipling's great dramatic monologue *McAndrew's Hymn* (1890) encapsulates the Calvinist ship's engineer in its tremendous opening lines:

LORD, Thou hast made this world below the shadow of a dream,
An', taught by time, I tak' it so—exceptin' always Steam.
From coupler-flange to spindle-guide I see Thy Hand, O God—
Predestination in the stride o' yon connectin'-rod.

McAndrew has kept the trade of the Empire going with no help from his bosses or the British class structure:

Not but that they're ceevil on the Board. Ye'll hear Sir Kenneth say:
"Good morn, McAndrew! Back again? An' how's your bilge to-day?"
Miscallin' technicalities but handin' me my chair
To drink Madeira wi' three Earls....

That minds me of our Viscount loon—Sir Kenneth's kin—the chap
Wi' Russia leather tennis-shoon an' spar-decked yachtin'-cap.
I showed him round last week, o'er all—an' at the last says he:
"Mister M'Andrew, don't you think steam spoils romance at sea?"
Damned ijjit! I'd been doon that morn to see what ailed the throws,
Manholin', on my back—the cranks three inches off my nose.

Not only engineers but also soldiers and administrators came disproportionately from Scotland. Colley (1996) quotes several studies that show that a quarter of the British army in the eighteenth century were Scots. Army service was a good way for the descendants of Jacobites to prove their loyalty to the Crown and the UK, and the aptitude of Highlanders for fighting—for the regime that had defeated many of them at Culloden—soon became legendary. So did the role of Scots administrators in India. At a time when Scotland contributed under 10 per cent of the UK population in the decade after 1775, some 47 per cent of the 249 men appointed to serve as writers in Bengal were Scots; and so were 60 per cent of the 371 men allowed to reside in Bengal as free merchants (Colley 1996: 134).

Irish attitudes to the Empire varied. There are three relevant groups of Irish people: northern ('Ulster-Scot') Protestants, southern Protestants, and Catholics.

Protestants from the north-east of Ireland were culturally very much like Scottish Protestants, many of them indeed descended from the 'Plantation of Ulster' with Presbyterians in the early seventeenth century. They led a huge wave of emigration to certain parts of the USA in the eighteenth century, settling especially at the then frontier in the Appalachian Mountains. American history knows them as 'Ulster-Scots' and they were heavily represented in the early leadership of the republic. However, American independence removes them from our story.

In the nineteenth century, northern Protestants were responsible for the industrialization of what is now Northern Ireland. This detached their interests from those of both other groups of Irishmen. Wolfe Tone, the Protestant leader of the 1798 Rebellion, was never replicated. Ulster-Scots' anti-Catholicism derived from their common Presbyterian culture with that of Scottish Protestants—they were equally the descendants of John Knox and the Covenanters, the best Catholic-haters of the sixteenth and seventeenth centuries. The closer and more numerous presence of the traditional enemy sharpened it. It was a cultural and economic hostility that took British politicians, not least Gladstone, completely by surprise in the 1880s. To Gladstone's discredit, he had not anticipated the 'Orange' obstacle to Irish Home Rule, even though, as noted in Chapter 3, Orange lodges, the institutional form of militant anti-Catholicism, date back to 1795 (Foster 1989: 272). Introducing his first Home Rule Bill, he said:

the voice of Ireland, as a whole, is at this moment clearly and Constitutionally spoken. I cannot say it is otherwise when five-sixths of its lawfully chosen Representatives are of one mind in this matter. There is a counter voice; and I wish to know what is the claim of those by whom that counter voice is spoken, and how much is the scope and allowance we can give them. Certainly, Sir, I cannot allow it to be said that a Protestant minority in Ulster, or elsewhere, is to rule the question at large for Ireland. (*Hansard* 8 April 1886, col 1053)

Charles Stewart Parnell's Irish Party machine had won seventeen of the thirty-three seats in Ulster, although Catholics were a minority of the population there. So, for the only time in British-Irish history, it was true that the Protestant minority held a minority of seats even in Ulster. This does not excuse Gladstone's myopia.

Ulster Protestant attitudes to the Empire, although less studied than Scottish attitudes, were probably very similar. Trade and professional networks in the two countries were close. Ulster Protestants went into trades and professions similar to those of Scots. Two of the three centres of shipping and shipbuilding were Glasgow and Belfast. The designers and engineer officers of the *Titanic*, built at Harland and Wolff's yard in Belfast, were real-life McAndrews. (They all stayed at their posts, and everyone died except some deck officers.) It is safe to conclude that the Empire bound Ulster Protestants to the Union.

Southern Protestants—the traditional 'Ascendancy' were a different matter. Southern Ireland never industrialized. The Ascendancy was a landed aristocracy in hard times, times that got worse for them during the nineteenth century. They were not even in the same church as the plurality of

Ulster Protestants. The latter was split roughly evenly between the established Church of Ireland and the nonconformist Presbyterian church. The
former belonged wholly to the established Church of Ireland. Establishment
meant that the entire population was liable to pay bitterly resented tithes to
this minority church. The politics of the Ascendancy was a long and ultimately unsuccessful struggle for church and land. The one imperial institution
in which southern Irish Protestants were deeply involved was the Army. This
certainly tended to bind them to Empire and Union, but it was a less intense
network than the one that linked Scots and (probably) Ulstermen to the
Empire.

Irish Catholics had no reason to love the Empire. The extent of their
hostility should not be exaggerated, as many of them were willing to fight
for it, notably in both the Napoleonic Wars and the First World War, when
they were part of it, and in the Second World War, when they had to all
intents and purposes left it. But organized Catholicism, both inside and
outside Ireland, was always hostile to the Union and the Empire. The Irish
Catholic diaspora was already well under way before the Famine of 1845–7.
That catastrophe of course speeded up the exodus. In Canada, the USA, and
Australia there sprang up organizations of bitter Irishmen who, in the words
of Flanders and Swann's *Song of Patriotic Prejudice* ('The English, the
English, the English are best', 1965)

blow up policemen, or so I have heard
And blame it on Cromwell and William the Third

Welsh attitudes to an Empire are the hardest to discern. Welsh culture was
highly distinctive. As late as 1901, 30 per cent of the population of Wales
spoke no English (Jenkins 2001: 60). The first Census in which fewer than
half of Welsh residents spoke Welsh was that of 1911, after massive anglophone migration into the south Wales coalfield. Colley's survey (1996: 310–
13) of responses to the military Volunteer movement during the Napoleonic
Wars shows very mixed results. In 1798 Wales, with Scotland, offered double
the population of Volunteers to England's (4 per cent and 2 per cent of the
population respectively). But in the survey of preparedness compiled in 1804,
which is Colley's main data source, the Welsh response was poorest: 'North
and central Wales especially remained at the start of the nineteenth century
the part of Great Britain most resistant to control from the centre' (Colley
1996: 312).

Within the UK, the years from 1800 to 1886 witnessed a series of nation-
building events, followed by the development of centre-periphery politics, as
various parts of the periphery organized their opposition to the core. Colley
(1996) identifies a set of nation-building events occurring close together at the
end of her period. They include Catholic Emancipation in 1829; the associ-

ated decline of hardline Protestantism in England (not in the peripheral countries); and the Reform Act of 1832. Of these the most interesting, and the most easily forgotten nowadays, is the decline of hardline (known in the nineteenth century as 'Ultra') Protestantism.

As we saw earlier, some political elites in England treated the Protestant Succession established in 1707 as a matter of national survival. Catholicism implied Jacobitism, which in turn implied the overthrow of the seventeenth-century settlement and subordination to the mortal enemy, France. That is the source of the requirement of the Act of Succession 1701 (still in force as we write in 2004) that the monarch of the UK must be Protestant, and of George III's disastrous veto in 1801.

The betrayers of Ultra Protestantism were two of their own: the Duke of Wellington and Sir Robert Peel. Essentially on grounds of public order, they agreed on the two great betrayals: Catholic Emancipation in 1829 and the Maynooth Grant in 1845. Once a reluctant Wellington—himself an Irish Protestant landowner—was convinced that these measures were needed to protect public order in Ireland, he acquiesced in them. His speech commending Maynooth to the House of Lords in 1845 is classic. Maynooth was a Catholic seminary that had fallen on hard times. To the fury of the Ultras, the Peel Administration proposed an increased state grant to it. In the Lords, Wellington pointed out that Ireland contained eight million people, a third of the UK population. Nearly 90 per cent of them were Catholics: 'we cannot avoid their being Roman Catholics'. Their priests must be educated somewhere. If the British government did not make provision in Maynooth, they would be educated in Italy, France, or another Catholic country—a much worse prospect from the perspective of public order. Priests dispensed political advice. At Maynooth, the British government could at least observe what they learnt and taught (*Hansard*, Lords, 2 June 1845, cc. 1160–74).

The last gasp of English Protestantism was Lord John Russell's Ecclesiastical Titles Act 1851, which forbade the Catholic Church from re-establishing its hierarchy—in Russell's charming phrase 'the mummery of superstition'—in England. Gladstone, who had earlier opposed the Maynooth grant on Protestant grounds, had by 1851 turned full circle, and spoke passionately against the bill—on the grounds, among others, that it was an insult to the eight million Catholic citizens of the UK. It was enacted but never enforced, and Gladstone's first administration repealed it in 1871.

It was the last gasp for two reasons. First, the end of the Napoleonic Wars meant the end of the politico-religious threat from France that had dominated British international thinking since 1688. Second, religiosity of any sort was in rapid decline. Hilton's (1988) influential 'atonement' hypothesis maintains that from about 1800 to about 1850 a certain style of Protestant evangelicalism, which maintained that Christ had died to atone for the sins of man but that man must repent practically by social action, underlay much of domestic politics. The thesis is controversial, but even Hilton agrees that political evangelicalism was in rapid decline by 1850. The religious census of 1851 was a terrible shock to the Church of England (and for that reason has never been repeated). The main results are in Table 4.1.

It showed that the established church scored only a plurality (not a majority) of church attendances in England, and a smaller plurality in England and Wales. In the year that Russell denounced the mummeries of superstition, there were three million attendances at the main Church of England service on Census Sunday, and $\frac{1}{4}$ million at Roman Catholic churches in England and Wales. When the overwhelmingly Catholic population of Ireland (not covered by the 1851 census) is added, Catholics can be estimated at somewhere around 29 per cent of the UK population.

In the following sections of this chapter we examine the roots of discontent with the Union in each of the three non-English parts of the Kingdom.

Scotland

Scotland in the nineteenth century did well out of the Union. It provided a labour supply for empire. At the start of the century the four Scottish universities were turning out more graduates a year than the only two English universities then extant, Oxford and Cambridge.

The most important Unionist in the early nineteenth century was Sir Walter Scott. In his novels, Scott celebrated a romantic Highland nationalism—but a nationalism tamed by the defeat of the clans in 1746. Scotland should continue to celebrate the romance but not the associated danger of Jacobite politics. As a nationalistic Tory, Scott put these views into practice. He was the mastermind of the visit of George IV to Scotland in 1822, when he forced the King's ample form into a kilt. It was the reigning monarch's first visit to Scotland since 1707. George IV's statute stands at the apex of Edinburgh's New Town, where Hanover St crosses George St, and George IV Bridge overleaps the Old Town to the south to open up new suburbs. The self-styled Highland Lady Elizabeth Grant missed the point comprehensively when she wrote:

A great mistake was made by the stage managers, one that offended all the southron Scots; the King wore at the Levee the highland dress. I daresay he thought the country all highland, expected no fertile plains, did not know the difference between the Saxon and the Celt. (Grant 1988, vol. II: 165–6)

In reality Scott created, and Queen Victoria's generation later reinforced, the harmless tartanry to which Scottish cultural nationalism turned. The kilt, a symbol of rebellion when it was banned after Culloden in 1746, became an

TABLE 4.1. *Number of persons present at the most numerously attended services on Sunday, March 30, 1851*

	Church of England	Protestant dissent	RC	Other	All	Total population	Attendances as % of population	C of E as % of attendances
England	2,838,318	2,629,590	243,701	21,110	5,732,719	16,738,986	34.25	49.51
Wales	132,940	481,192	5,688	3,683	623,503	1,188,914	52.44	21.32
Scotland					740,794	2,888,742	25.64	

Source: Cols 1–6 Census Reports 1851: England and Wales, and Scotland. Religious Worship/E & W Table N. Sc Table B. Cols 7–8: our calculations. The census takers for England and Wales warned that there could be over- and under-counting of individuals who attended more than one service; who attended services of more than one denomination; or who attended a service that was not the most numerously attended on Census Sunday. The Scottish enumerators merely counted attendances in 'morning', 'afternoon', and 'evening', and did not discriminate by denomination. The figures for 'morning' (the highest) are shown.

ornament of society. The whole apparatus of clan tartans ('If Your Name is Here We Have Your Tartan', as the Edinburgh tourist shops advertise[3]) was invented by Scott. Any connection with the pre-Culloden clan system is contingent and probably spurious.

Scott was a former pupil of the Royal High School, which had been Edinburgh's city school since the twelfth century. But he was one of the founders of a rival, more English-oriented school, the Edinburgh Academy. The Academy taught Latin with English pronunciation, and its mission was 'to enable Scots boys to compete with English public school boys for the more important posts in the Empire' (see the school history at *http://www. edinburghac.demon.co.uk/school.html*). Edinburgh Corporation vowed to have nothing to do with the Academy. In the multiply segregated world of Edinburgh schools nearly two centuries later—segregated by class, segregated by religion—the Academy now stands for one conception of Scotland: Unionist, integrationist, offering English as well as Scottish qualifications, and the Royal High another: local authority-run, culturally but not politically nationalist, offering Scottish but not English qualifications. The history of Edinburgh schools is the history of the Union in microcosm.

Before 1886 the biggest shock to the Union in Scotland was the Disruption crisis of 1843. Evangelicalism in Scotland had followed a different course to England. It had thrown itself into ministering, in extreme Calvinist style, to the population of the growing urban areas and of the poverty-stricken Highlands. Many ministers dissented from the established Church of Scotland. But those who were inside it wanted ministers to be nominated by their own congregations, not by outside patrons. By the 1830s, the General Assembly of the Church of Scotland was openly at war with the courts, each purporting to impose a minister of the parishes of Auchterarder and Marnoch and to depose the other's candidate. The inherent contradictions of a state church could not be ignored. (For more detail on church establishment in Scotland and England see McLean and Linsley 2004.)

The crisis remained an internal Scottish matter until Peel and his Home Secretary Sir James Graham decided to resolve it. Regarding the evangelicals as 'a band of crazed zealots' (Ferguson 1968: 311), Peel and Graham rejected their claim for spiritual independence of the Church. This split the established Church down the middle. In the General Assembly of 1843, about half of the ministers withdrew to an alternative hall they had already booked. Professing a belief in an established church, they effectively disestablished the Church of Scotland for the rest of the nineteenth century. The Free Church they founded was relatively stronger than the established Church in the poorer parts of

---

[3] Or the alternative version, to the tune of *Scotland the Brave*: 'Tartan breeches, tartan hats, Tartan for your dogs and cats, If your tartan isn't here you haven't got a name.'

Scotland. In the poorest of all, the Highlands, it became the standard-bearer for Liberalism and anti-landlordism. The established Church, as an instrument of social control, disappeared in Scotland in 1843. By the time it was reunited, in 1900, the time for churches to act as agents of the state had passed.

Wales

If they were not border gentry, the English only began to become aware of the otherness of Wales when the Napoleonic Wars cut them off from the Grand Tour of the Continent. Then, aided by the eighteenth-century guidebooks of Thomas Pennant and by their contemporary George Borrow, they started to discover the alien land on their doorstep.

It may be difficult for modern readers to realize how alien it was. According to Morgan (1963), the great political transformation in Wales came with the General Election of 1868. He quotes the pacifist dissenting minister Revd. Henry Richard as saying to the newly enfranchised electors of the borough of Merthyr Tydfil:

The people who speak this language [Welsh]..., who created and sustain these marvellous religious organization, the people forming three fourths of the people of Wales—have they not a right to say to this small propertied class.... *We are the Welsh people and not you?* (*Aberdare Times* 14.11.1868, quoted by Morgan 1963: v)

Richard won the seat, which he 'retained till his death, his majorities, whenever there was a contest, being overwhelming, and his expenses being always paid by his constituents' (*Old DNB*). The best picture of Wales at mid-century (or any other time) comes from George Borrow. His infectious travelogue *Wild Wales* (Borrow 1862/2002) depicts a Wales where the linguistic boundary is very sharp. In 1862, nobody spoke Welsh in Wrexham; everybody spoke Welsh in Llangollen ten miles away; nobody except commercial travellers spoke English in Dyffryn Ceiriog, only another ten miles into Wales. In 2004, the linguistic boundary is just as sharp and it passes through the same places, although the overall proportion of the population who speak Welsh is smaller. Dyffryn Ceiriog is still one of the most Welsh-speaking places in Wales, less than ten miles from the English border. Likewise, a few miles to the south, Dolanog and Llanfihangel-yng-Gwynfa are wholly Welsh; their market town Welshpool is wholly anglophone.

Borrow's main topics of conversation were poetry and sects. He must have infuriated his Welsh hearers by knowing, as an East Anglian, more Welsh poetry than they did, and correcting their mistakes in their native language. He also repeatedly extolled the established Anglican church and was disappointed by the stubborn Calvinist Methodism of most of the Welsh people he met.

Of the three classical defining features of Welshness, two were old in the time of Richard and Borrow, and one was relatively new. More than half the population still spoke the Welsh language, and a substantial proportion did not speak English. Welsh historians have argued that the language came under serious threat from anglicizing educators in the nineteenth century, although the most recent research suggests that this has been much exaggerated. At all events, as late as 1911, 7.9 per cent of the population spoke Welsh only and a further 32.5 per cent were bilingual in Welsh and English.

Farm size and tenure also differed from England. The hilly or mountainous terrain largely dictated that. Most farms were small family farms, usually of less than 100 acres held on annual leases without security of tenure. This put them somewhere between the arable farms of England and the desperate smallholdings of the west of Ireland.

Welsh religious distinctiveness was surprisingly recent at the time of Richard's call to arms. In 1800 the Methodists were still part of the established Church. The so-called Calvinist Methodists (more Calvinist than Methodist) seceded in 1811. By 1851 they were just the largest Nonconformist denomination in Wales, closely followed by the Congregationalists, with the Baptists and Wesleyans behind. Nonconformists as a whole outnumbered the established Church by at least two to one, or maybe more. As in Ireland and Scotland, religion mapped onto social class and vice versa. Only the landowning class was attached to the established Church; all other classes were predominantly Nonconformist. In the absence of a Welsh political party, Nonconformist ministers such as Richard took on themselves the role of national spokesmen. Borrow failed to see how his own church had become a partisan sect.

In 1868 the industrialization of Wales was well advanced. Merthyr Tydfil was the largest town in Wales. South Wales was starting to become one of the largest coal-mining areas in the world. However, until about the 1880s, this industrialization was fed by migration from within Wales rather than outside. Therefore the Welshness of industrial South Wales was scarcely diluted. The best-known miners' MP of the nineteenth century, 'Mabon' (William Abraham) was elected in 1885 and sat until 1920. His outlook on the world was purely Welsh, 'the pathos of his speech [in favour of church disestablishment in 1889] being heightened by his apparent unfamiliarity with the English language' (Morgan 1963: 81).

The party politics of Wales was overwhelmingly Liberal from 1868, the first election after the Second Reform Act, until 1906. Between 1868 and 1886, Welsh cultural nationalism made patchy progress. A motion to disestablish the Church in Wales, proposed after the Irish Church had been disestablished in 1869, got little support—its time had not yet come. But Gladstone agonized over finding a Welsh-speaking bishop, did find one for St Asaph in 1870. Most distinctively, one of a tiny number of Wales-only public Acts to be passed in the nineteenth century was the Welsh Sunday Closing Act 1881, which has left its mark on Wales almost until the present day (the last 'dry' areas of Wales only being permitted to open their pubs on a Sunday in 1996, and the 1881 Act effectively repealed in 2003). Three Welsh university colleges, albeit all of them tiny, were founded between 1872 and 1883.

Like all the other marginal farming areas of the UK, Wales was badly hit by the agricultural depression of the 1870s, when lower prices for cereals from the prairies of America undercut British produce. An appalling harvest in 1879 brought things to a head, in Wales as in Ireland. It helped to produce the Liberal sweep in rural Wales in the 1880, 1885, and even 1886 General Elections. These brought into Parliament a new generation of Welsh cultural nationalists, led by Tom Ellis (1859–99), and a cultural revivalist movement *Cymru Fydd* ('Wales of the Future' or 'Young Wales'—obviously an echo of the Young Ireland movement of the 1840s), both discussed in chapter 5.

Disestablishment and devolution were long in the future. But by the time of the crisis of 1886, there already existed a Welsh lobby in the Liberal Party, who had seen land and church reform in Ireland, and who wanted it for themselves.

Ireland

The Union of 1800 got off to a bad start. Its first twenty-five years were marked by efficient administration and anarchic rural protest. The most efficient administrator in nineteenth-century politics, Sir Robert Peel, was Chief Secretary for Ireland between 1812 and 1818. Like other Chief Secretaries and viceroys (the line between their responsibilities was unclear) he presided over the administration at Dublin Castle. As the task of British administration in Ireland was essentially one of social control, the Castle had to be efficient if British administration was to survive. It was, and it did, until 1919.

But the Castle could do nothing about rural violence. The Whiteboys and the Ribbonmen continued an already old tradition of violent anti-landlord protest. Among northern Protestants, Orangeism revived

amongst the vulgar classes, . . . very turbulent, bigoted, riotous and affronting, very saucy, and overbearing, almost proud of transgression, necessarily producing exasperation, and often leading to the effusion of blood. It is a rebellious and insurrectionary propensity gone astray, and running contradictorily in the channel of Allegiance. (Baron Smith to Sir William Gregory, 4.9.1813, quoted by Foster 1989: 303)

In 1821 and again in 1825, bills for Catholic emancipation passed the Commons but were defeated in the Lords. The stage was set for 'the

Liberator', Daniel O'Connell (1775–1847). Like Parnell fifty years later, O'Connell had a genius for political organization. A reasonable number of Catholics had the vote, although they were not allowed to run for office. O'Connell's Catholic Association collected a 'Catholic rent' to fund his organization. It culminated in O'Connell's successful election campaign in Co. Clare in 1828. The election was necessitated by Wellington's appointment of the sitting member to his Cabinet—this in those days required the member to resign and seek re-election. In the face of O'Connell's certain victory, he did not even stay in contention.

The election of O'Connell made emancipation inevitable, however much the Ultras denounced Wellington and Peel. Otherwise, Ireland would have been ungovernable, as a follower of O'Connell would top the poll in any seat in Catholic Ireland. The most obdurate opponent of emancipation was King George IV, but the conversion of Peel and Wellington meant that there was no alternative Protestant government available to him. From then until his death, O'Connell led the Repealers (of the Irish Union) in Parliament. But repeal was not practical politics unless either the Repealers held the balance of seats in the Commons or the cause could enlist allies in Britain. Neither of these conditions was to be met until 1885, and then they were both met at once.

A blight destroyed the potato crop after it had been lifted in the dark wet summer of 1845. Given the science of the time, nothing could prevent the subsequent starvation. (The fungus that caused the blight was not correctly identified until the 1880s.) The actual crop failure was worst in the east of Ireland but the starvation was worst in the west. The Irish Famine of 1845–7 perfectly exemplies Amartya Sen's argument (Sen 1981) that famine results not from a failure of food, but from a failure of entitlement. The peasants of western Ireland were outside the cash economy. When the potato crop failed, they had no money to buy any substitute, not even the fish that piled up rotting on Galway quay for lack of purchasers. The blight destroyed the seed potatoes for planting in 1846, the year in which the actual starvation was worst. Cholera followed. The total death toll was over a million. The population of Ireland, over 8 million in the 1841 census, was reduced to 6.5 million ten years later. Death and emigration each accounted for half of the decline (Mokyr 1983; Woodham-Smith 1962).

The immediate political consequence of the Famine seemed perverse. Far from encouraging the Repeal movement, the Famine seemed to kill it off. O'Connell died in 1847 and no comparable politician took his place. Catholic politics petered out into the romantic inconsequentiality of Young Ireland, and to the more consequential violent insurrectionary politics of bitter emigrants. The Fenian movement was founded in 1858, linking the secret Irish Republican Brotherhood (the distant forerunner of the IRA) in Ireland with the open Fenian Brotherhood, which was strongest in North America. The latter funded the former, a pattern that was to endure.

Gladstone and the Irish Nation

Gladstone and the Irish Nation is the title of what is still after sixty years the best monograph on the subject (Hammond 1938). It is also an appropriate title for this section, because the attempt to change British policy in 1886 was wholly the work of W. E. Gladstone. The politician who killed off the old regime in Ireland was Charles Stewart Parnell. This section must concentrate on these two compelling characters.

In December 1868, a young aristocrat called Evelyn Ashley was standing in Gladstone's park at Hawarden holding his coat, while Gladstone felled a tree. A telegraph boy appeared. Gladstone

took the telegram, opened it and read it, then handed it to me, speaking only two words, namely, 'Very significant', and at once resumed his work. The message merely stated that that General Grey would arrive that evening from Windsor. This, of course, implied that a mandate was coming from the Queen charging Mr Gladstone with the formation of his first Government. I said nothing, but waited while the well-directed blows resounded in regular cadence. After a few minutes the blows ceased and Mr Gladstone, resting on the handle of his axe, looked up, and with deep earnestness in his voice, and great intensity in his face, exclaimed: 'My mission is to pacify Ireland'. He then resumed his task, and never said another word until the tree was down. (E. Ashley in *National Review*, June 1898, quoted by Matthew 1999: 147)

Gladstone had already decided that the established Church and the land tenure system in Ireland were both beyond reform. With the Fenians in mind, he already saw it as an imperial question:

The Irish question which has long been grave is growing *awful*. In my opinion this Empire has but one danger. It is the danger expressed by the combination of the three names Ireland, United States and Canada. English policy should set its face two ways like a flint: to support public order, and to make the laws of Ireland such as they should be. (Gladstone to C. S. P. Fortescue, Dec. 1867, quoted in Matthew 1999: 146)

In 1869, during his first government, Gladstone disestablished the Church of Ireland. Given the High Anglican views set out in his theocratic tract *The State in its Relations with the Church,* this was a dramatic shift. But by 1868 he was signalling, as the new leader of the Liberal Party, that he thought establishment had become untenable. This prompted the Catholic Church to organize the vote vigorously in Ireland in the 1868 election to ensure that disestablishers won as many seats as possible. The Bishop and clergy of Galway resolved that they would refuse to support any candidate

who will not pledge himself both to support Mr Gladstone's resolutions against the Irish establishment ... and to assist in hurling from office any, and every ministry, which will refuse to make the said resolutions cabinet measures. (*Galway Vindicator*, 19.9.1868, quoted by Thornley 1964: 49)

The clergy succeeded in all bar three of the constituencies where they tried. This had two effects at least. It showed Irish politicians how effective a lobby of the relatively homogeneous Irish electorate could be. And it gave disestablishment an easy ride. The Liberals never had a majority of votes in the House of Lords, where the Tories were the largest party from 1800 until the elimination of most of the hereditary peers in 1999. The Tories were also the more unionist party. Most Union-weakening or pro-periphery proposals therefore were defeated in the Lords, or would have been if they had got there. But Lord Salisbury, the Tory leader in the Lords in 1869, let Irish disestablishment through on the grounds that 'it was not the business of the House of Lords to resist the nation's will' (Hammond 1938: 89). This was not a line that either Salisbury or his successors as Tory leaders in the Lords were to take consistently. A commoner line was that they, not the vulgar elected house, represented the true will of the people.

The path from disestablishment to Home Rule was long and winding. It started well for Gladstone and for his supporters in Ireland. He enacted two reforms of land tenure in Ireland, in 1870 and 1881. The 1870 Act, as he told Cardinal Manning (with instructions to pass the letter on to Cardinal Cullen, the overbearing leader of the Catholic Church in Ireland), was designed

to prevent the Landlord from using the terrible weapon of undue and unjust eviction by so framing the handle that it shall cut his hands with the sharp edge of pecuniary damages. (16.2.1870, quoted by Hammond 1938: 100)

But first the Whigs in his own Cabinet and then the House of Lords blunted it. A weapon that cut away any of the rights of landed property was too sharp for them.

The Liberals returned to office in 1880. By then, the Irish Party had been formed. Disappointed by the Land Act, a formerly Tory Irish lawyer called Isaac Butt had formed first a Home Government Association and then a Home Rule League to promote Home Rule for Ireland. In the General Election of 1874, the brand-new Home Rule League elected (as it claimed) 59 out of the 105 Irish members, in the process unseating Gladstone's former Irish secretary Chichester Fortescue. The senior Catholic clergy opposed Home Rule, but their parish clergy revolted (Thornley 1964: 176–204).

Butt's Irish Party was not cohesive, and Butt was elbowed aside by the more ruthless Parnell in 1877. But the 1874 election proved that the median voter in Ireland was a Home Ruler. Even Tories, to be elected in Catholic Ireland, must support Home Rule, as one of them explained to Disraeli in 1877:

I knew that unless I accepted the 'shibbolet' of Home Rule I must retire forever from public life. . . . It did not necessarily imply anything calculated to injure the integrity of the empire. (Sir G. Bowyer to Disraeli, 6.11.1877, quoted by Thornley 1964: 196)

By the next election, in 1880, Bowyer and his like had retired forever from public life. Nobody could be elected under the labels Tory or Liberal in Catholic Ireland. Parnell did not yet control the Home Rule party, but he was on the way to turning it into the first disciplined cadre party in the British Isles.

Gladstone's Conversion

As in 1845, the disastrous harvest of 1879 caused most misery where there was least entitlement, namely in the west of Ireland. But it exacerbated the decline in Ireland's competitive position for agriculture, so that all stake-holders throughout Ireland, from landowners to labourers, lost. Landowners may have lost more than proportionately (Foster 1989: p. 376, Fig. 3). But tenant farmers saw landlords as oppressors, not as fellow-sufferers. Simultaneously with Parnell's reshaping of the Irish Party, there arose a Land League, whose aims were to force landlords to sell out and to hold (or bring) rents down to their level in 1852. The methods of the Land League, and even more of unorganized protest, were not gentle. Captain Boycott, who unwillingly gave his name to the methods used against him, had to 'enlist fifty Orangemen, guarded by troops, to harvest his crops' (Hammond 1938: 193). The Land Leaguers' practice of maiming animals to reduce their value shocked the sentimental English.

Gladstone met the collapse of 1879 and the rise of the Land League with a second Land Act in 1881. This granted the campaigners' 'Three F's', namely fair rent (to be assessed by government arbitration), free sale (of interests in tenancies), and fixity of tenure. As in 1870, Gladstone had to take on the Whigs in his own party and the House of Lords. The opposition of the latter was blunted by the fact that the majority of Irish Conservatives (who sat in Protestant Ulster) voted for the bill. Irish landlords no longer commanded any seats in the elected house, and in the unelected house they were but a subset of Irish Unionists. The builders of the *Titanic* were fervent Unionists for sure, but they had neither stake nor interest in the Irish land question.

However, the Land Act did not restore public order, either in Ireland or in the Commons, where the Irish members had perfected methods of obstruction. In 1881 the government interned Parnell without trial for allegedly inflaming the land war. In 1882, by the so-called Treaty of Kilmainham Jail (which Gladstone angrily denied was a treaty), Parnell was released on the understanding that he would be a force for moderation. And so he was, even though within two days of his release terrorists unconnected with the Land League murdered Gladstone's new Chief Secretary Lord Frederick Cavendish in Phoenix Park, Dublin, only half a mile from Kilmainham where the 'Treaty' had just been agreed. Cavendish was the brother of Gladstone's main Whig colleague Lord Hartington, and his wife was Gladstone's wife's niece. The families had been very close.

Several studies have shown that, although the revelation of Gladstone's conversion to Home Rule was a bombshell, its development was long-drawn-out (see especially Hammond 1938: 404–54; Matthew 1999: 450–510). Others, including Chamberlain and Parnell, also proposed schemes of devolution. When Gladstone's administration was defeated on its budget in June 1885, Lord Salisbury took office in a minority Conservative government. Parnell decided to seek Home Rule from the Tories. This has shocked many historians but it made perfect sense. Parnell commanded a block of fifty seats in Ireland, a number bound to rise at the next election because the franchise had been widened in 1884. He was also believed to control a number of seats in Britain with a substantial Irish vote. He had no prior ideological commitment to either British party. The Salisbury minority government depended on Irish votes. Perhaps most important, the Tories no longer had an ideological nor an interest-based commitment to Irish landowners. As noted earlier, the latter controlled no seats in the elected house. Though heavily represented in the House of Lords, they would be unable to defeat a government led from that house by Lord Salisbury. Salisbury's Irish secretary Lord Carnarvon was sympathetic to Home Rule and gave Parnell misleading signals about how warm the government would be to it. That Salisbury might have enacted Home Rule is no more absurd than for Disraeli to have passed the Second Reform Act or Nixon to have visited China (McLean 2001a: 63–102). Parnell was quite clear-eyed about the situation. He knew that a Gladstone Home Rule Bill would be defeated in the Lords. A Salisbury Home Rule Bill might just carry there, according to Parnell's lieutenant Tim Healy:

We have to make the best fight we can for a small country, and clearly, if we put the Tories in and hold them dependent on us, that is our game. With the house of Lords behind them and our help, they could play ducks and drakes with the Union, were they so minded. (T. M. Healy to Henry Labouchere, 15.10.1885, quoted by Lyons 1977: 298–9)

Salisbury might even have been forced to act, but for the most disastrous leak in British political history. The general election of November 1885, in which Parnell urged the Irish in Britain to vote Tory, yielded a Home Rule bloc of eighty-six seats. The Liberals got 333 and the Tories 251. Parnell could thus put either party in government, providing it did not fracture. (It is frequently, but wrongly, stated that he could only put the Liberals in. That mistake combines retrospective reasoning with an inability to count.) Salisbury did not immediately resign. Carnarvon did, when Salisbury repudiated the deal he thought he had done with Parnell. But, critically, Carnarvon did not publicize his resignation. (His 'deal' with Parnell did not become public knowledge until 1925.) As of 17 December 1885, therefore, Parnell thought he had a deal with Salisbury; and Gladstone, anticipating the 'Nixon in China' logic, preferred to leave Salisbury in office so that he would be forced to introduce Home Rule rather than throw Salisbury out and take office himself.

On that day the following syndicated press release appeared in the *Pall Mall Gazette*:

Mr Gladstone has definitely adopted the policy of Home Rule for Ireland and there are well-founded hopes that he will win over the chief representatives of the moderate section of the party to his views.... Mr Gladstone is sanguine that this policy of settling the Irish question once for all, will commend itself to the majority of his party and to the English people, when it is clearly understood that no other course can bring real peace. If he is enabled to eject the [Salisbury] Government in this issue, he will have a large majority in the House of Commons for his Irish bill, and he believes that the House of Lords, weighing the gravity of the situation, will not reject it. Should there be a sufficient defection of the moderate Liberals to encourage the Lords to throw out the bill a dissolution would be inevitable, but ... the country would in all probability endorse Mr Gladstone's policy and give him an unmistakable mandate to carry it into law. There is reasonable expectation that both Lord Hartington and Mr Goschen will come round to Mr Gladstone's view, and Mr Chamberlain and Sir Charles Dilke, in spite of their present attitude, could not consistently oppose it. (*Pall Mall Gazette* 17.12.1885, quoted in Hammond 1938: 449–50)

The leak emanated from Gladstone's pro-Home Rule son Herbert, who thought he was doing Home Rule and his father a favour. He probably did them more harm even than the Phoenix Park murderers. Gladstone's plan might—just might—have worked if Herbert had kept it secret. The median member of each house was opposed to Home Rule. But Gladstone might have persuaded enough 'moderate Liberals' that public order required Home Rule to carry it in the Commons. The Lords might then have been cowed by the threat of a 'peers v. people' dissolution. But announcing his plan to all the main actors killed it. Salisbury immediately grabbed hold of the Hawarden Kite (as he nicknamed it) to float away from the embarrassment and recriminations that his repudiation of Parnell would have inevitably caused if it had become known. Hartington (brother of Lord Frederick Cavendish) and Goschen (later to be the most important Unionist Chancellor of the Exchequer) refused to join Gladstone's ensuing government. Chamberlain did, but walked out after two months. Gladstone's Home Rule bill was defeated in the Commons in June 1886 by 341 to 311—one of the largest votes in the Commons' history—with ninety-three Liberals including Chamberlain, Hartington, and Goschen voting against the government. The government resigned. In the ensuing General Election, Salisbury ensured that the Conservatives did not oppose the Liberals who had voted against Gladstone—now labelled Liberal Unionists.

Gladstone's Bill

Since at least the spring of 1885, Parnell had been discussing a possible Home Rule Bill with anyone who he thought might be in a position to deliver one: the Liberals Chamberlain and Gladstone, and the Conservatives Carnarvon and Randolph Churchill. Many Home Rule schemes were on offer. And for us, hindsight is as painful as it was for George V in 1930. The failure of Parliament to concede Home Rule in 1886 has brought such misery on Ireland, misery that is not yet over, that it is easier to condemn politicians' myopia than to understand it. To clear the ground, let us look first at two unfortunate contingencies and then at the real rocks that could have wrecked Home Rule even with goodwill and mutual understanding.

The first contingency is that the English and the Catholic Irish hated each other (Foster 1993). O'Connell and Cullen among others had made Catholicism a badge of national as well as of religious identity in Ireland. There was enough popular Protestantism in England to mistrust the Irish on that ground alone. Popular Protestantism was reflected in high places as late as Russell's Ecclesiastical Titles Act of 1851. Protestants thought that Catholics were disloyal, owing allegiance to a pope over the water and willing to ally with the hated French when it suited them (as some Irish nationalists had done in 1798). Irish Catholics thought that Protestant policy towards them was, at best, discriminatory and, at worst, genocidal. The latter included Cromwell's campaigns in the 1640s (where the belief was well founded) and the Famine two centuries later (where it was not).

The people who had the strongest economic reason to hate the Irish were those only just above them in the social scale. People from rural Ireland, driven by famine or need to seek work in Britain, lacked even such skills as the native working class could acquire in the first decades of the Industrial Revolution. They could become navvies but not engine-drivers. But any gains that working-class people could make in the Victorian labour market through their non-substitutable skills, or their trade unions, were fragile. The biggest threat to them was deskilling and wage competition—which Irish workers supplied. Throw in the fact that Irish people could be easily recognized by their accents and often their appearance, and you have the perfect breeding ground for intense ethnic hatred. It was for the Irish from the 1850s to the 1880s as it was to be for Jews in the 1900s; Afro-Caribbeans in the 1960s; south Asians in the 1970s; and asylum seekers in the 2000s. And all for fundamentally the same reason.

This drove a wedge between the Irish Party and their natural allies in Britain. In 1886, the Liberal Party was becoming more and more the party of the peripheries: the geographical, religious, and class peripheries. The Tories were the party of the established Church, of financial interests, and of the south-east of England. The Liberals were the converse. Some of them (including Chamberlain and Dilke, but not Gladstone) wished to make explicit links to the working class. All of them championed the religious periphery—those excluded from, or discriminated against by, the Church of England. Their electoral strength was in the geographical periphery— south-west England, the northern industrial cities, Scotland, and Wales. But for religion and economic rivalries, Ireland would have fitted naturally. The Catholic religion was just as downtrodden as English Nonconformity. But they could or would not make common cause. And those who might otherwise have been the natural allies of the Irish tended to be their most bitter enemies. After 1886, this crippled the Liberals, and the Irish Party with them, and enabled the Unionists to form a new cross-class coalition that reached its zenith between 1895 and 1905.

The Structure of British Politics at the Accession of Lord Salisbury

The crisis of 1885–6 made Unionism an issue dimension in the whole of the UK. The Irish Party, or its fractions, completely dominated Catholic Ireland. Although the fractions fought amongst themselves, no candidate could win a Catholic-majority seat in Ireland unless he was from one or other fraction of Parnell's party. The Unionists, now specifically labelled Ulster Unionists, had equally monolithic control over Protestant Ireland. Southern Protestant interests—essentially those of the Church of Ireland Ascendancy—held at most one seat (South Co. Dublin) in the Commons, although they retained considerable power in the Lords. From 1886, the ideology of Irish Unionism was mostly the ideology of Ulster Unionism.

In Scotland, the Disruption had provided the material basis for a two-party system, in which the urban (plus Highland) and lower-class Free Church interest might form one bloc of class and religion, and the suburban, rural (less the Highlands), and upper-class Church of Scotland interest might form the other (MacLaren 1974). But the cleavage was not actualized until the split of 1886. When it was actualized, it fell exactly the way that a sociologist of class cleavage would predict. The former bloc stayed with the Gladstonian

Liberals, the latter went Liberal Unionist. Scotland became a competitive two-party system, with Unionist strength in Edinburgh and the more prosperous burghs and county divisions (Pelling 1967: ch. 16). This had the effect of forcing two rival class and religious blocs into the same camp, for Scotland's large Catholic community, mostly of Irish descent, were forced into sometimes uneasy alliance with the Gladstonians. The ardent Presbyterian lion lay down with the Catholic lamb. Up to November 1885 it was possible to believe that either UK party could deliver Home Rule. From that date, only the Gladstonian Liberals could. The Irish in Britain could only ally with them.

Wales remained the stronghold of Gladstonian Liberalism. Neither class nor religion gave enough succour to Unionism for it to establish an electoral base. But Wales was small; England was large. The coalition—as it became by 1887—of the Conservatives and the Liberal Unionists became the hegemonic force in England until 1906. Geographically, the Unionists dominated England south-east of a line between the Wash and Portland Bill; the Liberals north-west of that line. The blocs were also defined by class and by religion—in fact, by religion more than by class, as Pelling (1967) suspected and Wald (1983) proved. The Unionists were the party of the Church of England; the Liberals, the party both of Protestant dissent and of Roman Catholicism.

In summary, the geography of Unionism from 1886 to 1910 lay on a gradient with Ulster at the top of the slope; southern England and some parts of prosperous Scotland next, followed by northern England, the rest of Scotland, Wales, and Catholic Ireland in that order. Assuming that opponents of the Union did more agenda-setting than its defenders, we should expect more action in the following decades in Ireland than in Wales, and more in Wales than in Scotland. In England, the Union as such was not questioned, but Unionism was very much alive.

5

The High Noon of Unionism: 1886–1921

Gladstone's conversion to Home Rule forced unionism out into the open. Before 1886, Victorian politicians outside Ireland had been instinctive Unionists, but their arguments were mostly unspoken. Prominent landmarks in the ideological history of the British Empire included Viscount Palmerston's 'Don Pacifico' speech in 1850 and Disraeli's Crystal Palace speech in 1872. The first boasted that any subject of the Queen living abroad could seek the protection of the British Navy.[1] The second stated that the Tory Party 'had three great objects: to maintain our institutions, to uphold the empire, and to elevate the condition of the people' (Monypenny and Buckle 1920 V: 194).

Of Disraeli's three principles, the first sounded banal but was not. 'Maintaining our institutions' served the political interests of Disraeli's party. Of Britain's central institutions, the House of Lords was always Conservative; the Church of England usually was; so was the monarch. King George III, King George IV, King George V, and Queen Victoria, all obstructed their Prime Ministers' efforts to pacify Ireland. Disraeli's third principle sounded

---

[1] David ('Don') Pacifico was born in Gibraltar and therefore Palmerston, the Foreign Secretary, claimed that he was a British subject entitled to the Queen's protection. He had become Portuguese consul in Athens, where his house was ransacked by a mob. The House of Lords had censured Palmerston's imperial adventures including a gunboat sent to Athens to demand restitution for Pacifico. Palmerston's speech concluded:
'I maintain that the principles which can be traced through all our foreign transactions, as the guiding rule and directing spirit of our proceedings, are such as deserve approbation. I therefore fearlessly challenge the verdict which this House, as representing a political, a commercial, a constitutional country, is to give on the question now brought before it; whether the principles on which the foreign policy of Her Majesty's Government has been conducted, and the sense of duty which has led us to think ourselves bound to afford protection to our fellow subjects abroad, are proper and fitting guides for those who are charged with the Government of England; and whether, as the Roman, in days of old, held himself free from indignity, when he could say *Civis Romanus sum*; so also a British subject, in whatever land he may be, shall feel confident that the watchful eye and the strong arm of England, will protect him against injustice and wrong' (*Hansard* 3rd ser. 112: 444).

banal and was. The second confirmed him as the leading political entrepreneur of his age (McLean 2001a: 59–76). Upholding the Empire turned out to be hugely popular in England, Scotland, and Protestant Ireland. In 1872 Disraeli had no detailed imperial ideas in mind but he improvised brilliantly. In 1875–6 he purchased shares in the Suez Canal Company and made Queen Victoria Empress of India (her idea, not his; but the pomp and flattery was all his). These were brilliant cheap-talk gestures. They made Britons feel good without costing British lives or a lot of money.

Later Conservatives followed through. Salisbury was a more consistent imperialist than Disraeli. He took over the private enterprise Primrose League from its founder Randolph Churchill and turned it into the vanguard of mass Conservatism. This linked the causes of Queen, Lords, Union, and Empire. Pugh (1985: 91) reports that in 1890

300 members of Ribblesdale (Settle) Habitation [of the Primrose League] . . . [heard] a two-hour lecture on the colonies which comprised one hundred limelight views designed to portray the vastness of empire and its commercial potential.

The entire population of Ribblesdale is barely 2000, and it was Liberal territory (Pelling 1967: Table 34; Skipton constituency).

Gladstone was an imperialist too, but he got no credit for it. Some of his followers were certainly 'Little Englanders' and Unionists managed to tar his whole party with that brush. The Queen led the charge. In 1885, after the death of General Gordon, who had been disobeying orders when he marched on Khartoum in pursuit of no discernible British interest, the Queen telegraphed Prime Minister Gladstone *en clair* (not in code):

These news from Khartoum are frightful and to think that all this might have been prevented and many precious lives saved by earlier action is too fearful.

Gladstone received this missive at Carnforth Station (where *Brief Encounter* was later filmed). He replied magnificently:

Mr Gladstone does not presume to estimate the means of judgement possessed by Your Majesty, but so far as his information and recollection at the moment go, he is not altogether able to follow the conclusion which Your Majesty has been pleased thus to announce. (Both quoted in Jenkins 1995: 513–14)

But the damage was done. The Unionists inverted Gladstone's nickname 'GOM' for Grand Old Man to MOG for Murderer Of Gordon. After 1886, the Liberals were tied to the Irish Party to the detriment of both. The Irish had no other possible allies after Parnell's 'vote Tory' strategy in 1885 had been destroyed by Salisbury's repudiation of Carnavron (Chapter 4). The Liberals kept their embarrassing allies at arms' length. After Gladstone retired, no leading British Liberal was keen on Irish Home Rule for its own sake. There were votes to be lost and none to be gained by espousing it. The Catholic Irish in Britain had nowhere else to go, and already supported the Liberals; some of the Protestant Irish and non-Irish in Britain could go Unionist in response to racist or imperialist anti-Catholic appeals. Therefore Irish Home Rule would reappear on the political agenda when, and only when, the Irish Party held the balance in the House of Commons. That occurred between 1892 and 1895, and from January 1910 until the start of the first wartime coalition government in May 1915.

Wales: Language, Religion, and Home Rule

Most of this chapter is therefore about Ireland. However, the period also witnessed the first stirrings of devolution in Wales and the development of a two-party system in Scotland.

Before 1886, Wales was the strongest Liberal area in the UK. Wales was overwhelmingly Nonconformist, and therefore the privileged position of the Anglican Church in Wales was resented almost as much as the equivalent situation in Ireland and more so than in England. One of the main denominations, the Calvinist Methodists, was purely Welsh. There was no district in England where Church of England loyalty was as low as in Wales and Ireland. In the 1851 census (the only one before 2001 to survey religion), 80 per cent of attendances on census Sunday in Wales were at Nonconformist chapels (Table 4.1). The Welsh language got no official encouragement and some Welsh-speakers thought that there was a British government plot to suppress it. In the first industrial town in Wales, Merthyr Tydfil, there was a long-standing tradition of Welsh-speaking radicalism, going back to the 1830s, through Henry Richard (Chapter 4), and onto Keir Hardie, elected there in 1900.

However, Welsh nationalism was mainly a rural movement. So, although in the 1868 general election the partial enfranchisement of the 1867 Act led to the unseating of some landlords and Radical gains, Welsh radicalism could not consolidate until the rural electorate was expanded in the Third Reform Act of 1884. The Liberal hegemony of 1868 was lost in 1874 and regained in 1880 but from 1885 on it would be unshakeable. Save for the replacement of the Liberals by Labour it has remained unshakeable up to the present day. In the general election of 1885 the Liberals obtained 58.3 per cent of the vote in contested seats (more than in any other UK region) and twenty-nine of the thirty-four seats, with a thirtieth going to William Abraham, the Welsh speaking Lib-Lab miners' leader. They also gained control of all bar one the Welsh county councils at their first election in 1889 (Morgan 1963: 107).

As already noted, the first Welsh public Act after the revival of Welsh radicalism was the Sunday Closing Act 1881, which kept the pubs of some parts of Wales closed on Sundays until 1996. It was not repealed until 2003 (see *http://www.culture.gov.uk/global/press_notices/archive_2003/dcms86_03. htm*). Other distinctively Welsh issues included the lack of higher and further education; alleged discrimination against the Welsh language; and above all, the privileges of the minority Anglican church. The agricultural depression of the late 1870s hit all the UK's marginal farm areas, including Wales, but unlike in Ireland and Scotland, gave rise to no Welsh land campaign. What would otherwise have been the land campaign was subsumed into the more general campaigning of *Cymru Fydd* ('Young Wales').

In the Parliament of 1886–92, the Unionists had a clear majority in the Commons and were at no risk of defeat there. However, unlike England and Scotland, Wales was infertile ground for Liberal Unionism. The Welsh Liberals formed themselves into a coherent group with a militant extra-Parliamentary wing, *Cymru Fydd,* under the leadership of Tom Ellis, MP for Merioneth. *Cymru Fydd* demonstrated strength in weakness, or weakness in strength. It stood for causes that went deep in rural Wales: language, education, temperance, disestablishment, land reform. But the agricultural crisis combined with the coal and iron boom in South Wales to lead to a huge shift of the Welsh population. Initially, the Valleys of South Wales were culturally similar to rural North Wales. They retained the chapels, the language, and Sunday closing. But with migration from outside Wales and a divergence in their material interests from about 1900, south and north Wales went their different ways. Like the other non-English territories, Wales should have been a veto player in the 'hung parliaments' of 1892–5 and 1910–15. For various reasons, it was not.

The demand for Welsh Home Rule was the weakest from any of the three non-English territories. Ellis got little response from his campaigning, per-haps because of the cultural division between north and south Wales. *Cymru Fydd* fell apart across that division (Morgan 1963: 160–5). While Gladstone remained in office, almost nothing except Irish Home Rule commanded attention (although a preliminary bill for Welsh disestablishment was in the 1893 Queen's Speech); on the defeat of Home Rule in the Lords in 1893, the leadership passed to the ineffective Lord Rosebery. Disestablishment bills in 1894 and 1895 got nowhere.

In the Parliament of 1906–10, the Lords vetoed every Welsh measure—non-denominational education in 1906; licensing in 1908; and disestablish-ment (again) in 1909, when the government did not even bother to put it up to the Lords. But the Welsh wielded no veto and their incomparably best politician, Lloyd George, had moved on to other things after his start as Tom Ellis's disciple in the 1890s.

By the hung parliaments of 1910, there was no longer a unified Welsh interest. Labour now had a toehold in the south; but more important, the interests of the median voter in southern constituencies had shifted away from education, disestablishment, and Home Rule to class and industrial issues. Disestablishment at last had a clear run after the Parliament Act 1911. Introduced in 1912, it was of course defeated twice in the Lords and carried under the terms of the Parliament Act in 1914. Like Irish Home Rule, it was suspended on the outbreak of war, and finally enacted in 1920. To this day, each Welsh County Council controls a Welsh Church Act Fund, the proceeds of the disendowment of 1920, that councillors may use to restore Nonconformist chapels and village halls.

Thus Wales was simultaneously the most culturally distinct and the smallest threat to the Union of the three non-English territories. Scotland had a minister and (probably more important) a bureaucracy of its own; a stronger stake in the Empire than Wales; its church controversies did not threaten the state; and consequently it too posed no threat to the Union in this period.

Scotland: Crofters, Church, and Empire

Curiously, the most significant threat from Scotland occurred right in the shadow of the Irish crisis in 1886. But it was resolved so swiftly that it has been almost forgotten. It is time to disinter it.

The 1885 general election was the first in which any of the rural poor had a voice. Five independent Liberals were elected from the far north-west of Scotland, who became known as the 'Crofters' Party'. The Highlands of Scotland shared several features with the West of Ireland, including absentee landlords, a history of famine and emigration, and subsistence farming on below-subsistence plots. When 'Bonnie Prince Charlie' raised his standard at Glenfinnan in 1745 (in one of the districts that elected a Crofter in 1885) he chose the best place for the Jacobite challenge to the Union. The writ of the UK did not run to Glenfinnan. The people differed by language, religion, and occupation from the rest of the Scots, let alone the English. After Culloden in 1746, the government consolidated the Union in the Highlands in various ways. Highlanders became soldiers or emigrated; their chiefs were anglicized; those who had been on the losing side (though most had not) were expropriated.

In the nineteenth century, Highland society was almost as desperate as the west of Ireland. It too suffered from the potato blight in 1845–7. But unlike the west of Ireland, the Highlands were not chronically over-populated, because of the notorious 'Clearances' which came in two waves, one at the start of the nineteenth century and the other at the end of it. In the 1820s the landowners cleared the glens for sheep. In the 1880s, after the Queen had popularized the Highlands for sport, they depopulated them again for deer.

By the late 1870s, therefore, the Gaelic-speaking peasants were confined to marginal land on the west coast and the islands. There had been some rural disorder there, although a pale shadow of the Irish Land Campaign of 1879–85. As soon as local male householders were enfranchised, they elected MPs who pressed their grievances. The 'revolutionary Crofters Act 1886', as Kellas (1980: 155) appropriately calls it, gave security of tenure to crofters even without legal title to the land they farmed. It created a Crofters' Commission, which was renewed in 1955, to protect crofting tenure (Darling 1955: 6–11; *http://www.crofterscommission. org.uk/ccframe.htm*). A croft is a (very) small holding. One of the defining quotations in the *Oxford English Dictionary*, from an 1851 government report, explains, 'The crofting system was first introduced, by the arable part of the small farms previously held in common being divided among the joint tenants in separate crofts, the pasture remaining in common' (OED 2nd edn. Online, s.v. *croft*). In 1884 it was claimed that the largest croft on the Isle of Skye was of only seven acres. Hence crofting tenure comprises a secure tenancy of a house; a unique right to farm land immediately around it; and common rights, shared with other crofters, to grazing and peat extraction on the unenclosed land beyond. The 1886 framework remains in place in the Highlands to this day. Unlike in Ireland, land grievances were kept apart from nationalist grievances. Settling the land question in the Highlands restored peace, though it did not bring prosperity. Because no party had an overall majority in the Parliament of 1885–6, the five Crofter MPs got a signal concession for their constituents. The Crofters' Party disintegrated in 1886 because some of them joined the Liberal Unionists and some the Gladstonian Liberals. But their job was done.

Most of Scotland was not like the West Highlands. Table 5.1 shows that the Unionist vote in Scotland leapt up between 1885 and 1886.

Scotland had been a one-party state since 1832; the emergence of the Liberal Unionists turned it into a two-party state. The cleavage lines were around ideology and ethnicity rather than class. At the Disruption of 1843, the Free Church had been, paradoxically, a disestablished church that believed in establishment. Now, and more logically, an influential section of the Free Church campaigned for disestablishment, a campaign that (perhaps surprisingly) was more successful in Scotland than in Wales. It was then that antidisestablishmentarianism (the word and the thing) arose. Antidisestablishmentarians flocked to the Liberal Unionists. So did Orangemen, especially in the west of Scotland, where Irish politics and Irish sectarianism spilt over into Glasgow politics. As Irish Catholics formed their institutions of civil society (especially Celtic and Hibernian football teams in Glasgow

TABLE 5.1 Seats and votes in the four territories of the UK, general elections 1885–1910

		England		Wales		Scotland		Ireland		UK	
		Seats	Vote share (%)	Seats	Vote share (%)	Seats	Vote share (%)	Seats	Vote share (%)	Seats	Vote share (%)
1885	Unionist	213	47.5	4	38.9	8	34.3	16	24.8	249	43.5
	Anti-Unionist	243	52.5	30	61.1	62	65.7	85	75.2	421	56.5
1886	Unionist	332	52.6	8	46.1	27	46.4	17	50.4	393	51.4
	Anti-Unionist	124	47.4	26	53.9	43	53.6	84	49.6	277	48.6
1892	Unionist	261	51.1	3	37.2	19	44.4	21	20.6	313	47.0
	Anti-Unionist	195	48.9	31	62.8	51	55.6	80	79.4	357	53.0
1895	Unionist	343	51.9	9	42.2	31	47.4	19	26.0	411	49.1
	Anti-Unionist	113	48.1	25	57.8	39	52.6	82	74.0	259	50.9
1900	Unionist	332	52.4	6	37.6	36	49.0	19	32.2	402	50.3
	Anti-Unionist	124	47.6	28	62.4	34	51.0	82	67.8	268	49.7
1906	Unionist	122	44.3	0	33.8	10	38.2	15	47.0	156	43.4
	Anti-Unionist	334	55.7	34	66.2	60	61.8	86	53.0	514	56.6
1910J	Unionist	233	49.3	2	31.9	9	39.6	19	32.7	272	46.8
	Anti-Unionist	223	50.7	32	68.1	61	60.4	82	67.3	398	53.2
1910D	Unionist	233	48.8	3	33.8	9	42.6	17	28.6	271	46.6
	Anti-Unionist	223	51.2	31	66.2	61	57.4	84	71.4	399	53.4

Notes:
University seats not counted in territorial totals but included in UK total.
'Unionist' = Conservative (+ Liberal Unionist from 1886 onwards)
'Anti-Unionist': all other parties.
Vote share calculations are unreliable in Ireland, because of unopposed Nationalist returns.
Source: Adapted from Craig (1989: Tables 1.13 to 1.20).

and Edinburgh), so did their Protestant enemies (Rangers and Hearts). As the Liberals and the Irish Party were linked in their mutually destructive union, the Orange vote went Liberal Unionist and, later, just Unionist.

A Scottish Home Rule Association was founded in 1886. It drew its authority from Gladstone's guarded encouragement of 'Home Rule All Round' in his Midlothian Campaign in 1879. But it became too much identified with one faction—a smaller faction in Scotland than in Wales—to succeed. Most notably, however, it employed one J. Ramsay MacDonald as its London organizer. When his fellow Scot Keir Hardie stood as an Independent Labour candidate in the Mid-Lanark by-election of 1888, Mac-Donald wrote, as secretary of the SHRA, the first letter to pass between the two Scotsmen who were to create the Labour Party:

I cannot refrain from wishing you God-speed in your election contest. . . . The powers of darkness—Scottish newspapers with English editors . . . , partisan wire-pullers, and the other etceteras of political squabbles—are leagued against us. But let the consequences be what they may, do not withdraw. The cause of Labour and of Scottish Nationality will suffer much thereby. Your defeat will awaken Scotland, and your victory will re-construct Scottish Liberalism. (MacDonald to Hardie, 1888, in Stewart 1921: 40)

In this letter, MacDonald mentions three causes—Liberalism, Labour, and Scottish Nationality—as if they were the same, or at least overlapping. They were all anti-Unionist, but that did not make them either hegemonic or identical. In Scotland especially, much historiography of the period focuses on the rise of Labour. A better approach, however, is to focus on the resilience of Unionism. Despite the sterling efforts of a few historians including Pelling (1967), Wald (1983), and Pugh (1985), the historiography of the period has far too much to say about the tiny Labour Party, which for our purpose is simply a successor to part but not all of the Gladstonian vote, and far too little to say about the hegemonic Unionists. From the most detailed ecological analysis, due to Pelling (1967: 372–413), We can see that there were several distinctive components of Scottish Unionism:

• Military and imperial. The disproportionate recruitment of Scots to the Army has already been discussed. The 1900 general election was fought at a high point in the Boer War. Several poor constituencies elected Unionists, notably Inverness District and Sutherland, for what Pelling surmises were military reasons.
• The Irish, orange and green. Orange anti-Catholicism was a steady influence in the working-class vote in the West of Scotland, delivering what (from their class composition) might have been expected to be Liberal or Labour seats to the Unionists. This effect persisted in local elections until 1921 (McLean 1999: ch. 16). But the Liberals could not always rely on the

Catholic Irish either. Strong local chapters of the United Irish League decided how to cast their vote. Notably (and ironically, in view of what was to happen later), they claimed responsibility for the 1900 defeat of the Liberal in the most working-class seat of Glasgow, in favour of the Unionist Andrew Bonar Law.

• Church politics and establishment. As noted earlier, the Free Church (and the Liberal Party) favoured disestablishment by 1892. But a countercurrent arose in the Highlands, where the Free Church was very strong but very poor. Its ministers favoured establishment, breaking away to form the 'Wee Frees' in 1900, and controversially taking the property of the Free Church with them. Theologically conservative, the Wee Frees seem also to have been Unionists on the whole.

Putting all this together, Scotland contributed substantial Unionist support. Its average Unionist vote between 1886 and 1910 was 43.0 per cent compared with 50.8 per cent in England, 38.6 per cent in Wales, and about 20 per cent in Ireland (Pelling 1967: Table 52; Craig 1989: Tables 1.14–1.20—but Irish numbers are unreliable because of uncontested Nationalist seats). Before turning to Ireland, however, we must note one other small component of unionism. There were nine University seats, whose electors were the graduates of the university or group of universities in question. They were by far the most reliable component of British Unionism. One solitary Liberal University member was elected in 1885. For the rest of the period, all nine seats went Unionist in every election. But for the University seats, the Liberals would have had an overall majority in the Commons in 1885. The solidity of graduate unionism is easy to explain. The two most obvious career destinations for graduates were the Church and the Empire (including its armed forces). Both careers gave graduates a very strong material reason to vote for Unionists. They did.

The Unionists Turn to Ulster

In 1912, Unionist policy switched rather suddenly from defence of the Union to defence of Ulster. This was always likely to happen because of the disappearance of the Ascendancy from the House of Commons, but its timing was an accident arising from the fractious history of Unionism after Salisbury's retirement in 1902.

Several events led from Unionist domination of the 1900 general election to catastrophe in 1906. The long-delayed conclusion of the Boer War, not complete till 1902, showed that imperialism was not wholly cheap talk. Sometimes it cost British lives and money. But the fatal blow was Joseph Chamberlain's Tariff Reform campaign. Launched in summer 1903, its effect was extraordinarily similar to that which Euroscepticism was to have in the Conservative Party ninety years later. The party activists loved it. Half of the front bench hated it. The leader vainly tried to paper over the divisions. The party turned inwards, not noticing that its favourite policy was a turn-off for the electorate. This description fits the Unionist Party under A. J. Balfour from 1903 to 1911 as well as it fits the Conservatives under John Major, William Hague, Iain Duncan Smith, and Michael Howard from 1990 to 2004.

The Liberals won the General Election of 1906, on a platform of cheap bread and no Chinese labour in South Africa. Although they gained less than half of the vote (just over half if the Labour vote is counted in with the Liberal vote), the electoral system rewarded them, as usual in British election, with a landslide of seats. Therefore they had no need of the Irish Party and proposed no Home Rule Bill. Still consumed with the war between Tariff Reformers and Free Traders, the Unionists opened a second front in 1909 when their Lords leaders rejected Lloyd George's 'People's Budget'. The evidence suggests that the idea of turning it into a 'Peers versus People' campaign occurred rather late to Lloyd George. Provoking the peers was not his original motive, but when they reacted mulishly in defence of their landed acres, he provoked them outrageously, calling them '500 men chosen accidentally from the ranks of the unemployed' who preserved the land as the prerogative of 10,000 people and left the rest of the population 'trespassers in the land of our birth'. The Unionist leaders fell straight into Lloyd George's trap. By rejecting the Budget, they deprived the Government of finance and therefore forced the general election of January 1910, offering Lloyd George and Asquith the best campaign slogan of the twentieth century.

The 'Peers v. People' election produced a hung parliament. This proves, not Unionist success, but Unionist failure. The run of by-election results before the rejection of the Budget implies that without that the Unionists would have won the general election. The Liberals now depended on Irish votes. Although the Irish Party had not liked the People's Budget because of its whiskey duties, they were at one with the Liberals on the House of Lords. They had a common interest in curbing it—the Liberals so that they could enact social reform, and the Irish Party so that they could enact Home Rule. Both of these would otherwise be vetoed by the Lords. The Liberals had no principled commitment to Home Rule. During the summer of 1910 Lloyd George offered a coalition to the centrist Unionists. As he was consistently to try for the next twelve years, he wanted to form a hegemonic centrist party that would exclude the three groups of extremists—Irish Catholics, Irish Protestants, and the Labour Party. The Unionist leaders took his approach seriously but in the end rejected it because of opposition from the parliamentary rank and file (Jenkins 1968: 161–6). The new king, George V, had succeeded in May 1910. More of an ideological Unionist than his father, he refused to create the 500 peers that would be needed to enact the Parliament Bill without another dissolution and another general election.

The forced general election of December 1910 produced an identical result, in aggregate, to that of January. The condition for the King's reluctant agreement to create peers was now met. The Irish Party was pivotal but the Labour Party was not. The threat to create peers meant that in the end the Lords had no choice but to pass the Parliament Bill, which was enacted in August 1911. They took their defeat hard. 'We were beaten by the Bishops and the rats', said the former Unionist minister George Wyndham (Butler and Butler 1994: 266). Many blamed Balfour for his failure to lead his unleadable party. John Major would have understood. Balfour's resignation in November 1911 produced the most remarkable leadership contest of the century. There were two main contenders. Austen Chamberlain would have been a competent leader, but was associated with Tariff Reform and the Lords diehards. Walter Long had rural rank-and-file support but would not have been a competent leader. He was short-tempered (not a fatal defect) and lacked insight (not good in the face of Asquith and Lloyd George). But most importantly, Chamberlain and Long detested each other passionately. Through the middle came the almost unknown Bonar Law. Born in Canada of Ulster-Scots parents, he moved to Glasgow as a child, and his invalid father retired to Ulster. The Andrew Bonar after whom he was named was one of the heroes of the Disruption of 1843 (Chapter 4). After Benjamin Disraeli and Iain Duncan Smith, he is the unlikeliest leader the Unionists have ever produced. He remains the only Conservative leader in history with Ulster roots and the only one until Margaret Thatcher not to be a member of the Church of England.[2]

The new Tory leader signalled his intention to break with his languid predecessor. 'I am afraid I shall have to show myself very vicious, Mr Asquith, this session. I hope you will understand.' So he said to the Prime Minister as they walked together back from the King's Speech to the Commons in 1912, according to Asquith's later statement (Asquith 1928: vol. I, 202). This implies that Law's verbal violence in 1912 was tactical. The weight of evidence suggests otherwise. He later told Austen Chamberlain, with whom he remained on good terms (as he did with Long—perhaps this was the secret of his unlikely success), that 'before the war, he cared intensely about only two things: Tariff Reform and Ulster; all the rest was only part of the game' (Blake 1955: 97). His two main speeches on Ulster in 1912 were memorably intense.

---

[2] This is, admittedly, to class Disraeli as an Anglican. Culturally and theologically, he was a very odd one.

At Balmoral (the Belfast suburb, not the royal holiday home) in April 1912 the Unionist rally opened with Psalm 90.[3] Law said:

Once again you hold the pass for the Empire. You are a besieged city.... The Government by their Parliament Act have erected a boom against you, a boom to cut you off from the help of the British people. You will burst that boom.

Three months later he went still further. Law spoke on 29 July 1912 at Blenheim Palace. Blenheim was not only the palace built for John Churchill, Duke of Marlborough, *eminence grise* of Union in 1707, but also the seat of Randolph Churchill when he had said 'Ulster will fight, and Ulster will be right' and 'The Orange card will be the card to play: pray God it will be ace of trumps and not the two' in 1886. Law said that Unionists regarded the Government as 'a Revolutionary Committee which has seized upon despotic power by fraud'. He went on:

I repeat now with a full sense of the responsibility which attaches to my position, that ... I can imagine no length of resistance to which Ulster can go in which I should not be prepared to support them, and in which, in my belief, they would not be supported by the overwhelming majority of the British people. (Both speeches as quoted by Blake 1955: 129–30)

These were extraordinary pronouncements. No other Leader of the Opposition has said anything remotely comparable since 1832. Law was inviting the Ulster Protestants to overthrow the UK Government (at least in Ulster), by force if necessary. He did this in the full knowledge that they would have two years in which to do so. The Home Rule Bill was introduced in 1912. As it was bound to be defeated twice in the Lords, it would not pass until 1914 when, under the provisions of the 1911 Parliament Act, it would pass the Commons in the third consecutive session and would be enacted without Lords' assent.

The Unionist leaders in Ulster organized an Ulster Covenant (the Presbyterian imagery was deliberately modelled on the Scottish National Covenants of 1638 and 1643). It committed those who signed it to 'us[e] all means which may be found necessary to defeat the present conspiracy to set up a Home Rule Parliament in Ireland' (Stewart 1967: 62). While Asquith could not believe that Law was serious, the paramilitary organization of the Ulster

---

[3] 1 Lord, thou hast been our dwelling place in all generations.
   2 Before the mountains were brought forth, or ever thou hadst formed the earth and the world, even from everlasting to everlasting, thou art God.
   3 Thou turnest man to destruction; and sayest, Return, ye children of men.
   4 For a thousand years in thy sight are but as yesterday when it is past, and as a watch in the night. (Psalm 90:1–4)
Psalm 90 and Psalm 124 buttressed Unionist belief in destiny. For the parallel political iconography of Psalm 124, see McLean (1999: 98–9). The 'besieged city' and 'boom' language of the Balmoral speech is a direct reference to the Protestant icon, the siege of Londonderry in 1689.

Covenant grew rapidly. The organizers claimed that over 200,000 Ulstermen signed the Covenant. The same number of women, who were regarded as ineligible to sign the Covenant, signed an accompanying declaration. The Covenanters decided to raise a military force, to be known as the Ulster Volunteer Force and limited it to 100,000 men. The UVF started drilling and gunrunning. Its most spectacular coup was to land between 20,000 and 30,000 German rifles and three million rounds of ammunition in Larne in April 1914. The chief gunrunner stated in two manuscripts written in 1914 and 1915 that he had met Law and Long before going to Germany to buy the rifles. He saw Long first, then Law, who

said, with a twinkle in his eye, 'I have heard of you before, Mr Crawford'. I had a private letter from the Chief [Sir Edward Carson], whom I left in Belfast, to him. I had to see W[alter] L[ong] about the finances of the business, and make my final arrangements for paying [a] very large cheque. (F. Crawford, Diary of the Gun-Running, PRONI D/1700/5/17/2, quoted by Jackson 2003: 133)

Jackson immediately goes on to stress that Crawford is an unreliable witness, but cites some circumstantial evidence suggesting that the story is true. If true, it is truly revolutionary. The three leaders of Unionism were complicit in arming an insurrection against the Government of the UK. The insurrection never occurred because it was not needed. By August 1914 it was obvious to all that Protestant Ulster could not be included in Home Rule. The Home Rule Bill was enacted in September and immediately suspended, along with Welsh disestablishment, for the duration of the First World War, which had so providentially broken out. The German guns went various ways. Some armed the 'Black and Tans' recruited by the British during the Anglo-Irish war in 1920; some the Protestant 'B Specials' in Northern Ireland; and some, Ethiopian guerrillas fighting against their Italian occupation under British direction in 1941 (Stewart 1967: 248–9). The UVF itself became the 36th Ulster Division on the outbreak of war. They went over the top on the first day of the Battle of the Somme, 1 July 1916, the date originally celebrated as the anniversary of the Battle of the Boyne. Shouting 'No Surrender' and 'Remember 1690' they marched straight into the German lines, losing 5,500, killed and wounded. This exceeds the total death toll from violence in Northern Ireland since 1967.

Two things remain to be explained. Why did Unionist primordialism capture the official Opposition so violently? And how did UK Unionism transmute into Ulster Unionism? The explanation for both lies with Bonar Law. Before Law, all Unionists with material interests in Ireland—from the Duke of Wellington to Sir Edward Carson and Lord Lansdowne—had been Southerners, members of the Church of England and the Protestant Ascendancy. The Ascendancy's material interest in Ireland had eroded and was almost extinct by 1906, having been first crushed by agricultural depression and then bought out for twenty years under the banner of killing Home Rule by kindness. Their constitutional veto remained until 1911. Having lost the Lords veto, the Unionists still considered a desperate throw with the King. In May 1912 Bonar Law urged him to veto the Home Rule Bill (Blake 1955: 133). The following year the King pleaded with Asquith to withdraw the bill, saying,

Whatever I do I shall offend half the population. One alternative would certainly result in alienating the Ulster Protestants from me, and whatever happens the result must be detrimental to me personally and to the Crown in general. (George V to Asquith, 11.8.1913, in Jenkins 1964: 283)

This was more direct even than Victoria's *en clair* telegram to Carnforth. Asquith replied unflinchingly:

The Sovereign undoubtedly has the power of changing his advisers, but it is relevant to point out that there has been, during the last 130 years, one occasion only on which the King has dismissed the Ministry which still possessed the confidence of the House of Commons. This was in 1834, when William IV (one of the least wise of British monarchs) called upon Lord Melbourne to resign.... The Parliament Act was not intended in any way to affect, and it is submitted has not affected, the Constitutional position of the Sovereign. It deals only with differences between the two Houses. When the two Houses are in agreement (as is always the case when there is a Conservative majority in the House of Commons), the Act is a dead letter. When they differ, it provides that, after a considerable interval, the thrice repeated decision of the Commons shall prevail, without the necessity for a dissolution of Parliament.... [A]t a dissolution following such a dismissal of Ministers as has just been referred to, it is no exaggeration to say that the Crown would become the football of contending factions. This is a Constitutional catastrophe which it is the duty of every wise statesman to do the utmost in his power to avert. ('The Constitutional position of the Sovereign', 09.1913, in Jenkins 1964: 544–5)[4]

It used to be an old staple university exam question: *When did Britain come nearest to revolution: 1832, 1866, 1912, 1919, 1926...?* The documents just quoted show that the correct answer is none of these, but spring and summer 1914. Thanks to three anti-Irish politicians and encouraged by one anti-Irish King, the UK came close to violent disintegration, saved only by the First World War, by Asquith's imperturbability, and by the King pulling back from his thoughts of vetoing the Home Rule Bill.

---

[4] Both the tone and the content of this letter uncannily resemble Pitt's to George III in the almost identical situation in 1801 (Chapter 3). Did Asquith know of Pitt's letter? Although he did not have a strong interest in recent history, he had two eminent historians for colleagues and former colleagues. John Morley was the biographer of Gladstone. Lord Rosebery had written a life of Pitt (*Pitt*) in 1890.

The Unionist sense of outrage can be traced back to Disraeli's apparent banality that the object of the Tory Party was to 'maintain our institutions'. It was in the Unionists' material interest to uphold Lords, Church of England, and monarchy, all of which generally supported them. This led them to believe that attacks on any of these were unconstitutional and illegitimate. Gladstone had finally (and with great anguish, given his own religious views) disestablished the Anglican Church in Ireland. He dared not do the same in Wales; and his deference to the monarchy and the Lords was so great that he repeatedly protected Queen Victoria from the consequences of her partisan stupidity, and repeatedly ennobled Whig magnates who almost all joined the Unionists during the 1880s. Lloyd George and Asquith were less deferential than Gladstone; the Unionists in the Lords became more reckless; George V was as prejudiced against the Liberals and the Irish as his grandmother. It required only the accession of the bigoted and inexperienced Bonar Law in 1911 to complete the ingredients for explosion.

The hysterical phase of Unionism began with the passage of the Parliament Act. Unionists regarded it as a coerced cheat. A. V. Dicey developed a new constitutional doctrine that fundamentally contradicted his well-known doctrine of Parliamentary sovereignty. He now said:

The Parliament Act gives unlimited authority to a parliamentary or rather House of Commons majority. The wisdom or experience of the House of Lords is ... thereby deprived of all influence.... [T]he referendum might ... increase the authority of voters not deeply pledged to the dogmas of any party. (Dicey 1915: xcvii)

The new attraction of the referendum was asymmetrical. It could check Liberal and Irish tyranny. It was never intended to check Unionist tyranny. Dicey proposed a referendum in Britain (apparently excluding Ireland) on whether the Home Rule Bill should be enacted. He did not countenance a referendum in Ireland, or any part of Ireland, on whether it should remain in the Union.

The emotional force of primordial Unionism derived from either neglect or hatred of the (Catholic) Irish. The Governments of 1906 and 1910 had as much popular support in the UK as their Unionist predecessors. But that support included the voters for the Irish Party, whom Unionists preferred not to count—even though they were unwilling partners in that same Union. In October 1912 Bonar Law told a Catholic correspondent who 'had urged him to avoid attacks on her faith' (Blake 1955: 126):

The Ulster ... population ... is homogeneous and determined to be treated in the same way as citizens of the UK. In my opinion from every point of view they have the right to take this attitude. (Law to Lady Ninian Crichton Stuart, 7.10.1912, in Blake 1955: 126)

This is multiply astonishing. The Ulster population was remarkably hetero-
geneous; but all of them already were citizens of the UK. Until 1912, the
Unionist demand had been that the 'Ulster' that should be excluded from
Home Rule should be the nine counties of historic Ulster: i.e., the present-
day Northern Ireland plus Cavan, Monaghan, and Donegal. That 'Ulster'
was almost exactly half Protestant and half Catholic. In the Parliaments of
1885, 1886, and 1906 a majority of MPs from the nine counties of Ulster had
been Nationalists. By 1912 Carson, but not yet Law, had come to realize that
nine-county exclusion from Home Rule was untenable. Even the six counties
that now make up Northern Ireland had a substantial Catholic and nationalist minority—probably between 35 and 40 per cent of the population in
1912. But the Catholics of Ulster were invisible to Bonar Law and to many
Unionist politicians. For them, the causes of Ulster and of Protestantism
were the same. In the abortive Buckingham Palace conference of July 1914 to
discuss partition, the Unionists still insisted on the exclusion of all nine
counties (Jenkins 1964: 318–21).

Winston Churchill, contrary to his father, is the most eloquent narrator of
what happened next:

I remember on the eve of the Great War . . . for a long time . . . after the failure of the
Buckingham Palace Conference, we discussed the boundaries of Fermanagh and
Tyrone. Both of the great political parties were at each other's throats. The air was
full of talk of civil war. . . . The differences had been narrowed down . . . to parishes and
groups inside the areas of Fermanagh and Tyrone, and yet, even when the differences
had been so narrowed down, the problem appeared to be as insuperable as ever, and
neither side would agree to reach any conclusion. Then came the Great War. . . . Every
institution, almost, in the world was strained. Great Empires have been overturned. The
whole map of Europe has changed. The position of countries has been violently altered.
The mode and thought of men, the whole outlook on affairs, the grouping of parties, all
have encountered violent and tremendous changes in the deluge of the world, but as the
deluge subsides and the waters fall we see the dreary steeples of Fermanagh and Tyrone
emerging once again. The integrity of their quarrel is one of the few institutions that
have been unaltered in the cataclysm that has swept the world. (Speech introducing the
Irish Free State Bill, 16.2.1922; quoted in Churchill 1929: 319–20.)

We might summarize in the drier language of political science: the Irish
Question had become an Ulster Question; the Ulster Question was an intractable intercommunal conflict; the parties perceived it as a zero-sum game.
In the light of Churchill's brilliant summary, the puzzle is not that the Ulster
Question has bloodily returned to UK politics since 1968, but that it was ever
quiescent. That most of Ireland left the UK in 1921 without provoking civil
war in Britain (although it did provoke civil war in the Irish Free State) is the
supreme achievement of Lloyd George. But not only his. It required a sharp
retreat from Unionist primordialism.

The Unionist Retreat and the Free State Advance, 1916–25

The Irish crisis got worse before it got better. The Easter Rising led by Padraig Pearse and James Connolly in 1916 was not a serious threat to the Union, even though Sir Roger Casement was landed by a German submarine in Tralee to join the rebels. Irish opinion was still loyal to the Union; the Irish leader John Redmond had done the same as the Ulster Protestant leaders, and urged his followers to join the Allied armies. (However, in 1914 Kitchener had refused requests from Redmond and Lloyd George to form an Irish and a Welsh Division. He permitted the UVF's transformation into the 36th Ulster Division, with the tragic consequences described earlier.)

But where Padraig Pearse and Roger Casement failed, the British military succeeded. Their long-drawn-out round-up and execution of the leaders of the Easter Rising during April and May 1916 turned Pearse and his colleagues into martyrs (and, more recently, into Ireland's mainline railway stations) and fatally damaged the Home Rule party. It was already doomed to be damaged by talk of partition. It had seen Home Rule enacted in 1914, only to be immediately suspended. The threat of Protestant paramilitary violence meant that any settlement was now bound to involve partition, turning Parnell's posthumous triumph of 1914 to dust. Lloyd George floated a partition plan in 1916. True to later form, he gave the Irish Party leaders to understand that any exclusion of Protestant Ulster would be temporary; he gave the leaders of Protestant Ulster to understand that it would be permanent (see, e.g., Laffan 1999: 56–8; Jackson 2003: 155–71). In 1917 another all-party convention discussed partition but got nowhere. In the 1918 general election, the Irish Party was wiped out by Sinn Fein, which won almost all the seats in Catholic Ireland (although by no means all the votes—with proportional representation the Irish Party would not have been wiped out). The Sinn Fein MPs elected in 1918 refused to take their seats in Westminster, but constituted themselves as the first Dail Eireann, sitting in Dublin. The authority of the UK government in Catholic Ireland eroded steadily, and violence rose to the level of full-scale guerrilla war, until the British Government abruptly called a truce in July 1921.

But even as the Irish Party imploded, the Unionists retreated from indefensible primordialism to a tenable defence of Protestant Ulster. All three Unionist insurgents of 1914—Carson, Law, and Long—retreated to more moderate positions during World War I. Carson retreated first, being a pragmatist behind his show of defiance. Law and Long both became ministers in the first wartime coalition under Asquith, from May 1915 onwards. In the second coalition under Lloyd George, beginning in December 1916, Law became a permanent member of the War Cabinet. Long remained a minister, and took charge of what became the Government of Ireland Act 1920.

Earlier in his career, Long had been an Irish, but not Ulster, Unionist. His grandfather had owned an estate in Co. Wicklow. He was briefly Chief Secretary for Ireland in 1905. In the 1906 Parliament he sat for South Co. Dublin, the only Irish constituency outside Ulster to return a Unionist (and still today, as symbolized by the fortified Church of Ireland church at Monkstown, the heartland of what remains of the Ascendancy). He started moving in 1913, supporting Bonar Law's plan for the exclusion of Ulster from Home Rule against their Lords leader Lansdowne, a southern Unionist who wanted to keep the whole of Ireland in the Union. 'It may be necessary to sacrifice [the Southern Irish Unionists, whose MP he had recently been] in order to escape from civil war', he wrote (Kendle 1992: 79). In 1916 he had swung back to Lansdowne's side, objecting to Lloyd George's partition scheme. Lloyd George's typical response was to bring Long into the Cabinet as Colonial Secretary with responsibility for an Irish bill. Long became interested in a federal solution, in which the UK would have had five federal components, namely, England, Scotland, Wales, northern Ireland, and southern Ireland. Lloyd George brusquely told Long that this idea was a non-starter, but in his next bill, introduced in October 1919, Long proposed a mini-federal solution with a government for northern Ireland and one for southern Ireland. He still wanted 'northern Ireland' to comprise the nine counties of historic Ulster. But the leader of the Ulster Protestants, James Craig, wanted a Goldilocks-sized state that guaranteed Protestant supremacy. For Craig, nine counties were too big; four counties excluding Fermanagh and Tyrone were too small; six counties were just right. In a letter written just before his death when a Boundary Commission (see later) was beginning to sit, Long said that, in return for Ulster Unionist support for his bill, he had been forced in 1920 to concede to Craig that 'the Six Counties . . . should be theirs for good and all and there should be no interference with the boundaries . . . [except] to get rid of projecting bits, etc.' (Long to Lord Selborne, 18.12.1924, in Kendle 1992: 190–1).

The Government of Ireland Act 1920 offered watered-down federalism. It provided for bicameral parliaments for each of southern and northern Ireland. It defined the latter 'for the purposes of this Act' as the six counties of present-day Northern Ireland. 'With a view to eventual establishment of a Parliament for the whole of Ireland', s.3 provided for a Council of Ireland to run common services and to prepare for unity; s.12 and 75 show that Diceyans still had trouble with federalism. In particular, s.75 declaimed that 'the supreme authority of the Parliament of the UK shall remain unaffected and undiminished over all persons, matters, and things in Ireland and every part thereof'.

It did not—not in either part thereof. The Army and police were telling Lloyd George's Cabinet what they wished to hear about the security position in Ireland. They wished to hear that Home Rule was salvageable. It was not. In the only elections to the Parliament of southern Ireland under the 1920 Act, Sinn Fein again swept the board. Its elected members again refused to sit, and constituted themselves as the second Dail Eireann. The Unionist members elected for Trinity College, Dublin, met once and adjourned, and that was the end of the government of southern Ireland under the 1920 Act. In Northern Ireland, the Unionists who had earlier bitterly rejected Home Rule now came to see how it might work for them—in Craig's notorious words of 1934—as 'a Protestant parliament and a Protestant state' (quoted in Jackson 2003: 229). The 1920 Act became the Constitution of Northern Ireland. In the light of the declaration of the Republic of Ireland in 1948, the (UK) Ireland Act 1949 affirms that 'in no event will Northern Ireland or any part thereof cease to be part of His Majesty's dominions and of the UK without the consent of the Parliament of Northern Ireland'. However, s.75 of the 1920 Act finally came into its own in 1972, when the UK Government suspended the Government of Northern Ireland and imposed direct rule. The 1920 and 1949 Acts were superseded by the Northern Ireland Act 1973, which switches the locus of approval from the Parliament to the people of Northern Ireland. Northern Ireland will remain part of the UK unless and until a referendum of the people of Northern Ireland decides otherwise (Mansergh 1991: 346). The Anglo-Irish Agreement ('Good Friday Agreement') of 1998 confirms this position.

The story of the creation of the Irish Free State in 1921 has been told many times. We will not repeat the full account in McLean (2001a), and for more detail readers are referred to that book and the sources cited there. After declaring earlier that the UK Government had 'murder by the throat', Lloyd George abruptly reversed direction and called a truce in the summer of 1921. Although later Unionist commentators made much of admissions by Michael Collins (the leader of the Irish guerrilla force) that his forces were near to collapse when the truce was called, the truth is that the UK Government had no real choice but to seek a deal with the Irish. Apart from the military position, the administration of justice in most of Ireland was gone beyond recall, with the population having recourse to Sinn Fein courts and ignoring the UK machinery. The Royal Irish Constabulary and Dublin Metropolitan Police were riddled with spies and cowed by murders of their officers. Most worryingly of all, the USA and the Dominions, all with substantial Irish Catholic communities, were more and more uneasy with the 'Black and Tan war'.

Lloyd George's genius was to secure a Treaty in the small hours of 6 December 1921, when he controlled none of the three relevant legislatures and only one of the three executives. His Coalition Liberals held the barest possible majority (11 to 10) in the UK Cabinet and were in a minority in the Commons. The Unionists held more than half the seats in the Commons (and as usual controlled the Lords and the monarchy), and could therefore have deposed Lloyd George at any time, as they finally did in October 1922. Lloyd George had no direct influence at all in the governments or parliaments of northern or southern Ireland. The secrets of his success were the sequential game he imposed on the Irish negotiators; the Boundary Commission; and his co-optation of the UK Unionist leaders. We have dealt with the first two in McLean (2001a: ch. 7), and will be brief here, although it is necessary to follow the Boundary Commission story to the end in 1925 (or 1969).

The Irish president Eamon De Valera appointed a balanced delegation of plenipotentiaries to negotiate a treaty. Irish politicians were already divided between those (led by Arthur Griffith) who wished to negotiate and those (led by Austin Stack and Cathal Brugha, born Charles Burgess) who wanted to fight on. De Valera sided with the latter camp but did not go to London himself. Of his five negotiators, two (Griffith and Duggan) were likely to agree to a treaty; two (Barton and Gavan Duffy) were likely to reject it. The non-voting secretary to the delegation, Erskine Childers, was on the militant side. Michael Collins, the Irish army leader, was the swing voter. Lloyd George swung him on the day of the Treaty itself. Collins' memorandum has been frequently quoted but must be quoted once more for what it reveals about Lloyd George:

[Lloyd George] remarked that I myself pointed out on a previous occasion that the North would be forced economically to come in. I assented but I said that the position was so serious . . . that for my part I was anxious to secure a definite reply from Craig and his colleagues, and that I was agreeable to a reply rejecting [entry to the proposed Free State] as [to a reply] accepting. In view of the former we would save Tyrone and Fermanagh, parts of Derry, Armagh and Down by the Boundary Commission. . . . Mr Lloyd George expressed the view that this might be put to Craig. (Memo by Michael Collins, 5.12.1921, in Dáil Éireann [1972]: 304–6)

Lloyd George told no lies (on this occasion). He deftly caught Collins' aspirations for the squeezing of the North and bounced them back so that Collins came to believe that Lloyd George had promised that he *would* squeeze it. By a sequence of incredible threats and bullying, but with more credible threats at his back, Lloyd George put each of the five Irish negotiators in turn into a position where he either agreed to the draft treaty or would be responsible for restarting war. Though in the long run Ireland would certainly win such a war, in the short run it would lose. All five negotiators signed, and all five voted for the Treaty when it narrowly carried in the Irish Cabinet and Dail. But for one vote (Robert Barton's, in the Irish

Cabinet), the Treaty would not have been ratified in Ireland (McLean 2001a: 171–97).

A Boundary Commission was not a new idea, nor was the idea of using it to make incompatible promises to north and south. Lloyd George had done something similar in 1916. But in 1921 he persuaded the two sides to believe opposite things about what the Commission would do. Because of the Irish civil war (1922–3) and instability in the UK with three general elections in quick succession, the Boundary Commission got to work only in 1924 under the MacDonald Labour Government, which appointed a South African judge to chair it. The Government of the Irish Free State nominated a member; the Government of Northern Ireland refused to, and the UK Government therefore appointed an Ulster journalist, J. R. Fisher, to represent the Protestant Unionist interest. This he did with a will. The Commission proposed to expand Northern Ireland and make it a more defensible Protestant state by taking in part of east Donegal and giving up part of south Armagh. Fisher's vision was explicitly military:

With North Monaghan *in* Ulster and South Armagh *out*, we should have a solid ethnographic and strategic frontier to the South, and a hostile 'Afghanistan' on our north-west frontier [i.e., Co. Donegal] would be placed in safe keeping. (J. R. Fisher, 1922, in Gwynn 1950: 215–16; stress in original)

The draft was leaked to the most Unionist paper, the *Morning Post*, probably by Fisher. If he was the leaker, he was too clever by half. The Free State nominee immediately resigned, and Craig repeated his slogans of 'Not an Inch' and 'No Surrender'. The UK Government held an emergency meeting with both the Free State and Northern Ireland Governments with Prime Minister Stanley Baldwin's wife placed at lunch 'as the 'Boundary' between Craig and O'Higgins' according to the diary of assistant Cabinet Secretary Tom Jones (Jones 1971, diary for 29.11.1925). The Free State Government believed that 'Hostile feeling had been dying away; adoption of Boundary Commission report would resurrect heat and hate' (opinion of President W. T. Cosgrave, according to Jones, diary entry for 25.11.1925). The meeting ended with surprising harmony among all three governments, with Cosgrave and Craig, according to Jones, agreeing that they both disliked the Single Transferable Vote, which the British had imposed on both of their territories. All three governments agreed to leave the boundary where it was and to suppress the Boundary Commission report, which was not published until 1969.

Fisher had indeed seen further than Craig. If the Ulster Unionists had ceded South Armagh to the Free State, the area round Newry, Forkhill, and Crossmaglen would not have become one of the heartlands of republican terrorism after 1968. As it was, even Long's 'projecting bits' were left to project, especially between Cavan and Fermanagh, making for an extremely permeable boundary when violence restarted.

The third feature of the 1921 settlement was Lloyd George's incorporation of the Unionists. It helped that Law and Long both retired through ill health in 1921. In the autumn of that year, Law threatened to return. This probably helped Lloyd George rather than hindering him, as he was able to confront the Irish negotiators with a choice between a negotiation with him and a return to hardline British Unionism under Law. Bonar Law was indeed to return as Prime Minister on Lloyd George's overthrow in October 1922 but, already fatally ill, did not dismantle the settlement. The British Unionist negotiators of the Irish treaty were Austen Chamberlain, F. E. Smith (Lord Birkenhead), and Winston Churchill, who, although still nominally a Liberal, behaved in the Treaty negotiations as a Unionist military strategist. Although Birkenhead had earlier backed the Ulster rebels, he and Chamberlain proved themselves very flexible. In particular, Birkenhead formed a strong tactical alliance with Michael Collins to write a declaration of the status of the Irish Free State within the Empire that satisfied them both. It failed to satisfy Eamon De Valera, and therefore led to the Irish Civil War, which the Free Staters won in 1923. In 1933, De Valera came to power peacefully. He did not take the logical step of declaring the Free State a republic, although his External Relations Act 1936 all but did so. The final step was taken by a coalition government in 1948.

Thus by 1921 the Union question had resolved into a Northern Ireland question and an imperial question. It left two ragged ends from the 1886 attempt to settle it, namely representation and finance in the outlying parts of the Union. These matters are the subject of the chapters that follow.

6

Ulster Unionism since 1921

Unionism may be either primordial or instrumental. A Unionist (person or attitude) is primordial if he/she/it regards the Union as a value in and of itself. A Unionist is instrumental if he/she regards the Union as good because it has good consequences.

Almost all nineteenth-century British politicians were primordial Unionists, although some were also instrumental Unionists. The most articulate ideologues of primordial Union were A. V. Dicey in the nineteenth century and Enoch Powell in the twentieth. The fury of Unionist opposition to Home Rule between 1910 and 1918 was partly accountable by its primordial nature. How else could Bonar Law say in 1912 'I can imagine no lengths of resistance to which Ulster can go in which I should not be prepared to support them'? (see Chapter 5). He was making the preservation of Ulster in the Union the supreme goal of politics, and quite openly encouraging paramilitary action. Law was not bluffing, nor was he taking a line in which the preservation of Ulster was a means to some other desired end, such as the replacement of the incumbent government. For the Unionist leaders between 1910 and 1914 the priority was opposite. They wished above all to supplant or turn aside the incumbent government as a means to the end of preserving the Union. Union and Empire pointed the same way.

The process leading to the Government of Ireland Act 1920 drove a wedge between British and Ulster Unionists as the former came to see the latter as a sectional interest rather than a bulwark of Union. After the Act and the Treaty, British politicians' attitude to Northern Ireland and the Union became instrumental, consequential. Retaining it in the Union remained important, but it could be overridden by more pressing concerns. Union and Empire might now point in opposite ways, as there was no particular sympathy for Ulster Unionism elsewhere in the British Empire (e.g., Wilson 1985: 160–6). Two prime ministers—Neville Chamberlain and (even) Winston Churchill—were prepared to negotiate with the Irish Prime Minister Eamon De Valera for a united Ireland, in return for concessions that De

Valera refused to make. The only period in which British government attitudes to Northern Ireland returned to a faint shadow of Unionist primordialism was from De Valera's final rejection of Irish entry to the Second World
War on the Allied side in 1942 until the passage of the Ireland Act 1949. This
section examines the gulf between primordial unionism in Northern Ireland
and instrumental unionism in Britain. Of course, many Northern Irish
arguments for union are also instrumental. Unionists argue for the material
or liberal benefits of the Union as they see them. But there are primordial
strains. This chapter is about the latter.

Three Primordial Streams

Major says he is not going to be a 'persuader' for a united Ireland. What the fuck
does he think the government has been since 1969? The sugar plum fairy? The Tories
took away the B Specials, they took away Stormont, they pissed on every bloody
proposal the unionist majority made. Thatcher sends my son and thousands of other
squaddies to defend fifty sheep shaggers on the far side of the globe and then signs us
away in the Anglo-Irish accord. If that is not acting as a persuader for the Free State
then what the fuck is it? (Unionist paramilitary supporter, *c.*1992, interviewed by
Bruce 1994: 150)

At the end of the day my politics are not divisible from my faith. It's Protestantism
versus Rome. (Alan Wright, Salvation Army and Ulster Clubs activist, *c.*1985. Bruce
1994: 25)

Unner-Editor (Inglis an Ulster-Scotch) for the Chaummer o the Scrievit Account
(Hansard). 6-month leemited-tairm contraick. Sellerie: £13,737 tae £19,215

- It's noo apen fur tae pit in jab foarms fur tha ontak o Unner-Editor (Inglis an
  Ulster-Scotch) wi tha Chaummer o tha Scrievit Accoont (*Hansard*) o tha New
  Ulster Semmlie sittin at tha Toisel Biggins, Stormont, Bilfawst. A start wull be
  gien fur sax month, wi anither contraick aiblins forbye.

- Yins ats pit in fur it maun hae GCSE/GCE "O" level Grade A or B fur Inglis Leid,
  or less a like exam taen and hauden tae bear the same gree or abain. Aa thir maun be
  wi iz afore tha hinmaist day an hoor gien.

- Ilka yin on tha leet wull be gart sit a sey piece fur tae kythe: a perfit guid hannlin o
  tha Inglis, takin in gin yer fit or no fur tae owreset the wurds spake intil aisy read
  scrievin, houlin tha much ye can o tha taakeris ain wyes an gates; a guid braid
  kennin; an a unnerstaunin o daeins anent parliament an pairty ettlins, maist o aa
  adae wi Norlin Airlann; an—a guid hannlin o tha Ulster-Scotch leid. . . .

- The Semmlie wull be gye blithe fur tae get job foarms on tha leet pit in wi onie weel-fitted boadie nae matter thair kirk, sex, ills, race, quhit partie ye houl wi, aild, merriet or no, or sexual airt. Ilka job foarms, wull be preed anent abilitie an naethin else ava. (Job advertisement, *Belfast Telegraph*, 9.2.2001)

Three intertwined strands of primordial unionism coexist in modern Northern Ireland. There are probably others. But for sure, there are the Gunmen, the Evangelicals (both of those labels from Bruce 1994), and the Ulster-Scots intellectuals. The Gunmen are primarily urban and working class; the Evangelicals more rural and working class or from farm families; and the intellectuals are middle class and likely to have spent time in Scottish as well as Northern Irish universities.

Unionist paramilitary violence goes back a long way. The Orange Order was founded in 1795. Though not itself a paramilitary organization, it has always attracted people who have believed that physical force was needed to save the Union or to protect their community against Catholics. From the late eighteenth century there were Protestant and Catholic secret societies in (mostly rural) Ireland, and there was violence in both camps. From the time when Belfast started to grow rapidly, in the second half of the nineteenth century, Protestant paramilitarism became more urban and more obviously defensive. It was obviously defensive in the sense that it flared up most when the status of Protestant working-class people seemed most under threat. Boyd (1969) and Gibbon (1975) catalogue the serious rioting in Belfast in 1857, 1864, 1872, 1886, 1893, 1920–2, and 1964. In response to the Anglo-Irish agreement of 1985, Loyalist paramilitary groups increased their attacks on Catholics and also targeted RUC officers—peaking between March and May of 1986. New political parties representing the Loyalist paramilitary groups such as the Progressive Unionist Party (PUP) came into being. One of their leaders, Billy Hutchinson, who has spent time in prison for sectarian offences, recently stated:

Previous to the outbreak of violence there was little opportunity or inclination for anyone from a background such as mine . . . young, working-class and Unionist . . . to become involved in Politics. There was certainly no meaningful role for me in the Unionist Party, even if I had wanted to be part of it, and even less opportunity for my political views if I had of become part of it. (*http://www.pup-ni.org.uk/statements/ speech_BH.htm*)

Bruce (1994) interviewed a number of people associated with the main Loyalist paramilitary groupings in 1992 and 1993. The predominant sentiment is 'betrayal'. Both Ulster and UK leaders had promised to protect Protestantism and the Union. The slogan of Sir James Craig was 'No Surrender' even as the Protestants of Londonderry had refused to surrender when besieged by a Catholic army in 1689. But from the Loyalist perspective, as in the first epigraph to this section, all their political leaders have betrayed them. The Protestant share of the Northern Ireland population is in a long slow decline (Table 6.1) and the aristocracy of labour has gone with the shipyards and the linen industry. In modern Northern Ireland, there are more Unner Editors than shipwrights.

Table 6.1 needs to be interpreted with some caution. For all recent censuses, some respondents have probably hidden their religious affiliation in the 'Not stated' option. And the results for 1981 are distorted by a boycott urged by some nationalist politicians at the time, which probably depresses the numbers in the 'Catholic' column and raises those in the 'Not stated' column above their trends, as well as perhaps depressing the entire reported population. The long-term trend it shows is more subtle than the militant Loyalist interpretation, shared by Bruce's 'Gunmen' and 'Evangelicals', that Protestant Ulster will soon sink under a Catholic wave.

The first qualification is that the Catholic share of the population of Northern Ireland fits a U-shape, not a straight line. It was higher in 1861 than it (probably) is in 2001. Of course, Northern Ireland was not a political entity until 1920. Over the generations, higher Catholic fecundity has been balanced by higher Catholic net emigration. The latter was probably highest in the decades following the creation of Northern Ireland, hence the trough in 1926 and 1937. The current trend is upward, probably because net emigration is less unequal. Extrapolation would make Northern Ireland a majority-Catholic society by 2041 or 2051.

That would not necessarily generate a majority in favour of a United Ireland. Table 6.2 shows a much higher proportion of Catholics preferring to remain in the UK than of Protestants preferring a United Ireland. Nevertheless, the trend feeds Loyalist feelings of insecurity and betrayal. So does the increased spatial segregation of the two communities, in both local and province-wide geographies. Locally, there have been thirty years of intimidation of families living in the 'wrong' community. But also, as with any segregated population, it is only necessary to posit that the median member of a group would prefer her neighbourhood to be slightly or predominantly made up of people from her own community for all communities to 'tip' towards total segregation. This tipping process can be mathematically modelled. In working-class urban Northern Ireland, this tipping probably strengthens the Gunmen in each community. At a wider level, it has the effect that the west and south of the province are becoming (or are once again becoming) more Catholic, and the east outside Belfast more Protestant. Belfast contains large but segregated communities of each religion. The effects of segregation are perhaps felt most by those who live most closely to the other community. Local violence is most intense in what have become known as 'interface areas' where working-class Catholics and Protestants are separated by mere metres.

TABLE 6.1. *Religious affiliation in Northern Ireland, 1861–2001*

Year of Enumeration	Total population	Roman Catholic number (%)	Presbyterian number (%)	Church of Ireland number (%)	Methodist number (%)	Other denominations[1] number (%)	Not stated[2]
1861	1,396,453	571,890 (40.9)	457,119 (32.7)	320,634 (23.0)	27,919 (2.0)	18,646 (1.3)	445 (0.1)
1871	1,359,190	534,441 (39.3)	435,731 (32.1)	329,279 (24.2)	26,536 (2.0)	32,816 (2.4)	387 (0.0)
1881	1,304,816	495,559 (38.0)	414,236 (31.7)	321,998 (24.7)	31,179 (2.4)	40,317 (3.1)	1,527 (0.1)
1891	1,236,056	448,304 (38.3)	393,505 (31.8)	313,299 (25.3)	36,987 (3.0)	41,958 (3.4)	2,005 (0.2)
1901	1,236,952	430,380 (34.8)	396,582 (32.0)	318,825 (25.8)	44,134 (3.6)	47,971 (3.9)	1,070 (0.1)
1911	1,250,531	430,161 (34.4)	395,039 (31.8)	327,078 (26.1)	45,942 (3.7)	49,827 (4.0)	2,486 (0.2)
1926	1,256,561	420,428 (33.5)	393,374 (31.3)	338,724 (27.0)	49,554 (3.9)	52,177 (4.1)	2,304 (0.2)
1937	1,279,745	428,290 (33.5)	390,931 (30.5)	345,474 (27.0)	55,135 (4.3)	57,541 (4.5)	2,374 (0.2)
1951	1,370,921	471,460 (34.4)	410,215 (29.9)	353,245 (25.8)	66,639 (4.9)	63,497 (4.6)	5,865 (0.4)
1961	1,425,042	497,547 (34.9)	413,113 (29.0)	344,800 (24.2)	71,865 (5.0)	71,299 (5.0)	26,418 (1.9)
1971	1,519,540	477,921 (31.4)	405,717 (26.7)	334,318 (22.0)	71,235 (4.7)	87,838 (5.8)	142,511 (9.4)
1981	1,481,959	414,532 (28.0)	339,818 (22.9)	281,472 (19.0)	58,731 (4.0)	112,822 (7.6)	274,584 (18.5)
1991	1,577,836	605,639 (38.4)	336,891 (21.3)	279,280 (17.7)	59,517 (3.8)	122,448 (7.8)	173,061 (11.0)
2001	1,685,267	678,462 (40.3)	348,742 (20.7)	257,788 (15.3)	59,173 (3.5)	107,249 (6.4)	233,853 (13.9)

Note: [1] 2001—'Other Christian . . .' and 'Other religions and philosophies'; [2] includes 'None', asked only in 1991 and 2001.
Sources: (1861–1991): derived from *Northern Ireland Census 1991: Religion Report* as tabulated at *http://cain.ulst.ac.uk/ni/religion.htm#1a* with some arithmetic errors corrected; (2001), Northern Ireland, Census 2001, online table at *http://ww-v.nisra.gov.uk/census/Excel/cas_tables/CAS308ni.xls*; authors' calculations.

TABLE 6.2. *Religion and constitutional preference, Northern Ireland, 1994*

Option	Protestants	Catholics	Others	n
Remain part of the UK (%)	90	24	66	492
Reunify Ireland (%)	6	60	15	192
Other/DK/n.a. (%)	4	16	19	78
n	789	518	212	

Note: In this table the number of respondents in each category is unweighted, although to calculate the percentages the data was standardized so as to allow for the different number of occupants in each household. For further details see the Technical Report to NISA 1994.
Source: *Social Attitudes in Northern Ireland: The Fifth Report, 1995–1996*; Northern Ireland Social Attitudes Survey 1994.

The Evangelicals have a very different profile to the Gunmen. Gunmen are mostly urban and secular; Evangelicals are more rural and (obviously) religious. Typically, their religious definition is more fundamental than their political definition. Ian Paisley, for instance, was a religious leader before he became a political leader. Northern Irish evangelicalism derives from the specifically Scottish character of the Plantation of Ulster in the early seventeenth century. The Scottish Reformation was ideologically anti-Catholic in a way that the English Reformation originally was not. Religion and nationhood were intertwined. Scottish religious leaders drew up the National Covenant of 1638 and the Solemn League and Covenant of 1643. These were undertakings to protect and disseminate 'God's true and Christian Religion' and to 'extirpate popery and episcopacy' (Mitchison 1970: 195, 213). There has always been a strain of anti-Catholicism in the theology of the Church of England as well. As we saw in Chapter 3, English anti-Catholicism dealt a fatal blow to the 1800 Union when the King refused the Catholic emancipation that Pitt had offered the Irish as a quid pro quo for Union. But it never ran so deep as in Scotland or Ulster, and it declined rapidly after the Tractarian and Maynooth disputes of the 1840s. Its last hurrah was the Ecclesiastical Titles Act of 1851—Russell's attack on the 'mummeries of superstition'—which Gladstone described as one of the three 'actual misdeeds of the Legislature during the last half-century' (Matthew 1999: 338).

But in Scotland and Northern Ireland, the enemies of mummery remained vigorous. The Presbyterian churches in each retained their strains of primordial anti-Catholicism. The religious revival in north Antrim in 1859 (in what became Revd. Ian Paisley's constituency) brought Protestant fundamentalism into Ulster politics (Gibbon 1975: ch. III). That the Ulster Protestant campaign against Home Rule devised another Covenant—the Ulster Covenant of 1912—was no accident. 'You couldn't do better than take the old Scotch Covenant', a friend said to Craig, who drafted it, with a copy of a

History of Scotland by him as he did so. Craig submitted his draft to the Protestant churches for their approval (Stewart 1967: 61).

Bruce's (1986: 249) assertion that 'the Northern Ireland conflict is a religious conflict' has been controversial. But it does his subjects the courtesy of believing what they say. There is no reason to doubt the sincerity of Protestant Evangelicals whose mission in life is to attack the Roman Catholic Church. They stand in 400 years of Ulster, and Scottish, Protestant tradition. And they are a quite distinct strain to the Gunmen. Bruce (1994: 33–4) points out that a 1967 sectarian murder defendant's alleged confession 'I am terribly sorry I ever heard of that man Paisley or decided to follow him' is very likely to have been a police fabrication—'it is worth considering how little that statement approximates to working-class Belfast speech patterns'. Yet that confession, which is regularly repeated in political attacks on Paisley, is the only even semi-credible evidence directly linking him with political violence. When the Gunmen and the Evangelicals form an alliance, as in the Ulster Workers' Council strike of 1974 and the Drumcree Church protests since 1995, it is an alliance, not a fusion.

The Ulster-Scots intellectuals are different again. Their quiet voice is hard to pick out in the raucousness of Loyalist politics, and they are best approached through their own scholarly monographs (notably Stewart 1967, 1977; Wilson 1989). One of their strongest points is their protest against the 'map-image' of Ireland. Nationalist history and politics takes it as an axiom that the island of Ireland is a natural unit: as canonically stated in De Valera's 1937 Constitution, Article 2, *The national territory consists of the whole island of Ireland, its islands and the territorial seas.* But, as the Dutch geographer M. W. Heslinga (1962: 41) observed, 'To many Irishmen it is almost a dogma that the Creator has predestined Ireland to be a national and political unit, because it is a "perfect geographical entity", in the sense of a natural (physical) entity. This belief [is] a typical instance of confusion between natural features and Divine will.'

But until the eighteenth century most transport was by sea. From the north coast of Ulster to the west coast of Scotland is only about twelve miles at the narrowest point. Close links between the two long antedate the Ulster Plantation. In the heyday of the Celtic church, monks moved back and forth across the Celtic Sea. The Book of Kells may actually have been written in St Columba's Monastery on Iona, where a hillock at the south of the island is called Carn Cul ri Eireinn (The Cairn of [Turning] the Back to Ireland). Scots and Irish Gaelic are essentially the same language.

The Plantation of Ulster was really two events. After a rebellion by local Catholic chieftains, their clan lands were taken by the Crown in 1607. The Crown at the time was James I of England, ruling separately as James VI of Scotland. He settled English-speaking Scots Protestants in western Ulster.

The Plantation counties were Fermanagh, Tyrone, Derry, and Armagh, together with two of the three Ulster counties that entered the Irish Free State in 1921, namely, Cavan and Donegal. As befits a colonial settlement, the 'planted' settlers dominated the small towns of the regions such as Enniskillen and Omagh. The Catholics were forced on to the remotest and worst land. Eastern Ulster (Antrim and Down) was not formally part of the Plantation, but a large influx of Scots arrived by private arrangements during the seventeenth century. (Heslinga (1962) is a good non-partisan source for most but not all of these facts.)

After a further century, many of them moved on again. The term 'Ulster-Scots' was coined in the USA, where they are more widely recognized than in the UK. The first great wave of Irish emigration to (what is now) the USA was of Protestant Ulster Scots, settling especially in Appalachia and Arkansas. The tune that Americans know as the theme of Copland's 'Appalachian Spring' and Britons know as 'Lord of the Dance' is an Ulster-Scots folk tune. Ulster Scots played a prominent role in the first century of independent American politics, supplying, they say, fourteen Presidents, the last of whom was Woodrow Wilson.

The Ulster and Appalachian branches of Scots Protestantism formed part of the Scottish Enlightenment. That is the proper light in which to see the Society of United Irishmen, founded in 1791, one of the sponsors of the abortive revolt of 1798 (Chapter 3). Almost the only time that Protestants appear in Irish nationalist historiography is in celebration of Wolfe Tone, the Protestant leader of that rebellion. But Ulster-Scot historiography (e.g., Wilson 1989: 18–20) gives a deeper account of what was going on. In the 1790s Belfast, like Edinburgh, Glasgow, and Birmingham but unlike London, was a centre for Enlightenment intellectuals who opposed the established Anglican Church and welcomed the American and (to begin with) the French Revolution. The language of the Rights of Man was crafted by opposition Whigs beginning with Locke and his contemporaries at the time of the English 'Glorious Revolution' of 1688. The Scottish philosophers and theologians who taught Thomas Jefferson and James Madison exported opposition Whig ideology to US revolutionary thought. It was celebrated in prose by Tom Paine and in poetry by Robert Burns. Presbyterian ground was the most fertile for the egalitarianism of the Scottish Enlightenment.

Which is where the language comes in. Ulster-Scots ('Ullans') has equal status with English and Irish by the terms of the Belfast Agreement ('Good Friday Agreement') 1998. The Ulster Scots took a leaf out of the book of Arthur Griffith and Eamon De Valera, for whom the Irish language became a defining symbol of Sinn Fein in the early twentieth century. Ullans would be a wonderful language if it took hold. It is in direct descent from the language of Burns (and, for that matter of Adam Smith and David Hume, whose spoken English probably sounded quite a lot like Ullans). Here is Robert Burns:

What though on hamely fare we dine,
Wear hoddin grey, an' a that?
Gie fools their silks, and knaves their wine –
A man's a man for a' that.
For a' that, an' a' that,
Their tinsel show, an' a' that,
The honest man, tho' e'er sae poor,
Is king o' men for a' that.
(*Is There for Honest Poverty*, 1792)

And here, again, is Ulster-Scots:

The Semmlie wull be gye blithe fur tae get jab foarms on tha leet pit in wi onie weel-fitted boadie nae matter thair kirk, sex, ills, race, quhit partie ye houl wi, aild, merriet or no, or sexual airt. Ilka job foarms, wull be preed anent abilitie an naethin else ava.

Here is the lifeless English which that passage translates:

The Assembly welcomes applications from all suitably qualified candidates irrespective of religion, gender, disability, race, political opinion, age, marital status, or sexual orientation. All applications for employment are considered strictly on merit.

Compare *onie weel-fitted boadie nae matter thair kirk, sex, ills, race* with *all suitably qualified candidates irrespective of religion, gender, disability, race*. There is no contest. It wad be gye blithe if yins ats pit in fur joabs had a guid hannlin o tha Ulster-Scotch leid but it winnae happen. Ulster-Scots is no more a viable national language than is Irish in the Republic. Irish is the language of planning applications in Dublin. Developers who hope that nobody will notice what they propose publish their statutory notices in the first official language. The Ulster Scots Agency (or 'tha Boord o Ulstèr-Scotch') has an annual budget of £1.4 million. It is widely suspected of being a gravy train for cheerfully cynical anti-Assembly Unionists who are spending British and Irish public money (e.g., Hoggart 2000).

What do the three strands of primordial Unionism have in common? A worldview in which they are a special people who struggle grimly against huge odds but with Divine assistance. The uniting Unionist experiences seem to be not so much King Billy and the Battle of the Boyne—for they are too raucously appropriated by one of the three strands—but the First (especially) and Second World Wars. As noted earlier, Lord Kitchener refused requests from Lloyd George and John Redmond to create Welsh and Irish divisions in the British Expeditionary Force, but accepted the request of Carson and Craig to turn the Ulster Protestant paramilitaries into the 36th Ulster division. This piece of military Unionist primordialism would have tragic consequences.

Fellow soldiers noted with awe how the 36th Ulster Division went over the top on 1 July 1916 with their Bibles and their faith. The *Official History of the War* states:

All ranks felt that they were engaged in a Holy War under Divine guidance and protection, and the remembrance that that day was the anniversary of the Battle of the Boyne filled every Ulsterman's heart with a certainty of victory. (cited by Loughlin 1995: 83)

Blasphemously, one cannot help wondering what went wrong with the Divine guidance and protection. As many as 5,500 men of the 36th Ulster Division were killed or wounded (Stewart 1967: 241). A division formed from the pre-war Ulster Volunteer Force died en masse only three months after a few rebels in Dublin had tried to overthrow the British Empire with German help. Many of the murals in UVF-dominated areas of Belfast make some mention of the 36th Ulster Division linking present-day UVF paramilitary activities with the sacrifices during the First World War. An example can be seen at *http://cain.ulst.ac.uk/mccormick/photos/no1760.htm#photo*. The most symbolic atrocity of the whole Northern Ireland conflict was the Remembrance Day bomb in Enniskillen in 1987, which killed eleven people (and injured sixty-three) in the garrison town created by the planters of Ulster in 1607.

However, these have become strictly *Ulster* Unionist concerns. In the next section we maintain that no UK Government since 1920 has been primordially Unionist.

The End of Primordial Irish Unionism in Britain

No UK Government since 1920 has regarded the retention of (Northern) Ireland in the Union as a primary policy to be pursued for its own sake. To substantiate this, we look at the main political events touching the constitutional status of Ireland since the 1921 Treaty.

- *The battle of Pettigo and Belleek, 1922.* Pettigo and Belleek are two villages on the border between Fermanagh (Northern Ireland) and Donegal (Irish Free State, now Irish Republic). The border passes through the middle of Pettigo. Belleek is the westernmost settlement in the UK. They lie at a doubly strategic point. Lough Erne almost cuts off the two villages from the rest of Northern Ireland. But the western border salient at Belleek also almost completely cuts off Co. Donegal from the rest of the Free State at this point. J. R. Fisher, the Unionist mapmaker on the Boundary Commission, would see the Belleek salient as a strategic protection of the Unionists' north-west frontier.

In June 1922, raiders on the republican side in the incipient Irish Civil War tried to capture the two villages. This raid engaged the full military attention of Winston Churchill, UK Government minister and one-time soldier on the bigger North-West Frontier. The full record of British Cabinet discussions being kept by assistant Cabinet Secretary Tom Jones shows both Churchill and Lloyd George in their characteristic poses—Churchill ready to lead a military expedition, Lloyd George deflating his colleague by pretending to take him seriously. In the end, the republicans withdrew with little bloodshed and Lloyd George's 'desire to celebrate the victory of Belleek led him to sing "Scots wha hae" putting in Winston's name wherever he could' (Jones 1969: 201, source of quotation; 1971: 199–212). Three weeks later, Churchill was to make grimmer contingency plans to retake Dublin in the event that the Free State Government failed to end the republican occupation of the Four Courts there. Luckily for all except the republicans, Churchill's plan was never implemented.

But the battle of Pettigo and Belleek froze out the Government of Northern Ireland. Churchill and Lloyd George were alike furious that the new Craig government had its own military strategist (Sir Henry Wilson, shortly to be assassinated by the IRA in London) and its own paramilitary force (the so-called B Specials, a Protestant gendarmerie). Security on the Border was for the UK Government, not the Government of Northern Ireland. At Belleek, Churchill and Lloyd George acted as military strategists, not as primordial Unionists.

• *The Boundary Commission, 1924–5.* The Commission had been Lloyd George's masterstroke in 1921. He persuaded Craig that it would preserve the integrity of Northern Ireland while persuading Collins that 'the North would be forced economically to come in'. As already noted, J. R. Fisher saw the boundary as an opportunity to close off the hostile north-west frontier. Fisher's Afghanistan was Co. Donegal—the north-west corner of Ireland, to which the ancestors of Catholics dispossessed by the Plantation had been forced. The safe keeping comprised the Belleek salient, which almost completely cuts Donegal off, plus a transfer of some of the eastern and historically more Protestant (plantation) parts of Donegal to Northern Ireland.

Fisher's leak of the report to the *Morning Post* led to the suppression of the report on the grounds that publishing it would lead to more bloodshed than keeping it secret. It was published for the first time in 1969 (Hand 1969). On 1911 figures, which were the latest available to the Commissioners as civil disorder had prevented a Census from taking place in 1921 in either part of Ireland, it would have moved 31,319 people from Northern Ireland to the Irish Free State and 7,594 the other way. In communitarian terms it would have moved 32,673 people the 'right' way (viz. Catholics into the Free

State and Protestants into Northern Ireland) as against 6,240 people the 'wrong' way (viz. Catholics into Northern Ireland plus Protestants into the Free State).

Perhaps Fisher reasoned that other Unionists would agree that the Boundary Commission had delivered a more defensible Protestant state. However, the consequences of the leak were not good for his military strategy. Craig, sloganeering on 'not an inch' and 'no surrender', achieved an unchanged Northern Ireland, but when intercommunal violence returned in the 1960s, his successors would have preferred a more defensible space. But, once again, the matter was settled between the British and Irish Governments without regard to the primordial Unionist interests of Ireland. The Protestants of Donegal and Monaghan were left out of the UK because the UK Government had bigger fish to fry.

- *The External Relations Act 1936, and De Valera's 1937 Constitution.* In 1932 an Irish general election led (to the surprise of some) to a peaceful transition from the pro-Treaty to the anti-Treaty side, and Eamon De Valera became prime minister. To British ministers, he remained as slippery as Lloyd George had found him to be ('like picking up mercury with a fork' in 1921). He did not make the final break with the Crown and Dominions that had been widely expected. Instead, he took the opportunity offered by the abdication of Edward VIII in 1936 to enact the 'external association' that he had vainly sought in 1921. The Free State's External Relations Act 1936 provides that overseas representatives of the Free State are appointed, and treaties signed by its Executive Council, and no longer by the 'Crown'. The Act kept the Free State inside the club of the white dominions but a cigarette-paper's thickness away from a republic. The new Constitution the following year upset Northern Irish Unionists more than the External Relations Act did. Its most notorious articles were nos. 2, 3, 4, and 44:

  2. The national territory consists of the whole island of Ireland, its islands and the territorial seas.
  3. Pending the re-integration of the national territory, and without prejudice to the right of the Parliament and Government established by this Constitution to exercise jurisdiction over the whole of that territory, the laws enacted by that Parliament shall have the like area and extent of application as the laws of Saorstát Eireann and the like territorial effect.
  4. The name of the State is Éire, or in the English language, *Ireland*.

  Article 44 stated, in part, that the State 'recognizes the special position of the Holy Catholic Apostolic and Roman Church as the guardian of the Faith possessed by the great majority of the citizens'.

  The constitution was ratified in a referendum in June 1937. It had two features deeply offensive to primordial Unionists. The first was the privileged position of the Roman Catholic Church, evident in the confessional language of the preamble and the constitutionalization of Catholic social teaching in Articles 41–3 as well as the explicit wording of Article 44. Whether or not Unionists knew it, the entire draft had been shown to the pope (Bowman 1989: 152). It was a standing affront to the Evangelicals. It seemed to justify the old slogan 'Home Rule is Rome Rule'. Although, as explained below, Articles 2, 3, and 44 have all been altered, the preamble and Catholic social teaching remain offensive to Evangelicals in Northern Ireland, however unnoticed they go in the rest of the world.

The second offence to Unionists was the irredentist claim to Northern Ireland expressed in Articles 2–4—what Unionists call the fallacy of the map-image. British politicians finessed Article 4 and ignored Articles 2 and 3. The finesse copied Lloyd George's gambit of July 1921, when he had tried to wish away an Irish republic by translation (McLean 2001: 173, 181). If the Irish Constitution said that the name of the state in the national language was Éire, then that was what British government documents would call it, thus avoiding any commitment to calling De Valera's state, in the English language, Ireland. British ministers probably knew that Articles 2 and 3 were symbolic, and that the irredentist claim made in Article 2 was for practical purposes negated in Article 3. They guessed that De Valera, beneath his genius for gesture politics, was not going to invade the North. 'An armed attack on Ulster was not, however anticipated', the UK Cabinet minuted on De Valera's accession.[1]

- *The Handover of the Treaty Ports.* The military clauses of the Treaty, due to Winston Churchill, had guaranteed British access (including for air defence) in time of peace to Brerehaven in Bantry Bay in the south-west, Queenstown (now Cobh) in the south, and Lough Swilly in the north-west of the Free State. In time of 'war or of strained relations with a Foreign Power', the Treaty guaranteed the British access to 'such harbour and other facilities as the British Government may require' for the defence of Britain and Ireland. In 1938 the Chamberlain Government decided to improve relations with Eire, in the hope of persuading De Valera to end his economic war with the UK. Some have suggested that the motivation was geopolitical—that Chamberlain wanted De Valera's assistance to develop the peaceful restraint of Hitler through the League of Nations. De Valera, concerned at a possible German invasion of Ireland, wanted control of his own defences. The outcome was the Anglo-Irish Agreement of April 1938, in which De Valera called off the Economic War and gained control of the Treaty ports. Malcolm MacDonald, the main UK negotiator, had been

---

[1] CAB 23/71 37(32)2, 22.06.1932. Quoted by Bowman (1989: 111).

willing to announce that the UK would not veto reunification of Ireland if the North supported it (Bowman 1989: 178).

- *The Second World War*. Winston Churchill never disguised his view that the handover of the Treaty Ports was a serious mistake. Eire remained neutral at the outbreak of war, and in 1940 the Chamberlain Government started talks with a view to trying to bring it into the war on the Allied side. In May 1940 the UK representative in Eire asked De Valera, on Chamberlain's behalf, 'If the Partition were solved today would you automatically be our active Ally?' De Valera reportedly replied, 'I feel convinced that that would probably be the consequence.' He authorized staff talks to prepare for UK help in the event of a German invasion of Eire. The UK sent Malcolm MacDonald to Dublin to warn De Valera that such an invasion would be over in a matter of hours and that De Valera would be shot by the Nazis. The War Cabinet decided that if he gave UK forces access to Eire, the UK would make a declaration in principle in favour of a united Ireland without consulting Craig (by now Lord Craigavon) in advance (Bowman 1989: 219–29, documents quoted on p. 220).

This initiative came to nothing. The expected German invasion of Ireland did not occur, and that of Britain was stalled in the Battle of Britain. Churchill succeeded Chamberlain as Prime Minister. Because of his continuing anger over the Treaty Ports ('A more feckless act can hardly be imagined—and at such a time'—Churchill 1948: 216), he was at first unwilling to treat with De Valera. But the very surrender of the Treaty Ports made it essential. Writing in 1948 after the Battle of the Atlantic, Churchill stated that the loss of Brerehaven and Queenstown had reduced the range of the anti-U-boat destroyer flotillas by 'more than 400 miles out and home' (Churchill 1948: 215). Churchill had succeeded Chamberlain by the time that De Valera rejected the latter's offer in July 1940. In 1940 and 1941, both the US and the Canadian Governments considering trying to lease the Treaty Ports, but both desisted on deciding that De Valera now cared more about neutrality than about ending partition. But the day after Pearl Harbor, Churchill sent De Valera the following telegram:

Begins. Now is your chance. Now or never. A Nation once again. Am very ready to meet you at any time. Ends. (Churchill to De Valera, 7.12.1941, quoted by Bowman 1989: 246)

Many people, beginning with Churchill's Dominions Secretary the same day as the telegram, have strenuously denied that the telegram means what it obviously seems to mean. We think it does mean what it seems to mean. Despite (maybe because of) his fury at the loss of the Treaty Ports, Churchill was willing to offer De Valera a united Ireland if it was the price of getting the treaty ports back. De Valera again declined. Eire remained neutral; Northern Ireland remained in the UK; the Allies did not get the treaty ports back; many more Allied lives and supplies had already been lost in the Battle of the Atlantic than if they had been available.

In *Their Finest Hour* (Churchill 1949: 529), Churchill describes how, after the fall of France, Allied shipping in the Atlantic could no longer go south of Ireland: 'all had to come in around Northern Ireland. Here, by the grace of God, Ulster stood a faithful sentinel.' One of the master stylists of the English language here uses the language of Ulster evangelical primordialism—of Covenanting deliverance, of the first day of the Somme. Does that make him a primordial Unionist? No. A primordial Unionist would never have spoken, as Churchill did in 1922, of 'the dreary steeples of Fermanagh and Tyrone emerging once again' (Churchill 1929: 319–20, see longer extract in Chapter 5).

He did not have to put it like that. But he did, and he was sufficiently pleased with his imagery to include it in *The World Crisis* seven years later. Every time the dreary steeple of Drumcree Church (admittedly not in Fermanagh or Tyrone) has appeared on our TV screens since 1995, Churchill's image returns irresistibly to mind.

• *The Republic of Ireland Act 1948 (ROI) and the Ireland Act 1949 (UK)*. By 1948, Eire had a less subtle leader than De Valera, and the UK a less poetic one than Churchill. The Inter-Party Government elected in 1948 declared Ireland a republic in their Republic of Ireland Act. This was merely to clarify what had all along been implied by the External Relations Act and the 1937 Constitution. But it provoked the British Labour Government of Clement Attlee into the closest approach to primordial Unionism of any UK Government since 1921—and the only UK policy towards (Northern) Ireland that was discussed ahead of time with the Government of Northern Ireland. Drafts of what became the Ireland Act 1949 were shared with the Prime Minister of Northern Ireland before it was laid before the UK Parliament and the two governments remained in close contact throughout its Parliamentary passage (Jackson 2003: 349). The Second World War surely influenced this warmth. The Ireland Act declares resoundingly at s.1(2):

It is hereby declared that Northern Ireland remains part of His Majesty's dominions and of the United Kingdom and it is hereby affirmed that in no event will Northern Ireland or any part cease to be part of His Majesty's dominions and of the United Kingdom without the consent of the Parliament of Northern Ireland.

But even this declaration of primordial Unionism is compromised—ironically because of the most primordial Unionist of them all, A. V. Dicey. Dicey's constitutional doctrine holds that 'Parliament [understood as "the King, the House of Lords, and the House of Commons"] has, under the English constitution, the right to make and unmake any law whatever' (Dicey 1885: 38).

From this it follows that there is only one thing that a Parliament cannot do, namely, bind its successor. The supremacy of the UK Parliament over 'all persons, matters, and things in Ireland and every part thereof' was expressly, if redundantly, written into the Government of Ireland Act at s.75. That section, still in force as regards Northern Ireland in 1949, seems to be contradicted by the declaration in s.1(2) of the 1949 Act. Normally, in Diceyan doctrine, a later statute overrides an earlier one. But the supremacy of Parliament was more of a baseline principle than the 1949 Act. Interpreting the 1949 Act has always been difficult during the long periods since then when there has been no Parliament of Northern Ireland.

- *The 'Troubles' 1968–85.* The literature on the return of communal violence to Northern Ireland beginning in 1968 is huge. We need focus on one issue only: how far have the concerns of Ulster Unionism been shared at Westminster? The only possible answer is: hardly at all. The 'Troubles' broke out under the Wilson Labour Government of 1966–70. Harold Wilson was probably the prime minister least sympathetic to Unionism of any since the fall of Lloyd George. He repeatedly denounced the Ulster Unionist MPs at Westminster as merely protectors of Conservative hegemony with their then automatic support for Conservative governments. But the Unionists fared no better under Wilson's successor Edward Heath, during whose premiership their link with the Conservatives was forever broken. In March 1972, the worst year for sectarian violence in the whole history of the 'Troubles', Heath demanded that the Northern Ireland Government surrender its powers over law and order to the UK Government. When it refused, he brusquely prorogued Stormont and direct rule from Westminster began. Section 75 of the 1920 Act had proven mightier than s.1(2) of the 1949 Act.

At the start of the Troubles, the Irish Prime Minister, Jack Lynch, had done some Valerian grandstanding—for instance, announcing that he would set up field hospitals near the border to rescue any northern Catholics injured in communal violence. But he was no friend of Sinn Fein, and sacked two leading ministers, including the future Prime Minister Charles Haughey, for their alleged involvement in a gun-running plot. The UK and the Irish republic joined the European Common Market together in January 1973. Heath and Lynch had a common interest in solving a dispute on what then became an internal Common Market boundary. Lynch was the first Irish leader to make a symbolic concession to the Evangelicals in Ulster by sponsoring the 1972 amendment to the 1937 Constitution that repealed the Article 44 reference to the special status of the Roman Catholic Church.

Since 1973, all UK constitutional initiatives in Northern Ireland have taken place in consultation with the Government of the Republic. None has involved prior consultation with the Government of Northern Ireland—one good reason being that for most of the time since 1972, there has been no elected government of Northern Ireland. The first such after the suspension of Stormont was the power-sharing Executive and Sunningdale Agreement of 1973. The Northern Ireland Constitution Act 1973 amended some 1920 features and re-enacted others. It restored proportional representation for Northern Ireland elections, which Craig had removed in the 1920s. Like more recent such attempts, it envisaged a power-sharing Executive in which moderate nationalist and moderate Unionist parties would govern together. It re-enacted s.75 of the 1920 Act. And it handed the power to consent (or not) to changes in the constitutional status of Northern Ireland, which the 1949 Act had conferred on the now-vanished Parliament of Northern Ireland, to the people of Northern Ireland in referendum.

The Sunningdale Agreement added some formal North–South arrangements to the mix. However, the power-sharing Executive fell to a coalition of the Evangelicals and the Gunmen in the Ulster Workers' Council strike of May 1974. It had already been weakened by the February 1974 UK general election. In that election, Unionists who rejected their (former) leader Brian Faulkner's entry to the power-sharing Executive swept the board, winning all but one of the 12 seats from Northern Ireland and getting over half the vote. Therefore, a temporary coalition of (at least) the Gunmen and the Evangelicals, with at least the tacit support of the Ulster-Scots intellectuals as well, could argue that the power-sharing assembly had no democratic legitimacy. The Ulster Workers' Council strike began in electricity generation. Northern Ireland had very limited links to the grids in either Great Britain or the Republic, so the veto power of the power station workers was huge. Within two weeks, the power-sharing Executive and the Sunningdale Agreement were dead; direct rule returned for many years more.

Nevertheless, Sunningdale was the first precursor of the Good Friday Agreement. The Anglo-Irish Agreement 1985 was the second. All three agreements envisaged institutions of north–south cooperation. All three were drafted in cooperation between the British and the Irish Governments. None of the three involved prior consultation with the Ulster Unionists.

Probably the prime mover in the 1985 Agreement was Garret FitzGerald, Irish Prime Minister from 1982 to 1987. The son of a Northern Presbyterian mother and a Southern Catholic father, FitzGerald had already (cf. FitzGerald 1973) demonstrated more understanding of Unionism than any of his predecessors. Like those predecessors back to Lynch, he had the opportunity to talk face to face to the British Prime Minister at every biannual meeting of the European Council. Margaret Thatcher must have seemed the most unpromising of these, especially given that the IRA had murdered her closest ally Airey Neave in 1979, and bombed the 1984 Conservative Party conference in Brighton. One of her ministers described her as 'the most Unionist politician in Downing Street since the war' (Young 1990: 465). She swung round dramatically from a violent rejection of inter-governmental cooperation in November 1984 to an agreement with the Government of the Irish Republic a year later that entirely excluded the Unionists. Enoch Powell called her a Jezebel.[2] That can only have speeded her reconceptualization of Unionists from loyal friendship to being 'terrified of their plantation extremism' as one of her ministers told her biographer Young (1990: 470). The Unionist MPs resigned en bloc from Westminster in protest against the Agreement. In the ensuing by-elections one of them lost his seat. The mass resignations only demonstrated their impotence at Westminster. There was no repetition of the 1974 strike.

- *The Good Friday Agreement 1998.* As with the long history of the Troubles, so the short history of the Good Friday Agreement has already spawned a massive literature, some of it of high quality. The salient points are the same as in the previous subsection. On the side of the Irish Republic, a more mature understanding of Northern Unionism; on the side of the UK Government, a determination that Unionist politicians should have no veto over the constitutional status of Northern Ireland. Both of these were bipartisan in domestic politics. On the Irish side, the agreement included a referendum to amend Articles 2 and 3 of the 1937 Constitution to remove the irredentist claim of the Republic over Northern Ireland. That was approved by 94.4–5.6 per cent in May 1998. The amended text reads:

Article 2. It is the entitlement and birthright of every person born in the island of Ireland, which includes its islands and seas, to be part of the Irish Nation. That is also the entitlement of all persons otherwise qualified in accordance with law to be citizens of Ireland. Furthermore, the Irish nation cherishes its special affinity with people of Irish ancestry living abroad who share its cultural identity and heritage.

Article 3–1. It is the firm will of the Irish Nation, in harmony and friendship, to unite all the people who share the territory of the island of Ireland, in all the diversity of their identities and traditions, recognising that a united Ireland shall be brought about only by peaceful means with the consent of a majority of the people, democratically expressed, in both jurisdictions in the island. Until then, the laws enacted by the Parliament established by this Constitution shall have the like area and extent of application as the laws enacted by the Parliament that existed immediately before the coming into operation of this Constitution.

2. Institutions with executive powers and functions that are shared between those jurisdictions may be established by their respective responsible authorities for

---

[2] Young (1990: 472). *Jezebel:* 'Name of the infamous wife of Ahab king of Israel (1 Kings 14: 31; 19: 1–2; 21; 2 Kings 9: 30–37); hence used allusively for a wicked, impudent, or abandoned woman (cf. Rev. 2: 20) or for a woman who paints her face' (*OED Online*). It is a term of abuse frequently hurled by Ulster Protestants at Catholics.

stated purposes and may exercise powers and functions in respect of all or any part of the island.

The two main parties in the Republic are the historic descendants of the two sides in the Irish Civil War. Fianna Fail, today the hegemonic party in Ireland, descends from the losing Republican side of De Valera. Finc Gael, the main Opposition party, descends from the winning Free State side of Michael Collins. However, in 1998 no political leader of any standing took the No side.

On the British side, the peace initiative passed intact from the outgoing Conservative to the incoming Labour government. A counterpart to the Irish removal of De Valera's Articles 2 and 3 was the repeal of the 1920 Government of Ireland Act, including of course s.75. Both governments are now aligned on the position that a change in the constitutional status of Northern Ireland will come only with the consent of the people of Northern Ireland.

In Northern Ireland itself, the vote to accept the Agreement was closer, with a 71.2 per cent Yes in the May referendum there. It had been agreed that an overall Yes required a Yes from both the Unionist and nationalist communities, and the pro-agreement majority among Unionists was meagre. The second election for the Northern Ireland Assembly, which was deadlocked over the implementation of the Good Friday Agreement and suspended, finally took place in November 2003. The more extreme parties on each side—Paisley's Democratic Unionists and Sinn Fein—each beat their moderate counterparts the Ulster Unionists and the SDLP. The Assembly remained suspended. Primordial unionism lives on in Ulster. In Britain, it is no more.

7

Unionism in Britain since 1961:
Elite Attitudes

Unionism Instinctive but Instrumental, 1921–1961

As British politics shook down in the 1920s, it was changed radically in two ways. One was the departure of Ireland. The other was the replacement of the Liberals by Labour as the party in contention with the Conservatives to govern the UK. In the general elections of 1918, 1922, and 1923, it was not clear even to a well-informed voter which opposition party would come out on top. The Labour and Liberal Parties obtained a comparable number of votes and seats in each of these general elections. Although the Labour Party had the edge in seats each time, this was an artefact of the electoral system. Because Labour's vote was more concentrated than the Liberals' a given number of votes won Labour more seats than it did the Liberals. However, the general election of 1924 confirmed that only Labour could mount a nationwide opposition to the Conservatives.

British politics is governed by Duverger's law (1954: 217), which states 'The simple-majority single-ballot system favours the two-party system.' Because votes that do not go to a party that is capable of coming first or second locally appear to be 'wasted', there are powerful incentives for both voters and politicians to converge on to two parties. Voters will tend to abandon any party that seems to have no hope locally, thus confirming that it has no hope. Politicians will aim to make their party one of the leading two. If they fail, they will abandon it. Lloyd George tried for twelve years to make the Liberals the hegemonic party of the left. When he finally failed in 1922, he never returned to office—a fact that would have astonished his contemporaries if anyone had predicted it in 1922. As the Liberal Party faded, ambitious politicians transferred their allegiances to a party that could win—either Labour or the Conservatives. Most, but not all, ambitious Liberals transferred to Labour. So did most, but not all, of the Liberal vote.

But in the simple-majority single-ballot system, voters vote in constituencies. Understood properly, Duverger's law explains what happens in constituencies under the first-past-the-post system, not what happens in the nation. There may be different patterns of two-party competition in different sets of districts. Most relevant to this book, there may be parties that wish to alter the Union, but operate only in the parts of the UK whose status they wish to change. There have been parties wishing to dissolve or weaken the Union in Ireland since 1832 (albeit with a break from the death of Daniel O'Connell in 1847 to the rise of Isaac Butt in 1874). Parties that wished to strengthen the Union in Ireland may be dated to 1886. Parties wishing to weaken the Union in Wales and Scotland made their hesitant starts in the same year (with *Cymru Fydd* and the Crofters' Party), but did not become serious contenders in their parts of the UK until the 1960s. The Ulster Unionists were an integral part of the Conservative party; Ulster nationalists appeared fitfully if at all at Westminster, winning few seats, and then sometimes following the Sinn Fein tradition of refusing to attend the Commons.

The period from 1924 to 1961 was therefore one of two-party hegemony in the UK. Both parties were firmly Unionist, the Conservatives mostly for strategic and imperial reasons but increasingly for welfarist reasons. With Labour the reasons came in the opposite order, but they were the same.

It is easy to forget how much the Empire mattered and for how long. Between the world wars, perhaps a third of the world was still painted pink on the maps that hung in every primary school classroom. Admittedly, the combination of Mercator's Projection and thousands of square miles of uninhabitable Arctic Canada gave children a misleading impression of how vast the British Empire was, but impressions are a large part of reality. The 'white dominions' of Ireland, Canada, Australia, New Zealand, South Africa, and Newfoundland became almost fully self-governing under the terms of the Statute of Westminster of 1931. India, and the tropical empire, did not become independent until after the Second World War: India in 1947 and tropical Africa and the West Indies from 1960 onwards. The Empire remained the UK's main trading bloc until the 1960s. Australia, with a population then of ten million, was the UK's largest trading partner in the 1950s (Milward 2002: 4). Most of the Commonwealth (except Canada) was in the Sterling Area, which persisted as a currency zone until 1973, when the UK's entry to the European Union (EU) killed it off.

Militarily, the Empire still mattered. In the Second World War, all the independent dominions except Ireland automatically joined the Allies. Despite their small populations, their worldwide distribution was immensely important to naval and air operations. The not-yet-independent government of India supplied many thousands of troops.

All of these, and associated matters such as the role of the Crown in the Dominions, occupied a huge amount of politicians' time until the UK's turn from empire to Europe in the 1960s. In the nature of things, they appealed most to Unionists in the Conservative Party, but the Labour Party was no less Unionist when in government. The Statute of Westminster was developed under the MacDonald Labour Government (although not enacted until after its fall); Indian independence under the Crown was enacted under the Attlee Labour Government in 1947; the same government coped in a Unionist way with the declaration of the Irish republic in 1949. The declaration of an Indian republic in the same year forced the Attlee Government into constitutional contortions, from which it emerged that a nation could be a member of the Commonwealth without allowing allegiance to King George VI.

The welfare state was inherently Unionist. From the outset, with old age pensions in 1909 and National Insurance against sickness and unemployment in 1911, welfare benefits were set at uniform values in cash or kind throughout the UK. Taken in conjunction with the tax system, they therefore represented a double redistribution from rich to poor. They redistributed resources from rich people to poor people. As people live in places, this also implied redistribution from rich places to poor places. Policymakers deeply involved in the creation of the welfare state understood this from the beginning; other politicians caught on more gradually.

That incomparable study of policymaking, William Braithwaite's *Lloyd George's Ambulance Wagon* (1957: 222–4), reveals the civil servants' fury in 1911 at being forced to create four separate sets of Commissioners, one for each country of the UK:

[t]he Irish party had sent in their demands. . . . The political position was such, with the Parliament bill on hand and Home Rule in the offing, that these demands had to be acceded to . . . without question. . . . When the other 'nations' saw them the fat was in the fire. First the Scots and then the Welsh Liberal members demanded separate Commissions for their countries. . . . All this was most heart-breaking and vexatious.

Thus the politics of territory intruded even into national insurance. Lloyd George turned it to advantage by using what he called the 'Celts' to wring policy concessions from English interest groups.

Politicians more distant from policy absorbed these issues more slowly. The Labour Party became the official opposition in 1918 still as an offshoot of the Home Ruling Gladstonian Liberals. Its leader from 1922 was that same Ramsay MacDonald whom we last met as the secretary of the Scottish Home Rule Association. Scottish backbenchers promoted Scottish Home Rule Bills in 1924 and 1928. Curiously, the first gross paradox of Unionism after 1918 came, not from English members imposing uniformity on Scotland but from Scottish members interfering in a rare England-only matter. In 1927 and 1928 the proposed Church of England Prayer Book was rejected twice in the Commons—on the votes of Scottish and Welsh MPs objecting to its allegedly popish tendencies. If only English MPs had voted, the Prayer Book would have been carried (McLean 1999: 208). What we have learnt to call the 'West Lothian Question' (see below) is truly venerable.

By the 1930s, the Labour Party's Home Rule origins had been buried. In the age of mass unemployment, politics was decisively about place and about uniformity of standards. In the words of Gordon Brown (1982: 527), later to become Chancellor of the Exchequer:

[T]he real problem for Scottish Labour was that it wanted to be Scottish and British at the same time. No theorist attempted in sufficient depth to reconcile the conflicting aspirations for home rule and a British socialist advance. In particular, no one was able to show how capturing power in Britain—and legislating for minimum levels of welfare, for example, could be combined with a policy of devolution for Scotland.

The Conservative-dominated National Government developed policies to alleviate distress in the 'special areas' of high unemployment. And in the bipartisan consensus of the Home Front in the Second World War, the Beveridge Report of 1942 envisaged a nationally uniform scheme of social insurance. William Beveridge, who had been one of Braithwaite's colleagues in 1911, would have no truck with regional variation in rates or rights. In Scotland, a few Scottish unions, led by the Scottish Farm Servants' Union and the magnificently named Scottish Horse and Motormen's Association, held out for independence in trades where they felt they were better organized or better paid than their English equivalents (Keating and Bleiman 1979: 92). Similarly, the Scottish TUC retained its independence of the national TUC. But the overwhelming tide flowed the other way—in Wales even more than in Scotland. By far the largest and most powerful union in Wales was the South Wales Miners' Federation. Through bitter defeats in 1921 and 1926 the miners tried vainly to hold out for nationwide, not local, pay bargaining. That was because local pay bargaining was against their interest. South Wales coal has high value added but is expensive to dig out because of narrow seams and hilly terrain—a combination that was to prove literally lethal in 1966 (McLean and Johnes 2000). Although the structure of the National Union of Mineworkers remained federal, it was not in its members' interests after 1926 to negotiate for regional pay deals— certainly not for its economically weak Welsh or Scottish members. A Wales-only miners' union would certainly have to concede lower wages than a UK-wide union.

The final defeat, as it seemed, for Home Rule came during the Second World War, when the UK was united as a nation as never before (or since), and when 'nationalism' had become associated with Nazism or fascism. The Union was at its strongest. Although the wartime Secretary of State for Scotland, Tom Johnston, shrewdly used the alleged Scottish Nationalist threat in order to secure pork for Scotland (Morrison 1960: 199; Walker

1988: 162), the Scottish Nationalist victory in the Motherwell by-election in 1945 was universally, and rightly, dismissed as a fluke consequence of the wartime truce between the major parties. The SNP held the seat for a mere two months (Brand 1978: 242).

The First Nationalist Challenge, 1961–70

In what became the favourite Aunt Sally for British politics examiners, Peter Pulzer famously wrote in 1967, 'Class is the basis of British party politics; all else is embellishment and detail' (Pulzer 1975: 102). It was ceasing to be true as he wrote.

The SNP first threatened Labour by its respectable performance in two by-elections in Labour-held seats. These were Glasgow Bridgeton in 1961 and, iconically, West Lothian in 1962 (McLean 1969; Brand 1978: 258–61). The 1962 by-election returned Tam Dalyell as the Labour MP for a constituency whose name would be attached to the hardest devolution question. At every election in West Lothian and its successor seat since 1962, the contest has been between Dalyell (still the local MP, and Father of the House, as we write, although he has announced his intention to retire) and the SNP.

The SNP was beginning its journey from the fringe to credibility. Earlier, it had been preoccupied by cultural issues, such as the title of the Queen on accession (there had been no previous Queen Elizabeth of Scotland) and the student stunt of capturing the Stone of Scone from Westminster Abbey in 1950. But it had contained a wild anglophobic fringe ('I, for one, am fully agreed that Scotland's arch-enemy is not Germany, but England'—letter to *Scots Independent*, December 1938, quoted by McLean 1969: 25). Its economic policy had been primitive and autarkic, and its long-time leader, Arthur Donaldson, knew no economics and so managed to get the consequences of the 1949 devaluation upside down in a policy pamphlet (interview, IM with the late A. Donaldson, Forfar, 1968). Its policy statement, drafted in 1946 and still force in 1969, stated:

Scottish Nationalism is based primarily on spiritual values, on the recognition of the needs of the individual, and the right to express himself fully and freely within the framework of a community.... The economic safeguard of democracy lies in the diffusion of economic power.... Grain stores, cooperative societies not under immediate control, multiple firms and similar bodies, must be restricted in operation in the interests of local communities. Those under alien control will not be permitted in Scotland. (SNP, policy statement, 1946, cited by McLean 1969: 129; cf. Hanham 1969 172–6; Miller 1999)

However, by 1961 a new generation of leaders, including the Bridgeton and West Lothian candidates, were social democrats complaining about

Scotland's economic decline. As soon as Hanham (1969) reminded the world of the SNP's autarkic economics, it disowned them.

Social democracy was a more credible threat to Labour under a Labour Government. Accordingly, the SNP's next advance came when the Labour Government of 1964–70 ran into serious economic difficulty beginning in mid-1966. It did well in a by-election in Glasgow Pollok and then sensationally captured Labour's safest seat in Scotland, at Hamilton, in November 1967.

Plaid Cymru's social base was narrower, but its first scalp came earlier. Unlike the SNP it remained a party of cultural protest, whose manifesto would have seemed familiar to Tom Ellis. Its strength lay in Welsh-speaking, rural, chapel-going Wales. There the politics of Tom Ellis ran deep. But even under the generous treatment of the Boundary Commissioners, who have always allowed rural Wales to have some of the smallest population constituencies in the UK (Johnston and McLean 2005), there are only a maximum of six Ellisian seats. Unluckily for Labour, one of them, Carmarthen, became vacant with the death of Lloyd George's daughter Megan in 1966. The leader of Plaid Cymru, Gwynfor Evans, captured it. From this base, the party then did well in subsequent by-elections in the Labour heartlands of the south Wales Valleys (Madgwick 1973; Philip 1975).

By the 1970 general election, the nationalist threat had subsided. The SNP lost Hamilton, although it gained the most culturally distinctive (and smallest) seat in Scotland, the Western Isles—the only constituency in the UK in which the Gaelic language remains viable, and the constituency with the largest number of crofts and of adherents of the 'Wee Free' Free Church of Scotland (McLean 1970). Politicians could therefore pigeon-hole the two Celtic nationalist parties as just that—parties of cultural protest confined to their declining cultural ghettoes. The Conservatives, led by the Scot Sir Alec Douglas-Home, became more devolutionist, with their 1968 Declaration of Perth committing them to a form of Scottish devolution (Kellas 2005). Labour, under the non-Scottish Harold Wilson, did not follow.

It's Whose Oil? 1970–1979[1]

North Sea Oil changed everything. In the 1966–70 Parliament, Wilson had set up a leisurely Royal Commission on the Constitution, to report on the

---

[1] From 1973 to 1979, one of us (IM) was an elected member of Tyne and Wear Metropolitan County Council, serving successively as vice-chairman and chairman of its Economic Development Committee. As such he was closely involved in the events described in this section, being jointly responsible with the leader and chief executive of the County Council for its policy and networking in this area. Facts not supported by citations are from his recollections and contemporary records. (See also Guthrie and McLean 1978.)

relationship of the UK with all its non-English parts and neighbours, including the Channel Islands and the Isle of Man. These last were the giveaway. The Royal Commission was a device not to find the truth or to recommend changes, but to give the impression that the Government was looking at the issue and would not be in a position to make a commitment until after the next general election. It was a device Wilson used in other policy areas. In this case it succeeded. Devolution was scarcely an issue in the 1970 general election. However, Labour lost it. The Royal Commission reported in 1973 under its second chairman the Scottish judge Lord Kilbrandon, recommending devolved assemblies for Scotland and Wales. By then the SNP was rising fast again, because it had discovered its most effective slogan ever: 'It's Scotland's Oil...'. One version of the poster, featuring a haggard-looking old lady, went on: 'so why do 50,000 people in Scotland a year die from hypothermia?' International lawyers gravely disputed whether it was in fact Scotland's oil.[2] Should Scotland declare independence, the international boundary would run north-east, not due east, from Berwick-on-Tweed, thus putting a third of the North Sea oilfields into the English sector (Grant 1976). Another third was off Shetland, which was then making the same demands for separation from Scotland that the SNP was making for separation from England. These subtleties did not spoil a great slogan. The SNP won another by-election in 'safe Labour' Govan within a week of Kilbrandon reporting.

Labour politicians started to panic. They had more to lose immediately from an SNP upsurge than the governing Conservatives. At this point, there were few principled devolutionists in the national Labour party, although one influential one was the Oxford academic Norman Hunt (Lord Crowther-Hunt), a member of the Kilbrandon Commission who was to be Wilson's key adviser in the events that followed. The rest of the national Labour leadership were like the Tory peers in 1911: divided into hedgers and ditchers. The hedgers, led by Harold Wilson, believed that making some gestures to devolution would head off the Scottish Nationalist threat. For them, devolution was a purely pragmatic move, to be taken with no deep thought as to its constitutional implications. The ditchers, led politically by Labour's once and future Scottish Secretary Willie Ross and intellectually by Tam Dalyell, believed that any concession to the SNP was dangerous. For them, devolution was a dangerous precedent, a slippery slope, the start of the breakup of Britain.

In the February 1974 general election, the SNP held Western Isles and gained six more seats, four from the Conservatives and two from Labour, while just failing to hold its by-election gain in Govan. It won 22 per cent of

---

[2] And policy specialists gravely disputed whether in fact 50,000 people a year died of hypothermia in Scotland.

the Scottish vote. Astute politicians knew that, while the electoral system had protected Labour by giving the SNP only 10 per cent of the Scottish seats for its 22 per cent of the vote, it would swing round viciously if the SNP vote share were to rise by another 10 percentage points or so. On a vote share of somewhere between 30 and 35 per cent, the SNP would flip from victim of the electoral system to its beneficiary. With an evenly distributed 35 per cent of the vote, it could win more than half of the seats in Scotland—Labour had just won 40 out of 71 seats (i.e., 56 per cent) in Scotland on 37 per cent of the vote. Were it to do so, it would start to negotiate for Scottish independence. Bang would go the UK and (as important for national Labour politicians) Labour's chance of forming a governing majority, which utterly depended on its forty Scottish seats.

Through the year 1974, ministers in the Labour minority government focused on these governing realities, while its Scottish elite focused more on the pros and cons of devolution per se. This led to the confused events of June to August. On 22 June 1974, Scotland were playing Yugoslavia in the World Cup. A thinly attended meeting of the Labour Party's Scottish Executive was evenly divided between hedgers and ditchers when, in Dalyell's account (1977: 101):

all eyes turned to . . . the petite and comely Mrs Sadie Hutton of Glasgow, who had drifted in after doing her morning's shopping. Loyal to her [ditcher] Chairman, and resentful of the pressure that was being put on him from Transport House, she raised her hand. . . . So, by six votes to five, the Scottish Executive of the Labour Party reaffirmed their policy that an Assembly was 'irrelevant to the real needs of Scotland'.

To reverse this embarrassing decision, the national leadership of the Labour Party called on their trade union shock troops. In July, the national executive of the party resolved that it 'recognize[d] the desire of the Scottish people for the establishment of an elected legislative Assembly within the context of the political and economic unity of the United Kingdom'. The unions were sent with their card votes to a special Scottish conference in the middle of the school holidays on 17 August in the Dalintober Street Co-operative Halls in Glasgow. This duly reversed the Scottish Executive's position. By command of the National Executive, the uncertainly devolved Scottish Executive announced that it was now in favour of devolution.

Tam Dalyell's bitter but entertaining diary records John Smith as having said that devolutionists 'could not have their cake and eat it, by insisting that they keep the office of Secretary of State for Scotland, and all seventy-one MPs'. But that was precisely the position the party adopted. In Keating and Bleiman's words (1979: 167), 'the difficulties over which devolutionists had agonised for years were solved at a stroke by incorporating in the successful propositions the principal demands of both devolutionist and unionist factions'. John Smith, the most successful and only committedly devolution-ist Labour minister in the ensuing struggle to legislate, helped to enact the Scotland and Wales Acts 1978, which provided precisely for devolved assemblies in each country while retaining its Secretary of State and its full slate of Westminster MPs.

In the October 1974 general election, the SNP advanced further, to eleven seats and 30 per cent of the Scottish vote. Then the most extreme pro-devolutionists in Scottish Labour split off to form the Scottish Labour Party. It seemed that the ditchers had been right, and that the Union was not to be saved by card vote manoeuvres in the school holidays. In the next four years, they turned out to be wrong. During the Parliament of 1974–9, the SNP message became confused. SNP members contradicted one another on the floor of the Commons on whether they would concede to Shetland the same autonomy for 'Shetland's Oil' as they claimed for 'Scotland's Oil' (Hansard: 5th series, Vol. 924: 17–28 January 1977, cols. 1608–19; McLean 1977: 427). The Scottish Labour Party fizzled out (Drucker 1978). As the 1979 general election approached, the SNP-backed confidence motion that precipitated it was ridiculed as 'turkeys voting for Christmas'. The SNP was reduced from eleven seats to two. The Scottish Labour Party lost its two sitting MPs. After the election, Margaret Thatcher immediately repealed the Scotland and Wales Acts, which had failed to gain the referendum support that hostile amendments to the government bills had inserted. The Scots failed to rise up in wrath, and devolution went to sleep until the creation of the Scottish Constitutional Convention in 1989.

Dalyell (1977: 108) records the following conversation with Crowther-Hunt on the night of Dalintober Street:

The real trouble is that he thinks that the SNP exists because people want a different constitutional set-up; Ronnie [TD's agent] and I know the SNP flourishes on account of the greed of the people for North Sea Oil revenues, disgust at local council corruption scandals, stirring up Rangers supporters' clubs by Orangemen because there are too many Catholics in the Labour Party, and a host of other matters, which are well known to those of us who struggle along in the gutter of political life, but which are somewhat novel, if known at all, in Oxford University Common Rooms frequented by Norman.

Dalyell exaggerates, but he was closer to the truth than Crowther-Hunt. However, by that time the Government's devolution flagship was in full sail. It was shortly to be wrecked off Whitley Bay.

The first Scotland and Wales Bill was introduced in 1976. It offered legislative assemblies to each country, with powers to act on a range of devolved powers specified in detailed schedules. The philosophy of the bill was that everything was 'reserved' to the UK Parliament unless listed as

devolved in a schedule. Scotland and Wales were to retain their full comple-
ment of MPs, and their Secretaries of State. The administration of devolved
government would fall to the Scottish and Welsh Offices, which already
administered most, if not all, the matters to be devolved. Harold Wilson's
statecraft in piloting devolution[3] (cf. Bulpitt 1983) involved preserving the
capacity of Labour to govern the UK (what Bulpitt calls 'high politics') while
sacrificing local issues to a devolved administration ('low politics').

Wilson's statecraft worked in Scotland. It failed in Wales and, most
important, it failed in England. In Scotland, the demand for devolution,
although real, was skin-deep (Chapter 8). Wilson's statecraft therefore
saved the Union—by accident. During 1975, its prospects looked grim. The
SNP was riding high in the polls; as mentioned earlier, two Scottish Labour
MPs broke away to form the Scottish Labour Party. A general election in
1975 would probably have given the SNP and Scottish Labour Party between
them a majority of Scottish seats. But the combination of internal divisions
within the SNP, including over Europe; the low salience of the issue; and the
perception that 'something was being done' saved Labour's bacon. In a
particularly astute move, Wilson reportedly offered Winifred Ewing, the
victor of the Hamilton by-election, a seat in the then-nominated European
Parliament on the following terms: 'You Nats can have a seat in the European Parliament, but we need to know by 6 pm or the [Ulster] Unionists get
it' (Miller 1999: 23; based on interview with W. Ewing MEP, 10.12.1998).
Ewing took the seat and held it for twenty years. This killed two birds with
one stone. It split the SNP and distracted their most eloquent MP. Ewing lost
her Commons seat in 1979.

The decision to offer devolution to Wales as well as to Scotland was
presumably taken on grounds of consistency. Plaid Cymru posed no threat
of comparable credibility to the SNP's. In the October 1974 general election
it had won only three seats, all of them in Welsh-speaking Wales, and two of
them (Caernarvon and Merioneth) tiny and vulnerable to amalgamation in
any subsequent boundary review. English-speaking Welsh people turned out
to be suspicious of devolution as a device to promote the interests of a
'Welsh-speaking mafia'—a perception that contributed to the overwhelming
defeat of devolution there in the 1979 referendum.

But the territory where Wilson's statecraft caused most trouble was England. The newly created metropolitan county councils in the northern English
conurbations provided a ready-made network for English disquiet about the
proposals for Scotland (and Wales; but like most others, the metropolitan
county leaders regarded Wales as an inconsequential add-on). The campaign

---

[3] We ascribe the statecraft to Wilson, although he had retired in favour of Jim Callaghan by
the time the Scotland and Wales Bill was finally introduced.

originated in 1975, in Tyne and Wear County Council. This council covered the most urbanized part of the north-east of England, with about half its population. By local networking, the council persuaded the other north-eastern counties of Northumberland, Durham, and Cleveland to join the campaign, and later added Merseyside and South Yorkshire to the list.

Some civil servants and academics shared the councillors' unease. Bevan Waide, an economist who led the public sector North Region Strategy Team, published a report drawing attention to the differentials in public spending per head between the northern region and Scotland. The former was equally deprived, but received substantially less public spending per head (NRST 1976). After leaving the UK civil service, Waide explained:

The Department of the Environment—indeed all Departments of Central Government—were, needless to say, extremely sceptical about the utility of this approach, and saw Ministers as vulnerable to awkward Parliamentary questions; it was not easy to get them to agree to publish.... (E. B. Waide to D. McConaghy, 22.6.1978; quoted by kind permission of the recipient)

Ministers responded by saying that there was no demand for either an English parliament or a set of English regional assemblies. In a poorly received (Griffith 1976; Senior 1977) white paper *Devolution: The English Dimension* (Office of the Lord President of the Council 1976), the government stated:

Some people have ... proposed a series of regional assemblies for England. But ... setting up regional assemblies with legislative powers would mean that the legislative framework for such matters as education, health, local government and land use would be largely determined at regional level, leading to possibly marked differences over short differences.... The Government therefore rule out from further consideration not only the creation of an English Assembly but also a series of regional assemblies with legislative powers. (Office of the Lord President of the Council 1976: para. 20)

But if every reference to English regions in that passage is replaced by a reference to Scotland and Wales, the argument against Scottish and Welsh legislative assemblies is equally compelling. The Government was therefore committed to asymmetric devolution, although it did envisage regional development agencies whose annual reports to Parliament would be '[n]o doubt ... carefully scrutinised by Members representing other parts of the United Kingdom' (para. 37).

Though intellectually weak, this white paper was therefore in a sense perceptive. Any concession to English regions would generate distributive, zero-sum, spatial politics. But so did the refusal to make any concession to them. After the publication of the white paper, the northern counties' Labour leaders lobbied their local MPs to oppose the Bill. Harold Wilson made a rare post-retirement speech in the Commons debate acknowledging genuine fears and anxieties in the English regions . . . especially in some of the hardest-hit regions such as the North-West, the Northern region, Yorkshire, the south-west and others . . . that the powers available under decentralisation for Scotland and Wales will give those two countries an unfair advantage. . . . [T]he English regions cannot be totally ignored. (*Hansard* 5s. v. 922 cols. 1010-11, 13.12.1976)

Indeed they could not—but only because the Government lacked an overall majority of seats. Elected in October 1974 with a wafer-thin majority over all other parties, it had by now lost it through defections and by-election defeats. Therefore it was vulnerable to any opposition coalition, including (for the first time since 1885) a territorial coalition from within its own ranks. The Scotland and Wales Bill was defeated on a guillotine motion in February 1977. The rebels were coordinated from northern England but also included Scottish and Welsh Labour MPs hostile to devolution. As with Mrs Thatcher and the poll tax thirteen years later, the self-proclaimed 'flagship' policy of the Government had sunk.

The Government responded to the failure of its Welsh statecraft by splitting the bill, reintroducing it as two separate bills, one each for Scotland and Wales. As they may have calculated, this might involve sacrificing Welsh devolution (which did not matter for Unionist statecraft) in order to save Scottish (which did). Further revolts imposed two hostile amendments on both bills. The first insisted that each assembly would be activated only if ratified by a popular majority in a referendum. The second was the 'Cunningham amendment', moved by an expatriate Scot, George Cunningham, who sat for a London seat. This required that a 'Yes' vote in such a referendum was not to bind the Government to create the assembly unless it comprised more than 40 per cent of the territory's *electorate*: a majority of those voting would not suffice if it did not meet the Cunningham threshold.

The bills were enacted (as the Scotland and Wales Acts 1978). But the first of these amendments killed Welsh devolution. As already noted, the 1979 referendum led to a 4–1 defeat of devolution. Apparently, the outgoing government had totally misread Welsh opinion in offering devolution there. The Cunningham amendment killed Scottish devolution. In one perspective it was outrageous. Only in 1931 has the winning party in a UK election ever secured the votes of more than 40 per cent of the electorate.[4] The Cunningham amendment applied to devolution a criterion that Government had never applied to itself. But in another perspective it was brilliant statecraft. In the Scottish referendum in 1979, devolution was just approved, by a margin of 52–48 per cent. But the 52 per cent of votes for 'Yes' comprised only 33 per cent of the Scottish electorate. The Conservatives

---

[4] In 1951, the Labour Party secured the votes of more than 40 per cent of the electorate. But it lost the election, because the Conservatives won more seats on fewer votes.

moved a vote of no confidence. The SNP 'turkeys voting for Christmas' (Butler and Kavanagh 1980: 125) had to support the no-confidence motion, although it was common knowledge that their support in Scotland was slumping. Because Labour had no overall majority, any minority group could bargain for pork. But in the end Callaghan's frantic search for votes failed by one. The 1979 general election was called; Mrs Thatcher and her Conservatives won. She immediately repealed the 1978 Act. There were no riots in the streets of Edinburgh. Devolution went into cold storage. Harold Wilson's party had lost the election, but his statecraft had, for the time being, saved the Union.

But at the cost of arousing the English dog from its sleep. After the guillotine defeat of February 1977, the Government realized that it had to placate the northern English regions. Some of its moves were short term and now seem quaint. Jim Callaghan's immediate responses to the Geordie revolt were two. First, he brought the newly elected US President Jimmy Carter to Newcastle, where in a well-coached (but alas hopelessly inaccurate) Geordie accent Carter welcomed the crowds with the Geordie greeting *Ha'way the lads!* Second, Callaghan directed the nationalized electricity generator, the CEGB, to buy a turbo-generator set for a power station it said it did not need (Drax B in Yorkshire) from a supplier it had not planned to use (Reyrolle Parsons in Newcastle).

There were longer-term consequences though. They were the Treasury Needs Assessment; the Barnett Formula; and the first airing of the arguments for English regional government.

In 1978, the Treasury started to calculate the relative 'needs' of England, Scotland, and Wales for the services that would have been devolved under the Scotland and Wales Acts. There had long been a Treasury perception that Scotland and Northern Ireland were overgenerously funded (for Northern Ireland see Bogdanor 1999: ch. 3; Mitchell 2004). In Scotland, Treasury officials had long believed, along with 'all Departments other than the Scottish Office and all MPs other than Scottish ones that the Scots had been getting away with financial murder', in the words of a Scottish Office civil servant in charge of devolution policy at the time (Ross 1985). The Needs Assessment was produced with the very reluctant cooperation of the territorial departments. It was reportedly very hard to reach inter-departmental agreement even on the very meagre published results, which are summarized in Table 7.1.

If (and it is a big if) the numbers in Table 7.1 are reliable, then in 1976–7 Scotland and Northern Ireland were receiving public expenditure in excess of their 'needs' for the services that would have been devolved under the 1978 Act. The Goschen Proportion, devised in 1888 (Chapter 10), certainly played a part here. The Goschen Proportion was 11:80. Over time, as Scotland's

TABLE 7.1. *HM Treasury 'Needs' Assessment 1979 (data for 1976–1977)*

	England	Scotland	Wales	Northern Ireland
Needs	100	116	109	131
Spending per head	100	122	106	135

Source: HM Treasury (1979).

relative population declined, the 11:80 ratio of public spending between Scotland and the rest of Great Britain came to exceed Scotland's share of population by more and more, and hence any tranche of public spending that was divided up in the Goschen Proportions gave Scotland a bigger and bigger advantage, per head, as time went on (Table 7.2). By 1971, the last Census year before Barnett, this advantage had reached 28.2 per cent. The Secretary of State for Scotland could always demand at least the Goschen share of any spending that came up for discussion, and sometimes more (Mitchell 2003: ch. 8; Levitt 1999).

Wales, however, was receiving less than her 'needs' so defined. That is consistent with the relative threat potential of the three territories. Scotland had had devolved institutions and a seat at Cabinet since 1885. Ireland had had a seat (or two) at Cabinet from 1800 till 1921, and Northern Ireland had had devolved institutions since its start in 1920. Although there was at the

TABLE 7.2. *Relative populations of England & Wales and Scotland, Censuses 1881–1971 (Population, '000s)*

Census	England and Wales	Scotland	Scotland (England & Wales=80)	Value of Goschen grants per head in Scotland (England=100)
1881	25,974	3,736	11.51	95.59
1891	29,003	4,026	11.11	99.05
1901	32,528	4,472	11.00	100.01
1911	36,070	4,761	10.56	104.17
1921	37,887	4,882	10.31	106.71
1931	39,952	4,843	9.70	113.43
1939	41,460	5,007	9.66	113.86
1951	43,758	5,096	9.32	118.07
1961	46,105	5,179	8.99	122.41
1971	48,750	5,229	8.58	128.19

Note: 1939 mid-year estimate.
Source: *British Historical Statistics*, Mitchell (1988).

time no Secretary of State for Northern Ireland, there were established relationships of a colonial sort between the Treasury and finance officials in Northern Ireland, in which the colonial masters complained furiously at the colonists' fecklessness and monetary demands, and then paid them (Mitchell 2004). Wales on the other hand had had a Secretary of State only since 1964. The aftermath of the Aberfan disaster, between 1967 and 1970, had cruelly revealed that the Welsh Office was at the bottom of the Whitehall pecking order. More powerful departments—in the Aberfan case, the Ministry of Power—trampled over it (McLean and Johnes 2000).

Northern Ireland could threaten secession and bloodshed. Scotland could threaten secession, although it could not plausibly threaten bloodshed. Wales threatened a little civil disorder, when language campaigners took direct action, extending to burning down the holiday cottages of English-speaking incomers. But even this, violent though it was, affected only a small part of Wales and a few cottages. Wales posed much the least credible threat to the Union. And it got the least money in relation to its needs. Hence the relativities of the Needs Assessment.

But the most enduring result of Harold Wilson's failed English statecraft was the Barnett Formula. In the dying days of the Callaghan Government, Chief Secretary to the Treasury Joel Barnett approved a formula drafted by his officials that aimed to redress what they saw as overspending in Scotland. The Barnett Formula was designed to do two main things. In the short run it was designed to replace bargaining one programme at a time by a single annual bargain, in order to reduce the opportunity for the Scots to use the Goschen Proportion as a floor (never a ceiling) every time they negotiated a block of spending. In the long run it was designed to bring about convergence. The details are too technical to go into here (see Bell and Christie 2001; McLean and McMillan 2003a). The important thing to understand is that, if allowed to run unhindered by political interference, the Barnett Formula would have brought public spending in all four territories to converge on equal spending per head. It was applied from 1978 to Scotland and Wales, and from about 1980 to Northern Ireland as well.

Thus if applied mechanically, Barnett would have undershot. According to the Needs Assessment, all three territories had higher needs for public spending per head on devolved services than England. A formula that eliminated their per-head advantages would have brought Scotland and Northern Ireland down to their 'needs'. But then it would have sailed past those needs heading downwards, until it brought each of them to a level of spending parity, but needs disparity, with England. As to Wales, if the Treasury numbers in Table 7.1 were correct, then Barnett should never have been applied there. Spending in Wales was already below 'needs'. A formula that led it to converge on equal per-head spending with England would be taking Wales further away from, not closer to, her needs (McLean and McMillan 2003a).

All of this refinement was lost outside the tiny Barnett policy community after 1979. Its revival in 1997 belongs later in our story. The 1979 general election seemed to confirm that it was the UK's oil, and that the UK would continue united.

The Big Chill and the Small Thaw, 1979–97

One of Mrs Thatcher's Cabinet colleagues described her as 'the most Unionist politician in Downing Street since the war' (Young 1990: 465). He was referring to Northern Ireland (see earlier) but the point is general. Under Wilson and Callaghan, the entire Scottish political class had been gearing up for devolution. The defeat of the referendum under the Cunningham amendment, followed immediately and consequentially by the change of government, left them poleaxed. It is eloquent testimony to the non-salience of devolution that nothing happened. Devolution was a dog that didn't bark in Scotland for ten years more, and in Wales for fifteen.

Not only did Mrs Thatcher snatch away Scotland's devolution, but she did so without ever having a majority of seats in Scotland, nor did her successor John Major. The Conservatives' position in Scotland and Wales in their four UK general election victories under Thatcher and Major is shown in Table 7.3.

Table 7.3 shows that in both Scotland and Wales, the Conservatives did less well than in England. In all the Conservative governments, the Conservative seat majority depended on England alone. Never were they the largest party in Scotland or in Wales. That might have been expected to give rise to huge 'West Lothian' complaints in Scotland and Wales. When he raised the West Lothian Question in 1977, Tam Dalyell used it to

TABLE 7.3. *Conservative votes and seats, Scotland and Wales, 1979–1992*

	1979		1983		1987		1992	
	Vote share%	Seats	Vote share%	Seats	Vote share%	Seats	Vote share%	Seats
Scotland	31.4	22	28.4	21	24.1	10	25.7	11
Wales	32.2	11	31.0	14	29.6	8	28.6	6
England	47.2	306	46.0	362	46.3	358	45.5	319
UK	43.9	339	42.4	397	42.3	376	41.9	336

Source: Butler and Kavanagh (1980, 1984, 1992).

complain that under devolution he as a Scottish MP would be able to vote on conditions in England but not in Scotland. English Conservatives retorted that, in 1977, the Scots could determine policy in England, when their party was in a minority of seats there. In the 1980s that situation was reversed. The English majority party could impose policy on Scotland and Wales. But the surprise was that political and constitutional protest was quite muted. It did not get under way until 1989 in Scotland and later than that in Wales.

It may also have resulted from killing Home Rule by kindness. That ancient Unionist technique was revived under the Thatcher and Major Conservative Governments. The most skilled mercy killers were the last two Conservative Secretaries of State for Scotland (Ian Lang and Michael Forsyth) and the second Conservative Secretary of State for Wales (Peter Walker). Their ideology differed widely—in contemporary terminology Walker was a 'wet' and the two Scots were 'dry'—Forsyth being of Chilean desert levels of desiccation. But their policy was identical. To contain the separatist threat in their territory, they had to kill Home Rule by kindness. Walker did this in the obvious way—by showering Wales with public spending and big projects. The two Scots did so more subtly, by quiet bypasses of the Barnett Formula to ensure that Scotland did not after all start to converge on the English level of public spending per head. Forsyth also used a louder but more dangerous tactic. In 1992 Lang initiated a statistical series, which still continues, called *Government Expenditure and Revenue in Scotland.* In his memoirs (Lang 2002: 183), Lang states that it was explicitly intended to show how much more public expenditure Scotland received per head than England, and that government expenditure in Scotland substantially exceeded government revenue raised in Scotland, and would do so even if North Sea Oil taxation receipts were wholly assigned to Scotland. Chancellor Norman Lamont objected to its publication, according to Lang, on the grounds that it 'would create resentment and demands for higher expenditure in other parts of the country', but Prime Minister Major backed Lang on Unionist grounds. Major's side of the story (Major 1999: 419) implies that he was less gung-ho than Lang in this Unionist strategy. Its aim, expressed fairly quietly by Lang and more stridently by Forsyth, was to persuade Scots that they got a very good deal out of the Union and the Barnett Formula, and that they would lose heavily from devolution, and still more from independence. The risk was that their numbers might be noticed in England, and bring about the very fate they were trying to avoid. Lang, indeed, boasted that he was saving Barnett when it might be truer to say that he was waiving Barnett. He demanded extra money bypassing Barnett whenever he could claim that the Union was in danger from a nationalist resurgence. He makes this explicit in his memoirs (Lang 2002: 194). He was playing the Tom Johnston gambit.

But these subtle moves were overshadowed by the Poll Tax. In Scotland there was a revaluation of properties for rating purposes in 1984. Governments always hate periodic property revaluations. The owners of properties that have become relatively more valuable lose from the re-rating, and complain volubly. Gainers from the re-rating keep quiet. For this reason, the Conservatives had avoided any revaluation in England. Allegedly, Mrs Thatcher's first local government secretary Michael Heseltine had told her in 1979, 'We've got this problem' of rating revaluation; to which she replied 'There's no problem. We're not doing it' (Butler et al. 1994: 61). In Scotland, the losers tended to be rich houseowners, who were disproportionately likely to be Conservatives. The protests echoed through Scottish Conservative associations, which persuaded Mrs Thatcher that she must get rid of the rates.

Accordingly, the Poll Tax was piloted in Scotland a year ahead of England. The Scottish bill was introduced in 1986 and enacted ahead of the 1987 general election, in which all the Scottish Conservatives who had promoted it lost their seats. This should perhaps have been a warning but was not. Nobody attributed their losses to the Poll Tax (Butler and Kavanagh 1988: 89–113). Throughout Britain in the 1987 general election, Labour was extremely quiet about the Poll Tax. Its leader, Neil Kinnock, had just noisily expelled the hard left of the militant tendency from the party, and the party desperately wished to avoid being seen as the patron of 'loony left councils'. But as the extent of the Poll Tax disaster for the Conservatives unrolled during 1988, so did their legitimacy in Scotland. The poll tax had been enacted by a party holding twenty-one of Scotland's seventy-two seats, but after the general election it had been reduced to ten (Table 7.3). At long last, this revived the constitutional issue of devolution.

Labour's return to devolution was therefore home-grown and rationally explicable. In the 1974 Dalintober Street coup, the Labour Party in London had had to override an anti-devolution Labour Party in Scotland to force devolution on it—a manoeuvre made possible only by the un-devolved structure of the Labour Party. In 1988, by contrast, the Labour Party in Scotland helped promote a Claim of Right for Scotland, followed by a Constitutional Convention. The Claim of Right intoned:

We, gathered as the Scottish Constitutional Convention, do hereby acknowledge the sovereign right of the Scottish people to determine the form of Government best suited to their needs, and do hereby declare and pledge that in all our actions and deliberations their interests shall be paramount.

Labour worked together with the Liberal Democrats, the churches, trade unions, and other civil society bodies on the Constitutional Convention. The Scottish Nationalists hesitated but stayed outside. The Conservatives stayed out without hesitation. The Constitutional Convention's final report in 1995 recommended a 129-seat parliament elected by an additional member system of proportional representation (AMS). It would have a power to vary the UK rate of income tax up or down by 3p in the pound. Public finance should continue to be governed by the Barnett Formula. All of these provisions went into the Labour manifesto and, almost unaltered, into the Scotland Act 1998, so that they now govern the Scottish Parliament.

Wales was different. There, the heirs of Nye Bevan, including for a while Neil Kinnock, repeated the Bevanite argument that devolution imperilled socialism—an argument endorsed by future Chancellor Gordon Brown in his doctoral thesis. Welsh Labour was deeply divided, so that its leader, Ron Davies, wrote a painful compromise for the 1997 Labour manifesto, which offered powers over secondary but not primary legislation to the proposed Welsh Assembly. On the cultural front, however, things moved faster in Wales than in Scotland. Ellisian rural politics could only gain Plaid Cymru, at maximum, the six seats in Welsh-speaking Wales. Only once, in 1979, when the failing Callaghan Government had lost its majority, were Plaid Cymru able to force a concession from it (namely, giving the slate quarrymen of Bethesda and Blaenau Ffestiniog the same rights to silicosis compensation as the coal miners of Gwaun cae Curwen and Tredegar). And that was in the same year that the Welsh Assembly crashed to defeat in a referendum. In that referendum, the antis made effective use of the complaint that devolution would privilege a Welsh-speaking elite, who they alleged would monopolize public-sector jobs and force children in Newport to waste time learning Welsh at school. Though the *Yes* campaign used the Lloyd George trick of saying in their Welsh-language literature that devolution would protect the language while denying in their English-language literature that it would (Ellis 1979), the 'Welsh mafia' objection was probably decisive.

But things changed between 1979 and 1997. UK politicians realized that language concessions in Wales were what the economists call cheap talk. They did not cost much to implement, and most of the costs could be spread thinly around the rest of the UK. The most costly innovation by far has been Welsh-language television. S4C (Sianel Pedwar Cymru) has been a great political, as well as broadcasting, success. It increased the visibility of the language, gave non-Welsh-speakers for the first time an attractive incentive to learn it—and most of the costs were absorbed by the 95 per cent of UK licence payers and consumers of advertising who are not in Wales. Likewise, the Welsh Language Act 1993 proved to be successful cheap talk. And the inclusion of Welsh in the national curriculum, although it causes problems in recruiting primary school teachers, was an enormous step in safeguarding the future of the language. The language, so explosive (sometimes literally) in the years up to 1979, had ceased to be an issue by 1997.

The Last Unionists—Enoch Powell and John Major

Enoch Powell was the last English primordial Unionist, and it was fitting that he ended his Commons career as the MP for North Down in Northern Ireland. His extraordinary career is well known. Born in Birmingham, he emigrated to Australia to be Professor of Greek at Sydney in his twenties. In 1939 he resigned to volunteer for the British Army as a private. He ended the war as a brigadier—one of only two people in the British Army to achieve that feat between 1939 and 1945. His last job in the army was to prepare for the post-war defence of India, which he assumed would remain the jewel in the imperial crown. He entered Conservative politics on demobilization in the hope that he could work his way up to Viceroy of India (Heffer 1998: 99). Indian independence in 1947 ended that phase of romantic imperialism, but Powell found another. Elected MP (Cons.) for Wolverhampton SW in 1950, he became a specialist on imperial and constitutional affairs. From 1951 he began his attack on the British Nationality Act 1948, which had become 'that most evil statute' (although Powell had not said so in 1948, when he worked on the subject at Conservative Central Office). The 1948 Act had created the status of 'citizen of the United Kingdom and Colonies' in response to a Canadian statute that had defined Canadian citizenship (Hansen 2000). To Powell this was to 'make a differentiation in the eyes of the law between two categories of British subjects' (Heffer 1998: 173), destroying his Diceyan view of the British Empire as a world-wide collection of subjects of the King, governed by the King-in-Parliament. (Slight problem here: Canada is a sovereign state entitled to make its own laws.) Powell's Diceyan imperialism did not reach wider attention until 1968.

Powell will be forever remembered for the speech that led the Conservative leader Edward Heath to dismiss him from the front bench. Speaking to the Conservative Political Centre in Birmingham on 20 April 1968, Powell opened by saying that 'The supreme function of statesmanship is to provide against preventable evils'. He went on to quote a constituent who had told Powell that he and his family planned to emigrate because

in this country in fifteen or twenty years time the black man will have the whip hand over the white man'. I can already hear the chorus of execration. How dare I say such a horrible thing? How dare I stir up trouble and inflame feelings by repeating such a conversation? . . . I do not have the right not to do so.

Powell stated that his constituent was voicing the sentiments of 'thousands and hundreds of thousands' of others about the 'areas that are already undergoing the total transformation to which there is no parallel in a thousand years of English history'. He went on to quote another story, purporting to come from a correspondent in Northumberland describing a friend of hers in Wolverhampton.

Eight years ago in a respectable street in Wolverhampton a house was sold to a Negro. Now only one white (a woman old-age pensioner) lives there. This is her story. She lost her husband and both her sons in the war. So she turned her seven-roomed house, her only asset, into a boarding-house. She worked hard and did well, paid off her mortgage and began to put something by for her old age. Then the immigrants moved in. With growing fear, she saw one house after another taken over. The quiet street became a place of noise and confusion. Regretfully, her white tenants moved out.

The day after the last one left, she was awakened at seven a.m. by two Negroes who wanted to use her phone to contact their employer. When she refused, as she would have refused any stranger at such an hour, she was abused and feared she would have been attacked but for the chain on her door. . . .

She is becoming afraid to go out. Windows are broken. She finds excreta pushed through her letter-box. When she goes to the shops, she is followed by children, charming, wide-grinning piccaninnies. They cannot speak English, but one word they know. 'Racialist', they chant. When the new Race Relations bill is passed, this woman is convinced she will go to prison. . . .

As I look ahead, I am filled with foreboding. Like the Roman, I seem to see 'the River Tiber foaming with much blood'. The tragic and intractable phenomenon which we watch with horror on the other side of the Atlantic but which is there interwoven with the history and existence of the States itself, is coming upon us here by our own volition and our own neglect. (Powell 1991: 373–9)

Afterwards, Powell expressed regret that he had not checked the quotation from Virgil which he translated as 'the River Tiber foaming with much blood', nor given it in Latin (*Et Thybrim multo spumantem sanguine cerno*; Virgil, *Aeneid,* vi: 87). 'I can't find the Roman', he told his friend John Biffen shortly afterwards, and was agitated to find that Virgil attributes the words to the Sybil, a prophet, and not to a Roman (Shepherd 1996: 359–60). Despite diligent research by the *Wolverhampton Express & Star* and others, nobody has ever located the landlady (or the grinning piccaninnies).

The two parts of Powell's imperialism were inconsistent. If the British Empire was, as Palmerston had said back in 1850, one where any subject was equally entitled to the protection of the Queen, that should be equally true whether that subject of the Queen lived in Bombay or Bilston. But like Joseph Chamberlain before him (on whom he wrote a very revealing book— Powell 1977), Powell could not accept that the rest of the Empire and Commonwealth comprised independent states who would take their own decisions on citizenship and immigration. Once they started to do so, it was an inevitable concomitant of Powell's Palmerstonian conception of British subjecthood that British subjects should use their unfettered right to enter the UK. The Conservatives fettered it in 1961 and 1962, but this risked leaving British subjects stateless, as duly happened when the governments of Kenya and Uganda expelled thousands of their Indian fellow-citizens in 1967–8.

Powell's imperialism was thus incoherent. What about his Diceyan attitude to Parliament? He expressed it most powerfully in his opposition to UK membership of the EU. He opposed the European Communities bill 1972 fundamentally and bitterly:

For this House, lacking the necessary authority either out-of-doors or indoors, legislatively to give away the independence and sovereignty of this House now and for the future is an unthinkable act.... The very stones of this place would cry out against us if we dared such a thing. (*Hansard* 5s v. 831: 707, 17.02.1972)

In what was widely seen as an encouragement to vote Labour in February 1974, he described Prime Minister Edward Heath as

the first Prime Minister in 300 years who entertained, let alone executed, the intention of depriving parliament of its sole right to make the laws and impose the taxes of the country and who then, without either electoral or parliamentary authority, took it upon himself to commit this country to economic and monetary unification with eight other nations of western Europe. (at Mecca Dance Hall, Birmingham, 23.2.1974, quoted by Heffer 1998: 706)

Elsewhere, we have calculated that Powell was decisive in swinging the 1970 general election to the Conservatives—and, possibly, the February 1974 general election to Labour (McLean 2001a: Appendix to ch. 5). Both triumphs were disasters for Powell. The Heath Conservative Government enacted the European Communities Bill, and the UK joined the EU in 1973. The Wilson Labour Government failed to take the UK out. It was itself divided, and Wilson put the matter to a referendum, where in 1975 the people voted by 2–1 to stay in the EU.

In its time, Powell's constitutional objection to EU membership was overshadowed by other objections. Since then, it has become the bedrock of Euroscepticism. The Single European Act 1986 provided for extension of the single market by qualified majority decision on the Council of Ministers. Member states might pay lip service to the single market while seeking to protect their special interests. The UK was no exception. The Merchant Shipping Act 1988 purported to prevent non-British fishing companies from acquiring British fishing quotas. In a series of cases bearing the common name *Factortame*, a Spanish fishery company of that name overturned the law by persuading both the British and the European courts that the 1988 Act violated the 1972 Act as amended in 1986.

To any Diceyan, *Factortame* was the end. Under Diceyan doctrine, Parliament may do anything except bind its successor. But here the UK courts were holding that an earlier law trumped a later one, thus fundamentally denying parliamentary sovereignty. The surrender was voluntary, said Lord Bridge in the Law Lords' judgment:

Thus, whatever limitation of its sovereignty Parliament accepted when it enacted the European Communities Act 1972 was entirely voluntary. Under the terms of the Act of 1972 it has always been clear that it was the duty of a United Kingdom court, when delivering final judgment., to override any rule of national law found to be in conflict with any directly enforceable rule of Community law. Similarly, when decisions of the Court of Justice have exposed areas of United Kingdom statute law which failed to implement Council directives, Parliament has always loyally accepted the obligation to make appropriate and prompt amendments. (*R.* v. *Transport Secretary ex p. Factortame (No. 2)* 1991 1 A.C. 603–83 at 659)

But this is both the end of Diceyanism and a signal that Diceyans have nowhere to go. The UK could indeed legislate to leave the EU and (although the EU might not want to let it go) such legislation would de facto be effective. But that is not practical politics because no large party supports it, although quite a lot of the British public do. This marks out not only Powell's personal failure but the intellectual failure of Diceyanism. In its pure form it denies that constitutional legislation exists. *Parliament may do anything except bind its successor.* But that grand negation sweeps up the Acts of Union 1707 and 1800, the Parliament Act 1911, the Government of Ireland Acts 1914 and 1920, the Ireland Act 1949, and the European Communities Act 1972 as fully as any other Act—they can have no entrenched status, they are nothing special. And yet Diceyans themselves, when it suits them, wish to argue that some Acts are fundamental constitutional legislation. Unionists say this about the 1707 Act and until 1921 they said it about the 1800 Act. At the deepest level Diceyan doctrine is inconsistent, as Dicey himself showed by his behaviour between 1911 and 1914. It is somehow typical of Enoch Powell that he should be the only consistent follower of a radically incoherent doctrine.

John Major succeeded Mrs Thatcher as Conservative leader and Prime Minister after her fall on Thanksgiving Day 1990. In 1992 he won an unexpected general election victory that featured a slight Conservative rally in Scotland (Table 7.3). Nevertheless, his government was plunged into a crisis that began with the ejection of the pound from the European Monetary System in September 1992 and ended with the landslide defeat of the Conservatives in the 1997 general election. The ejection of the pound destroyed the Conservatives' reputation for economic competence. It was actually rather good for the UK economy but that did the Conservatives no good. In the face of polls suggesting that they were doomed to lose, factions of Conservatism turned on one another. The most persistent were the Eurosceptics who rallied, twenty years late, to Powell's cry that membership of the European Union was destroying British sovereignty. The Eurosceptics had expected Major to be their man, as had the increasingly Eurosceptic Mrs Thatcher when she let it be known that she preferred him to his rivals in 1990. They were bitterly disappointed in him. Internecine war in the party forced him to offer himself for re-election as party leader in 1995. He won, but did not silence the Eurosceptics, whose continued hostility to government policy helped to bring about the electoral catastrophe of 1997.

It was nevertheless natural for Major to parade his instinctive unionism. Borrowing from Orwell, he said in 1992 that

Fifty years on from now, Britain will still be the country of long shadows on county grounds, warm beer, invincible green suburbs, dog lovers and old maids bicycling to Holy Communion through the morning mist. (*http://www.number-10.gov.uk/output/page125.asp*)

The statement was much mocked but it has several interesting features. It recalls Stanley Baldwin as much as it does Orwell. Like Baldwin, Major was attempting to spin a myth—but how much did each of these Conservative Prime Ministers know that it was a myth? It is possible to know that few people attend county cricket matches, that only the CAMRA (Campaign for Real Ale) generation now in their forties and upward still prefer warm beer to chilled lager, that not many old maids (or anybody else) bike to Holy Communion nowadays—and yet still regard these as 'the essential' England. That is recognizably what many current popular authors on England and the English do (Bryson 1995; Paxman 1998; Jenkins 1999, 2003).

Essential England, but not essential UK. None of these symbols resonates in Wales, Scotland, or Northern Ireland. The Church of England and county cricket feature in none of the three; warm beer never caught on in Ulster or Scotland (although Brain's Dark ensured that it did in Wales). Like Powell, (and indeed Baldwin, Kipling, and Orwell), when Major reached for symbols of UK unionism, he found symbols of English unionism (mostly southern English at that—from the parts of England where the Unionists have always won most votes and seats). Jenkins' 1,000 greatest houses and 1,000 greatest churches have a similar southern slant.

Major's fight with the Eurosceptics cut him off from another ground of Powellite Unionism. Any prime minister who wishes the UK to remain in the EU—even if only to extend the single market and benefit from free trade within the union—must forswear Dicey, and Powell. The remaining ground for unionism was therefore defence of the United Kingdom against devolution. Mrs Thatcher had simply ignored it; Major went on the attack. In the Conservatives' 1997 Scottish manifesto, Major wrote that the election

will be the 290th anniversary—to the exact day—of the implementation of the Act of union which created Great Britain and from which so many benefits have derived for both Scotland and England. It would be a tragedy if the votes cast on that anniversary were to undermine and eventually destroy our Union and the stability and prosperity it guarantees....

Nearer home, the menace of separatism—introduced through the Trojan Horse of devolution—would blight the lives of Scots for generations to come. The failure of the Labour and Liberal Democrat parties to answer the West Lothian Question after twenty years and the prospect of Scottish MPs being excluded from English and Welsh legislation are chilling portents of disintegration. (Major 1997)

The paragraph on the West Lothian Question is puzzling, as the most plausible answer to it is precisely to exclude Scottish MPs from English and Welsh legislation, as Gladstone had briefly proposed in 1893 and as Major's successor William Hague was to propose in 1999.

The 1997 election was unionism's last stand. In choosing to make a stand on unionism, Major was influenced by the Conservatives' gain in Scotland against the UK trend in 1992 (Major 1999: ch. 18). His fervent cries to save the Union in 1992 and 1997 were driven, he says, by many things including the fear that a UK without Scotland would lose its entitlement to a permanent seat in the UN Security Council (Major 1999: 415). However, in the 1997 general election the Conservatives lost every single one of their eleven seats in Scotland, and every one of their eight seats in Wales. They had held no Ulster seats since the rift with the Unionists in 1972 (Chapter 6). In the 1997 Parliament, the Conservatives were an England-only party.[5] They have retreated to the territory of warm beer and county grounds.

Meanwhile, however, the Conservatives do hold seats proportionate to their vote share in the Scottish Parliament and the National Assembly for Wales. Donald Dewar, the promoter of the Scotland Act 1998, described Labour's grant of proportional representation (PR) to the Scottish Parliament as 'a great act of charity' (D. Dewar, speech to British Academy conference, Edinburgh, 1997) on the grounds that it would deprive Labour of what would otherwise be a certain majority. If so, it was charity with a soupçon of self-interest. For Dewar had not forgotten 1974. If PR deprived Labour of an overall majority in the Scottish Parliament, it also deprived the SNP of one. It was Dewar's way of saving the Union—very different from John Major's. And so diluted in its consequences that it is hard to call it unionism at all. For devolution sets in train a set of consequences that may not destroy the Union as Tam Dalyell feared, but will certainly change it utterly. One of these consequences is that in Scotland and Wales the Conservatives now have a stake in the PR Parliaments whose creation their leaders up to Major opposed so bitterly. We turn more generally to these consequences in the final section of this book.

---

[5] In 2001, they regained one seat in Scotland. They still hold none in Wales or Northern Ireland.

8

The Union since 1961—Mass Attitudes

Men make their own history, but they do not make it just as they please; they do not make it under circumstances chosen by themselves, but under circumstances directly encountered, given and transmitted from the past.

(K. Marx, *The 18th Brumaire of Louis Bonaparte,* 2nd para.)

Introduction: Kilbrandon and Scotland's Oil

This chapter analyses the bases for support for devolution in Scotland and Wales in the 1970s and since. As it was events in the mid-1970s that set the path that devolution subsequently followed, we focus most closely on that period. Did devolution emerge as a consequence of changing attitudes, or changing party alignments? How much was support for devolution a proxy for other (temporary?) political attitudes such as disillusionment with the main parties? Was support for SNP a result of its stand on independence, or a more general shift away from Labour and Conservative parties? Was there a significant difference between attitudes in England and those in Scotland and Wales with regard to regional self-government? The circumstances of devolution today are, as Marx realized, circumstances directly encountered, given, and transmitted from the past.

The issue of Scottish devolution leapt to prominence when the SNP snatched the safest Labour seat in Scotland in the Hamilton by-election of November 1967 (Chapter 7). It was part of Prime Minister Harold Wilson's statecraft to send difficult issues such as devolution and trade union reform to a stately Royal Commission with a distant reporting date. His response to Hamilton was to appoint the Crowther (later Kilbrandon) Royal Commission on the Constitution, which was constituted in 1969 and reported in 1973. It commissioned research on attitudes to devolution (OPCS/SCPR 1973), which we reanalyse in this chapter. Kilbrandon's research, which was conducted in 1970, remains the only Great Britain-wide survey whose samples were big enough in each region of England, as well as in Scotland and Wales, to compare attitudes to devolution across each of them. They turned out to be remarkably uniform (Table 8.1).

Table 8.1 shows that Scotland was, as predicted, the region where the demand for self-determination was highest, but it was closely followed by East Anglia and the south of England. However, the East Anglia National Party and the Southern Separatist Party failed to materialize. Albeit within a narrow range, demand for self-determination was lowest in Wales and in south-west England.

The conclusions of this attitude survey did not deflect Lord Kilbrandon (a Scottish judge), nor Lord Crowther-Hunt (a member of the Kilbrandon Commission who was Wilson's constitutional adviser during the preparation of the Scotland and Wales Bills in 1974–7). Although there was no evidence that demand for devolution was higher in Scotland than elsewhere, and some evidence that it was weaker in Wales than elsewhere, the Royal Commission majority proposed a legislative assembly for Scotland to deal with matters that would be transferred from Westminster under a devolution statute that specified the transferred powers and reserved all others to Westminster.

When Kilbrandon reported, the SNP was rising fast again, because it had discovered its most effective slogan ever: 'It's Scotland's Oil ...'. Oil was discovered in marketable quantities in the North Sea in the 1960s, but not until just after the 1970 general election did it emerge as a potent political issue (Chapter 7). The SNP won a by-election in 'safe Labour' Govan within a week of Kilbrandon reporting.

Table 8.2 gives the time series for vote intention and actual votes in Scotland from the 1966 to the October 1974 general elections.

In the February 1974 general election, the SNP won 22 per cent of the Scottish vote. The electoral system had protected Labour by giving the SNP only 10 per cent of the Scottish seats for this 22 per cent of the vote, but if the SNP vote share were to rise to somewhere between 30 and 35 per cent, the system would flip from punishing the SNP to rewarding it—*and politicians knew that*. The plurality electoral system treats concentrated and dispersed parties differently. Small concentrated parties—as the SNP was in 1970, and as Plaid Cymru and all the Northern Ireland parties have always been—can achieve their population share of seats or more, because their votes are efficiently distributed to win seats in just the few places where they are strong. So the SNP won the Western Isles in 1970, and Plaid Cymru has held at least one of the half-dozen Welsh-speaking seats since 1966. Large concentrated parties, such as Labour in 1983 and the Conservatives in 1906 and 1997, when each remained strong in its heartlands but lost badly in the rest of the country, win a smaller share of seats than of votes.

TABLE 8.1. *Attitudes to devolution, regions of Great Britain, 1970*

	England	Wales	Scotland	North	Yorkshire	North-west	West Midlands	South-west	East Midlands	East Anglia	South-east	Greater London	South	Total (unweighted)
Leave as they are	14.0	15.2	6.5	10.7	15.8	8.5	14.7	20.6	12.2	16.6	13.7	16.4	10.9	12.9
Keep things much the same but more govt understanding	24.1	27.1	20.2	26.4	23.3	19.2	23.0	28.2	22.6	24.3	28.6	24.4	23.1	23.8
Keep the present system but more regional decisions	24.0	21.1	26.1	25.8	23.5	30.0	26.1	19.6	26.2	17.2	20.6	23.6	19.9	23.9
Have a new system of governing the region	20.2	23.4	24.2	20.1	20.0	23.7	17.7	17.2	21.3	21.3	20.0	18.8	25.0	21.4
Let the region take over complete responsibility	16.1	12.9	22.1	15.7	16.0	15.4	17.1	12.4	17.7	20.1	15.8	14.3	20.5	16.7
Do not know	1.6	0.3	0.9	1.3	1.4	3.1	1.4	1.9		0.6	1.3	2.4	0.6	1.3
Total	100	100	100	100	100	100	100	100	100	100	100	100	100	100
n	3058	697	815	154	478	409	459	196	150	158	436	460	144	4569

Source: Kilbrandon (1973) survey.

TABLE 8.2. *Vote and vote intention (adjusted to exclude*
'Don't know/Didn't vote'), Scotland, 1966–1974

	SNP	Lab	Cons	Lib	Other
(%)					
General election 1966	5.0	49.9	37.7	6.8	6.0
NOP, November 1967	24.0	41.0	25.0	9.0	1.0
MIS, for BBC, May 1968	43.0	22.0	30.0	4.0	1.0
NOP, January 1969	20.9	39.3	33.5	5.7	0.6
Gallup, March 1970	12.5	37.5	43.0	6.5	0.5
General election 1970	11.4	44.5	38.0	5.5	0.6
General election Feb 1974	21.9	36.6	32.9	8.0	0.7
MORI, August 1974	25.2	41.4	26.1	6.9	0.4
BES, October 1974	28.2	38.2	25.4	7.9	0.4
General election Oct 1974	30.4	36.3	24.7	8.3	0.3
General election 1979	17.3	41.5	31.4	9.0	0.1

Source: Kellas (1971: 455); Bennie et al. (1997: 50, Table 3.2).

With dispersed parties, the effects are opposite. A small dispersed party, such as the Green Party, will win no seats at all. When it was a small party within Scotland, neither did the SNP. But as it became large, dispersal would turn from a curse to a blessing. With an evenly distributed 35 per cent of the vote, it could win more than half of the seats in Scotland as Labour did in most elections. Were it to do so, it would start to negotiate for Scottish independence. Through the year 1974, Labour's national elite focused on retaining the party's capacity to govern the UK. This entailed changing its policy from the welfare-state unionism it had espoused for forty years (Chapter 7) to welcoming devolution.

After thirty years, participants' memories are clouding. James Callaghan (1987: 503), who as prime minister commanded Labour's devolution flag-ship, misremembers that devolution was in the February 1974 Labour mani-festo, as a response to Kilbrandon. It was not. It is important to trace the sequence accurately, as it turns out to depend crucially on polls conducted in the summer of 1974. Only after the February 1974 election led to a Labour minority government did the party move. Shirley Williams had been asked to prepare a rival prospectus to Kilbrandon (Ziegler 1993: 451). According to Wilson (1979: 48) she led an ad hoc subcommittee of the NEC, which provided much of the draft for the White Paper that launched the Scotland and Wales Bill. Idi Amin, the dictator of Uganda, came out in favour: 'I call upon you seriously to consider granting freedom and full independence to Scotland, Wales and Northern Ireland, whose people have repeatedly demanded . . . their respective eagerness and wishes to become independent of London' (Ziegler 1993: 452, from Wilson papers, 11.10.1974). Roy Jenkins 'broke in angrily to protest that it would be insanity to break up the United Kingdom for the sake of a few extra seats at a general election' (Ziegler 1993: 452). Ziegler (1993: 453) suggests that Wilson thought that devolution was necessary to bring government nearer to Scots, appeasing moderate opinion whilst maintaining the unity of the UK in the aftermath of the February 1974 general election. With Labour and Conservatives evenly matched in terms of seats, the Liberal, Ulster Unionist, and nationalist parties held the balance of power. Harold Wilson's decision to use the Queen's Speech to announce that the Government would consider devolution proposals and the publication of a White Paper in September 1974 came without any prior manifesto commitment. According to Rose (1982: 189–90), the Labour devolution pledge was a panicky response to the threat to Labour posed by the SNP, sparked by an unpublished MORI poll that was interpreted (possibly mistakenly) as showing strong support for a devolution pledge. By revisiting this MORI poll (courtesy of MORI and the UK Data-Archive (Worcester and Gosschalk 1977)) we can examine the extent to which the Labour response was a correct reading of national attitudes, and how it compared with other assessments of opinion regarding devolution carried out at the same time.

The Labour Party MORI poll was carried out in August 1974, interviewing 976 people using a quota sample in 36 Scottish constituencies. Amongst those who expressed a vote preference, 41.4 per cent said they would vote Labour, compared to 25.2 per cent SNP, 26.1 per cent Conservative, and 6.9 per cent Liberal. This suggested a swing since February away from the Conservatives, and towards Labour and the SNP. However, rumours at the time suggested that poll evidence showed the Labour party under threat. Bob Worcester of MORI is reported as claiming that, if the Labour Party did not change its policy on devolution, the party would lose up to thirteen seats (Keating and Bleiman 1979: 165).[1]

Looking again at the August 1974 MORI survey, it is not clear how attitudes to devolution relate to changing patterns of party support. Whilst it does ascertain respondents' views on devolution, and their party preferences if a general election were held immediately, there is no question regarding their vote in February 1974, or in earlier elections. At a first glance, the evidence for strong support for devolution seems sparse. Without prompting, only 6.9 per cent of respondents mentioned the creation of a

---

[1] Keating also reports Bob Worcester making 'a clandestine trip to Glasgow in the summer, posing as a visiting American sociologist', in order to gauge feeling within the Scottish Labour Party. Keating is sceptical about the information gleaned from this trip, although impressed by the consumption of beer and sandwiches. 'Unfortunately... the sample consisted of those who were on the telephone, lacked prior engagements and were interested in talking to American sociologists, and was dominated by academics with English accents' (Keating and Bleiman 1979: 208 fn. 28).

Scottish Parliament/Assembly as the most important issue, behind inflation (33.1 per cent), unemployment (17.3 per cent), and North Sea Oil (8.9 per cent), and just ahead of strikes (6.6 per cent), balance of payments (5.9 per cent), and housing (5.0 per cent). Of those who mentioned a Scottish Parliament/Assembly as the most important issue, 60 per cent were SNP supporters, the remainder split between Conservative and Labour.

According to Rose, Labour concern was sparked by a question presenting three options for Scottish constitutional reform:

q. 11c. . . . would you personally like to see . . .
A completely independent Scottish Parliament separate from England (20.8 per cent)
A Scottish Assembly part of Britain but with substantial powers (58.1 per cent)
No change from the present system (17.2 per cent)
Don't know (3.7 per cent)

But as Rose notes, the evidence illustrated by this response is 'ambiguous', since the question of 'substantial' powers is highly subjective (Rose 1982: 189). The question itself was asked as a follow-up to one presenting more detailed options:

q. 11a. For running Scotland as a whole which of these alternatives would you prefer, overall?
Leave things as they are at present (10.3 per cent)
Keep things much the same as they are now but make sure the needs of Scotland are better understood by the Government (17.2 per cent)
Keep the present system but allow more decisions to be made in Scotland (26.6 per cent)
Have a new system of governing Scotland so that as many decisions as possible are made in the area (21.7 per cent)
Let Scotland take over complete responsibility for running things in Scotland (21.1 per cent)
Don't know (2.7 per cent)

Asking the question in this way indicates support for the status quo plus tinkering (the first three options) stands at 54.1 per cent. Support for a devolved assembly with substantial powers (option 4) came from only 21.7 per cent of the respondents. Looking at the 58.1 per cent of respondents who answered q. 11c in favour of a Scottish Assembly, and comparing their views on the more detailed option listed in q. 11a, shows just under a third (32.6 per cent) associating a Scottish Assembly with option 4, a new system of government, and 6.9 per cent associating it with a completely independent assembly. The majority, however, saw a Scottish Assembly as a means of allowing more decisions to be made in Scotland (36.6 per cent) or ensuring the needs of Scotland were better understood (20.2 per cent), whilst maintaining the present system. Tables 8.3–8.7 present our reanalysis of that fateful poll.

TABLE 8.3. *Constitutional preference by vote intention, Scotland, 1974*

	Vote next general election?				Definite	Unsure
	Con (%)	Lab (%)	Lib (%)	SNP (%)	Lab (%)	Lab (%)
No change	7.5	18.7	7.7	2.5	19.6	14.5
More understanding	24.1	21.5	17.3	6.4	22.5	16.4
More decisions	38.2	27.6	25.0	10.4	28.0	25.5
New system	23.1	19.0	34.6	20.8	18.5	21.8
Scottish independence	7.1	13.2	15.4	59.9	11.4	21.8
No change	18.4	28.0	16.7	1.5	30.0	18.2
Scottish Assembly	74.9	59.7	68.5	41.5	58.1	67.3
Complete independence	6.8	12.3	14.8	57.1	11.9	14.5
n=792						

Source: MORI.

TABLE 8.4a. *Second preference by vote intention, Scotland, 1974*

	Vote at a general election				Definite	Unsure
	Con	Lab	Lib	SNP	Lab (%)	Lab (%)
Con	—	3.0	16.1	12.6	2.2	6.8
Lab	1.4	—	19.6	25.2	—	—
Lib	28.6	10.7	—	24.8	11.8	5.1
SNP	26.3	33.1	23.2	—	28.3	55.9
Other/none	43.7	53.3	41.1	37.4	57.7	32.2

TABLE 8.4b. *'Mainly a protest vote?' (SNP 1st and 2nd preference voters only)*

	Vote SNP (%)	2nd preference SNP (%)
Disagree	62.6	38.4
Agree	26.7	46.5
Other	10.7	15.2

Source: MORI.

Table 8.3 shows attitudes expressed regarding constitutional reform in Scotland, broken down by party support. Labour supporters are the most widely dispersed across the range of options. Although a majority of Labour supporters favoured a Scottish Assembly, they also had the highest proportion in favour of no change. The SNP vote was clearly skewed towards the independence option, and both the Conservative and Liberal supporters clustered around the range of options offering more Scottish autonomy

TABLE 8.5. *Perceptions of party positions, Scotland, 1974*

q. 11b And which of these alternatives comes closest to xxx party policy on Scotland?

| | Lab position | | Con position | | Lib position | | SNP position | |
	All	Lab voters	All	Con voters	All	Lib voters	All	SNP voters
No change	19.3	13.3	26.8	12.7	7.4	5.4	0.2	—
More understanding	18.6	21.9	17.7	28.6	10.0	10.7	0.5	—
More decisions	19.9	23.4	14.1	26.3	12.3	16.1	0.9	1.0
New system	12.3	18.3	10.2	16.0	17.5	35.7	2.7	5.3
Scottish independence	2.3	3.8	0.9	1.9	4.1	7.1	76.3	84.5
Don't know	27.6	19.2	30.3	14.6	48.8	25.0	19.4	9.2
n=813								

Source: MORI.

TABLE 8.6. *Mechanics of devolution, Scotland, 1974*

| | Scots Assembly if fewer MPs | | | Scots Assembly if no SoS | | |
	Yes	No	Don't know	Yes	No	Don't know
Completely independent (%)	63.5	21.7	14.8	56.2	29.6	14.3
Scottish Assembly (%)	49.3	33.8	16.9	33.3	53.2	13.6
No change (%)	21.4	57.1	21.4	13.7	66.1	20.2
All (%)	47.4	35.4	17.3	34.7	50.4	14.9
n=939						

Source: MORI.

with an Assembly. Respondents who expressed a preference over the party they were likely to vote for at the next general election were also asked if they had definitely made up their mind; 80 per cent of respondents said they had, with the Labour vote appearing solid (82.5 per cent definite). The right-hand side of Table 8.3 distinguishes between those Labour supporters who said they had definitely made up their minds, and those who were unsure. Whilst the Labour core support appears to be slightly more likely to be against change, and those who are unsure slightly more likely to favour Scottish independence or an Assembly, the differences are not significant when measured using a chi-squared statistic.

In order to examine the solidity of the Labour and SNP votes, respondents' second preferences were examined (q. 7 If you were not to vote for *xxx* how would you vote instead?). Table 8.4a shows (reading across) that the SNP was favourite recipient party of other parties' second preferences, although a substantial proportion of both Labour and Conservative supporters declared their support to be non-transferable. Reading down, it shows, as might be expected, that unsure Labour supporters were much more likely to award a second preference to the SNP than were definite Labour supporters. Voters whose first or second preference was for the SNP were asked whether an SNP vote was mainly a protest vote. Table 8.4b shows that the two categories diverged sharply. Modally, firm SNP supporters denied that it was a protest vote, while second preference SNP supporters believed that it was.

Table 8.5 shows that respondents were unclear about the parties' constitutional position, with one glaring exception. They were overwhelmingly convinced that the SNP stood for independence. However, their beliefs as to the constitutional position of Labour and Conservatives were evenly spread. This was not surprising, as both parties' constitutional positions had recently changed and were internally controversial.

Table 8.6 shows what each group of constitutional choosers would think about a Scottish Assembly if the number of Scottish MPs at Westminster were to be cut, and/or if the post of Secretary of State for Scotland were abolished. The results have to be treated with caution. It was a hypothetical question about remote constitutional matters generating a high proportion of 'Don't knows'. But it was probably the crucial question in the survey for political reasons. Labour politicians—according to Dalyell (1977: 106–7) they included John Smith—had warned the Scots that they could not have devolution and expect to retain their overrepresentation (McLean 1995) in the shape of seventy-one seats in the House of Commons, in addition to a Secretary of State for Scotland remaining in the Cabinet. Respondents cared more about keeping a Secretary of State than about keeping seventy-one MPs. Probably the crucial number in Table 8.6 is that 53.2 per cent of those favouring a Scottish Assembly would no longer favour it if the post of Secretary of State were abolished. Within days of these findings, the Dalintober Street 'compromise', as Keating and Bleiman (1979: 167) quaintly call it, was to set in stone the pattern of devolution that we now have. Labour's national executive 'compromised' by offering the Assembly, that one side wanted, and retaining the seventy-one MPs and the Secretary of State, as the other side demanded.

'Rich Scots or Poor Britons' was one slogan of the SNP oil campaign. Almost as important as the results of Table 8.6 are those of Table 8.7.

Table 8.7 shows that Labour supporters were less likely to display a 'unionist' attitude towards the distribution of government spending and North Sea oil revenue than the population at large. The Labour profile to each of these three questions lies in between the SNP profile and that of Liberal and Conservative supporters, but clearly Labour and SNP voters form one cluster and Conservative and Liberal voters form another. The first cluster believed strongly that 'profits from North Sea Oil should be kept for

TABLE 8.7. *Attitudes to North Sea oil by party preference, Scotland, 1974*

	Con	Lab	Lib	SNP	All
Profits from North Sea oil should be kept for the benefit of the Scottish people					
Disagree	42.7	19.8	32.1	12.1	24.7
Agree	45.5	71.9	51.8	83.5	66.5
Other/n.a.	11.7	8.3	16.1	4.4	8.7
Profits from North Sea oil should be used to help the less prosperous regions in the United Kingdom					
Disagree	27.7	35.8	26.8	44.7	35.3
Agree	54.5	45.9	62.5	43.2	48.6
Other/n.a.	17.8	18.3	10.7	12.1	16.1
Scotland gets less than its fair share of economic help from the British government					
Disagree	17.4	12.1	14.3	6.3	12.2
Agree	68.5	75.4	69.6	87.4	76.3
Other/n.a.	14.1	12.4	16.1	6.3	11.6
$n=813$					

Source: MORI.

the benefit of the Scottish people' and that 'Scotland gets less than its fair share of economic help from the British government'. The responses to Table 8.7 confirmed how terribly dangerous the SNP oil campaign was to Labour. Labour promoted its own oil policy (viz. to take a majority stake in North Sea oil) with the magnificently ambiguous slogan *Make Sure It's Your Oil, Vote Labour*. The almost complete segregation of the Scottish and UK media helped. Very few Scottish readers saw papers originating in England—the English broadsheets had trivial circulations in Scotland, and the mass-market papers all had Scottish editions. Because the Borders are thinly populated, almost nobody in Scotland picked up English broadcasts. BBC broadcasts all emanated from BBC Scotland. As to ITV, there was a very small broadcaster called Border TV, which covered the Scottish Borders, Carlisle, and the Lake District.[2] Butler and Kavanagh (1975: 131) suggest that *Make Sure It's Your Oil, Vote Labour* was only used in Scotland. A Labour party election broadcast in October 1974, screened only in Scotland,

---

[2] One of us (IM), then a lecturer in the University of Newcastle, was called in by Border to help with their February 1974 general election coverage. He came in straight from a walk over the Lakeland fells, and therefore had no clothes suitable for a pundit. He was fetched from Keswick Bus Station by Border's (singular) car and offered Border's (singular) jacket and tie to wear in the studio.

repeatedly described the proposed Scottish Assembly as a 'Parliament . . . primed by North Sea Oil so that the benefits of oil go to the ordinary working people of Scotland'—somewhat more than was offered by the party's manifesto published in London. (Miller 1980: 20)[3]

A few bemused viewers in Carlisle and Keswick may have realized what Labour was up to; almost nobody else outside Scotland did.

The MORI poll from August 1974 does not give a clear picture of the changing pattern of party support in Scotland, since it only records their political preference at one point in time. More academically useful, although less politically important at the time, is the British Election Study, which was carried out in the aftermath of the October poll. The survey included a special booster survey in Scotland, interviewing 1,178 people (69 per cent of the 1,704 targeted), and asking them a similar range of questions touching on devolution and political attitudes to the MORI poll, but including questions on voting behaviour in 1970 and the two 1974 election. This poll, therefore, allows a more accurate picture of the changing nature of party affiliation in Scotland over this period.

Table 8.8 shows the distribution of party support for each of the three general elections in the early 1970s, as recalled by Scots after the October 1974 election. The figures show a slightly lower recall of voting for the SNP in 1970 than their actual vote share (which was 11.4 per cent, see Table 8.1). However, the general shift shown in the responses is roughly in line with what actually happened, showing the SNP steadily gaining; the Labour party losing support between 1970 and February 1974, but holding its vote share between February and October; and the Liberals gaining very slightly between the first and second general elections in the period.

In order to examine how people recorded their changing party votes over the period, the pattern of vote switching/retention is examined in Table 8.9. The two matrices in Table 8.9 show how party supporters in the 1974 elections had voted in the previous general election, illustrating the inflow of party support from one election to the next. The top row shows that 85.6 per cent of those who said that they voted Conservative in February 1974 said that they voted Conservative in 1970; that 1.5 per cent of those who said that they voted Conservative in February 1974 said that they voted Labour

---

[3] The quotations from the PEB are from the transcript. The October 1974 Labour national manifesto promised only to 'set up new development agencies in Scotland and in Wales, financed by the United Kingdom Exchequer, with extra funds to reflect the revenue from offshore oil. . . . The next Labour Government will create elected assemblies in Scotland and Wales.' The Conservative manifesto promise on oil revenue for Scotland was Downsianly identical: 'The Scottish people must enjoy more of the financial benefits from oil, and they must be given a far greater say over its operation in Scotland. We will, therefore, establish a Scottish Development Fund' (*The Times* 1974 quoted on pp. 303, 307, 320).

TABLE 8.8. *Party support over three elections; recall of vote from BES Scottish Cross-Section Sample, October 1974*

	SNP	Lab	Con	Lib	Other
(%)					
General election 1970	7.9	46.5	39.2	6.2	0.2
General election Feb 1974	20.3	39.2	31.9	8.1	0.5
General election Oct 1974	28.2	38.2	25.4	7.9	0.4

Source: BES Scottish Cross-Section Sample, October 1974.

in 1970; and so on. The figures suggest that both the Labour and Conservative parties were dependent on their core support, gaining few converts from other parties in each of the 1974 general elections. For the SNP, which gained the most votes over the period examined here, the table indicates that it gained most support in February 1974 from those who had not voted in 1970. It also managed to pull in support from those who had voted Labour in 1970 (22.6 per cent of its February 1974 support) and Conservatives (15.4 per cent). Between February and October 1974 the party gained support mainly from Conservative voters.

The questions in the British Election Study were similar,[4] but not identical to those asked in the earlier MORI poll. The pattern of responses shows a similar enthusiasm for some constitutional change that would reflect Scottish concerns. The proportion of people favouring the status quo (8.0 per cent of those who expressed a view) and Scottish independence (21.3 per cent) was very similar to the earlier study. This left a large proportion who wanted better understanding from the London government (26.2 per cent) or more decisions to be made in Scotland (44.5 per cent). Asked if they were in favour of a Scottish Assembly, 82.3 per cent of respondents with an opinion were either very much or somewhat in favour. Again, whilst the concept of a Scottish Assembly undoubtedly had very different implications for respondents, it had an extremely high level of support.

---

[4] v080. There has been a lot of discussion recently about giving more power to Scotland. Which of the statements on this card comes closest to what you yourself feel should be done?

  1. Keep the governing of Scotland as it is now.
  2. Make sure the needs of Scotland are better understood by the Government in London.
  3. Allow more decisions to be made in Scotland.
  4. Scotland should completely run its own affairs.

v085. People have different views about the need for a separate Scottish Assembly. How about you? Which of the views on this card comes closest to what you yourself feel? Are you:

  1. Very much in favour of a separate Scottish Assembly
  2. Somewhat in favour of a separate Scottish Assembly
  3. Somewhat against a separate Scottish Assembly
  4. Very much against a separate Scottish Assembly

The relationship between partisanship and preferences for Scottish constitutional reform is shown in Table 8.10. This compares the constitutional preferences of those who supported Labour for each of the three elections, the core Labour vote, and who said that they switched from either Labour supporting or another option to voting for SNP in either February or October 1974.

Table 8.10 shows that all those who switched to supporting the SNP favoured some form of constitutional change, but not all of them were in favour of the most extreme option of Scotland running its own affairs. Of those who switched from Labour to SNP between 1970 and February 1974,

TABLE 8.9. *Inflows of vote for 1970/Feb 1974 and Feb/Oct 1974*

		Vote 1970				
		Con	Lab	Lib	SNP	Non-vote/NR*
	Con	85.6	1.5	1.2	1.2	10.4
Vote Feb	Lab	5.2	83.0	0.7	1.2	9.7
1974 (%)	Lib	16.9	18.1	43.4	3.6	18.1
	SNP	15.4	22.6	5.3	27.9	28.8
	Non-vote NR	9.4	18.1	1.9	1.9	68.8

		Vote Feb 1974				
		Con	Lab	Lib	SNP	Non-vote/NR*
	Con	90.6	2.0	2.7	0.4	4.3
Vote Oct	Lab	1.6	85.9	1.3	4.2	7.0
1974 (%)	Lib	19.0	2.5	59.5	6.3	12.7
	SNP	15.5	11.0	6.7	59.0	7.8
	Non-vote NR	16.9	18.6	2.8	10.7	50.8

* Non-vote/NR indicates those who said that they did not vote, did not respond to the question, could not recall how they voted, or voted for a party other than the four parties listed here.
Source: British Election Study.

TABLE 8.10. *Constitutional preference by party preference, Scotland, 1974*

	Labour constant	Lab to SNP for Feb 1974	Other to SNP for Feb 1974	Lab to SNP for Oct 1974	Other to SNP for Oct 1974	Rest
Keep much as now	12.0	—	—	—	—	9.6
Better understood	32.4	10.0	10.7	20.0	15.6	28.9
More decisions	39.1	50.0	41.7	32.0	46.9	47.2
Run own affairs	16.4	40.0	47.6	48.0	37.5	14.3
n	225	40	84	25	64	509

Source: British Election Study.

60 per cent were in favour of one of the more moderate options, whereas, of the smaller number who switched between February and October 1974, 52 per cent were in favour of the more moderate options. Whilst any conclusions based on such small numbers (only sixty-five respondents in all) have to be extremely tentative, it does support the view that the Labour commitment to constitutional reform may have had some influence in reducing the number of people who switched to the SNP in October 1974. Whether the Labour party would have lost thirteen seats without its commitment to devolution is hard to say. Miller (1980), using the recall and perception data from the 1974 BES (our Tables 8.8 and 8.10), estimates that Labour would have lost fifteen seats had it not moved (in Scotland only) closer to the SNP position than did the Conservatives. However, his method necessarily involves heroic extrapolation and his estimate cannot be robust.

Change Over Time in Scotland

Table 8.11 gives a time series for constitutional options in Scotland, drawn from six surveys conducted between 1970 and 1979. Inevitably, differences in question wording cloud interpretation, but the overall picture is clear, especially if the first pair, and the second pair, of options are grouped. The second pair have to be grouped because option 4 was not always asked, and the pattern of response when it was not suggests that its supporters then defaulted to option 3 and not to option 5. The first pair should also be grouped as 'Keep things much the same but more govt understanding' is constitutionally no different from 'leave as they are'. (Indeed, given option 2, it is hard to understand why any attentive respondent chose option 1. People who wanted less government understanding, presumably.) Support for the status quo varies only from a low of 26.7 per cent in 1970 to a high of around 34 per cent in October 1974 and 1979. Support for independence is in the remarkably narrow range from 21.0 per cent (1979) to 24.1 per cent (1975). It thus varies much less than does support for the SNP (Table 8.2). By subtraction, support for intermediate options is also very stable.

Table 8.11 shows that the Conservatives were on safe ground when they abandoned their support for Scottish devolution in 1975. As related in Chapter 7 they had been the first of the major parties to swing toward devolution, with their Declaration of Perth in 1968. However, the accession of Margaret Thatcher to the leadership in 1975 swung them back. An instinctive unionist, Mrs Thatcher took constitutional advice from the Oxford political scientist Nevil Johnson. Johnson, a believer in the Diceyan sovereignty of Parliament, was bitterly opposed to the Labour Government's devolution plans (Thatcher 1995: 324; Johnson 1980, 2004). Abandoning the

Declaration of Perth, as Mrs Thatcher did in 1975, fitted her own constitutional instincts. The Conservatives' private pollster, ORC, provided her with evidence that it did not put their vote at risk (see Table 8.11, col. 5).

There is a long-standing belief that Scots are more left-wing than English people, and that Scottish support for devolution has been linked with that. To be sure, devolution attracted some left-wing Scots because it held the promise that they could develop more left-wing—or at any rate more statist—policies than their counterparts in England, as has happened since 1997.

For two decades Professor William Miller and associates have been studying the hypothesis that the Scots are more left-wing than the English. They have never found any evidence for it. Their most recent evidence comes from massive paired samples of the British ($n = 2060$) and Scottish ($n = 1255$) people in 1996. The samples overlapped—255 of the Scots were also in the British sample (Miller et al. 1997: 371, 464–6). Table 8.12 shows the differences between social attitudes in Scotland and in Britain.

It is very interesting that the only issue on which Scottish opinion is to the left of British by as many as 10 points out of 200 is 'sympathy for the socially disadvantaged'. That is a core theme of Scotland's second-greatest thinker, Adam Smith, in his *Theory of Moral Sentiments* (1759), whose key concept is 'sympathy'. Most Scots have not read Adam Smith. But they have read his popularizer Robert Burns, the last stanza of whose 'To a Louse' summarizes Smith in two lines: *O wad some Pow'r the giftie gie us/To see oursels as ithers see us!*

This is not to deny that there was a big shift in Scottish opinion between 1979, when the majority in favour of devolution was too small for it to be enacted, and 1997, when both the Parliament and its tax-raising powers were

TABLE 8.11. *Time series of support for constitutional options, Scotland, 1970–1979*

	Kilbrandon Survey (1970)	BES Feb 1974	MORI Aug 1974	BES Oct 1974	ORC Dec 1975	SES May 1979
Leave as they are	6.5	7.8	10.3	8.0	10.5	7.9
Keep things much the same but more govt understanding	20.2	24.1	17.2	26.2	15.8	25.8
Keep the present system but more regional decisions	26.1	46.6	26.6	44.5	27.1	43.9
Have a new system of governing the region	24.2	—	21.7	—	19.0	—
Let the region take over complete responsibility	22.1	21.6	21.1	21.3	24.1	21.0
Do not know	0.9	0.0	2.7	0.0	3.4	1.4
n	815	232	946	947	1,276	961

TABLE 8.12. *Differences between Scottish and British political attitudes*

Subject	Average British score	Average Scottish score	Difference
Liberty	−25	−25	0
Equality	55	61	+6
Respect for authority	39	39	0
Respect for traditional values	37	39	+2
Wealth creation	53	58	+5
Tolerance	3	2	−1
Limited government	1	1	0
Right to speak out	35	34	−1
Right to protest and rebel	31	35	+4
Self-reliance	13	9	−4
Economic equality	46	53	+7
Caring	79	84	+5
Equal rights	40	45	+5
Protection	53	52	−1
Right to know	87	90	+3
Sympathy for socially disadvantaged	18	28	+10

Source: Adapted from Miller et al. (1996), Tables 11.1 and 11.2. The scores summarize answers to a large number of attitude questions (for question wording see Miller et al. 1996: 480–98). A positive value means support for the property shown. The range of possible scores is from −100 to +100.

approved by comfortable majorities. But it is wrong to read that shift as reflecting something fundamental about Scottish culture or attitudes.

And to a Lesser Extent Wales

It has ever been the fate of Wales to be tacked on to other people's devolution plans, usually with the condescending phrase 'and to a lesser extent Wales' popping up in the description. The majority report of the Kilbrandon committee proposed an elected assembly for Wales: 'some members would give it legislative functions and others deliberative and advisory functions'. The minority report by Lord Crowther-Hunt and Alan Peacock proposed seven 'Assemblies and Governments' of equal standing, one each for Scotland, Wales, and five regions of England (Cmnd 5460, para. 1217; Cmnd 5460-I, para. 16).

Table 8.13 gives the only time series we have been able to construct for constitutional preference in Wales. Typically for its 'lesser extent' status, far fewer opinion surveys were conducted there than in Scotland, so unfortunately we are unable to track the dramatic move in opinion that occurred between February 1974 and 1979.

TABLE 8.13. *Constitutional preferences in Wales, 1970–1979*

Kilbrandon Survey (1970)		BES Feb 1974		WES May 1979	
For running... (Name region) as a whole, which of these five alternatives would you prefer overall?		There has been a lot of discussion recently about giving more power to Wales. Which of the statements on this card comes closest to what you yourself feel should be done?		Ideal form of government for Wales should be	
Leave as they are	15.2	Keep the Governing of Wales much as it is now	23.7	No change	71.4
Keep things much the same but more govt understanding	27.1	Make sure the needs of Wales are better understood by the Government in London	33.6		
Keep the present system but more regional decisions	21.1	Allow more decisions to be made in Wales	27.5	Proposed Assembly	7.1
Have a new system of governing the region	23.4			Stronger Assembly	11.7
Let the region take over complete responsibility	12.9	Wales should completely run its own affairs	9.9	Complete self-government	5.0
Do not know	0.3	Do not know	5.3	Do not know	4.8
n	697		131		858

Source: Kilbrandon Survey, OPCS/SCPR 1974; BES Feb 1974; Alt et al. 1976; WES May 1979; Balsom et al. (1981).

As already noted, Wales began the 1970s with one of the lowest levels of nationalist support of any GB region. Despite the existence of Plaid Cymru ('Party of Wales'), the Kilbrandon cross-section found fewer separatists in Wales than in East Anglia or southern England. By February 1974 devolution is more popular, although the level of support for 'Wales should completely run its own affairs' is less than half that for Scotland, and the status quo support is double the Scottish level. The 1979 survey was taken after the devolution scheme in the Wales Act 1978 had been rejected by a 4–1 margin in the referendum of March 1979. 'No change' then got, at 71.4 per cent, more than double the share of the vote that it ever got, in any territory of Great Britain, in any year of the decade.

The absence of surveys between 1974 and 1979 robs us of detail but not of the big picture. Many accounts confirm that Wales was divided politically and socially between the rural, chapel-going, Welsh-speaking north and west and the rest of Wales (e.g., Madgwick et al. 1973; Philip 1975). The Plaid Cymru vote was concentrated heavily in the former, which accounts for only about 20 per cent of the population of Wales. It has always been more a cultural nationalist party, and less a party of economic grievance, than the SNP. Accordingly, the very features of Welsh devolution that appealed most to its Welsh-speaking supporters appealed least to its non-Welsh-speaking opponents. Both saw it as an institution that would preserve (privilege) the language and culture of north Wales. In 1979, the 'Yes' campaigners' Welsh-language publicity stated that a 'Yes' vote would protect the special status of the language. Its English-language publicity denied that it would give Welsh speakers any special status (Ellis 1979). Unfortunately for the 'Yes' campaign, the former perception leaked into anglophone Wales.

According to the Kilbrandon Survey in Wales, there was some association between attitudes towards constitutional change and those respondents who spoke Welsh. This was particularly apparent when Welsh speakers were divided into fluent and non-fluent speakers (Table 8.14a). Fluent Welsh speakers were more likely to favour a new system of regional government or the option of letting government take over complete responsibility. The Welsh Election Survey of 1979, which included 242 Welsh-speaking respondents (out of a total of 858, or 28.2 per cent), also showed a distinction in attitudes towards devolution between Welsh speakers and other respondents (Table 8.14b). In this survey there was little difference between the attitudes of fluent and non-fluent Welsh speakers. Welsh speakers were more likely to favour the reform options than non-Welsh speakers. Whilst over half of the Welsh speakers in the sample (55.8 per cent) lived in the 'North-West and West' region of Wales, no distinctive regional effect on attitudes towards devolution is evident from the survey data. However, the linguistic basis of Plaid Cymru is clear. Table 8.15 shows that Plaid Cymru gained almost all its support from Welsh-speaking respondents (who comprised 80 per cent of the total number of supporters). As Table 8.16 shows, the Plaid Cymru supporters were the subset of all Welsh speakers with very strong pro-devolution views.

The Rebirth of Devolution

The story of the rebirth of devolution is told elsewhere in this book. Was it driven by public opinion, or did the elites drive it? Much earlier in this book

TABLE 8.14a. *Language and attitudes to devolution in Wales, 1970*

	Do you speak Welsh		
	Fluently (%)	A little (%)	Not at all (%)
Leave as they are	10.9	18.3	15.7
Keep things much the same but more govt understanding	19.2	27.9	29.7
Keep the present system but more regional decisions	21.2	19.2	21.3
Have a new system of governing the region	30.8	23.1	21.1
Let the region take over complete responsibility	17.3	10.6	12.1
	100	100	100
n	156	104	464

Source: Kilbrandon Survey, OPCS/SCPR 1974.

TABLE 8.14b. *Language and attitudes to devolution in Wales, 1979*

	Do you speak Welsh (%)	
	Yes	No
No change	59.9	76.1
Proposed assembly	9.1	6.4
Stronger assembly	18.6	9.0
Complete self Government	7.0	4.1
Don't know	5.4	4.6
	100	100
n	242	614

chi sq. = 25.3**, 5 df

Source: WES 1979, Balsom and Madgwick 1981.

TABLE 8.15. *Language and vote in 1979 general election, Wales*

	Welsh speakers (%)	Non-Welsh speakers (%)
Conservative	22.9	36.3
Labour	51.9	53.3
Liberal	6.2	8.4
Plaid Cymru	19.0	1.9
	100	100
n	210	523

Source: WES (1979); Balsom and Madgwick (1981).

(Table 1.1 and Figure 1.1) we showed the time-series for the 'Moreno question', which asks people to choose between their local (English/Welsh/Scottish) identity and a British identity. That series shows that in Scotland a high and stable 60 per cent or more of respondents prefer one of the more Scottish self-descriptions to a neutral or more British one. In Wales, the

TABLE 8.16. *Vote and attitudes amongst Welsh speakers, 1979*

	Welsh speakers voting PC	Welsh speakers voting for other parties
No change	20.0	72.4
Proposed Assembly	12.5	8.2
Stronger Assembly	42.5	12.9
Complete self government	17.5	2.9
Don't know	7.5	3.5
	100	100
n	40	170

Source: WES (1979); Balsom and Madgwick (1981).

proportion choosing a more Welsh identity rose sharply (just) in time for, and after, the 1997 referendum and the creation of the National Assembly. In England, the proportion choosing 'English' rather than 'British' seems to be slowly rising, perhaps in reaction to devolution elsewhere in the UK, but it is not a majority choice (Figure 1.1).

This evidence postdates the rebirth of devolution among political elites, which can be dated back to the creation of the Scottish Constitutional Convention in 1989 (Chapter 7). Unfortunately, we cannot prove cause and effect. The first measurement of attitudes to the Moreno question was in 1992. At the previous general election in 1987, nobody had thought to ask the Moreno question, so we simply cannot say whether a popular ground-swell of devolutionism antedated the creation of the Convention. Our best guess is that there was a groundswell of grumpiness, as people in Scotland and Wales became aware that a government that they had not voted for introduced the highly unpopular Poll Tax. But, if public opinion in 1989 resembled that in the 1970s, it is unlikely that there was a strong demand for Scottish autonomy.

If the return of devolution to Scotland in 1989 was elite-led, it is fair to add that by 1997 the elites had the people with them. By the 1997 referendum campaign, a peak of 37 per cent of Scottish respondents wished to see Scotland independent from the UK. Most of those, however, voted for, not against, the offer of a devolved parliament (SNP fundamentalists were unable to convince many people to vote against the Scottish Parliament in the hope of getting Scottish independence later on). By the time of the first Scottish Parliament election in 1999, the Scots were more satisfied with what they had. Support for independence had dropped to 26 per cent, and over half (51 per cent) of respondents most preferred what they had got, namely a Scottish Parliament with tax-varying powers (Paterson et al. 2001: Table 6.1).

The place where opinion changed most between 1979 and 1999 was Wales. This went in two distinct steps, the first leading up to the referendum in 1997, and the second from there to the first National Assembly for Wales election in 1999. Whereas in 1979 support for a Welsh Assembly was highly localized to Welsh speakers and Plaid Cymru supporters (Tables 8.15 and 8.16), by 1997 it had spread to supporters of all parties except the Conservatives. The biggest movement was among Labour identifiers. In 1979, Labour was perceived as divided (because it was). In 1997, although there were still Labour antis, almost everybody in Wales perceived Labour, as well as Plaid Cymru, as favouring a 'Yes'; the Conservatives, again correctly, as favouring a 'No'; and they tended not to know where the Liberals stood (Wyn Jones and Trystan 1999, Table 4.3). This sufficed to bring the majority of Labour identifiers who voted into the 'Yes' camp (ibid.: Table 4.1), and hence to the knife-edge 'Yes' victory. Table 8.17 shows how, although fluent Welsh speakers were still the core of the 'Yes' vote, the 'Yes' camp, unlike in 1979, made significant inroads into the rest of the Welsh electorate. However, only the higher turnout of Welsh speakers than of non-Welsh speakers delivered a 'Yes' on the night.

The second step-change took place from 1997 to 1999, and it was probably concentrated in the immediate run-up to the first National Assembly election in 1999. As related above, Labour decided to introduce an Additional Member System of proportional representation in both Scotland and Wales. In Scotland, Donald Dewar's statecraft involved protecting the UK from an SNP majority in the Scottish Parliament—that could (can) only arrive if the SNP attain nearly 50 per cent of the vote. In Wales, Ron Davies' unacknowledged statecraft was probably to avoid a National Assembly with an overwhelming Labour majority in terms of seats, which might in itself have reduced the legitimacy of the National Assembly. However, Labour was so hegemonic in Wales that everybody expected it to control the National Assembly comfortably even with PR. In the event, there was a 'quiet

TABLE 8.17. *Language and attitudes to devolution in Wales, 1997*

	Welsh speaker		
	Fluent (%)	Non-fluent (%)	Not at all (%)
Yes	61	31	24
No	18	34	33
Did not vote	21	33	43
	100	100	100
n	111	83	485

Source: Welsh Referendum Study (1997), as reported in Wyn Jones and Trystan (1999: Table 4.11).

earthquake' that deprived Labour of an overall majority of seats. The results are at Table 11.2. More detailed analysis (Trystan et al. 2003) shows that Plaid Cymru benefited from differential turnout (like the 'Yes' side in the 1997 referendum). Trystan et al.'s logistic regression model, shown in simplified form in Table 8.18, reveals the social grounding of Welsh politics.

Table 8.18 shows that attitudes to constitutional futures and national identity were the best predictors of a vote for Plaid Cymru. Welsh speakers were less inclined to vote for any of the other parties than were non-Welsh speakers. Otherwise, the strongest predictors of vote for or against the two big UK parties were UK orientations, such as social class (significant only for Conservative voting) and attitudes to UK issues. As often, Liberal voters were harder to characterize, although the non-Welsh born were significantly more pro-Liberal than the Welsh-born.

In both Scotland and Wales, the second devolved assembly elections, in 2003, had a feel of a return to 'normal politics'. In Scotland, support for independence had dwindled from its peak of 37 per cent at the time of the referendum to 26 per cent, while support for the new status quo of a Scottish Parliament with taxing powers was the modal preference, at 48 per cent. In Wales, too, the status quo was the modal preference—41 per cent opting for an assembly without taxation or law-making powers. It was rather grumpy support. The blissful dawn of both assemblies had turned into grumbling; and most people by 2003 believed (once again) that the UK Government had more influence than the devolved assembly on how their country was governed. Most Scots and Welsh respondents thought that their assembly had made no difference to the quality of their government, although those who

TABLE 8.18. *Significant predictors of National Assembly vote by party, Wales, 1999*

	Lab	Con	Plaid	Lib Dem
Class		+ + +		
Born in Wales	+			− −
Constitutional preference		− − −	+ + +	− −
Welsh speaker	− − −	− − −	+ + +	−
Moreno identity scale			+ +	
Anti-(UK) govt views	− − −	+ + +	+ +	
Welsh issues			+ + +	
UK considerations	+ + +	+ +	−	

Key: + + +, − − −: $p < 0.01$
+ +, − −: $p < 0.05$
+, −: $p < 0.1$
Blank in cell: this variable is not a significant predictor of voting for or against this party.
For description of variables (where not obvious) and direction of coding, see source.
Source: Trystan et al. (2003: Table 4).

thought it had got better outnumbered those who thought it had got worse by about 20 percentage points (Curtice 2004, from Figures 9.6–9.8). In both countries, the nationalist parties fell back sharply in the 2003 elections (Tables 11.1 and 11.2).

Conclusion: Giving Them Devolution versus Giving Them More

We can now return to the questions posed at the start of this chapter. To answer them, we must return to the 1970s, when the present stance of the UK parties was set in stone, and the events that were to lead to devolution set in train, even though they then stalled for eighteen years.

Did devolution emerge as a consequence of changing attitudes, or changing party alignments? Attitudes to devolution did not change much in England or in Scotland between 1970 and 1979. In Wales, they became weakly more favourable and then strongly more hostile. Devolution did not emerge as a consequence of changing attitudes. It did emerge as a consequence of changing party alignments. Those changed in Scotland only, in the shape of a rise in SNP support at the expense mostly of the Conservatives but also of Labour. But they induced government proposals for devolution to both Scotland and Wales.

How much was support for devolution a proxy for other (temporary?) political attitudes (such as disillusionment with the main parties)? Was support for SNP a result of its stand on independence, or a more general shift away from Labour and Conservative Parties? In relation to Scotland and the SNP we can take these questions together. Our tables show that the answers are '*a proxy for other political attitudes*' and '*a more general shift away from Labour and Conservative Parties*'. That shift was fuelled by an increase in the demand not for independence, but for North Sea Oil proceeds. Labour and the Conservatives moved (the former in Scotland only) in a Downsian way towards the policy position of the SNP on this. Table 8.7 shows that such a move may have been necessary for Labour to save its position.

In relation to Plaid Cymru, and support for devolution in Wales we have limited survey evidence for this period (because of the small size of the 1979 Welsh sample) and must also rely on other sources (McLean 1976, 1977). All aggregate evidence suggests that support for devolution and for Plaid Cymru were very highly correlated with each other and with the ability to speak Welsh. Therefore, for Wales, support for devolution was a proxy for other (at root cultural) attitudes, and was not part of a more general shift away from the Labour or Conservative Parties. Plaid Cymru did score some by-election victories in anglophone Wales, which may have fitted the SNP pattern, but did not sustain those gains.

Was there a significant difference between attitudes in England and those in Scotland and Wales with regard to regional self-government? For Wales, see the previous paragraph. Between England and Scotland, the answer is 'No'. Although the only survey where the numbers for the English regions are large enough to be worth reporting in full is the Kilbrandon Survey (Table 8.1), Table 8.14 adds some suggestive details from the 1979 BES cross-section.

Table 8.19 reports the constitutional preferences for Scotland and Wales of the people of those territories, of England, and of the English regions that border on Scotland and Wales. The Northern Region of England was the only one to border Scotland.[5]

The West Midlands is the English region with the longest border with Wales. The cases differ sharply. Respondents in the Northern Region were distinctly hostile to Scottish devolution, unlike those in Scotland or in

TABLE 8.19. *Constitutional preferences in Britain, and selected regions, 1979*

q. 33 (M000122) After the recent referendum, opinion is still divided on whether or not to set up an elected assembly for Scotland. By an 'elected assembly' we mean a special parliament in Scotland for dealing with Scottish affairs. Which of the following statements comes closest to your view?

	England	Wales	Scotland	All	*Northern*
Complete independence	6.3	9.7	7.7	6.6	*5.0*
Elected Assembly	12.5	15.5	21.7	13.4	*10.0*
Find some other way	35.8	31.1	53.8	36.9	*25.8*
Keep government as has been	35.0	40.8	15.4	33.8	*53.3*
Don't know	10.4	2.9	1.4	9.3	*5.8*
	100	100	100	100	*100*
n	1619	103	143	1865	*120*

q. 34 (M000123) And next, thinking about Wales. Which of the following statements comes closest to your view about an elected assembly for Wales?

	England	Wales	Scotland	All	*Northern*	*West Midlands*
Complete independence	4.4	3.9	3.5	4.3	*5.8*	7.0
Elected Assembly	9.8	10.7	13.3	10.1	*10.8*	10.5
Find some other way	32.5	30.1	46.9	33.4	*25.8*	36.5
Keep government as has been	42.8	54.4	24.5	42.1	*57.1*	39.0
Don't know	10.5	1.0	11.9	10.1	*5.8*	7.0
	100	100	100	100	*100*	100
n	1620	103	143	1866	*120*	200

Source: BES (1979); Crewe et al. (1981).

[5] Cumbria, now in the north-west region, was in 1979 in the northern region.

England as a whole. This probably reflects the local politics of the devolution defeat in 1977 and Northern complaints of unfair treatment (Guthrie and McLean 1978). They also disliked devolution for Wales. In contrast, respondents in the West Midlands were keener on devolution or independence for Wales than were the Welsh.

The 1974 offer of devolution to Scotland and Wales was double overkill. The offer to Wales was not justified by anything in Welsh public opinion, as the Kilbrandon Commission's own opinion research showed. The offer to Scotland was well founded, from the perspective of Labour Party statecraft. However, it created constitutional problems that have still not been resolved. Perhaps it achieved nothing that the tripartisan willingness to siphon off North Sea oil revenue into Scottish public expenditure would not have sufficed to achieve. It is dangerous to form policy while ignoring (1970) or overinterpreting (1974) the survey evidence that you have gone to the trouble of collecting.

None of this implies that the grant of devolution in 1998 was trivial, nor that there is any great likelihood of a reversal. Devolution is here to stay. If the settlement unwinds, the reason will probably be some mixture of representational (Chapter 9) or fiscal (Chapter 10) instability. To these we must now turn.

9

Representation in a Union State

The Unionists defeated the Government of Ireland Bills 1886 and 1893 mostly for emotional and imperial reasons. But even on their own terms Gladstone's Bills had three huge defects. They failed to provide for the Unionists of Ulster; and solved neither the problem of representation nor that of finance in an asymmetrical Union. We have discussed Ulster earlier in this book. This chapter deals with representation, and Chapter 10 with finance.

Representation in an asymmetric Union and Sir William Harcourt's baby

The 1886 Bill proposed that Irish members would no longer sit at Westminster. As the Irish were deeply unpopular in Britain and had perfected the technique of parliamentary obstruction, that idea had a gut appeal. But it was untenable. It treated Ireland as a colony, but attempted to govern it as the UK had governed its American colonies up to 1776. That is, it imposed taxation without representation. Gladstone could not devolve taxation to Ireland, as Ireland was much poorer than Great Britain. Devolving taxation, as in a fully colonial model, would have led Ireland straight off a fiscal cliff. Without adjustment, the Irish would suddenly have to submit to both higher taxes and a lower standard of living. But devolving representation without taxation was unsustainable. If the 1886 Bill had got any further than it did, it would have been wrecked on that reef. As it was, it gave Joseph Chamberlain one of the four excuses for his exit. Enoch Powell describes the scene at the Cabinet when Gladstone outlined his plan.

[Chamberlain] put four questions across the table to the prime minister:

1. Was Irish representation at Westminster to cease?
2. Was the power of taxation, including customs and excise, to be given to the Irish legislature?
3. Was the appointment of judges and magistrates to vest in the Irish authority?

4. Was the Irish legislature to have authority in every matter not specifically excluded by the Act constituting it or only in matters specifically delegated to it by statute?

Gladstone, for once, did not refine or prevaricate. He answered 'Yes' to every one of the questions.[1] 'Then', said Chamberlain, 'I resign', whereupon he left the Cabinet room at once. (Powell 1977: 8)

This reflects as much how Powell would have liked to resign as how Chamberlain actually did resign, but most of the many ministers who were keeping diaries confirm its general outline (Cooke and Vincent 1974: 384–91).

In 1893, therefore, Gladstone toyed with what became known as the 'in and out solution'—that Irish MPs were to be elected to Westminster in their correct electoral proportion, but they should be permitted to vote only on 'Imperial' (to include UK-wide) business, not on purely Great Britain business. In 1886 he had already thought of this idea, but then rejected it on the twin grounds that 'it passes the wit of man' to draw the distinction between these two classes of business, and that it was 'impossible (because opinion touches responsibility)' (Gladstone's speech and speaking notes, 8.4.1886, quoted by Bogdanor 1999: 30). The latter objection was that if Irish members attended for some business and were excluded for other business, the Government of the day might well be unable to carry one class of its business. If Ireland had been given Home Rule on the basis of the 1893 Bill with proportionate representation of Ireland, so that eighty-five Irish Home Rulers had sat in every UK Parliament since then, this situation would have arisen in the Parliaments of 1892, twice in 1910, 1922, 1923, 1929, 1950, 1951, 1955, 1959, 1964, 1966, 1970, twice in 1974, 1979, and 1992. Those seventeen Parliaments comprise 63 per cent of all the Parliaments since 1893. So, at any time there would be a 5/8 chance that the partisan majority in the UK House would differ from the partisan majority in Great Britain. That suffices to show that the 'in and out' solution is untenable. Gladstone dropped it during the passage of the 1893 Bill. Conservative leader William Hague briefly revived it in 1999 under the slogan 'English votes on English laws'. It was not mentioned in the 2001 Conservative manifesto, but Hague's successor-but-one Michael Howard revived it again in 2004. The 'in and out' solution has popular appeal to judge by a poll conducted by the online polling organization YouGov in February 2004. This found that substantial popular majorities on both sides of the border (66 per cent of respondents in England and Wales; 78 per cent in Scotland) believed that 'Scottish Westminster MPs should not be allowed to vote on matters that affect only England and Wales'. A plurality (41 per cent) of English and Welsh respondents thought that Scotland should have fewer MPs than her popula-

---

[1] The only possible answer to Chamberlain's fourth question was 'Yes'.

tion proportion. A strong majority (75 per cent) of Scottish respondents thought that Scotland should retain her population proportion of MPs (King 2004).

The partisan attractions of 'in and out' to the modern Conservative Party are obvious. Their chances of winning a Commons majority in England greatly outweigh their chances of winning a Commons majority in Great Britain. But 'in and out' is just unworkable, as Gladstone decided, and as Howard may decide in due course. Therefore, Gladstone turned next to the idea of reduced Irish representation at Westminster. His awkward follower Sir William Harcourt pointed out, uncomfortably, but correctly, that

[t]he proposal of course is supposed to get rid of the objection to Irish interference with British affairs, but though it may lessen the *amount* it does not really touch the *principle* of the objection. When parties are pretty equally divided fifty Irish votes may be as decisive as 100 . . . and when you have once conceded the objection to Irish interference you don't get rid of it any more than the young woman did of the baby by saying it's such a little one. (Harcourt to Gladstone, 27.10.1889, quoted by Lyons 1977: 449)

Repeating our counterfactual, if Ireland had been given Home Rule on the basis of the 1893 Bill with half its population share of seats, so that forty Irish Home Rulers had sat in every UK Parliament since then, the housemaid's baby would have been pivotal in the Parliaments of 1892, 1910 (twice), 1923, 1929, 1950, 1951, 1964, 1970, 1974 (twice), 1979, and 1992. This still represents 13/27, just under half, of all the Parliaments since 1893. In its final version, the 1893 Bill provided for eighty Irish members to sit at Westminster (down from 105). The Government of Ireland Act 1914 reduced Irish representation further, to forty-two Irish members at Westminster (4 & 5 Geo. V, c.90, Schedule 1). But it (and Welsh disestablishment) were simultaneously suspended under the Suspensory Act 1914 (4 & 5 Geo. V., c. 88). In the 1918 general election, therefore, there remained 101 territorial seats in Ireland. The seventy-two Sinn Fein members elected constituted themselves as the first Dail Eireann, and the events that led to the 1921 treaty started to unfold (McLean 2001a).

By a schedule of the 1920 Government of Ireland Act, Northern Ireland was reduced to about two-thirds of its population share of seats. It had twelve seats in the Parliaments of 1922–79 inclusive. Three times—in the Parliaments of 1923, February 1974, and from 1976 (when Labour lost its overall majority) until the end of the October 1974 Parliament—those seats were pivotal. Labour Prime Minister Harold Wilson complained frequently during the 1964 Parliament that the twelve Ulster Unionist MPs, then an integral part of the Conservative Party in Parliament, were able to vote on Great Britain legislation that did not affect Ulster. He toyed again with the 'in and out solution' (Jackson 2003: 86[2]). In fact, the Ulster Unionists were never quite pivotal in the 1964 Parliament. On the three occasions when they *were* pivotal, so was everybody else. The classic 'hung parliaments' of 1923 and 1974 were so finely balanced that *every* small group had a veto. This included the Ulster Unionists but it also included their deadly enemies, the Catholic nationalist members from Northern Ireland. Any constitutional change in Northern Ireland would, *per impossibile,* have needed the support of both of those groups. Sir William Harcourt's baby had become so small that it vanished down the plughole. As a result of the last-minute bargaining while Prime Minister Callaghan vainly tried to save the Labour Government in 1979, Northern Ireland's seat total was raised to its population proportion of 17. Although this change arose from horse-trading, it could be justified on the grounds that Northern Ireland no longer had its own parliament, so the reason for under-representation at Westminster had gone.

What if Home Rule All Round had been enacted in 1886, 1893, or 1914, with Home Rule parliaments in Scotland and Wales as well as Ireland? We can repeat the same counterfactual exercise as above. If Ireland, Scotland, and Wales had been given Home Rule in 1893 but retained full representation at Westminster with their 1892 total of 205 territorial seats, then only in 1931 and 1935 could the possibility of a parliamentary majority for 'imperial' business differing from the parliamentary majority for English business be ruled out. Only on those two occasions out of twenty-seven has the leading party won enough seats in England alone to be certain of controlling this counterfactual UK Parliament (which, remember, would have eighty or so seats for southern Ireland). This would have been totally untenable. If Scotland, Ireland, and Wales had been represented at half-strength, they would jointly have held over 100 seats, which as we saw above would suffice to throw control of the Commons into doubt in at least 5/8 of the Parliaments since 1893. Still untenable. Furthermore, although many British politicians were happy to see the backs of the Irish, that did not apply to either the Scots or the Welsh. It was true that the Unionists' partisan advantage lay in throwing Wales out, as Wales was so monolithically Liberal (unsurprisingly, with the Unionist-dominated unelected house as determined to block Welsh disestablishment as Irish Home Rule). But they were, after all, Unionists. Giving equal consideration to all parts of the Union was their core ideology. And Scotland, unlike Wales, had a viable two-party system (e.g., Burness 2003), so that cutting Scottish representation would harm both large parties. This remained true until 1959, although it is no longer true.

[2] Original documents are PREM 13/1663, 1965, concerning the representation of Northern Ireland in the UK Parliament, correspondence between the Lord President and Attorney General.

The left-wing parties—Liberal, and then Labour—could not countenance any seat reduction in Scotland or Wales. Their material interest lay directly in retaining these countries at full strength or more in the House of Commons. Most left-wing governments since 1880 have been in a minority in England, and have depended on the rest of the UK for their Commons majority. As it was the same left-wing parties who were more sympathetic to Home Rule All Round than the Unionists, it is not surprising that Home Rule All Round, if it came, would not be accompanied by a reduced number of seats. Indeed, the separate identity of Scotland and Wales was used as an argument in the opposite direction—to give them *more* than their population share of seats in the House of Commons. We have reviewed the story elsewhere, where readers are referred for a fuller account (McLean 1995).The data are in Tables 9.1 and 9.2.

TABLE 9.1. *Scottish representation in the House of Commons, 1707–2001*

Year	Scottish seats	UK seats	Scottish share of UK seats	Scottish share of UK population	Scottish share of UK electorate	Scottish seat share/ population share	Scottish seat share/ electorate share
1707	45	558	0.081	0.151		0.532	
1800	45	658	0.068	0.100		0.683	
1832	53	658	0.081	0.098	0.079	0.819	1.016
1868	60	658	0.091	0.107	0.097	0.854	0.942
1885	72	670	0.107	0.107	0.100	1.004	1.070
1918	74	707	0.105	0.104	0.104	1.009	1.003
1922	74	615	0.120	0.111	0.108	1.085	1.110
1945	74	640	0.116	0.101	0.102	1.139	1.128
1950	71	625	0.114	0.101	0.098	1.120	1.160
1955	71	630	0.113	0.101	0.097	1.111	1.159
1974	71	635	0.112	0.094	0.092	1.187	1.216
1983	72	650	0.111	0.092	0.092	1.202	1.202
2001	72	659	0.109	0.086	0.088	1.269	1.247

Sources for Tables 9.1 and 9.2:
Population: 1707 and 1800, P. Deane and W. Cole, *British Economic Growth 1688–1959* (2nd edn., Cambridge University Press, 1967), Table 2.
1832–1983, nearest Census year from OPCS, *Census Report for Great Britain 1991* (Part I), vol. 1 (HMSO, 1993), calculated by interpolation.
2001, *www.statistics.gov.uk*, various pages from 2001 Census and 2002 Electoral Statistics.
Electorate: too misleading to calculate before 1832.
1832–85, F. W. S. Craig, *British Parliamentary Election Results 1832–1885* (London: Macmillan, 1977).
1918–83, D. E. Butler and G. Butler, *British Political Facts 1900–1994* (London: Macmillan, 1994).

TABLE 9.2. *Welsh representation in the House of Commons, 1832–2001*

Year	Welsh seats	UK seats	Welsh share of UK seats	Welsh share of UK population	Welsh share of UK electorate	Welsh seat share/ population share	Welsh seat share/ electorate share
1832	31	658	0.047	0.038	0.051	1.251	0.917
1868	33	658	0.050	0.045	0.051	1.114	0.978
1885	34	670	0.051	0.045	0.049	1.126	1.026
1918	37	707	0.052	0.056	0.055	0.928	0.956
1922	37	615	0.060	0.060	0.059	0.997	1.016
1945	37	640	0.058	0.052	0.054	1.117	1.069
1950	36	625	0.058	0.052	0.052	1.113	1.100
1955	36	630	0.057	0.052	0.052	1.104	1.106
1974	36	635	0.057	0.049	0.050	1.152	1.131
1983	38	650	0.058	0.050	0.050	1.167	1.167
2001	40	659	0.061	0.049	0.050	1.229	1.210

Scotland was under-represented before 1867, proportionately represented in 1885 and 1918, and has been over-represented since then. Judging by population share, Wales was over-represented until the 1885 apportionment, under-represented in 1918, and thereafter (like Scotland) over-represented on a gradually upward trend until the present day. Judging by electorate share, Wales was under-represented until 1885. In the nineteenth century, electorates and populations did not vary closely together as they now do. A relatively high proportion of the Welsh population had the vote in the nineteenth century and a relatively low proportion of the Scottish population did, hence the divergence between the two series.

Scotland's forty-five seats in the 1707 treaty were only some half of the number that could have been claimed on an equal population basis. The idea that Parliament existed to represent people was scarcely developed in the eighteenth century; rather, it existed to represent interests. Forty-five was the number bargained by the treaty negotiators: less than Scotland's population share, more than her share of tax revenue for the new kingdom. By 1800 Scotland was less under-represented, more because of change in the denominator than in the numerator. The population of Scotland had grown since 1707, but that of England and Wales had grown faster. Therefore forty-five seats in a 558-member Commons were closer to being a proportionate ratio. Scotland's increase to fifty-three seats in 1832, together with a further slight decline of Scotland's relative population, raised Scotland's ratio of representation to 0.85. Based on electorate rather than population, it was raised to 0.94, reflecting the highly restricted Scottish electorate (Table 9.1). Wales fared quite well. Its twenty-seven members of 1831 (fourteen county and thirteen borough) rose to thirty-one in 1832, with populous counties and the industrial towns of Merthyr and Swansea gaining a member each, while tiny boroughs such as Montgomery and Beaumaris retained their members.

The Representation of the People (Scotland) Act 1868 unexpectedly annihilated seven English borough seats to create seven extra Scottish seats. This coup took place at dinner-time against (the minority) government advice but was not based on any obvious principle. By the time of the Third Reform Bill in 1884, Ireland was slightly over-represented, but Gladstone was determined to preserve Irish numbers in order to placate Parnell and his party. This led Scottish MPs to complain 'When generosity to one part of the country inflicted, or threatened to inflict, injustice on another part, its Representatives could not hold their peace'. Gladstone offered them 12 extra seats, which they regarded as an 'irreducible minimum'. Gladstone wrote to Hartington that reduction in Irish numbers would 'entail reduction for Wales: and this would I suppose entail County amalgamation: and this would run into Scotland' (quoted in Jones 1972: 127, 222, and 182 in that order). For the first time, the representation package was presented in a unified bill for the whole UK. Neither Gladstone nor any other party leader was yet committed to the idea of equal-population electoral districts *within* each component part of the UK, but the politics of the bill entailed an effort to get proportionality *among* them. Tables 9.1 and 9.2 show that Scotland and Wales were proportionately represented for the first time.

Redistribution was the least controversial of the matters settled by the Representation of the People Act 1918. A Speaker's Conference was sprung by Walter Long, the Unionist Chairman of the Local Government Board, on his unsuspecting colleagues to deal with suffrage extension, proportional representation, and seat redistribution. The Speaker selected the members, after consulting the party whips, during a shooting party at Nuneham Courtenay, Oxon. They comprised thirteen Unionists, twelve Liberals, four Irish Nationalists, and three Labour members. Of the twenty-seven MPs among them, four represented Irish seats, three Scottish seats (one of them a university member), and none Welsh seats. Ireland and Scotland were thus over-represented in the Conference itself.

The Speaker's Conference recommended 'that each vote recorded shall, as far as possible, command an equal share of representation in the House of Commons', whose overall size should stay substantially unchanged. The target population for an average seat should be 70,000. The resulting instructions to the Boundary Commissioners for England and Wales, and for Scotland, gave the target population of 70,000 in identical wording. However, the instructions for Ireland forbade changing (that is, reducing) the total number of seats in Ireland. Thus, as in 1885, roughly proportionate representation was secured for England, Scotland, and Wales. The principle of equal representation both within and among the countries of Great Britain was accepted for the first time.

It was breached by the next Speaker's Conference, which sat during the Second World War. In the debate on setting it up, the redoubtable Labour Unionist Secretary of State for Scotland, Tom Johnston, argued:

> At the time of the Union of the Parliaments —it is sometimes forgotten that we are here by Treaty rights—we had reserved to us a proportion of the Members of the House. In 1707 we had 45 Members. That was when we had a population of just over a million. It is now well over 4,500,000 and we have 74 Members. (*Hansard* 5.s 396, 1234–5, 1944)

Johnston went on to point out that, if a standard electorate was imposed throughout the UK, 17 of the Scottish seats would be too small and would have to be amalgamated or expanded. Johnston was a noted historian as well as a politician. Thus he may have created the pervasive myth that the Union guaranteed Scottish over-representation. He pointed out that Scotland's population had quadrupled and its representation had less than doubled. He did not add that the population of the rest of the UK had gone up by more and its seat numbers had gone up by less. Immediately after him, D. R. Grenfell (Lab., Gower) made an 'us-too' claim for Wales.

The 1944 Speaker's Conference, like its predecessor of 1916–17, had thirty-two members besides the Speaker. It comprised seventeen Conservative representatives, nine Labour, two Liberal, one National Liberal, one Independent Labour Party (ILP), and two independents. Its own membership over-represented Scotland (five members) and, unlike its predecessor, Wales (three members). The minutes and evidence of this Speaker's Conference remained closed to the public until they were released at our request in 1995. They show how the over-representation of Scotland and Wales in Parliament arose. A briefing note, written by its secretaries 'at the direction of the Speaker', first pointed out that Northern Ireland had less than its proportionate share of MPs, but that its 12 territorial seats had been specified in a schedule to the Government of Ireland Act 1920. Turning to Scotland and Wales, the document notes that on 1939 figures, the average English constituency had 54,775 electors, compared to 44,642 in Scotland and 47,220 in Wales. However, 'It is clearly out of the question to instruct the Boundary Commissioners to apply only a strict mathematical test' in Scotland and Wales. Apart from the problem of sparse population in the Highlands, the document does not explain why the Speaker thought it was out of the question. In the conference,

> [I]t was pointed out that a strict application of the quota for the whole of Great Britain would result in a considerable decrease in the existing number of Scottish and Welsh seats, but that in practice, in view of the proposal that the Boundary Commis-

sioners should be permitted to pay special consideration to geographical considerations, it was...unlikely that there would be any substantial reduction. It was
strongly urged that...it would be very desirable, on political grounds, to state from
the outset quite clearly that the number of Scottish and Welsh seats should not be
diminished. The absence of any such assurance might give rise to a good deal of
political feeling and would lend support to the separatist movements in both countries. (Minutes of the 9th meeting, quoted in McLean 1995: 262–3)

Accordingly, the Conference resolved not to cut the number of seats in either
Scotland or Wales and to establish a separate Boundary Commission in
Wales.

At the next meeting, somebody pointed out the logical inconsistency of the
conference's position: that its decisions to hold the total size of the House
constant while not cutting the numbers of seats in Scotland, Wales, and
Northern Ireland 'might be represented as meaning that only England
could suffer any reduction in representation. It was pointed out, however,
that in fact England's position would be adequately covered by the formula
for calculating the quota by dividing the electorate by the number of seats,
and the Conference agreed that it was unnecessary to amend the Rules to
meet this possible line of argument. Politicians are sometimes accused of
wishing everybody to be richer than average. Here they were content to agree
that on average every constituency in England should be larger than average.

The 1944 recommendations have provided a template for all subsequent
legislation, and created some problems with which the Boundary Commissions have had to deal ever since. To this day, the statutory instructions to the
Boundary Commissions reflect the illogic of the 1944 Speaker's Conference.
They embody the contradictory requirements to protect seat minima in
Scotland and Wales, and to restrain the overall size of the House of Commons (McLean and Mortimore 1992; Rossiter et al. 1999). From a contradiction, anything follows. Therefore the rules are radically incoherent.

Tables 9.1 and 9.2 shows that by 2001 Scotland was over-represented in the
Commons by 25 per cent, and Wales by 21 per cent. If seats in the UK were
equally distributed, therefore, Scotland would be reduced from seventy-two
to fifty-seven, and Wales from forty to thirty-three. They might claim one or
two extra seats each to allow for their remote rural areas, but nowhere near
their present number. The Scotland Act 1998 (Section 86) requires the
Boundary Commission at its next review, in progress as we write, to apply
the same electoral quota in Scotland and England, and hence reduce Scottish
over-representation at Westminster. The Wales Act contains no equivalent
provision. As of autumn 2004, the Boundary Commission for Scotland
has recommended a reduction to fifty-nine seats there (see *http://www.
bcomm-scotland.gov.uk/),* but the recommendation has not been sent up for
parliamentary approval. It is likely, but not certain, that the new Scottish

boundaries will be in force for the 2005 general election. When the adjustment is complete, Scotland will have been reduced to, but not below, its population share of seats, and Wales will remain above its population share. In neither country, therefore, will the reduction discussed by Gladstone and Harcourt, supported by the English YouGov respondents, and enforced in Northern Ireland between 1922 and 1979, apply. Northern Ireland itself returned to proportional representation in 1983.

The UK thus remains an asymmetric Union with asymmetric representation. The asymmetry of representation is in the wrong direction. Wales, and up to 2005/6 Scotland are over-represented at Westminster, not under-represented, even though they have domestic governments of their own. Therefore it exacerbates the classic West Lothian Question (hereinafter WLQ), as constantly posed by the anti-devolution MP for West Lothian (now Linlithgow), Tam Dalyell, since 1974. However, as this chapter shows, it really goes back to 1886. If the 'in and out' solution is deemed impracticable, as everybody who has looked at seriously since (and including) Gladstone has come to agree, then MPs for territories with devolved governments must have different roles to MPs for territories without devolved governments. The Imperial Parliament has bound itself not to interfere in the internal affairs of the devolved territories. However, the notorious s.75 of the Government of Ireland Act 1920 asserts the supremacy of the Westminster Parliament over 'all matters, persons, and things in Ireland and every part thereof', and the Scotland Act 1998 contains a similar provision (Scotland Act 1998 c.46, s. 28(7)). The ghost of A. V. Dicey continues to haunt devolution.

Because the degree of devolution to the three non-English parts of the UK differs, the WLQ also differs in respect of each part of the country. It is least pressing in Wales, because the Government of Wales Act confers no primary legislative powers on the National Assembly of Wales. Primary legislation affecting Wales must therefore pass through Parliament (as and when it can), which legitimizes the role of Welsh MPs more fully than their Scottish and Northern Irish counterparts. But even in Wales, the majority of domestic policy is devolved. Wales has adopted a different, and more Old Labour, set of policies on health and education since devolution than those applying in England. First Minister Rhodri Morgan spoke on his accession of putting 'clear red water' between Cardiff and London (Osmond 2003: 12).

In Scotland, the Scottish and UK Governments have used 'Sewel motions' much more than anticipated in 1998. During the passage of the Scotland Act 1998 the junior minister Lord Sewel said:

Clause 27 [to become s.28 of the Act] makes it clear that the devolution of legislative competence to the Scottish parliament does not affect the ability of Westminster to legislate for Scotland even in relation to devolved matters. Indeed, as paragraph 4.4 of the White Paper explained, we envisage that there could be instances where it would be more convenient for legislation on devolved matters to be passed by the United Kingdom Parliament. However, as happened in Northern Ireland earlier in the century, we would expect a convention to be established that Westminster would not normally legislate with regard to devolved matters in Scotland without the consent of the Scottish parliament. (*Hansard*, House of Lords, 21.7.1998 c. 791)

Accordingly, a 'Sewel motion' is a proposal in the Scottish Parliament that the Executive permit Westminster to legislate on a devolved matter (Trench 2004: 29). Up to 10 October 2003, fifty Sewel motions had been debated in the Scottish Parliament chamber and 14 in committee (House of Commons Library 2003). Most controversially, the Executive used a Sewel motion to push a proposal to authorize civil partnerships (including same-sex civil partnerships) in Scotland back, like a poisoned chalice, to Westminster (Trench 2004: 29; *http://www.scottishgreens.org.uk/news/2003/nov/261103sewels.htm*). After a bruising row with Scottish social conservatives over previous proposals to liberalize homosexual law in Scotland, the Executive wished to duck further discussion, even though it was on a devolved matter.

In Northern Ireland, devolved matters are devolved to the Northern Ireland Assembly when there is one, but for long periods since 1972, including currently as we write, elected government in Northern Ireland has been suspended.

The WLQ has many forms. Its purest form is that in which Tam Dalyell originally asked it in 1977: by what logic could he, as MP for West Lothian, be allowed to 'vote on policy and money for . . . betting, bookies and gaming in Blackburn, Lancashire, but not Blackburn, West Lothian'? (Dalyell 1977: 248). This produces the two purest answers, with one post-1998 variant:

WLA1. Because that is precisely what asymmetric devolution involves. Parliament enacted it, and the people live with it.
WLA2. Because Parliament has retained the right to legislate for Blackburn, West Lothian . . .
WLA2A . . . and the Scottish Parliament sometimes invites it to, in a Sewel motion.

But the WLQ is now posed by English MPs and lobbies rather than by Scottish ones. In that form it becomes, *Why do Scottish, Welsh, and Northern Irish MPs have the right to meddle in our affairs, when we do not have the right to meddle in theirs?* Logically, it is the same question as in Dalyell's formulation, but now more dangerous. It expresses English resentment at the thought that an English majority in one direction can be outvoted by a Celtic majority in the other. Even without devolution, this drove Unionist resentment at the legislation of the 1886, 1892, and 1910 Liberal governments, as we saw earlier. Those who wish to minimize the WLQ, or who see it as merely an antidevolution rhetorical device, retort

WLA3. The dangerous case when an English Conservative majority is overridden by a UK anti-Conservative majority is uncommon (e.g., W. L. Miller cited in House of Commons Library 1998: 28).

However, it is commoner than Professor Miller admits. On his count, it had occurred since 1945 only in 1950 and 1974, and then, he says, the Government had refrained from passing contentious legislation. This may be queried on several grounds. In the Parliament of October 1974, there was a great deal of contentious legislation. Taking a starting date of 1945 obscures the fact that the WLQ has been around since 1886. And, most importantly, WLA3 fails to recognize that the WLQ applies to contentious issues *within* parties as well as between them.

As noted earlier, one of the most clear-cut cases of Celtic meddling in a purely English matter occurred in 1927–8. The Church of England is, since 1920, established in England only. The Church of Scotland Act 1921 confirms the position the Scottish church negotiators thought they had secured in 1707, namely that the church ran its own internal affairs, and the civil magistrate's responsibility was confined to the external protection of the church. Parliament had disturbed this by imposing lay patronage on the Church of Scotland in 1712, but a succession of events beginning with the Disruption and culminating in the 1921 Act restored the position that Carstares tried to secure in 1707 (McLean and Linsley 2004). Therefore, since 1921, only in England is Parliament the legislator of last resort for any church. Church of England legislation had no knock-on implications for church or society anywhere else in the UK. If ever there was an issue where Scots, Welsh, and Northern Irish MPs should have held back, it was this. But because of their Reformation histories, these were exactly the territories whose MPs were most likely to be unhappy at the allegedly papist tendencies of the proposed Church of England prayer book. Tom Johnston, then an opposition frontbencher, writes that they had decided not to vote 'as it was almost entirely an English issue'. However,

There came a powerful oration from Mr Rosslyn Mitchell [Lab., Paisley] against the new Prayer Book and as it proceeded there fell something like a sob from Willie Adamson [former leader of the PLP and Secretary for Scotland]: 'Tom', he whispered, 'I couldna' look ma forefolks in the face if I didna' vote the nicht'. And vote we all did! (Johnston 1952: 102; cf. also Kirkwood 1935: 238–40)

And so the proposed Prayer Book was defeated on Celtic votes. The Celts may have achieved rough justice for the failure of Parliament to enact Welsh disestablishment for decades after the majority of Welsh MPs voted for it and the majority of Welsh people had abandoned the Anglican church.

Other matters divide parties. Since devolution, the possibility has existed that a controversial policy that applies to less than the whole UK is enacted by the votes of MPs from constituencies where the policy will not apply. Although Labour has had a secure parliamentary majority for the whole period that devolution has been in effect, there have been a number of issues on which Labour MPs have been internally divided—notably, in 2003–4, foundation hospitals and university tuition fees in England, both of them forced through the Commons on the votes of Scottish and Welsh loyalist Labour MPs. There is, however, a partial retort:

WLA4. Even bills on devolved matters have knock-on implications for the devolved territories, so it is appropriate for their MPs to vote on them.

The Higher Education Bill introduced in January 2004, and finally enacted narrowly and painfully in July 2004, illustrates this in two ways. The first section of the bill would create an Arts and Humanities Research Council. This is a reserved matter, as scientific research (which is deemed to include an arts and humanities research council) is not devolved. An ingenious minister or parliamentary counsel can often, as in this case, find a UK matter to attach to an otherwise England-only bill. But secondly, the student funding regime for England has substantial knock-on consequences for the other three territories. It will affect the flow of students, of teachers, and of money in and out of the Scots, Welsh, and Northern Irish universities in complex ways, some of them predicted and some not. (There is evidence that the drafters of the antecedent White Paper were unaware of its devolution implications—McLean 2003b). Thus, it is said, it was legitimate for Celtic MPs to vote on the Second Reading, where the Government majority of 161 was cut to 5 (Hansard, 27.1.2004, Division 38). Tam Dalyell had earlier reportedly stated that his personal answer to his own question was not to vote on English bills. The sole Scottish Conservative MP followed the Dalyell/Hague strategy, and did not vote. Tam Dalyell, however, voted against the bill.

These examples also show that 'inverse WLQs' must not be ignored. Recall that the Unionists have been in a small minority in Wales since 1832; that neither main UK party has held any seats in Northern Ireland since 1972; and that Scotland was an anti-Unionist stronghold from 1832 to 1885 and again since 1987. It follows that governments of both main parties, but especially Unionist ones, often pass laws applying to the non-English territories that a majority of their MPs oppose. This does not touch the pure WLQ, which is a question about asymmetric devolution, but it powerfully touches the impure WLQ, which demands on what basis legislators from one territory decide the affairs of another. In the classic Victorian cases of Irish Home Rule and Welsh disestablishment, the wishes of the MPs from those territories were frustrated even with a Commons majority on their side, because of the veto of the unelected House of Lords. Even after the removal of the Lords' veto, the position of Conservative Secretaries of State in all three territories, and of Labour Secretaries of State in Northern Ireland, has been uncomfortably close to colonial governor. *Nemo me impune lacessit*, as it says on the edge of Scottish £1 coins (colloquial translation, *Wha daur meddle wi' me*; the epigraph of the Order of the Thistle, the main Scots order of chivalry, to which the great and good of Scotland are elected). Unfortunately for Unionists, the fact that they have been lacessing (to coin a phrase) the Scots with impunity since 1832 has been a powerful driver of the Scots demand for devolution.

Thus, none of the above WLAs (West Lothian Answers) is satisfactory. Harcourt and Dalyell are right. In a country with asymmetric devolution, there is no logically defensible answer to the WLQ. The only practical qualification is that if the number of MPs to whom the WLQ applies is small (e.g., the twelve Northern Irish members between 1922 and 1979), then the likelihood of WLQ crises is correspondingly small. In desperation, defenders of the status quo can only resort to Disraeli's jibe, 'England is governed not by logic but by parliament'.

10

Public Finance in an Asymmetric Union

W. E. Gladstone and Joseph Chamberlain both knew that the problem of finance was entangled with the problem of representation. The cleanest solution to the latter—removing Irish MPs from Westminster—fell at the first fence, that of 'taxation without representation'. There are two problems of public finance in an asymmetric Union. First, how do the people in the devolved territory pay for their share of 'Imperial' services? Second, how (if at all) arc equalization payments regulated? These problems were intractable even in 1886. In modern times, when the public sector accounts for about 40 per cent of GDP and people expect to pay reasonably comparable taxes and receive reasonably comparable services wherever they live, the problems are more intractable still. In the end, we come back, as in Chapter 9, to Sir William Harcourt and the housemaid's baby. 'It's only a little one' may be the only tolerable answer to the anomalies of devolution finance, as to the anomalies of devolution representation. Once the devolved territory exceeds a small proportion of the total, there may be no logical solution to the problem of devolved finance short of full-scale federalism.

The failure of the 1886 and 1893 bills ironically made 'killing Home Rule with kindness' easier, because both virtual and actual transfers to Ireland were hidden in the public accounts. Take imperial public goods first. We use 'public good' in its technical sense. A public good is anything with the property that, if it is provided at all, it is provided equally to everybody, and nobody can practicably be excluded from its provision. National defence is a public good. So is the central administration of the UK. So, in 1886, was the Empire. All citizens of the UK including Ireland received these goods to an equal extent. As Ireland was a poor country, tax receipts per head from Ireland were below the UK average. Therefore, Ireland paid less than its population share of the cost of defence, administration, and Empire. That was a virtual transfer from Great Britain to Ireland that Unionists were happy to tolerate. Any devolution, beginning with Northern Ireland in 1920, would start with an attempt to count the share of those costs that should fall to the devolved administration. Northern Ireland was required to pay what was always called an 'imperial contribution'. The payment was fictional. The net imperial contribution was massively negative, because the UK paid Northern Ireland to stay in the Empire far more than Northern Ireland paid the UK to sustain it. But devolution forced the issue into the semi-open.

Actual cash transfers are easy without devolution. The UK Parliament, as the legislature governing Ireland, passed laws governing railways, postal services, land redistribution, and what were called 'congested districts'[1] in Ireland. Acts such as the Congested Districts Board (Ireland) Act, 1899, or the Irish Land Purchase Act (the latter generally known, from its protagonist, as the Wyndham Land Act) of 1903 directed public expenditure, raised across the whole UK, into only one part of it. Generally speaking, the recipients were happy. The two acts just mentioned solved the Irish land problem at the expense of British taxpayers. The donors, who might have been unhappy under Liberal governments, were happy with (or ignorant of) the Unionist statecraft of killing Home Rule with kindness.

As we have seen in previous chapters, governments also killed Scottish Home Rule by kindness. The Crofters' Act 1886 was an unprecedented irruption into property rights in order to head off land wars in the Highlands. The other device of those years that survives to this day is formula funding of Scottish services.

The 'Goschen equivalent' or 'proportion' dates back to 1888. George Goschen was the safe, and Liberal-Unionist, pair of hands to whom Salisbury transferred the Treasury after succeeding Gladstone and later in 1886 getting rid of Lord Randolph Churchill. In his 1888 Budget speech, Goschen assigned some revenues from central to local government. As the network of County Councils across England was about to go live, they needed a secure revenue base especially for poor relief and what Goschen called 'disturnpiked roads'. He assigned them the revenue from some existing and new taxes and licences of a mostly local kind—including new taxes on wheeled carts (but excluding farm carts and bicycles) and on horses kept for pleasure. He accepted complaints that rates, a levy on real property, were bearing too much of the burden of local expenditure (this part of his speech has a very twenty-first-century air to it), and sought a personal property tax to redress the balance. Having rejected local income tax and an assignment of national income tax revenue, Goschen settled on Probate (estate) duty. The key territorial proposal was apparently to assign a share in this tax base to each of England (with Wales), Scotland, and Ireland.

---

[1] Overcrowded *rural* areas where holdings were below subsistence level.

However, it would be more correct to call it a block grant than an assignment. In a rather confused statement in his budget speech, Goschen announced that he would 'give each country a share of it [the probate receipts] in proportion to the general contributions of that country to the Exchequer'. On that basis, he announced the Goschen Proportions as 'England ... 80 per cent, Scotland ... 11 per cent, and Ireland ... 9 per cent'. The Scottish and Irish shares were to go to their territorial ministers 'to relieve ... ratepayers'. He had just said that the ratios for Probate Duty, the tax whose proceeds he had proposed to assign in part, were 85:10:5, and that even on a 'general contribution' basis, Ireland's share was only 8.7 per cent (G. J. Goschen, Budget speech 26.3.1888, *Hansard* 3s: 324, 268–317, quoted at cc. 294, 301, 302).

Thus Goschen assigned an arbitrary block, which was an assignment neither in proportion to the tax raised nor in proportion to population. Scotland's 'Goschen equivalent' block grant of 11/80 of English and Welsh expenditure began by disfavouring Scotland, but then came to favour Scotland more and more (Table 7.2). Block grant under Goschen could be compared to three standards: a standard of relative needs; an equal per capita (EPC) standard; or an assigned revenue standard. The only one for which data are readily available is an EPC standard. By that standard, the rightmost column of Table 7.2 shows that the Goschen equivalent was slightly ungenerous to Scotland in 1888. But, as Scotland's share of the British population steadily declined, so the Goschen equivalent became more and more favourable compared to an EPC standard. Compared to an assigned revenue standard, it must have been yet more favourable, because Scotland almost certainly generated less tax revenue per head than did England and Wales throughout the period that Goschen was regarded as a standard.

Did Goschen give Scotland more or less than her needs? The Scots (especially the Scottish Education Department) and the Treasury battled across these yards of Flanders mud for ninety years and got nowhere. Scots politicians and civil servants always asserted that Scotland's grant for any service was below her needs; Treasury civil servants and (when engaged) ministers always asserted the opposite. No attempt to assess relative need was made until 1978, and then it was highly controversial.

The Goschen formula merely transferred some tax revenues in a block for spending by their respective administrations in Edinburgh and Dublin. Here we must remember that although politics was not devolved, administration was. The Irish administration had been located in Dublin Castle since the days of Strongbow. The Scottish administration, formalized by the appointment of a Secretary for Scotland by Salisbury in 1885, actually had two wings until 1918. There was the Scotch Education Department, dating back to 1872 and formally a committee of the Privy Council (which never met). And there was the Scottish Office. This was formed in the 1885 reorganization. It took over functions that had lain with the Lord Advocate since 1707 (and which in his administration Pitt settled every night with Dundas over a bottle or six of port), plus others given up (probably gratefully) by the Home Office. English civil servants would no longer have to deal with the Scottish church affairs that had caused Peel and Sir James Graham endless trouble from 1841 to 1843. The two Scottish departments were merged in 1918 into the Scottish Office, which was united (mostly) under one roof in 1939 and changed seamlessly into the Scottish Executive in 1998 (Mitchell 2003: ch. 2). Dublin Castle was recreated in miniature at Stormont for the devolved government of Northern Ireland in 1920.

As there were separate administrations, so there were separate administrative interests. Whether or not formally part of the Home Civil Service,[2] senior bureaucrats in Dublin, Stormont, and Edinburgh made their careers there, not in London. So their stylized role was to extract as much money as possible from the Treasury, whose stylized role was to resist it. These stylized roles have not changed. In 1926, the Permanent Secretary to the Treasury sent this magnificent note to the prime minister:

Sir H. Craik [who by 1926 had become a Unionist MP] was himself a Civil Servant from 1870 to 1904, during the last nineteen years of the period being Secretary to the Scottish Education Department. He conceived that position as one of great importance, and the contemporary Treasury (unfortunately) never seems to have disguised its view that neither Sir Henry nor his post was of any particular importance. Hence an abiding resentment on his part in particular against the Treasury and in general against the Service. (Sir W. Fisher to S. Baldwin, 13.2.1926, quoted by Mitchell 2003: 150–1)

The key event in Scotland was probably the Education (Scotland) Act 1918. Passed at the height of the First World War, this was Scotland's Maynooth Grant. It established a network of fully supported Roman Catholic schools throughout Scotland to sit alongside the existing network of state schools that the SED had been developing since 1872. The origins of the 1918 Act deserve closer study. In part, it was certainly an attempt to buy out any Catholic resentment at poorer schools, and perhaps to make Scottish Catholic schoolchildren (mostly of Irish descent) into loyal citizens of the UK, not putative Sinn Feiners (McLean 1999: 189–92). The upshot was that, with two parallel systems and little aid from the churches, Scottish schooling was more expensive than English—and there were more school-age children in the Scottish population. Table 10.1, adapted from a note marked 'confidential' to the secretary of the SED in 1926, gives some comparative data.

---

[2] The Scotland Office and Scottish Executive remain part of the unified Home Civil Service. The Northern Ireland Civil Service never has been.

Table 10.1 shows how the parties could fight Goschen hand-to-hand across no-man's land. The Treasury could point out that Scotland got an extraordinarily good deal—well ahead of the Goschen equivalent (Table 10.1, line 2). The Scots could retort that Scotland had more school-children per 1,000 of population (line 5) and worse student–staff ratios (line 8). *Well, in that case, where is all the money going—you don't even seem to keep the kids in school?* (line 7). It still goes on all the time—currently between the Devolved Countries and Regions team of HM Treasury and finance officials in the three devolved administrations.

Fundamentally, the Secretary (of State) for Scotland always asked for at least Goschen, and preferably more, every time a service to be financed from block grant came up for discussion. The Treasury always resisted. The decision could turn on the credibility of the contemporary threat to the Union. Stanley Baldwin, as Chancellor of the Exchequer in 1923, fronted Treasury resistance to the Scots' demands but even then conceded that 'the Goschen proportion has been fairly well observed' and proposed to leave things at that, even while acknowledging that Scotland's relative population had declined (quoted by Levitt 1999: 100). More strikingly, the Unionist Government responded to the first appearance of the Scottish Nationalists in the 1930s with a gambit that was to be repeated by a later Unionist Secretary of State, Ian Lang, in 1992 (Chapter 7). They published a 'Parliamentary Return' in 1932 showing that Scotland's expenditure per head was above the Goschen line, whereas her tax receipts were below it (Levitt 1999: 103). Goschen remained the reference point for Scottish special pleading and Treasury resistance right up until the 1960s.

The Northern Ireland fiscal experiment has lasted since 1920. The Government of Ireland Act 1920 transferred extensive spending powers and

TABLE 10.1. *School costs in England and Scotland, 1913–1914.*

	England	Scotland	Scottish figure as % of English figure
$^{11}/_{80}$	80	11	13.75
Standard year [spending], 1913–14, £	13,470,966	2,306,835	17.12
Population, 1911	36,070,492	4,760,904	13.20
Scholars average enrolment 1914	6,288,103	857,000	13.63
Scholars as % of population	17.4	18.0	103.45
Teachers, 1914	174,502	20,800	11.92
Scholars ave attendance, 1914	5,569,805	765,621	13.75
Scholars per teacher 1914	31.9	36.8	115.36

Source: Derived from Mitchell 2003 Table 8.10, itself derived from National Archives of Scotland, SOE, 6/1/26. Percentages recalculated and missing percentages added.

almost no taxing powers to Northern Ireland. In that respect it continued the weakness of its three Gladstonian predecessors of 1886, 1893, and 1914. To separate the power to spend from the duty to tax is to encourage fiscal irresponsibility (to create a 'vertical fiscal imbalance', VFI), which Northern Irish politicians, being human, have always exercised to the full. The taxes transferred in 1920 (car license duty, stamp duty) raised no more than 20 per cent of Northern Irish tax revenue (Bogdanor 1999: 82; Kilbrandon 1973: para. 1273), and therefore less than 20 per cent of the average tax receipts per UK citizen (Northern Ireland being a poor part of the UK). The Government of Northern Ireland therefore possessed what Stanley Baldwin attributed to Lords Rothermere and Beaverbrook: 'power without responsibility, the prerogative of the harlot throughout the ages'. The main intergovernmental body was a Joint Exchequer Board, which was supposed to balance the books under the chairmanship of a neutral Scotsman (Mitchell 2004: 6).[3] It never did, and its UK Treasury members could never rise above impotent fury. Spending per head in Northern Ireland soared above the UK average; tax receipts per head slumped below. Stormont was prorogued in 1972 but these thoroughly unsatisfactory arrangements did not change until Northern Ireland was first brought into the Barnett regime around 1980 (below).

Administrative devolution to Wales in 1964 came by accident. The Labour general election manifesto stated briefly:

In Wales, the creation of a Secretary of State, to which we are pledged, will facilitate the new unified administration we need (*The Times* 1965: 272).

Not even in Wales, let alone outside it, had this pledge aroused much interest. On the other hand, in 1964 the Scots already had a Forth Road Bridge and the Welsh did not yet have a Severn Bridge. The conventional wisdom has it that the Labour leader, Harold Wilson, needed a berth for the popular but ineffective Jim Griffiths (Lab., Llanelli), who had served on Labour's National Executive for many years and had been a minister under Attlee and more recently deputy leader of the party. By 1964 he was over seventy. He duly became the first Secretary of State for Wales, serving for only eighteen months before retirement (Jones and Jones 2000). The Welsh Office was a cadet version of the Scottish Office, with fewer powers and a lower place in the Whitehall pecking order. Most of its initial powers were transferred from the old Ministry of Housing and Local Government. Its weakness was cruelly confirmed in the aftermath of the Aberfan disaster (21 October 1966).

---

[3] As follows: (NI population share of reserved tax proceeds) − (NI imperial contribution) + (transferred tax proceeds within NI) = (public expenditure in NI). The right-hand term exceeded the maximum possible sum of the left-hand terms in every year from 1922 onwards. By 1952 the supposedly neutral arbiter had become 'an aged Scottish judge (Lord Alness, who lives in Bournemouth)' (Treasury internal memo, 07.04.1952, PRO T/233/1475, in Mitchell 2004: 8).

Records released in 1997 show that the Welsh Office and the interests it represented were brutally pushed aside to protect the interests of the National Coal Board and the Ministry of Power, both of which were closer to high politics (McLean and Johnes 2000; for summary see *http://www.nuff. ox.ac.uk/politics/aberfan/home.htm*). Protecting the privileged position of the coal industry mattered more than mitigating the sufferings of Aberfan.

In the 1970s, the Welsh Office acquired more spending powers via the Welsh Development Agency, and in the 1980s it accrued more—Mrs Thatcher emulating the great Lord Salisbury and again killing Home Rule with kindness (Davies 1993: 665–6; Jones 2000: 19). Like Scotland, Wales had no devolved tax powers. But it was the weakest of three territories, precisely because it was the last to get a territorial administration. It had no Goschen equivalent to use as a bargaining power, nor the tools of (even nominal) intergovernmental finance available to the Government of Northern Ireland.

Needs, Barnett, and Needs Again

We have already discussed the origins of the Needs Assessment and the Barnett Formula. Labour, in office but scarcely in power from February 1974 until March 1979, had been badly scared by the Scots' apparent demand for devolution (Chapter 8). The reality of the SNP threat to the Union had been confirmed by their performance in the February and October 1974 general elections. The Welsh threat to the Union was more localized, but as in 1964, Labour absent-mindedly offered Wales what it was present-mindedly offering Scotland. Northern Ireland, meanwhile, had spun out of control, with murderous sectarian violence peaking in 1972 and the British Army apparently trapped in the midst of the conflict, deeply distrusted by (especially) nationalists. Stormont had been suspended and no permanent substitute had been found. The existing mechanisms for devolution finance could not be allowed to creak on.

Nobody would ever have devised the regime in place in 1977, when the defeat of the Scotland and Wales Bill forced the Government to go back to first base. It was committed to devolution of a sort for all three territories outside England, but in none of them were the financial arrangements either equitable or efficient. Equitable public finance in a federal state, or in a union state, implies that standards for nationally delivered services do not vary by geography. Efficiency implies that neither the upper-tier nor the lower-tier government faces perverse incentives; that services are delivered at the level at which it is most efficient to deliver them; and that citizens do not face perverse incentives to live in one place when it would increase everybody's welfare including their own if they lived somewhere else. (For a taster of the vast economic literature on efficient fiscal federalism see Buchanan 1950; Scott 1952; Oates 1972; Boadway and Flatters 1982. For recent applications to Australia see Garnaut and FitzGerald 2002; Brennan and Pincus 2002; McLean 2004*b*. For a book-length discussion see McLean 2005.)

The UK arrangements in force in 1977 did moderately well on equity, and appallingly badly on efficiency. They did moderately well on equity because by 1977 the largest domestic programmes were health and social security, which had purposely been designed by egalitarian governments on an all-UK basis with trivial exceptions. Their godfathers were two Liberals (William Beveridge and David Lloyd George) and one socialist (Aneurin Bevan). Although two of the three godfathers were Welsh, there was nothing different about health and social security in Wales from the rest of the UK. Lloyd George, as we saw earlier, was content to set up territorial boards for National Insurance for the 'Celts', but only to smooth the path of legislation. Bevan utterly deplored devolution, on socialist equity grounds. His National Health Service was to provide a truly uniform system of health everywhere in the UK. Social security did not come under the Goschen Proportion in Scotland, although education and sometimes health did. As to Northern Ireland, although these matters were nominally devolved to Stormont, policy there moved in lock step with Great Britain, and the finance moved with it.

Why then was the pattern of public expenditure only *moderately* equitable in 1977? Because some territories posed a credible threat against the UK and others did not. As we have seen, Scotland and Northern Ireland posed credible threats, and had institutions to fit (respectively, the Goschen Equivalent and the Joint Exchequer Board). Wales did not. Neither did the poorer regions of England. As soon as the politics of devolution unleashed the sleeping dog of English regionalism, these disparities would be noticed.

As explained in Chapter 7, the English backlash built up between 1975 and 1977. Why should a Labour Government favour people who were threatening to vote SNP over people who had always loyally voted Labour? More cerebrally, both academic economists and the government-sponsored Northern Region Strategy Team were examining flows of public expenditure around the regions of the UK. Table 10.2 is derived from one such attempt. Perhaps because it was so politically sensitive, the numbers originally presented in the source for Table 10.2 did not show expenditure per head. We have calculated expenditure per head from the population data mostly in the 1971 and 1981 Censuses.

Table 10.2 makes interesting and disturbing reading. The region receiving the most public spending per head was Northern Ireland. Scotland came next, then the South-East (which then included London). The North (that is, the present-day North-East plus Cumbria) and the South-West tied for

TABLE 10.2. *Public expenditure in the regions of the UK, 1975/1976*

Region	Expenditure, £m	Population	Expenditure per head, £	Exp/head (UK=100)
North	2,669.7	3,123,338	854.76	103.32
Yorks & Humber	3,476.2	4,858,262	715.52	86.49
East Mids.	2,763.7	3,726,031	741.73	89.66
East Anglia	1,340.2	1,770,556	756.94	91.50
South-East	14,757.2	16,863,193	875.11	105.78
South-West	3,593.2	4,214,749	852.53	103.05
West-Mids	3,662.0	5,128,962	713.98	86.30
North-West	5,028.6	6,505,514	772.98	93.43
Wales	2,309.9	2,761,528	836.46	101.11
Scotland	4,822.8	5,179,849	931.07	112.54
NI	1,631.2	1,537,200	1,061.15	128.27
UK	46,054.7	55,669,180	827.29	100.00

Source: Expenditure: Short and Nicholas (1981, Appendix 2, Table 12)
Population (GB): Census 1981 National Report Great Britain Part I, Table 3.
1976 interpolated from 1971 and 1981
Population (NI): Population Trends 4 (1976), Table 2.

fourth place. Wales came sixth. All the other regions of England received below-average public spending per head.

This map did not fit the known map of regional poverty. In particular, two regions richer than the North, namely Scotland and the South-East, were receiving not less but more public expenditure per head than the North. It looked to regional politicians as if the geography of public spending was determined as much by threat potential as by need.

While the equity of public expenditure appeared at best fair-to-middling, its efficiency was appalling. The literature on fiscal federalism teaches us that a federation should have low vertical fiscal imbalance—known to anoraks as VFI. A regime has VFI when, in aggregate, one level of government has more tax power than spending power, and others have more spending power than tax power. Almost all regimes have some degree of VFI, because the top tier of government can usually tax more efficiently than lower tiers. Only the top tier can efficiently capture the tax liability on incomes and corporate profits, which move around, whereas lower tiers can efficiently tax houses, shops, offices, and factories, which do not move around. Meanwhile, local governments have the responsibility to spend on local services. If their spending is simply funded by block grant from the top tier, then there is a degree of VFI.

The UK was not a federation, but an asymmetric union. Accordingly, it had an extreme degree of VFI. The three non-English territories had considerable administrative autonomy over spending. One of them had had an elected government for most of the period since 1920, and the other two were poised to get one each. But none of the three raised, or would raise, any tax themselves. Meanwhile in England most of public spending was raised centrally, but a lot of it was spent locally. Local authorities only raised in local taxes about half of what they spent. The rest came from rate support grant, as it was then called, from the central government.

VFI encourages fiscal irresponsibility. Politicians in the territories faced no budget constraint. The easiest platform for them would always be to promise (*a*) more spending in their territory than the other party, and (*b*) more spending than the UK Government was willing to permit. If the UK Government stopped them from spending, that only proved that the skinflint English were unwilling to provide for the basic needs of Scotland, Wales, and Northern Ireland. The party that was in government at UK level found it harder than others to make argument (*b*). But this constrained only one party at a time, and never constrained the Northern Irish Unionists, who were functionally distinct from the UK Conservatives. And all parties always made argument (*a*), whether in government or in opposition. The party in government could say, 'We will get more money than the other lot, and we have a Secretary of State in the Cabinet to make sure that we get it.' The party in opposition could always promise more for Wales and Scotland, especially as it could reasonably reckon that nobody outside each territory would see its manifesto for that territory (e.g., Kellas 2005 for the Conservatives in Scotland).

So territorial-spending politics became a zero-sum game. Politicians were not interested in using public expenditure efficiently, but only in claiming pork for their territory. The politicians of the North of England were no different. After defeating the Scotland and Wales Bill in 1977, their territorial demands were assuaged by the Government's placing an order in Newcastle for a generating set to go into a big power station in Yorkshire, over the protests of the Central Electricity Generating Board, which wanted neither the one nor the other (Guthrie and McLean 1978). It was left to the Treasury to work out a longer-term response—in fact, two conflicting responses.

The first was an attempt to assess the relative needs of the four territories of the UK. Needs are, of course, politically contested. Some may say that they are, as philosophers call it, an 'essentially contested concept'—that there is not and cannot be agreement as to what constitutes a need. In some federal regimes, an official body attempts to get to a needs-based definition of a uniform standard of public service. The most admired is probably the Australian Commonwealth Grants Commission (CGC).

The CGC was established in 1933. (A full description is in McLean 2004*b*.) Its most recent mission statement is:

The Commission's advice is based on the principle of fiscal equalisation which states that each State should be given the capacity to provide the average standard of State-type public services, assuming it does so at an average level of operational efficiency and makes an average effort to raise revenue from its own sources.

Equalisation is designed to equalise States' capacity to provide services, not their results. This is because the Commission's recommendations relate to untied general revenue grants and each State is free to decide its own priorities (*Source*: its website at *www.cgc.gov.au*, consulted on 9.2.2004)

This is at once highly egalitarian; uniform between the Australian States, but not within them; and respectful of state autonomy (as it constitutionally must be). It is highly egalitarian because it commits the Commission to equalize for three inequalities: *needs*; *resources*, and *costs*. A state has above average needs for a service if it has more clients per 1,000 of population for it. A state has below average resources if a given tax effort will produce below average tax proceeds per head. And a state may have above average costs of delivering public services because of sparsity (or alternatively congestion), or unusually high cost of its inputs. The regime aims to be uniform between, not within, states. In all states the services enjoyed by a remote rural dweller will probably be poorer than those delivered to a suburbanite. But the regime aims to equate remote rural dwellers in Northern Territory with their counterparts in South Australia, and suburbanites in Melbourne with their counterparts in Perth. The regime has to respect state autonomy as the states are constitutionally entrenched in Australia. Therefore neither it nor the Commonwealth Government has the power to order a state to deliver a particular service in a particular way, or indeed at all.

The only publicly known UK attempt to do anything similar is HM Treasury (1979). Much Whitehall lore surrounds this *Needs Assessment*. It was, as its subtitle states, a joint effort by the Treasury and the territorial departments. However, the Treasury held the whip hand. Civil servants in the territories are believed to have seen it as the Treasury's revenge for a century of frustration over Goschen and the Northern Irish Joint Exchequer Board. Much blood, it is said, was shed on the carpet. The departments failed to agree on the correct weighting to give for relative needs in the NHS.

The methodology of the Needs Assessment resembled that of the Commonwealth Grants Commission. The Treasury tried to divide drivers of 'need' into what it called objective and subjective. Objective drivers were those matters that were not the result of policy choices; subjective drivers resulted from policy choices. Examples of objective drivers were population structure, morbidity, and school-age population. The examples given of 'subjective' drivers of costs were bilingualism in Wales and denominational education in Northern Ireland. These subjective drivers were ignored *because* they resulted from policy choices. This replicates Australian procedures. The main published results of the Needs Assessment have already been given in

Table 7.1. Table 10.3 delves a little deeper to reveal the bloodstains on the carpet.

On one large block, current NHS hospital spending, the expert group could not agree. The minority produced numbers showing Scotland's and Northern Ireland's needs to be much higher than the majority. It is not hard to guess where the minority and majority civil servants hailed from. The overall results showed that, for the services to have been devolved in 1978, Scotland's needs per head were 16 per cent ahead of England's, Wales's 9 per cent and Northern Ireland's 31 per cent. Actual spending on those services was 22 per cent ahead in Scotland, 6 per cent ahead in Wales, and 35 per cent ahead in Northern Ireland.

The Needs Assessment should be interpreted with some, but not too much, caution (cf. HM Treasury 1979: para. 7.8). The services to be devolved in 1978 were fewer than those actually devolved in 1998. However, universities, police, and railways, to be reserved to the centre in 1978 but actually de-volved to the territories in 1998, probably incur higher per-head spending in Scotland and Northern Ireland (but not Wales) than in England. If a coarser model were taken, when the number of drivers of needs was reduced to a handful, the relativities remained robust. Accordingly, the conclusion that Scotland and Northern Ireland were receiving public spending ahead of their relative needs, and Wales behind, is also reasonably robust.

The 1979 Assessment, unlike the Australians, did not consider either resources or costs. It did not consider resources because the three territories had, in effect, zero power to tax or to vary tax rates. It did not consider the costs of delivering public services in different parts of the UK because it had no relevant data.

The Barnett Formula emerged at the same time as the Needs Assessment and in response to the same political stimuli. But it is quite different. It has

TABLE 10.3. *Needs Assessment 1979 (data for 1976–1977), showing disagreements between HM Treasury and territorial departments*

	England	Scotland	Wales	Northern Ireland
Hospitals and Community Health, Current (majority view)	100	108.6	105.3	108.4
Hospitals and Community Health, Current (minority view)	100	118	112.1	121.8
All services: needs	100	116	109	131
All services: actual expenditure	100	122	106	135

Source: HM Treasury (1979): Lines 1 and 2: Annex E, Para. 27 and footnote;
Line 3: Para. 6.5;
Line 4: Para. 2.15
All figures are per head (England = 100).

often been described (e.g., McLean and McMillan 2003; Bell and Christie 2001; House of Commons Library 2001; Heald and McLeod 2005), and a general book such as this is not the place for fine details. Here is an at attempt at the big Barnett picture.

The Barnett Formula was named after Joel Barnett (now Lord Barnett), who was Chief Secretary to the Treasury in the 1974–9 Government. He was for many years proud of giving his name to something that has become so famous, although he has now disowned it and asked for his name to be removed from it as he thinks it is so unfair. However, he did not personally either invent or name the Formula. He ascribes its invention to (Sir) Leo Pliatzky, most terrifying of Treasury mandarins (e.g., Pliatzky 1982, 1989). And it was given the name 'Barnett Formula' in 1980 by the public finance scholar David Heald, after it had already been in operation for two years.

The Barnett Formula had two purposes. The first was to secure a single block for each territory and obviate Goschen-style bargaining over each programme at a time. The second was to bring about convergence towards equal expenditure per head in each territory. It succeeded immediately in the first aim. To date, it has failed in the second; but equal per capita spending in each territory was never the correct target.

In evidence to the Treasury Select Committee in 1997, Lord Barnett said that he did not expect his Formula to last 'a year or even twenty minutes' (Barnett 1997: 1). It makes limited sense as a transitional device; it makes none as a long-term device. He added that it was intended to bring down spending in Scotland and Northern Ireland to the 'right' level, whereupon it would be succeeded by a needs assessment. That has not happened. Instead, the Scottish and Welsh White Papers of 1997 promised that the 'block and formula' arrangements for funding devolved services would continue. The arrangements are not statutory—they are not specified in the Scotland or Wales Acts. But could be argued that their inclusion in the White Papers put them on to the agenda on which the people of Scotland and Wales voted, and that they are legitimized thereby. More crudely, 'if it ain't broke, don't fix it'. However, the Barnett Formula is irretrievably broke.

It leaves untouched the baseline public spending per head on devolved services. The Needs Assessment showed that it was above 'needs' in Scotland and in Northern Ireland, and below them in Wales. However, it was above the equal-per-capita baseline of 100 in all three territories. Rather than touch the baseline, the Barnett Formula determines *changes* in the block grant to the territories from *changes* in the relevant public spending in England. Relevant spending is spending on a service that is devolved in one or more of the territories. To take a current example, higher education is a devolved function in each of the three territories. If, therefore, the Government increases public spending on higher education in England, each territory will get an increase in its block grant, known as a 'Barnett consequential', in the shape of its pro rata population equivalent of the extra expenditure in England. It may choose to spend this consequential on higher education but need not. Scientific research, on the other hand, is a non-devolved function. The 2003 Higher Education White Paper proposed to route some extra spending for English universities through the Higher Education Funding Council for England. This extra attracts a Barnett consequential. However, another block of the increased spending on universities that it proposes is increased spending on research support, routed in part through the Office of Science and Technology, which is part of the Department of Trade and Industry (DTI). As this is an all-UK function, the territories get no Barnett consequential for this component of the extra spending (McLean 2003).

In the long run, Barnett must converge towards equal spending per head (Bell and Christie 2001). This is because ultimately the original baseline becomes trivial by comparison with the successive increments, which are all assigned on an equal-per-head basis. But this cannot be the right target. The Needs Assessment showed that the needs of all three territories were above England's. In Wales, needs already exceeded spending in 1976/77, and therefore any convergence towards equal spending per head would be wrong from day one. In the other two territories, convergence would begin by bringing spending closer to needs. But it would then sail on downwards beyond the needs point and end with too little spending. The Northern Ireland Civil Service believes that Northern Ireland's block grant under Barnett is crashing through the needs line heading downwards. A second, independent, defect of the Formula is that it makes the block grant to the territories a function of expenditure in England—but that is a number over which they have no control. Both as an equity formula and as an efficiency formula, Barnett is a disaster.

For many years, the equity defects did not matter because Barnett was not enforced. It may seem strange that politicians should first create a formula and then ignore it. But in the light of the political economy of credible threats, that is not so strange. As shown in the previous chapters, Scotland posed a credible threat to the Union from the mid-1960s. Northern Ireland always has. Politicians had therefore to keep these territories in the Union however they could. Barnett, introduced in the wake of the English backlash of 1977, threatened to cut their public spending per head. If it threatened to cut it to the point where the opposition in these territories noticed, or the people noticed, then it would be sacrificed to measures to save the Union. As noted in Chapter 7, that is exactly what the territorial Secretaries of State did under the Conservatives from 1979 to 1997. They bypassed Barnett when enforcing Barnett might have threatened the Union.

When Labour entered office in 1997, they pledged to maintain the spending limits they inherited from the outgoing Conservatives for two years. This had the side effect of halting any Barnett convergence. If there is no increase in spending in England, there is no extra Barnett money for the Territories. But, starting in 1999, Labour implemented large real increases in public expenditure, especially in the Spending Reviews of 2000 and 2002, each running for two years. It follows from the mathematics of Barnett that the faster the real increases in England, the faster the convergence in the territories. They still get real increases in their expenditure, partly on programmes that do not go into the Barnett block and partly through the Barnett consequentials of the programmes that do. But their advantage in spending per head is being eroded. In Northern Ireland, the civil service believe that it is being eroded so fast that public expenditure will cross the needs line heading downwards during the lifetime of the 2002 Spending Review, which lasts until 2005.

The UK Government frequently states that it has no plans to alter the Barnett Formula. But sooner or later it will have to, whether it wants to or not. In Wales and in Northern Ireland, it will have to either bypass or ignore the Formula if it wishes to empower their Assemblies to deliver public services to the same standard as in England. In Scotland, this pressure will not arise until perhaps the mid-2010s. But in England it already has. Local media and local politicians in the poorer regions of England have returned to the politics of the 1970s. They notice, once again, that Scotland and London are richer than they are and yet receive more public expenditure per head. They blame Barnett.[4] Blaming Barnett is unfair because Barnett does not apply to the English regions, although it does help to explain why Scotland and Northern Ireland do well compared to them. But perceptions matter. Especially if elected regional assemblies in England materialize, but even if they do not, the crude parliamentary arithmetic is that there are more seats in the poor regions of England than there are in Scotland and Northern Ireland. That supplies another reason why Barnett is unsustainable.

Formula funding of the English regions does exist, but it takes quite different forms to Barnett. It is also broke. The regions *as regions* receive very little formula funding (Cameron et al. 2004). But all the main services to people in the regions, except social security, are delivered by formula. Social security, as throughout the UK, is demand-led. This means that it functions as an automatic stabilizer, between regions as well as in general macroeconomic management. If a region has high unemployment or above-average sickness or more pensioners than most, then to that extent it receives more

---

[4] A search in the Lexis-Nexis newspaper database for the string 'iniquitous Barnett formula' in September 2004 yielded 24 hits. Of these, 21 are from the *Journal* (Newcastle upon Tyne) and one each from *The Guardian*, *Daily Telegraph*, and *Northern Echo* (Darlington).

than average public spending out of the social security budget, which is the largest single spending programme of the UK Government.

After social security, the three next biggest distributive programmes are, in descending order, health, education, and law and order. Each of these is distributed around England by formula. The formula funding to each health authority and each local authority in a region adds up to the formula funding of the region. The fact, therefore, that the north-east of England receives less per head than Scotland is not purely a function of Barnett. It is also a function of the health and local government formulae. The formula for NHS spending works well and is politician-proof. The formula for local government services, including most of education and law and order, works badly, and politicians manipulate it as it is rational for them to do.

In principle both of these formulae are needs assessments. Like the Treasury's 1979 exercise, the planners of health and local government spending try to assess the needs of each area by reference to the objective characteristics of its population, such as morbidity, mortality, and the prevalence of old people and children. Why then do the health formulae work well and the local government formulae badly? For two main reasons, one neat and technical and the other political and rather disturbing.

The neat technical reason is that objective indicators are easier to come by for health. We know from the Office for National Statistics how many people are old, young, sick, and die in each region a year. None of these are manipulable by politicians, and only 'being sick' is manipulable by anyone else. In education, governments of both parties have been trying to get similarly objective indicators—this is one of the reasons for the proliferation of tests and school inspectors since the mid-1990s. But in other personal services it is much harder to get objective measures. Consider personal social services, which are delivered by local authorities. We would like to know whether people in Lambeth are happier than people in Lancashire. If they are sadder, we might want to spend more money per head there until the average happiness of the people is equal across all the local authorities of England. Since we cannot do that, we are forced back on very unsatisfactory measures. (How many social workers are there? What is their average case load? How many people a day do they see?) At worst, we are forced back on what the Office of the Deputy Prime Minister, the custodian of the formulae, calls 'regression on past spending'. If an authority has spent more than most on a service in the past, that apparently signals that it 'needs' to spend more on that service. In efficiency terms, a formula that regresses on past spending is as perverse as it could possibly be (McLean and McMillan 2003*a*, *b*).

There is worse to come. When we started working on this, a former Conservative minister warned us to 'look at the exemplifications'. When the local government department consults interested parties on possible changes to its formulae, it also publishes lists showing how each local authority would do under each of the proposed alternatives. That makes politicians' job fatally easy. A naive minister just runs a finger across the lists and chooses the formula under which the governing party's local authorities do best. A sophisticated minister runs a finger across the lists and chooses the formula under which the local authority containing the median voter (the voter whose vote will swing the next general election) does best. Either procedure violates both equity and efficiency. Empirical evidence (Ward and John 1999) confirms the hypothesis that ministers do what it is politically rational for them to do.

In summary, then, Barnett is broke, and so is formula funding to English local authorities. Distribution must be, in the classic Marxist formula, *to each according to his needs* (and tax policy must follow the other half of the maxim *from each according to his ability* to pay). A future government will have to build on the 1979 Needs Assessment by selecting objective measures of needs, and rejecting subjective ones. It should study the Australian model closely, as the Commonwealth Grants Committee is the only body in the world we know that manages to do such a job and avoid partisan political controversy.

That advice may be utopian. The Needs Assessment warned that it would be difficult (HM Treasury 1979: 7.10). If fine measurement of needs is impracticable, we have suggested elsewhere (McLean and McMillan 2003*a*, *b*) that coarse measurement may be a fallback. On this plan, the good part of Barnett would be kept, and extended from three regions of the UK to all 12. The bad part would be scrapped and replaced by a more appropriate formula.

The good part of Barnett is its convergence mechanism. Sir Leo Pliatzky's original intention was probably to achieve relatively painless convergence. The device to achieve it was that future *changes* of grant to one place depended on future *changes* of spending elsewhere. That feature of Barnett should be retained as it eases the necessarily painful adjustments.

But as we have shown, Barnett converges on the wrong thing, namely equal per capita spending in all regions. We suggest instead that convergence should be on relative GDP. The lower a region's GDP per head, the more needy it is. Both for equity and efficiency reasons, any government should be concentrating its spending on regions with low GDP per head in order to make their citizens richer, happier, and more productive. Furthermore, GDP is not directly something that governments produce. This minimizes the perverse incentives associated with Goodhart's Law ('If a measure becomes a target, it ceases to be a reliable measure'—McLean and McMillan 2003*b*).

Therefore we conclude by offering the McLean–McMillan Formula. Let there be a UK Territorial Grants Commission, a non-departmental public body responsible for allocating distributive expenditure, apart from social security, to all twelve regions of the UK. Let each territory have one vote at Commission meetings. Let there be a *unanimity rule with an inverse GDP default*. The unanimity rule states that the funding formula for the next time period must be unanimously agreed by all the territories it affects. This is to get over the problem of the differentially credible threats of some regions over others, which we have examined exhaustively in this book. A unanimity rule is the only one that makes all threats equally credible. However, on its own it would produce deadlock. The inverse GDP default part of the rule states that if the territories have not unanimously agreed a formula by the due date, then the formula for the next time period will be that the extra grant to each territory is an inverse function of its GDP.

Heald (1980) predicted that some day Joel Barnett would become as famous as Lord Goschen. That prediction has been amply fulfilled, unlike most predictions in social science. We do not aspire to become more famous than Lord Barnett, but we would not mind seeing our names in just a few, rather weak, lights.

11

Conclusion: A Union State without Unionism

Unionism in the UK always suffered from deep intellectual incoherence. For a long time that was masked by its usefulness to politicians and its popular appeal. Now that both of these have expired, can the union state survive without unionism?

The Death of Unionism

Unionism was an elite creed before it was a popular one. English politicians needed Union in 1707 because of the Scottish threat to the security of England after the death of Queen Anne. Scots politicians, their state bankrupt and subject to economic and military threats from England, had no realistic choice but to accept Union. However, they secured safeguards for their religion and laws, safeguards that have been (more or less) honoured ever since.

Popular unionism was in doubt for decades after 1707. Scotland seemed to have got no immediate benefits from the Union, and therefore the emotional support (in the Highlands) and non-resistance (elsewhere) to the Jacobite Rising of 1745 in Scotland comes as no surprise. In England, Jacobitism was weaker, but neither the Hanoverian kings nor the Scots were much loved. Politicians' attempts to cultivate popular unionism go back to the aftermath of the 1745. Most of the defeated Highland clans were treated leniently (by the standards of the time). They were incorporated into the British state by recruitment to the British Army and service in the British Empire. The noun *Briton* was coined, in its modern sense, by James Thomson, the author of *Rule Britannia*, set to music by Thomas Arne in 1740 and sung at the Last Night of the Proms every year.

Some of the greatest beneficiaries of Union were the Britons who settled in North America. The improved public finances of the new state enabled it to borrow more cheaply than its great rival France (Stasavage 2003), and hence contributed to British victories over France in the colonial wars in Canada and India known as the Seven Years War (1756–63). The victory in Canada removed French claims over a tourniquet from Pittsburgh to New Orleans, that would otherwise have strangled the westward ambitions of the Ulster Scots and other frontiersmen in the American colonies. British governments therefore decided that the colonists should cease to free-ride on the public good of (relative) peace on the frontier and decided to tax them to pay for the defence of the American colonies. This was, unfortunately, taxation without representation. And so the first British Empire fell apart. The defeat of the British by American and French forces in the American War of Independence proved, among other things, that the first empire had failed to solve the problems of representation or finance in a union state.

The American Revolution provoked the French: directly by example, and more subtly by bankrupting the French state and hence forcing Louis XVI to call the Estates-General in 1789. The bloody progress of the French Revolution placed Britain and the British Empire in the biggest danger they had encountered for a century. A mostly popular war stimulated popular unionism (see the regional recruitment statistics in Colley 1996). But the weakest point of the Union was now Ireland. The French-supported rebellion there in 1798 proved to the English that it was now necessary to incorporate Ireland into the Union. The majority of members of the Irish Parliament supported Union for various reasons, including better access to the Empire, greater stability in Ireland itself, and (for some) Catholic emancipation. But the royal veto over the last made the Irish Union illegitimate to most Irish people from the outset. It led to the Irish bloc in the Commons, which parliamentary arithmetic was bound to make decisive at some time, and finally did in 1885.

Outside Catholic Ireland, and even for some inside it, the nineteenth century was good for the Union. The growth of free-trade imperialism after the Repeal of the Corn Laws in 1846 led to substantial increases in wealth, even for the working class. It also led to expanded job opportunities in the Empire. India alone provided a career for every stratum of British society. They are all in Kipling, from Pagett MP and Morrowbie Jukes to Fleet Engineer McAndrew to Privates Ortheris, Learoyd, and Mulvaney. Mulvaney, by the way, is obviously a Catholic Irishman.

Nevertheless the breakup of Union, if not necessarily the bloody form it took between 1918 and 1923, was inevitable from 1886 onwards. That period revealed the intellectual incoherence of Diceyan unionism. However, its incoherence was masked by the simultaneous rise in welfare state unionism. David Lloyd George created the first welfare state, and the tax regime to fund it, between 1909 and 1914, and solved the Irish question for fifty years, in 1921. Both extraordinary feats preserved the Union—the first by giving a new ground for uniformity, and the second by removing the irreconcilable south of Ireland.

Welfare state unionism, sustained by both elite and mass attachment to the Empire and Commonwealth, subsisted until the late 1960s. The Empire disappeared first, with the UK's first application to join the European Common Market in 1961. The Welfare State remains. But sustaining it in a union state started to become complicated with the Scottish and Welsh nationalist gains at Carmarthen and Hamilton. In response to those, the UK-wide parties defended the Union in their own ways. Both parties, but especially the Conservatives, boosted Scotland's privileged share of public spending per head. Labour swung from unionism to Home Rule in 1974. Although the legislation of that Labour Government failed, it produced the features that have dominated territorial politics in the UK since—especially the contested assessment of needs; the Barnett formula; and the West Lothian Question.

The West Lothian Question in reverse led to the revival of devolution in Scotland. The Scottish Constitutional Convention was created in 1989, when Labour and the Liberal Democrats' dislike of each other was outweighed by their dislike of Conservatives governing Scotland on a small minority of the seats there. The change of government in 1997 led to the enactment of the Convention's ideas. Wales, as in 1974, was brought in as an afterthought.

Meanwhile, a separate set of events forced politicians to revisit the constitution of Northern Ireland. The resurgence of sectarian violence that began in 1969 and peaked in 1972 led to the end of the old devolved regime and an incomplete thirty-year march to a new one. The recognition, by the UK and Irish Governments, of the legitimacy of one another's interest in the constitution of Northern Ireland has led some to label Northern Ireland now as a 'federacy', not subject to unilateral UK control (O'Leary 2002). The supreme authority of the Parliament of the UK does not remain unaffected over all persons, matters, and things in (Northern) Ireland.

With the death of Enoch Powell and the retirement of John Major, unionism in British politics is dead outside Northern Ireland. Can a union state survive without unionism? Some unionists, and some separatists, have long had a common belief that it cannot, and that devolution to Scotland and Wales made a slippery slope down which they would be launched to independence. At the crudest level, that prediction has not been borne out. In both Scotland and Wales, the nationalist parties did less well in the second post-devolution national election in 2003 than at the first in 1999 (Tables 11.1 and 11.2).

Both parliaments use the Additional Member System of proportional representation. The parties' total representation is therefore close to being proportionate to their share of the list vote. In 1998 Donald Dewar described

TABLE 11.1. *Scottish Parliament election results 1999 and 2003*

Party	1999			2003		
	Constituency vote (%)	List vote (%)	Seats	Constituency vote (%)	List vote (%)	Seats
Labour	33.6	38.8	56	34.6	29.3	50
SNP	27.3	28.7	35	23.8	20.9	27
Conservative	15.4	15.6	18	16.6	15.5	18
Liberal Democrat	12.4	14.2	17	15.4	11.8	17
Green Party	3.6	0.0	1	0.0	6.9	7
Scottish Socialist Party	2.0	1.0	1	6.2	6.7	6
Other	5.7	1.7	1	3.4	8.9	4
Total	100	100	129	100	100	129

Sources: Scottish Parliament results site at *http://www.scottish.parliament.uk/ msps/results-03/*; our calculations.

TABLE 11.2. *National Assembly of Wales election results 1999 and 2003*

Party	1999			2003		
	Constituency vote (%)	List vote (%)	Seats	Constituency vote (%)	List vote (%)	Seats
Labour	37.6	35.4	28	40.0	36.6	30
Plaid Cymru	28.4	30.5	17	21.2	19.7	12
Conservative	15.8	16.5	9	19.9	19.2	11
Liberal Democrat	13.5	12.5	6	14.1	12.7	6
Other	4.7	5.1	0	4.8	11.8	1
Total	100	100	60	100	100	60

Source: (1999) Institute of Welsh Affairs, University of Wales, Aberystwyth, at *http:// www.aber.ac.uk/interpol/ IWP/IWP_elections.html*; (2003) (Osmond 2004: Fig. 3.4).

its adoption for Scotland as a 'great act of charity' by Labour, because it delivered Labour fewer seats than under the Westminster first-past-the-post system. This decision rankles with many Scottish Labour politicians. But as statecraft it was very wise. Although it prevents Labour from winning an outright majority in the Scottish Parliament, it also prevents the SNP from doing the same. That is why Dewar insisted on it. He was a cultural nationalist but a political unionist (McLean 2004*c*).

In Wales, everybody expected Labour to win an overall majority in the first National Assembly even with the AMS electoral system. But Labour's shambolic performance on the approach to the 1999 election helped to

deny them that. Plaid Cymru's strong performance was the obverse of Labour's weakness.

Labour went into coalition with the Liberal Democrats during the first parliament in both Scotland and Wales. That coalition continues in Scotland but in Wales Labour has formed a single-party administration without a majority of seats. It is thus still the dominant party in both parliaments after their second elections. But Scottish and Welsh Labour's relationship with Westminster Labour has subtly changed, precisely because of the weakness of both the SNP and Plaid Cymru in the 2003 elections. The credibility of the nationalist threat to the Union has subsided in both countries. Therefore the pragmatic unionist parties at Westminster—Labour and the Conservatives—have fewer reasons to make concessions. This bears more heavily on Labour, as it is in government as we write. In the first parliaments, there was little friction between the UK Labour Government and the Labour-dominated administrations in Edinburgh and Cardiff. Issues that might have caused trouble were to a remarkable extent settled informally within the Labour Party and personal connections. That situation will not long outlast the 2003 elections. As we argue below, the union state will have to change after the death of primordial unionism. These changes will cause pain in the London–Cardiff and London–Edinburgh axes. But Labour politicians in the devolved capitals no longer owe their colleagues of the same party in London any favours—and vice versa. For example, up to 2003 Labour politicians in the National Assembly knew that the Barnett Formula did no favours to Wales, but they dared not say so out loud because that would hand an election slogan to Plaid Cymru. The marginalization of Plaid Cymru removes that constraint. It equally makes Westminster Labour politicians from Wales less friendly to their party colleagues in the National Assembly, as witness Welsh Labour MPs' hostility to the National Assembly's Richard Commission, which in early 2004 demanded greater powers for the National Assembly. And the Labour Government of the UK has less reason to be tender to its party colleagues in Edinburgh and Cardiff. In autumn 2004 Malcolm Chisholm, the Scottish Health Minister, was rudely summoned to a meeting of Westminster Labour MPs to account for his programme of NHS rationalization. In a mature devolved UK, he could have retorted that it was none of their business. But he went; and, when he got home, the First Minister sacked him (*Herald*, 5.10.2004).

This tension could spell the doom of the Barnett Formula. As the union state of the UK evolves, it is predictable that its party systems will become more like those of Canada and Australia. In these systems, parties with the same name (e.g., Labor, Liberal, Conservative, New Democrat) contest both federal and provincial/state elections. But they are organizationally entirely separate. They resolve federal–state differences through the formal machinery for doing so, not inside the party.

Unionist Delusions

Letters on Unionist Delusions was the surprising title of one of Dicey's anti-Home Rule polemics (Dicey 1887). He meant the delusions of *Liberal* Unionists who wanted some compromise, or even reunion, with the Gladstonians. But in this section we aim to show that his own Unionism was based on a delusion. Or, if that is too harsh, on a contradiction.

To see why, we must first return one more time to 1707. The Treaty and Acts of Union were very cleverly drafted. The sequence was:

1. The treaty was debated and ratified by the Scottish Parliament, incorporating a Scottish Act for the establishment of the Presbyterian Church of Scotland. However, this Act contained two provisions to control the subsequent actions of the English Parliament. On the one hand, the Scottish Act ratified in advance 'whatever provision might be inserted by the English Parliament in the act of Union for the protection of the Church of England' (Dicey and Rait 1920: 219–20). On the other, the Act itself declared that it and the articles of Union were not binding in Scotland until they had been passed by the English Parliament. This document, ratified by the Scottish Parliament on 16 January 1707, is the document normally printed as the Act of Union.
3. The English Parliament now considered the articles. It recited them and the Scottish Act within the English Act, incorporating (as invited by the Scots) an act for the establishment of the Church of England. This document, although enacted after the Scottish Act, is referred to as the Act of Union 1706—because the English were still using the old calendar in which the year changed on 25 March, whereas Scotland had moved to the new calendar in which it changed on 1 January!

Two features of this process are of continuing constitutional relevance. They are the establishment of two churches with rival doctrines in the two parts of the uniting kingdom; and the attempt to entrench the Treaty and Acts for all time.

The incorporated Scottish act for the establishment of the Presbyterian Church states in part:

Her Majesty, with advice and consent of the said Estates of Parliament, doth hereby establish and confirm the said true Protestant religion, and the worship, discipline, and government of this Church to continue without any alteration to the people of this land in all succeeding generations; and more especially, Her Majesty, with advice and consent foresaid, ratifies, approves, and forever confirms the fifth Act of the first Parliament of King William and Queen Mary, entitled 'Act Ratifying the Confession of Faith, and Settling Presbyterian Church Government'.

The incorporated English act states in part

That after the Demise of her Majesty (whom God long preserve) the Sovereign next succeeding to her Majesty in the Royal Government of the Kingdom of *Great Britain*, and so for ever hereafter, every King or Queen succeeding and coming to the Royal Government of the Kingdom of *Great Britain*, at his or her Coronation, shall in the presence of all Persons who shall be attending, assisting, or otherwise then and there present, take and subscribe an Oath to maintain and preserve inviolably the said Settlement of the Church of *England*, and the Doctrine, Worship, Discipline, and Government thereof, as by Law established within the Kingdoms of *England* and *Ireland*, the Dominion of *Wales*, and Town of *Berwick* upon *Tweed*, and the Territories thereunto belonging.

To logical minds, this pair of provisions is problematic, especially in the Town of Berwick-on-Tweed. All the successors of Queen Anne have been bound to uphold rival churches in different parts of their united kingdom. As there can be at most one true Protestant religion, logicians and theologians must squirm. Historians and political scientists can relax. As Dicey and Rait (1920: 220) say, 'The Whigs of both countries . . . were fully determined that neither Bishop nor Presbyter should have power to raise a religious war which might break up the political union of the two countries.' The incorporation of two rival establishments is the clearest proof that the Treaty is indeed a treaty between two bargainers, neither of them powerless; and that the state it created is a union state, not a unitary state. The Act of Union forbids both any attempt by the bishops to establish Anglicanism in Scotland (which they had tried under Charles I) and any attempts by the presbyters to establish Presbyterianism in England (which they had tried during the English Civil War).

That is, assuming the words 'for ever', which appear in both of these clauses and in other places in the Acts, can be taken at face value. The treaty negotiators on both sides thought that they were trying to create an entity that could not be uncreated again. The English commissioners wanted to rule out forever the possibility of Scotland choosing a different king—and, therefore, in eighteenth-century terms a different government—to England. *But to those who believe in parliamentary sovereignty, those words* for ever *are empty. Parliament can do anything except bind its successor.*

Dicey himself put it as clearly and as brutally as anybody, as quoted in Chapter 1:

Neither the Act of Union with Scotland nor the Dentists Act, 1878, has more claim than the other to be considered a supreme law. . . . The one fundamental dogma of English constitutional law is the absolute legislative sovereignty or despotism of the King in Parliament. But this dogma is incompatible with the existence of a fundamental compact, the provisions of which control every authority existing under the constitution. (Dicey 1885: 141).

That is why Dicey and Rait (1920) is such a fascinating book. Writing jointly with the Historiographer-Royal for Scotland, Dicey wants to show, and on the whole succeeds in showing, that the 1707 Union is after all a fundamental constitutional document. This claim is in turn fundamental to Dicey's own Unionism, and his passionate denunciations of the Home Rule Bills of 1886, 1893, and 1912. But it is stark incompatible with parliamentary sovereignty, as he had famously delineated it in 1885. If parliamentary sovereignty is correct, primordial Unionism loses its intellectual grounding. The only way to save the Union is to abandon parliamentary sovereignty.

Who is Sovereign—Parliament or the People?

We said in Chapter 1 without explaining ourselves that we sided with polit-ical scientists and a few (mostly Scots) constitutional lawyers against the conventional wisdom of constitutional law. Here is our explanation.

Dicey's (and Enoch Powell's) claim that the King-in-Parliament is sover-eign over all persons, matters, and things in the UK is still the majority view of constitutional lawyers. But it rests on dubious history and on a logical contradiction. The contradiction we have just discussed. The dubious history is the claim that the Parliament of the UK is an enlarged continuation of the Parliament of England. As Dicey and Rait correctly say, the Union of 1707 was not the federation that the most far-sighted Scots, such as Fletcher of Saltoun, desired. No more was the Union of 1800 a federation. But it is the fallacy of the excluded middle to assert that the state created in 1707 must therefore have been a unitary state. To make that claim involves claiming that the Parliament of England, in which the doctrine of parliamentary supremacy, or sovereignty, had evolved over centuries, a civil war, and a deposition of a king, simply absorbed the Scots and continued on its way. But the history of the Union (Chapter 2 and this chapter) proves that this is wrong. The English Parliament was not a free agent when it made the English Act of Union 1706/7. Politically, it was not a free agent because it needed the Union to head off the Scots' threat to appoint a different monarch to the English. Constitutionally, it was not a free agent because the Scots had cleverly bound it, by the terms of the Scottish Act, to accept the Presbyterian settlement in Scotland. Reject that, and the Union would fail.

Therefore, we insist that the UK was a union state all along. From Rokkan and Urwin's definition of a 'union state', it features 'the survival in some areas of pre-union rights and institutional infrastructures which preserve some degree of regional autonomy' (Rokkan and Urwin 1982: 11).

The Irish Union was closer to the incorporating Union that the Scottish Union is so often wrongly believed to have been. Because the bargain between the British and Irish Parliaments that was made in 1800 was broken in 1801, it is harder to characterize the Irish Union as a bargain than the Scottish Union. The challenge to the Diceyanism of the 1920 Government of Ireland Act came not from constitutional law but from reality. In reality, southern Ireland never was, and Northern Ireland has not been since at least the Border Poll of 1973, subject to the unique jurisdiction of the Queen-in-Parliament. The people have a say as well.

There is a romantic notion that the idea of popular sovereignty in Scotland goes back to the Declaration of Arbroath in 1320. Addressed to the pope by a list of petitioners that ends '*and the other barons and freeholders and the whole community of the realm of Scotland*', it requests his support in the Scottish war of independence against England, continuing '*as long as but a hundred of us remain alive, never will we on any conditions be brought under English rule. It is in truth not for glory, nor riches, nor honours that we are fighting, but for freedom—for that alone, which no honest man gives up but with life itself*' (Translation at *http://www.geo.ed.ac.uk/home/scotland/arbroath_english.html*, accessed 29.3.04). Some have argued that the phrase 'community of the realm of Scotland' is a fourteenth-century appeal to popular sovereignty. We doubt it.

However, it is not necessary to claim popular sovereignty in order to deny parliamentary sovereignty. In *MacCormick* v. *Lord Advocate* in 1953 (the case in which MacCormick unsuccessfully challenged the title of Queen Elizabeth II in Scotland), the senior judge in Scotland at the time, Lord Cooper, made a striking statement in denial of Dicey. Although irrelevant to the outcome of the case, which MacCormick lost on other grounds, it has increasingly been seen as fundamentally important:

But lest this case should go further, I shall briefly express my opinion. The principle of the unlimited sovereignty of Parliament is a distinctively English principle which has no counterpart in Scottish constitutional law. It derives its origin from Coke and Blackstone, and was widely popularized during the nineteenth century by Bagehot and Dicey, the latter having stated the doctrine in its classic form in his *Constitutional Law*. Considering that the Union legislation extinguished the Parliaments of Scotland and England and replaced them by a new Parliament, I have difficulty in seeing why it should have been supposed that the new Parliament of Great Britain must inherit all the peculiar characteristics of the English Parliament but none of the Scottish Parliament, as if all that happened in 1707 was that Scottish representatives were admitted to the Parliament of England. That is not what was done. Further, the Treaty and the associated legislation, by which the Parliament of Great Britain was brought into being as the successor of the separate Parliaments of Scotland and England, contain some clauses which expressly reserve to the Parliament of Great Britain powers of subsequent modification, and other clauses which either contain no such power or emphatically exclude subsequent alteration by declarations that the provision shall be fundamental and unalterable in all time coming, or declarations of a like effect. I have never been able to understand how it is possible to reconcile with elementary canons of construction the adoption by the English constitutional theorists of the same attitude to these markedly different types of provisions.

The Lord Advocate conceded this point by admitting that the Parliament of Great Britain 'could not' repeal or alter such 'fundamental and essential' conditions. He was doubtless influenced in making this concession by the modified views expressed by Dicey in his later work entitled *Thoughts on the Scottish Union*, from which I take this passage [Dicey and Rait 1920: 252–4]: 'The statesmen of 1707, though giving full sovereign power to the Parliament of Great Britain, clearly believed in the possibility of creating an absolutely sovereign legislature which should yet be bound by unalterable laws.' After instancing the provisions as to Presbyterian Church government in Scotland with their emphatic prohibition against alteration, the author [sic] proceeds: 'It represents the conviction of the Parliament which passed the Act of Union that the Act for the security of the Church of Scotland ought to be morally or constitutionally unchangeable, even by the British Parliament. . . . A sovereign Parliament in short, though it cannot be logically bound to abstain from changing any given law, may, by the fact that an Act when it was passed had been declared to be unchangeable, receive a warning that it cannot be changed without grave danger to the Constitution of the country.'

(*Source*: [1953] SC 396, quoted from Lexis-Nexis database, accessed 31.3.2004. Minor inaccuracies of Lord Cooper's citation from Dicey and Rait silently corrected.)

The case went no further. But we agree with Lord Cooper. His remark about 'elementary canons of construction' is lethal. The Parliament of Great Britain was not a continuation of the Parliament of England. Therefore, the doctrine of parliamentary sovereignty cannot be carried over from the one to the other. As at least one of Dicey's two inconsistent arguments must be dropped, we prefer to drop the one that depends on bad history. That leaves open two possible implications for the union state:

• That (at least in Scotland and Northern Ireland) ultimate sovereignty rests not with the UK Parliament, but with the people;
• That the Acts of Union; the Scotland and Wales Acts; and the Acts governing the constitution of Northern Ireland are constitutional statutes with some entrenchment. They are therefore more difficult to repeal than the Dentists Act 1878.

In Scotland, the claim to popular sovereignty was revived in the Claim of Right 1989, made by the parties to the Constitutional Convention:

We, gathered as the Scottish Constitutional Convention, do hereby acknowledge the sovereign right of the Scottish people to determine the form of Government best suited to their needs, and do hereby declare and pledge that in all our actions and deliberations their interests shall be paramount. (Scottish Constitutional Convention 1995: 11)

This may be dismissed as windbaggery. But as MacCormick (1998) observes, it was signed by several senior Labour Party figures who went on to enact the Scotland Act 1998. In Northern Ireland the promise that Northern Ireland's status would not be changed without the consent of the people of Northern Ireland was enacted in 1973 and re-enacted in 1998. It implies that if (and only if) the people of Northern Ireland do vote for a change of status, then the Union legislation applying there may be changed.

There is of course some tension between the inference of popular sovereignty and the inference of entrenchment. If the people of Scotland and Northern Ireland are sovereign, that implies that they have the right to leave the Union; in which case the entrenched Acts would have to be amended as they apply to their territories. In Northern Ireland that right has been made explicit in legislation. It is also a matter of realpolitik. If a majority of the voters in Northern Ireland agreed in a future referendum that they would rather be in the Republic of Ireland than in the UK, the politicians and people of the rest of the UK would heave a unanimous sigh of relief. There are no primordial unionists left in Great Britain. And there is no instrumental reason for the British state to hold on to Northern Ireland. It costs money and sometimes lives; and it contributes no votes in the Commons to either a Conservative or a Labour government.

Scotland and Wales are both different. Though there is no primordial interest in maintaining the Scottish Union, there is an instrumental interest. In 1997 John Major expressed it when he said that a UK without Scotland would find it harder to justify its permanent seat in the UN Security Council. Labour's main instrumental interest remains those Scottish seats at Westminster—not needed in the Parliaments of 1997 or 2001 except to quell backbench rebellions on (English) tuition fees, but likely to be needed by a future Labour government. Therefore, both of the big UK parties would fight to retain Scotland as they would not fight to retain Northern Ireland. An SNP majority in the Scottish Parliament, and/or an SNP majority of Scottish seats at Westminster, might be necessary but would not be sufficient to dissolve the 1707 Union. There would certainly have to be a referendum. In Scotland (as in Quebec), popular support for independence runs below popular support for the pro-independence political party, so the union state is not under immediate threat as we write.

The National Assembly for Wales does not have primary legislative powers. Its Richard Commission reported in March 2004 in favour of upgrading the National Assembly to give it legislative and, preferably, tax-varying powers. The Commission (gratuitously and perhaps unwisely) points out that if the National Assembly's powers are upgraded, there would be pressure to reduce the number of Welsh MPs (Richard 2004: 261). That is sufficient to ensure that Richard's recommendations go nowhere, because it creates a lobby of up to forty implacable MPs, who are not prepared to risk their seats in the Parliament that would have to enact Richard's recommendations. If the National Assembly remains a body without primary legislative powers, the number of Welsh MPs will probably not be reduced, and the Wales Act is unlikely to be changed significantly. It is also less likely in Wales than in Scotland that the nationalist party could win a majority of seats in either Westminster or Cardiff, and much less likely that the nationalists could win an independence referendum.

For the foreseeable future therefore (where 'the foreseeable future' means 'the lifetime of this edition of this book'), we assume therefore that the union state will continue, although under pressure on representation and finance.

Where the Shoe Pinches

The unionism of the Welfare State continues, but we predict that it will cause increasing friction within the union state. As we have seen, the idea of uniform nationwide rates of welfare goes back to the introduction of old age pensions and National Insurance under Asquith and Lloyd George. The other founders of the Welfare State, Bevan and Beveridge, shared their vision of a nationally uniform service, where benefits are paid at a uniform rate throughout the UK, out of taxes that are also levied at a uniform rate throughout the UK. In that way, the Welfare State is an engine of geographical transfers as well as personal transfers. Since poor people tend to live in one place and rich people in another, the places where the rich live will contribute more per head in tax than average and the places where the poor live will receive more per head in benefits than average. Furthermore, the tax and benefit system acts as an automatic stabilizer in the event of a local economic shock—say massive closures in a geographically concentrated industry. The resulting unemployment leads to a rapid flow of transfer payments from the rest of the country to the affected region, thus to some extent dampening the shock.

With the trivial exception of the unused Scottish Variable Rate of Income Tax, neither the tax nor the benefit system is devolved. The tax-raising departments of Inland Revenue and Customs (to be merged in 2005), and the Department of Work and Pensions, are UK-wide operations, and neither the tax they raise nor benefits expenditure plays any role in the Barnett system of public expenditure allocation. But the shoe has started to pinch in three places:

- when governments run social policy through non-reserved departments, and fall into devolution confusions;

- when politicians start to ask whether Bevan's principle of national uniformity *is* being observed after all; and
- when another set of politicians start to ask whether it *should be*.

All three have been felt since 1997.

Much of the Welfare State is devolved. Education, health, and personal social services are the biggest examples, although there are others. The government elected in 1997 has made it a priority to reduce child poverty. It has done so partly through tax credits and partly through expenditure measures. For instance, the programme called Sure Start states on its website that it

is a Government programme which aims to achieve better outcomes for children, parents and communities by:

- increasing the availability of childcare for all children
- improving health, education and emotional development for young children
- supporting parents as parents and in their aspirations towards employment.

This will be achieved by:

- helping services development in disadvantaged areas alongside financial help for parents to afford childcare
- rolling out the principles driving the Sure Start approach to all services for children and parents. (*http://www.surestart.gov.uk/aboutsurestart/*, accessed 31.3.2004)

Part of Sure Start comes in the form of tax credits ('financial help for parents to afford childcare'), and part in the form of extra money available for nurseries and other facilities for pre-school children ('helping services development in disadvantaged areas'). But the first apply evenly throughout the UK. The second apply only in England, and carry over to the three devolved administrations only by the indirect means of their Barnett consequentials. The three devolved administrations have set up Sure Start on parallel lines (see *http://www.surestart.gov.uk/surestartservices/surestartlocalprogrammes/*, accessed 31.3.2004). But they did not have to. And the operation of the Barnett consequentials means that it and every other social programme in the devolved administrations is under a long-term squeeze.

This pinch point is almost imperceptible as we write. The Barnett squeeze has not yet imperilled services in Scotland; Scotland and Wales are governed by the same party (alone or in coalition) as the UK; and Northern Ireland is governed by direct rule ministers from that party. But that situation will not last forever. As social policy diverges, examples being student support, NHS reorgnization, and personal care for the elderly (Trench 2004: chs. 2, 3, 4, and 10), so the debate about Barnett consequentials will spread outside the tiny band of Barnett obsessives who debate them now.

Has the Bevan principle of national uniformity already gone? Not in taxation or social security. But on the Welfare State programmes that are run outside England by the Devolved Administrations, and inside England by local authorities, expenditure per head seems to have no relationship to GDP per head (McLean and McMillan 2003*a*), nor to social security expenditure per head (Bell and Christie 2001). One would expect it to be inversely related to the first and directly related to the second. The poorer a region, then the more per head one expects to be spent there both on social security and on the rest of the Welfare State, especially education, health, and personal social services. That is not the case. If one regresses expenditure per head on non-devolved services against GDP per head, spending in Scotland, Northern Ireland, and London is above the regression line, while spending in Wales and all the poor regions of England is below it (McLean and McMillan 2003*a*). Politicians in all these regions are asking why; the UK Government has not yet answered convincingly.

Thirdly, should benefit rates remain equal throughout the UK when the cost of living varies? In 2000, prices in London were 6.8 per cent above the UK average; those in the north-east were 4.7 per cent below (Baran and O'Donogue 2002). Therefore, any given transfer to an individual is worth 4.7 per cent more than average in the north-east and 6.8 per cent less in London. Though these differences are not extreme enough to have really perverse consequences, they do reduce mobility. A person who is unemployed in the north-east but who could get a job in London would have to raise their nominal wage considerably before they became better off from taking the job from remaining unemployed in the north-east. Although the issue has barely yet broken the surface, it could become contestable.

Is the Union Stable?

Almost every expert on the Soviet Union—political scientists included—regarded it as a stable state in the mid 1980s. We could be as badly wrong-footed as the sovietologists. But we predict that the union state of the UK will change little over the short term while changing radically over the long term. This prediction may be regarded as so vague that we should be newspaper astrologists. But we can justify its two parts separately.

In the short term, Northern Ireland will continue to have a majority Unionist population. Its government is deadlocked as we write. The 2003

Assembly election saw a swing in each community from moderates to extremists. Ian Paisley's Democratic Unionist Party is now the largest party in the suspended Assembly, and on the Nationalist side Sinn Fein holds more seats than the SDLP. It is not easy to see a way to restore the devolved institutions. On the other hand, paramilitary violence has subsided to historically low levels and there are no demonstrations in the street to end direct rule. It may jog along for a little while.

In Wales, the National Assembly would like more powers to legislate and to tax. It will not get them (Hazell 2003; Richard 2004). On the other hand, its legitimacy is secure. Although the referendum to establish it produced a 'Yes' vote by the narrowest possible margin, that vote determined the path from which Welsh politics cannot now be deflected. All parties including the Conservatives, who opposed the creation of the National Assembly, gain advantages from its continuation. So do all lobbyists.

In Scotland, expectations from the Scottish Parliament have been damped, and the biggest longest political story is the escalating cost of the Parliament's new building at Holyrood. But devolution remains 'the settled will of the Scottish people'. Even if it had not been so in 1998, it is in 2004, for the same reason as in Wales. All the political parties including the Conservatives and all lobby groups have adapted themselves to a world in which the Scottish Parliament exists.

In both Scotland and Wales, the Unionist hedgers have up to now been more correct than the Unionist ditchers. Since 1974, hedgers have argued that the best way to cope with the threat of Welsh and Scottish separatism is to give devolution. Ditchers have argued that devolution is a slippery slope to separatism. What ditchers fear is what separatists hope. Both assemblies use the Additional Member System of proportional representation. That makes it unlikely in current circumstances that the Nationalist parties could win a majority in either assembly. They have never reached 50 per cent of party support or identification in either country, and in a PR system they would not win a majority of seats unless they were at least close to 50 per cent of the vote. In the 2003 elections, the Nationalist parties fell back in both countries (Tables 11.1 and 11.2). The hedgers look wise, for the time being.

But the long term could be different in all three countries, and in England. In the medium rather than long term, the party composition of the four assemblies will diverge. From that point, they will have to start using the formal machinery of intergovernmental cooperation that was created in 1998 and has hardly been used at all. The parties themselves will start to diverge, as their UK leaderships and their leaderships in the devolved administrations go their own ways. To take some examples already apparent in 2004:

- the Conservative groups in the Scottish Parliament and the National Assembly support the continuation of these bodies, and the continuation of the PR electoral system which (alone in present circumstances) secures Conservatives a seat share commensurate with their share of the vote. The national Conservative leadership is uneasy with all of these;
- the Scottish Liberal Democrats favour fiscal autonomy for Scotland. Their national leadership favours local income tax, which is probably incompatible with the Scottish Variable Rate of Income Tax;
- the Welsh Labour Party is increasingly unhappy with the Barnett Formula, which the UK Labour Government has no plans to alter.

The likely path is towards Australia or Canada. In those countries, the parties organize separately for federal and for provincial elections. In Canada, parties may share the same name but almost nothing else, even when they fight elections in a given province both at provincial and at federal level.

In Northern Ireland, demographics will lead by mid-century to a Catholic majority, if present trends continue. That does not automatically translate to a nationalist majority, for a higher proportion of Catholics support unionist or cross-confessional parties than of Protestants support nationalist or cross-confessional parties. But the machinery for the UK to shed Northern Ireland is in place, and there is no political will to retain it against the majority wish of its population.

Neither the West Lothian Question (WLQ) nor the problem of devolution finance will go away. The WLQ is really insoluble, short of devolution (or federalism) all round, which is not practical politics, especially after the rejection of a North-East Assembly in a referendum in November 2004. In the foreseeable future, there will be neither an English Parliament nor nine English Assemblies with substantial power. The unelected Regional Development Agencies are accruing powers to fill the vaccuum.

At Westminster, the WLQ will explode when the political complexion of the UK Government differs from that of England. The likeliest scenario for this is a Labour or Labour-dominated UK Government, with the Conservatives (perhaps with allies) holding the majority of Commons seats in England. The benign view is that no constitutional crisis will ensue, for none ensued when the reverse situation obtained. Conservative governments have not had a crisis of legitimacy in Wales (where they have never had a majority of seats) nor in Scotland (where they last did in the Parliament of 1955–9). But these were not true WLQs because there was no devolved government, and therefore there was no class of MPs outside Northern Ireland voting on matters which were devolved (and hence none of their business) in their own constituencies. Now, there is. A likelier view, therefore, is that the WLQ will recur in earnest. It may knock on to decisions about the composition and powers of a reformed upper house, an issue that is parked (but will not go away) in 2004.

Finally, Barnett is unsustainable. It has lost its political support in Northern Ireland, is losing it in Wales, and is resented, albeit for different and not necessarily compatible reasons, in all nine English regions. Scotland will host Barnett's last stand. Even in Scotland, Barnett will come under great strain as the total block grant drops to equal a reasonable assessment of Scotland's needs, and then keeps on dropping. It makes fiscal responsibility in the Scottish Parliament unachievable. Influential members of three of the four biggest parties there have called for more fiscal autonomy, and the Scottish Liberal Democrats adopted it as party policy in March 2004 against their leaders' wishes (Barnes 2004). Its replacement is unknown, but is likely to include some reference to needs, and some formal intergovernmental machinery as in Canada and Australia (McLean 2003*b*, 2004*b*).

Can the union state survive these shocks without primordial unionism? On balance, we think so. Scotland, which is the hardest case to call, could become like Quebec or like Slovakia (McLean 2001*b*). The Quebec separatists have twice come close—very close the second time—to winning a referendum vote in favour of what they call sovereignty-association and their enemies call secession. But the long-run demographics of Quebec are probably against them, with anglophones and allophones (those whose first language is neither English nor French) jointly becoming a larger proportion of the population. Analogously, the pro-independence forces in Scotland may have seen their two best moments pass. In the months following both the October 1974 general election and the 1997 referendum their voting intention and pro-independence opinion both peaked, to settle down at a lower level where they again sit at the time of writing. Dewar's insistence on PR for the Scottish Parliament sets the SNP a particularly demanding threshold. An SNP-led coalition in a future parliament is by no means impossible, and they have a wide range of potential coalition partners (Conservatives, Liberal Democrats, Greens, and the Scottish Socialists are all possible and all have some attractions for a future SNP First Minister). But if the Parti Québécois cannot win a referendum on independence, we seriously doubt whether the SNP can.

By the Slovak scenario we mean one in which the smaller partner in a union state has routinely and noisily complained for decades, as part of normal politics, that it is not treated fairly and needs more autonomy, only to be taken by surprise when the larger partner unexpectedly offers it. Slovakia found itself independent in the 'velvet divorce' of Czechoslovakia in 1993, when the Czech leadership unexpectedly acceded to the the demands of the populist Slovak leader Vladimir Meciar. Where there had been one country, suddenly there were two, with no referendum in either part.

The Slovak scenario would be driven from England, not from Scotland. The English regions, beginning with London, have more autonomy. Everyone who wants to win an election in an English region has an interest in saying that that region is unfairly treated and draws attention to the 'unfair' beneficiaries. In every English region except London, these will appear to be London and Scotland. In London, the mayoral elections of 2000 and 2004 will show that the whipping-boy is Scotland. For reasons given above, Scotland will have lost its traditional allies in the fight to retain a favourable financial settlement, as the Barnett regime no longer favours Wales nor Northern Ireland. The English backlash will therefore force the UK Government to put a firmer and firmer squeeze on the Scottish expenditure block. Even if the UK Government and the Scottish Executive are led by the same party, that party's interests will be different in the two arenas. All parties in the Scottish Parliament except the one that forms the UK Government will protest furiously at the squeeze on the Scottish block, and demand at least a restoration of Scotland's spending advantage. The SNP and its allies will point out that you can never trust the English. Meanwhile, WLQ anomalies such as Scottish MPs voting on the future of tuition fees in England will exacerbate the English backlash. With most parties in Scotland calling for more fiscal autonomy, a future UK Government might just suddenly offer them it, and there would be a tartan divorce. Scotland would become a small open economy in the EU, and probably a member of the eurozone.

It might all happen. But it is more likely that the union state will lumber on, anomalies and all, for at least a few decades more. A union state without unionism can survive for a long time. But not, perhaps, forever.

Appendix: Principal Characters in 1707 and 1800

Argyll, Archibald Campbell, first Duke of (d. 1703)—Main perpetrator of the Massacre of Glencoe. Lord of Treasury, 1696.

Argyll, John Campbell, 2nd Duke of (1678–1743)—Soldier. Lord High Commissioner to the Scottish Parliament, 1705.

Belhaven, John Hamilton, 2nd Baron (1656–1708)—Anti-Union member of the last Scottish Parliament. Famous for anti-Union speech, 1706.

Beresford, John (1738–1805)—Irish politician. Privy Councillor, Member of Parliament for County Waterford and revenue commissioner.

Burke, Edmund (1729/30–1797)—Irish-born politician and writer. Gifted orator and parliamentarian

Castlereagh, Robert Stewart, Viscount (1769–1822)—Irish Privy Councillor. Enthusiastic and influential supporter of the Irish Union with Great Britain. Later Foreign Secretary and Leader of the House of Commons in the Westminster Parliament.

Carstares, William (1649–1715)—Scottish church leader; chaplain of William of Orange and Principal of University of Edinburgh.

Charlemont, Caulfeild, James, first Earl of (1728–99)—Irish politician and commander-in-chief of the Volunteers. Consistently opposed moves towards Irish Union with Great Britain.

Clerk of Penicuik, Sir John (1684–1755)—Diarist who wrote a memoir of the Union.

Cornwallis, Charles, 1st Marquess (1738–1805)—Lord Lieutenant of Ireland, 1797–1801. Previously unsuccessful British general in American War of Independence: surrendered to George Washington at Yorktown, 1781. Governor general of India 1786–93.

Defoe, Daniel (1661?–1731)—Novelist; English spy.

Dundas, Henry, first Viscount Melville (1742–1811)—Scottish politician. Close ally of Pitt the Younger during the passage of Irish Union.

Edgeworth, Richard Lovell (1744–1817)—Engineer and educational writer, who was friends with the Earl of Charlemont. Britsh born, but settled in Ireland.

Fitzgibbon, John, first Earl of Clare (1748–1802)—Lord Chancellor of Ireland. A supporter of Union with Great Britain, his speech of 1800 in the Irish House of Lords marked him as the chief propagandist of the measure.

Fitzwilliam, William Wentworth, 2nd Earl (1748–1833)—British politician and landowner. Whilst Lord Lieutenant of Ireland in 1795, he supported Catholic relief and was consequently recalled to Britain less than two months after taking the post.

Fletcher of Saltoun, Andrew (1655–1716)—Member of the last Scottish Parliament. Leading ideologue of the anti-Union side; a country Whig.

Foster, John, first Baron Oriel (1740–1828)—Irish politician. As speaker of the Irish House of Commons, he was opposed to the Union, and Catholic emancipation.

Fox, Charles James (1749–1806)—English politician. As an opposition leader during the passage of the Act of Union he had an ambivalent position on the statute itself, but was generally sympathetic to Irish patriotism.

Godolphin, Sidney, first Earl of (1645–1712)—English politician; Lord Treasurer between 1703 and 1710.

Grattan, Henry (*bap.* 1746–1820)—Gifted patriotic orator, and Irish politician under the patronage of the first Earl of Charlemont. Opponent of the Union, although suffered from an illness during its passage that prevented him from campaigning against the measure.

Grenville, William Wyndham, Baron Grenville (1759–1834)—As British foreign secretary and a close ally of Pitt, he was a key figure in the creation of the Irish Union.

Hamilton, James Douglas, 4th Duke of (1658–1712)—Leader of anti-Union faction in last Scottish Parliament. Missed crucial vote because of 'toothache'.

Harley, Robert, first Earl of Oxford (1661–1724)—English politician; English commissioner for Union.

Hussey Burgh, Walter (1742–83)—Irish MP, barrister, and orator. A close ally of Grattan, he was in favour of free trade with Britain, but against Union.

Loughborough, Alexander Wedderburn, Baron, later first Earl of Rosslyn (1733–1805)—British Lord Chancellor at the time of the Irish Union, he was a close adviser to King George III.

Marlborough, John Churchill, 1st Duke of (1650–1722)—British military leader; victor of Blenheim and Ramillies.

Pakington, Sir John (1671–1727)—Tory high church leader in English Parliament; opposed Union on grounds that it was inconsistent to support two established churches.

Paterson, William (1658–1719)—Scottish banker; founder of Bank of England; promoter of Darien company.

Pitt, William ('the Younger') (1759–1806)—British politician; Chancellor of the Exchequer 1783; Prime Minister 1784–1801; 1804–6.

Queensberry, James Douglas, 2nd Duke of (1662–1711)—Commissioner to the Scottish Parliament and secretary of state 1703–5; commissioner 1706.

Rothes, John Leslie, 8th Earl of (1679–1722)—Member of *Squadrone Volante*; made representative peer 1707; active in suppression of Jacobite rising 1715.

Roxburgh, John Ker, 5th Earl and 1st Duke of (d. 1741)—Member of the last Scottish Parliament. A member of the *Squadrone Volante*, who switched position from an anti-English to a pro-Union stance over the life of the Scottish Parliament of 1703–7. Scottish representative peer 1707.

Seafield, James Ogilvy, 1st Earl of (1664–1730)—Commissioner for Union with England; Scottish representative peer 1707.

Tone, Theodore Wolfe (1763–98)—Irish nationalist revolutionary and political writer. Notable as a Protestant agitator for Catholic emancipation, he led the 1798 rebellion.

Tweeddale, John Hay, 2nd Marquis of (1645–1713)—Lord High Chancellor of Scotland 1704–5. Became head of *Squadrone Volante*; made representative peer 1707.

References

Alt, J., Crewe, I. M., and Sarlvik, B. (1976). *British Election Study*, February 1974 [computer file]. Colchester, Essex: UK Data Archive [distributor]. SN: 359.

Armitage, D. (1995). 'The Scottish Vision of Empire: Intellectual Origins of the Darien Venture', in J. Robertson (ed.), *A Union for Empire: Political Thought and the British Union of 1707*. Cambridge: Cambridge University Press, 97–118.

Asquith, H. H. (Earl of Oxford and Asquith) (1928). *Memories and Reflections, 1852–1927*, 2 vols. London: Cassell.

Backhouse, R. E. (2002). *The Penguin History of Economics*. London: Penguin.

Balsom, D., and Madgwick P. J. (1981). *Welsh Election Study, 1979* [computer file]. Colchester, Essex: UK Data Archive [distributor]. SN: 1591.

Baran, D., and O'Donoghue, J. (2002). 'Price Levels in 2000 for London and the Regions Compared with the National Average', *Economic Trends*, 578 (January): 28–38.

Barbour, J. S. (1907). *A History of William Paterson and the Darien Company*. London: William Blackwood and Sons.

Barnes, E. (2004). 'Wallace defied by party faithful', *Scotland on Sunday*, 28 March.

Barnett, J. [Lord] (1997). 'Oral Evidence, 1–7', in House of Commons Treasury Committee, *The Barnett Formula: Second Report of Session 1997–8*, HC 341. London: Stationery Office.

Barrington, J. (1835). *Historic Memoirs of Ireland*, Vol. II. London.

Bartlett, T. (2003). ' "An Union for Empire": The Anglo-Irish Union as an Imperial Project', in M. Brown, P. Geoghegan, and J. Kelly (eds.), *The Irish Act of of Union, 1800: Bicentennial Essays*. Dublin: Irish Academic Press, 50–7.

Bayly, C. L. (1989). *Imperial Meridian: The British Empire and the World, 1780–1830*. London: Longman.

Beckett, J. C. (1966). *The Making of Modern Ireland 1603–1923*. London: Faber and Faber.

Bell, D., and Christie, A. (2001). 'Finance—The Barnett Formula: Nobody's Child?', in A. Trench (ed.), *The State of the Nations 2001: The Second Year of Devolution in the United Kingdom*. Thorverton: Imprint Academic, 135–51.

Bennett, G. V. (1969). 'Conflict in the Church', in G. Holmes (ed.), *Britain after the Glorious Revolution 1689–1714*. London: Macmillan, pp. 155–75.

Bennie, L., Brand, J., and Mitchell, J. (1997). *How Scotland Votes: Scottish Parties and Elections*. Manchester: Manchester University Press.

Blake, R. (1955). *The Unknown Prime Minister: The Life and Times of Andrew Bonar Law 1858–1923*. London: Eyre and Spottiswoode.

Blake, R. (1966). *Disraeli*. London: Eyre and Spottiswoode.

Boadway, R., and Flatters, F. (1982). 'Efficiency and Equalization Payments in a Federal System of Government—A Synthesis and Extension of Recent Results', *Canadian Journal of Economics*, 15 (4): 613–33.

Bogdanor, V. (1999). *Devolution in the United Kingdom*. Oxford: Oxford University Press.

Bolton, G. C. (1966). *The Passing of the Irish Act of Union: A Study of Parliamentary Politics*. Oxford: Oxford University Press.

Borrow, G. (1862/2002). *Wild Wales*. Original edn. London: John Murray. New edn. Wrexham: Bridge Books.

Bowman, J. (1989). *De Valera and the Ulster Question 1917–73*. Oxford: Oxford University Press.

Boyd, A. (1969). *Holy War in Belfast*. Tralee: Anvil.

—— (1705). *The History of the Reign of Queen Anne, Digested into Annals. Year the Third*. London: A. Roper.

Braithwaite, W. J. (1957). *Lloyd George's Ambulance Wagon*. London: Methuen.

Brand, J. (1978). *The National Movement in Scotland*. London: Routledge.

—— and Mitchell, J. (1997). 'Home Rule in Scotland: The Politics and Bases of a Movement', in J. Bradbury and J. Mawson (eds.), *British Regionalism and Devolution: The Challenges of State Reform and European Integration*. London: Jessica Kingsley.

Brennan, G., and Pincus, J. (2002). 'Fiscal Equalisation Revisited: Institutional Design and Reform'. Paper to Conference of Australian Economists, Glenelg, South Australia, October.

Brewer, J. (1989). *The Sinews of Power: War, Money and the English State, 1688–1783*. London: Unwin Hyman.

Brown, G. (1982). 'The Labour Party and Political Change in Scotland, 1918–1929: The Politics of Five Elections'. Edinburgh University, Ph.D. thesis.

Brown, K. M. (1992). *Kingdom or Province? Scotland and the Regal Union 1603–1715*. Basingstoke: Macmillan.

Brown, M., Geoghegan, P., and Kelly, J. (eds.) (2003). *The Irish Act of Union, 1800: Bicentennial Essays*. Dublin: Irish Academic Press.

Bruce, S. (1986). *God Save Ulster! The Religion and Politics of Paisleyism*. Oxford: Oxford University Press.

—— (1994). *The Edge of the Union*. Oxford: Oxford University Press.

Bryson, B. (1995). *Notes from a Small Island*. London: Doubleday.

Buchanan, J. M. (1950). 'Federalism and Fiscal Equity', *American Economic Review*, 40: 583–99.

Bulpitt, J. (1983). *Territory and Power in the United Kingdom*. Manchester: Manchester University Press.

Burness, C. (2003). *'Strange Associations': The Irish Question and the Making of Scottish Unionism, 1886–1918*. East Linton: Tuckwell Press.

Butler, D. E., and Butler, G. (1994). *British Political Facts 1900–1994*. London: Macmillan.

—— and Kavanagh, D. (1975). *The British General Election of October 1974*. Basingstoke: Macmillan.

—— —— (1980). *The British General Election of 1979*. London: Macmillan.

—— —— (1984). *The British General Election of 1983*. London: Macmillan.

—— —— (1988). *The British General Election of 1987*. London: Macmillan.

—— —— (1992). *The British General Election of 1992*. London: Macmillan.

—— and Pinto-Duschinsky, M. (eds.) (1971). *The British General Election of 1970*. London: Macmillan.

—— Adonis, A., and Travers, T. (1994). *Failure in British Government: The Politics of the Poll Tax*. Oxford: Oxford University Press.

Callaghan, J. (1987). *Time and Chance*. London: Collins.

Cameron, G., McLean, I., and Wlezien, C. (2004). 'Public Expenditure in the English Regions: Measurement Problems and (Partial) Solutions', *Political Quarterly*, 75(2): 121–31.

Carey, G. (2002). 'Holding Together: Church and Nation in the 21st Century', speech at Lambeth Palace, 23 April. London: transcript supplied by Lambeth Palace press office. Web version at *http://www.archbishopofcanterbury.org/carey/speeches/020423.htm*, accessed 3.11.04.

Churchill, W. S. (1929). *The World Crisis: The Aftermath*. London: Butterworth.

—— (1948). *The Second World War*, Vol. I: *The Gathering Storm*. London: Cassell.

—— (1949). *The Second World War*, Vol. II: *Their Finest Hour*. London: Cassell.

Clark, R. W. (1984). *The Survival of Charles Darwin: A Biography of a Man and an Idea*. London: Weidenfeld and Nicolson.

Clerk, J. (1892). *Memoirs of the Life of Sir John Clerk of Penicuik, Baronet, Baron of the Exchequer, extracted by himself from his own journals 1676–1755* (ed. John M. Gray). Edinburgh: Edinburgh University Press.

Colley, L. (1996). *Britons: Forging the Nation 1707–1837*. London: Vintage Books; originally published by Yale University Press, 1992.

Cook, C. (1972). 'The Liberal and Nationalist Revival', in D. McKie and C. Cook (eds.), *The Decade of Disillusion: British Politics in the Sixties*. London: Macmillan.

Cooke, A. B., and Vincent, J. (1974). *The Governing Passion*. Brighton: Harvester.

Craig. F. W. S. (1989). *British Electoral Facts 1832–1987*. Aldershot: Gower.

Crewe, I. M., Robertson, D. R., and Sarlvik, B. (1977). *British Election Study*: Scottish Cross-Section Sample, October 1974 [computer file]. Colchester, Essex: UK Data Archive [distributor]. SN: 681.

—— —— —— (1981). *British Election Study*, May 1979 [computer file]. Colchester, Essex: UK Data Archive [distributor]. SN: 1533.

Crowther-Hunt, Lord, and Peacock, A. (1973). *Royal Commission on the Constitution 1969–1973: Memorandum of Dissent Cmnd 5460–I*. London: HMSO.

Cullen, L. M. (1968). *Anglo-Irish Trade 1660–1800*. Manchester: Manchester University Press.

Curtice, J. (2004). 'Restoring Confidence and Legitimacy? Devolution and Public Opinion', in A. Trench (ed.), *Has Devolution Made a Difference? The State of the Nations 2004*. Exeter: Imprint Academic, 217–36.

Dáil Éireann (1972). *Private Sessions of the Second Dáil. Minutes of Proceedings 18.8.1921 to 14.9.1921 and Report of Debates 14.12.1921 to 6.1.1922*. Dublin: Stationery Office.

Dalyell, T. (1977). *Devolution: The End of Britain?* London: Jonathan Cape.

Darling, F. F. (1955). *West Highland Survey*. Oxford: Clarendon Press.

Davies, J. (1993). *A History of Wales*. Harmondsworth: Penguin.

Deane, P., and Cole W. (1967). *British Economic Growth 1688–1959*, 2nd edn. Cambridge: Cambridge University Press.

Defoe, D. (1786). *The History of the Union between England and Scotland, with a Collection of Original Papers Relating Thereto. By Daniel De Foe. With an introduction, in which the consequences and probability of a like union between this country and Ireland are considered. To which is prefixed, a life of Daniel De Foe, by George Chalmers* London: printed for John Stockdale. Originally published in 1709.

Devine, T. M. (1999). *The Scottish Nation 1700–2000*. London: Allen Lane.

—— (2003). *Scotland's Empire, 1600–1815*. London: Allen Lane.

Dicey, A. V. (1885). *Introduction to the Study of the Law of the Constitution*. London: Macmillan. 8th edn. 1915 with a new introduction. 8th edn. reprinted 1982 by Liberty Classics, Indianapolis.

—— (1887). *Letters on Unionist Delusions*. London: The Spectator.

—— and Rait, R. S. (1920). *Thoughts on the Union between England and Scotland*. London: Macmillan.

Dickson, D. (1983). 'Taxation and Disaffection in Late Eighteenth-Century Ireland', in S. Clark and J. S. Donnelly (eds.), *Irish Peasants: Violence and Political Unrest 1780–1914*. Dublin: Gill and Macmillan, 37–63.

Dickson, P. G. M. (1967). *The Financial Revolution in England: A Study in the Development of Public Credit 1688–1756*. London: Macmillan.

Ditchfield, G. M., Hayton, D., and Jones, C. (eds.) (1995). *British Parliamentary Lists, 1660–1800: A Register*. London: Habledon Press.

Doyle, W. (2000). 'The British–Irish Union of 1801: The Union in a European Context', *Transactions of the Royal Historical Society*, 10: 165–80.

Drucker, H. (1978). *Breakaway: The Scottish Labour Party*. Edinburgh: EUSPB.

Dunlop, A. I. (1967). *William Carstares and the Kirk by Law Established*. Edinburgh: Saint Andrew Press.

Duverger, M. (1954). *Political Parties*. London: Methuen. Originally published in French in 1951.

Ehrman, J. (1969). *The Younger Pitt: The Years of Acclaim*. London: Constable.

(1964). 'The Making of the Treaty of Union of 1707', *Scottish Historical Review*, 43 (136): 89–110.

Ellis, A. (1979). 'A Comparison between Separatism in Wales and Brittany'. Oxford University, P.P.E. thesis.

Evans, E. J. (1999). *William Pitt the Younger*. London: Routledge.

Ferguson, W. (1964). 'The Making of the Treaty of Union of 1707', *Scottish Historical Review*, 43(136): 89–110.

—— (1968). *Scotland, 1689 to the Present*. Edinburgh: Oliver and Boyd.

—— (1977). *Scotland's Relations with England: A Survey to 1707*. Edinburgh: John Donald.

FitzGerald, G. (1973). *Towards a New Ireland*. Dublin: Torc Books.

Foster, R. F. (1989). *Modern Ireland 1600–1972.* Harmondsworth: Penguin. Origin-ally published by Allen Lane in 1988.

—— (1993). *Paddy and Mr. Punch: Corrections in Irish and English History.* London: Allen Lane.

Fry, M. (2001). *The Scottish Empire.* Edinburgh: Tuckwell Press and Birlinn.

Fulton, J. (1991). *The Tragedy of Belief: Division, Politics, and Religion in Ireland.* Oxford: Clarendon.

Garnaut, R., and FitzGerald, V. (2002). *Review of Commonwealth-State Funding: Final Report.* Melbourne: Review of Commonwealth-State Funding.

Geoghegan, P. M. (1999). *The Irish Act of Union: A Study in High Politics 1798–1801.* Dublin: Gill and Macmillan.

—— (2003). 'The Irish House of Commons, 1799–1800', in M. Brown, P. Geoghegan, and J. Kelly (eds.), *The Irish Act of Union, 1800: Bicentennial Essays.* Dublin: Irish Academic Press,129–43.

Gibbon, P. (1975). *The Origins of Ulster Unionism.* Manchester: Manchester Univer-sity Press.

Goldie, M. (1996). 'Divergence and Union: Scotland and England, 1660–1707', in B. Bradshaw and J. Morill (eds.), *The British Problem, c.1534–1707: State Forma-tion in the Atlantic Archipelago.* London: Macmillan, 220–45.

Grant, E. (1988). *Memoirs of a Highland lady: Elizabeth Grant of Rothiemurchus,* edited with an introduction by Andrew Tod. Edinburgh: Canongate. Originally published in 1898.

Grant, J. P. (ed.) (1976). *Independence and Devolution: The Legal Implications for Scotland.* Edinburgh: W. Green and Son.

Griffith, J. A. G. (1976). 'The English Connection', *New Statesman*, 17 December, 864.

Guthrie, R., and McLean, I. (1978). 'Another Part of the Periphery: Reactions to Devolution in an English Development Area', *Parliamentary Affairs*, 31: 190–200.

Gwynn, D. (1950). *The History of Partition 1912–1925.* Dublin: Browne and Nolan.

Hague, W. (2004). *William Pitt the Younger.* London: HarperCollins.

Hall, F. G. (1949). *The Bank of Ireland 1783–1946.* Dublin: Hodges Figgis.

Hammond, J. L. (1938). *Gladstone and the Irish Nation.* London: Longmans Green.

Hand, G. (ed.) (1969). *Report of the Irish Boundary Commission 1925.* Dublin: Irish University Press.

Hanham, H. (1969). *Scottish Nationalism.* London: Faber and Faber.

Hansen, R. (2000). *Citizenship and Immigration in Post-war Britain: The Institutional Origins of a Multicultural Nation.* Oxford: Oxford University Press.

Hayton, D. (1996). 'Traces of Party Politics in Early Eighteenth-Century Scottish Elections', in C. Jones (ed.), *The Scots and Parliament.* Edinburgh: Edinburgh University Press, 74–99.

Hazell, R. (2003). 'If Ivor Richard Says Yes, Will London Say No?', in J. Osmond (ed.), *Second Term Challenge: Can the Welsh Assembly Government Hold Its Course?* Cardiff: Institute of Welsh Affairs, 97–107.

Heald, D. (1980). *Financing Devolution within the United Kingdom: A Study in the Lessons from Failure.* Canberra: ANU Press, Centre for Research on Federal Financial Relations, Research Monograph no. 12.

Heald, D. and McLeod, A. (2005). 'Scotland's Fiscal Relationships with England and the United Kingdom', in W. L. Miller (ed.), *Anglo-Scottish Relations from 1900 to Devolution and Beyond*. London: British Academy 95–112.

Heffer, S. (1998). *Like the Roman: The Life of Enoch Powell*. London: Weidenfeld and Nicolson.

HM Treasury (1979). *Needs Assessment Study: The Report of an Interdepartmental Study Coordinated by HM Treasury on the Relative Public Expenditure Needs in England, Scotland, Wales and Northern Ireland*. London: HM Treasury.

Heslinga, M. W. (1962). *The Irish Border as a Cultural Divide*. Assen: Van Gorcum.

Hilton, B. (1988). *The Age of Atonement: The Influence of Evangelicalism on Social and Economic Thought, 1795–1865*. Oxford: Clarendon Press.

Hoggart, S. (2000). 'Bringing a gleed o wut tae Westminster's lingua Scotia', *The Guardian*, 21 October.

Holmes, G. (1967). *British Politics in the Age of Anne*. London: Macmillan.

Horwitz, H. (1969). 'The Structure of Parliamentary Politics', in G. Holmes (ed.), *Britain after the Glorious Revolution 1689–1714*. London: Macmillan, 96–114.

House of Commons Library (1998). *The Scotland Bill: Some Constitutional and Representational Aspects*. Research paper 98/3, 7 January. *http://www.parliament. uk/commons/lib/research/rp98/rp98-003.pdf*.

House of Commons Library (2001). *The Barnett Formula*. Research paper 01/108, 30 November. *http://www.parliament.uk/commons/lib/research/rp2001/rp01-108.pdf*.

—— (2003). *An introduction to Devolution in the UK*. Research paper 03/84, 17 November. *http://www.parliament.uk/commons/lib/research/ rp2003/rp03-084.pdf*.

Insh, G. P. (1932). *The Company of Scotland Trading to Africa and the Indes*. London: Charles Scribner's Sons.

Jackson, A. (2003). *Home Rule: An Irish History 1800–2000*. London: Weidenfeld and Nicolson.

Jenkins, G. H. (2001). 'Terminal Decline? The Welsh Language in the Twentieth Century', *North American Journal of Welsh Studies*, 2(1): 59–67.

Jenkins, R. (1964). *Asquith*. London: Collins.

—— (1968). *Mr Balfour's Poodle*, 2nd edn. London: Collins.

—— (1995). *Gladstone*. London: Macmillan.

Jenkins, S. (1999). *England's Thousand Best Churches*. London: Allen Lane.

—— (2003). *England's Thousand Best Houses*. London: Allen Lane.

Johnson, N. (1980). *In Search of the Constitution*, 2nd edn. London: Methuen.

—— (2004). *Reshaping the British Constitution*. Basingstoke: Palgrave.

Johnston, E. M. (1963). *Great Britain and Ireland 1760–1800: A Study in Public Administration*. Edinburgh: Oliver and Boyd.

Johnston, R. J., and McLean, I. (2005). 'Choosing between Impossible Alternatives: Creating a New Constituency Map for Wales, 2004', *Political Quarterly* 76(1), 67–81.

Johnston, T. (1952). *Memories*. London: Collins.

Johnston-Lük, E. M. (2002). *History of the Irish Parliament 1692–1800: Commons, Constituencies and Statutes*. Belfast: Ulster Historical Foundation.

Jones, A. (1972). *The Politics of Reform 1884*. Cambridge: Cambridge University Press.

Jones, J. B. (2000). 'Changes to the Government of Wales', in J. B. Jones and D. Balsom (eds.), *The Road to the National Assembly of Wales*. Cardiff: University of Wales Press, 15–27.

Jones, R. M., and Jones, I. R. (2000). 'Labour and the Nation', in D. Tanner et al. (ed.), *The Labour Party in Wales 1900–2000*. Cardiff: University of Wales Press, 241–63.

Jones, T. (1969). *Whitehall Diary I: 1916–1925*. London: Oxford University Press.

—— (1971). *Whitehall Diary III: Ireland 1918–25* ed. R. K. Middlemas. London: Oxford University Press.

Jones, W. D. (2001). ' "Bold Adventurers": A Quantitative Analysis of the Darien Subscription List (1696)', *Scottish Economic and Social History*, 21(1): 22–42.

Keating, M., and Bleiman, D. (1979). *Labour and Scottish Nationalism*. London: Macmillan.

Kellas, J. (1971). 'Scottish Nationalism', in D. E. Butler and M. Pinto-Duschinsky (eds.), *The British General Election of 1970*. London: Macmillan, 446–62.

—— (1980). *Modern Scotland*, 2nd edn. London: Allen and Unwin.

—— (2005). 'After the Declaration of Perth, All Change', in W. L. Miller (ed.), *Anglo-Scottish Relations from 1900 to Devolution and Beyond*. London: British Academy, pp. 51–61.

Kelly, P. (1975). 'British and Irish Politics in 1785', *English Historical Review*, 90 (356): 536–63.

Kendle, J. (1992). *Walter Long, Ireland and the Union 1905–1920*. Montreal: McGill-Queens University Press.

Keogh, D., and Whelan, K. (2001). *Acts of Union: The Causes, Contexts and Consequences of the Acts of Union*. Dublin: Four Courts Press.

Kilbrandon, Lord (Chairman) (1973). *Report of the Royal Commission on the Constitution*. Cmnd 5460. London: HMSO.

King, A. (2004). 'Voters United on Both Sides of the Border', *Daily Telegraph*, 16, 10 February.

Kirkwood, D. (1935). *My Life of Revolt*. London: Harrap.

Laffan, M. (1999). *The Resurrection of Ireland: The Sinn Fein Party 1916–1923*. Cambridge: Cambridge University Press.

Lang, I. (2002). *Blue Remembered Years: A Political Memoir*. London: Politico's.

Lawson, P. (1993). *The East India Company: A History*. London: Longman.

Lecky, W. E. H. (1902). *A History of Ireland in the Eighteenth Century, Volume II*. London: Longmans.

Levack, B. P. (1987). *The Formation of the British State: England, Scotland and the Union 1603–1707*. Oxford: Clarendon Press.

Levitt, I. (1999). 'The Scottish Secretary, the Treasury, and the Scottish Grant Equivalent, 1888–1970', *Scottish Affairs*, 28: 93–116.

Lewis, R. (1979). *Enoch Powell: Principle in Politics*. London: Cassell.

Loughlin, J. (1995). *Ulster Unionism and British National Identity since 1885*. London: Pinter.

Lyons, F. S. L. (1977). *Charles Stewart Parnell*. Oxford: Oxford University Press.

MacCormick, N. (1998). 'The English Constitution, The British State, and the Scottish Anomaly', *Proceedings of the British Academy*, 101: 289–306.

Macinnes, A. I. (1990). 'Influencing the Vote: The Scottish Estates and the Treaty of Union, 1706–1707', *History Microcomputer Review*, 11–25.

MacLaren, A. A. (1974). *Religion and Social Class: The Disruption Years in Aberdeen*. London: Routledge.

Macree, D. (1973). 'Daniel Defoe, the Church of Scotland, and the Union of 1707', *Eighteenth-Century Studies*, 7(1): 62–77.

Madgwick, P. J., with Griffiths, N., and Walker, V. (1973). *The Politics of Rural Wales: A Study of Cardiganshire*. London: Hutchinson.

Major, J. (1997). 'Foreword', in *Fighting for Scotland: The Scottish Conservative & Unionist Manifesto 1997*. Edinburgh: Scottish Conservative and Unionist Party, 1–3.

—— (1999). *The Autobiography*. London: HarperCollins.

Malcomson, A. P. W. (1979). 'The Parliamentary Traffic of this Country', in T. Bartlett and D. W. Hayton (eds.), *Penal Era and Golden Age: Essays in Irish History, 1690–1800*. Belfast: Ulster Historical Foundation, 137–61.

Mansergh, N. (1991). *The Unresolved Question: The Anglo-Irish Settlement and its Undoing 1912–72*. New Haven, Conn.: Yale University Press.

Mathieson, W. L. (1905). *Scotland and the Union: A History of Scotland from 1695 to 1747*. Glasgow: James Maclehose and Sons.

Matthew, H. C. G. (1999). *Gladstone 1809–1898*. Oxford: Oxford University Press.

McCavery, T. (2000). 'Politics, Public Finance and the British–Irish Act of Union of 1801', *Transactions of the Royal Historical Society*, 10: 353–75.

McDowell, R. B. (1943). *Irish Public Opinion 1750–1800*. London: Faber and Faber.

—— (1979). *Ireland in the Age of Imperialism and Revolution 1760–1801*. Oxford: Clarendon.

McLean, I. (1969). 'Scottish Nationalism: Its Growth and Development, with Particular Reference to the Period since 1961', Oxford University, B.Phil. thesis.

McLean, I. (1970). 'The Rise and Fall of the Scottish National Party', *Political Studies*, 17: 357–72.

—— (1976). 'Devolution', *Political Quarterly*, 47: 221–7.

—— (1977). 'The Politics of Nationalism and Devolution', *Political Studies*, 25: 425–30.

—— (1995). 'Are Scotland and Wales Over-represented in the House of Commons?', *Political Quarterly*, 66: 250–68.

—— (1999). *The Legend of Red Clydeside*, 2nd edn. Edinburgh: John Donald.

—— (2001*a*). *Rational Choice and British Politics an Analysis of Rhetoric and Manipulation from Peel to Blair*. Oxford: Oxford University Press.

—— (2001*b*). 'Scotland: Towards Quebec or Slovakia?', *Regional Studies*, 35: 637–44.

—— (2003*a*). 'Devolution Bites', *Prospect*, March.

—— (2003*b*). 'Fiscal Federalism in Canada', Nuffield College Working Papers in Politics, 2003 W-17.

—— (2004*a*). 'Scottish Labour and British Politics', in G. Hassan (ed.), *The Scottish Labour Party: History, Institutions and Ideas*. Edinburgh: Edinburgh University Press.

—— (2004*b*). 'Fiscal Federalism in Australia', *Public Administration*, 82: 21–38.

—— (2004*c*). 'Dewar, Donald Campbell (1937–2000)', in H. C. G. Matthew and B. Harrison (eds.), *Oxford Dictionary of National Biography*, new edition, 60 vols. Oxford: Oxford University Press, and at *www.oxforddnb.com.*

—— (2005). *The Fiscal Crisis of the United Kingdom*. Basingstoke: Palgrave.

—— and Johnes, M. (2000). *Aberfan: Government and Disasters*. Cardiff: Welsh Academic Press.

—— and Linsley, B. (2004). *The Church of England and the State: Reforming Establishment for a Multi-faith Britain*. London: New Politics Network.

—— and McMillan, Λ. (2003*a*). 'The Distribution of Public Expenditure across the UK Regions', *Fiscal Studies*, 24: 45–71.

—— —— (2003*b*). *New Localism, New Finance*. London: New Local Government Network.

—— and Mortimore, R. G. (1992). 'Apportionment and the Boundary Commission for England', *Electoral Studies*, 11: 292–308.

McNeill, P. G. B., and MacQueen, H. L. (eds.) (1996). *Atlas of Scottish History to 1707*. Edinburgh: University of Edinburgh.

Miller, C. (1999). 'Independence in Europe: The SNP's Continental Shift'. P.P.E dissertation, Oxford University.

Miller, W. L. (1980). 'What Was the Profit in Following the Crowd? The Effectiveness of Party Strategies on Immigration and Devolution', *British Journal of Political Science*, 10: 15–38.

—— and Brand, J. A. (1981). *Scottish Election Study*, 1979 [computer file]. Colchester, Essex: UK Data Archive [distributor]. SN: 1604.

—— Timpson, A. M., and Lessnoff, M. (1996). *Political Culture in Contemporary Britain: People and Politicians, Principles and Practice*. Oxford: Clarendon Press.

Milward, A. S. (2002). *The UK and the European Community*, Vol. I: *The Rise and Fall of a National Strategy 1945–1963*. London: Whitehall History Publishing in association with Frank Cass.

Mitchell, B. R. (1988). *British Historical Statistics*. Cambridge: Cambridge University Press.

Mitchell, J. (2002). 'The Principles and Politics of Devolved Financial Arrangements I – the United Kingdom'. Paper to ESRC Devolution Programme conference, Birmingham, January.

—— (2003). *Governing Scotland: The Invention of Administrative Devolution*. Basingstoke: Palgrave.

—— (2004). 'Financing Devolution: Stormont and the Welfare State'. Paper to PSA Territorial Politics Group, Strathclyde, January.

Mitchison, R. (1970). *A History of Scotland*. London: Methuen.

—— (1983). *Lordship to Patronage: Scotland 1603–1745*. London: Edward Arnold.

Mokyr, J. (1983). *Why Ireland Starved: A Quantitative and Analytical History of the Irish Economy, 1800–1850*. London: Allen and Unwin.

Monypenny., W. F., and Buckle, G. E. (1910–20). *The Life of Benjamin Disraeli, Earl of Beaconsfield*, 6 vols. London: John Murray.

Morgan, K. O. (1963). *Wales in British Politics 1868–1922*. Cardiff: University of Wales Press. 2nd edn., 1970.

Morrison, H. (Lord Morrison of Lambeth) (1960). *Herbert Morrison: An Autobiography*. London: Odhams.

National Assembly for Wales. *Arrangements of the National Assembly for Wales*. Cardiff: National Assembly for Wales.

Neal, L. (1990). *The Rise of Financial Capitalism: International Capital Markets in the Age of Reason*. Cambridge: Cambridge University Press.

North, D. C., and Weingast, B. R. (1989). 'Constitutions and Commitment: The Evolution of Institutions Governing Public Choice in Seventeenth-Century England', *Journal of Economic History*, 49(4): 803–32.

Northern Regional Strategy Team (1976). *Public Expenditure in the Northern Region and Other British Regions 1969/70–1973/74*. Technical Report no. 12. Newcastle-upon-Tyne: NRST.

O'Brien, P. K. (1988). 'The Political Economy of British Taxation, 1660–1815', *Economic History Review* (second series), 41(1): 1–32.

O'Brien, P. (1998). 'Political Biography and Pitt the Younger as Chancellor of the Exchequer', *History*, 83(270): 225–33.

O'Leary, B. (2002). 'The Belfast Agreement and the British-Irish Agreement: Consociation, Confederal Institutions, a Federacy, and a Peace Process', in A. Reynolds (ed.), *The Architecture of Democracy: Constitutional Design, Conflict Management, and Democracy*. Oxford: Oxford University Press, 293–356.

Oates, W. E. (1972). *Fiscal Federalism*. New York: Harcourt Brace Jovanovich.

Office of Population Censuses and Surveys (OPCS) and Social & Community Planning Research (SCPR) (1973). *Devolution and Other Aspects of Government: An Attitudes Survey*. Royal Commission on the Constitution, Research Paper no. 7. London: HMSO.

Office of Population Censuses & Surveys (OPCS) and Social and Community Planning Research (SCPR) (1974). *Devolution and Other Aspects of Government: An Attitudes Survey* [computer file]. Colchester, Essex: UK Data Archive [distributor]. SN: 173.

Office of the Lord President of the Council (1976). *Devolution: The English Dimension. A Consultative Document*. London: HMSO.

Osmond, J. (ed.) (2003). *Second Term Challenge: Can the Welsh Assembly Government Hold Its Course?* Cardiff: Institute of Welsh Affairs.

—— (2004). 'Nation Building and the Assembly: The Emergence of a Welsh Civil Consciousness', in A. Trench (ed.) *Has Devolution Made a Difference? The State of the Nations 2004*. Exeter: Imprint Academic.

Pryde, G. S. (1950). *The Treaty of Union of Scotland and England, 1707*. London: Nelson, 43–77.

Paterson, L. et al. (2001). *New Scotland, New Politics?* Edinburgh: Polygon.

Paxman, J. (1998). *The English : A Portrait of a People*. London: Michael Joseph.

Pelling, H. (1967). *Social Geography of British Elections 1885–1910*. London: Macmillan.

Philip, A. B. (1975). *The Welsh Question: Nationalism in Welsh Politics 1945–1970*. Cardiff: University of Wales Press.

Pliatzky, L. (1982). *Getting and Spending: Public Expenditure, Employment and Inflation*. Oxford: Basil Blackwell.

—— (1989). *The Treasury under Mrs Thatcher*. Oxford: Basil Blackwell.

Powell, J. E. (1977). *Joseph Chamberlain*. London: Thames and Hudson.

—— (1991). *Reflections of a Statesman*. London: Bellew.

Powell, M. J. (2003). *Britain and Ireland in the Eighteenth-Century Crisis of Empire*. Palgrave: Basingstoke.

Pryde, G. S. (1950). *The Treaty of Union of Scotland and England, 1707*. London: Nelson.

Pugh, M. (1985). *The Tories and the People 1880–1935*. Oxford: Blackwell.

Pulzer, P. G. J. (1975). *Political Representation and Elections in Britain*, 3rd edn. London: Allen and Unwin. Originally published in 1967.

Rait, R. S (1901). *The Scottish Parliament before the Union of the Crowns*. London: Blackie and Son.

Reilly, R. (1979). *William Pitt the Younger*. New York: G. P. Putnam's Sons.

Richard of Ammanford, Lord (Chairman) (2004). *Report of the Commission on the Powers and Electoral*. Cardiff: The Richard Commission.

Riley, P. W. J. (1964). *The English Ministers and Scotland 1707–1727*. London: Athlone Press.

—— (1968). 'The Scottish Parliament of 1703', *Scottish Historical Review*, 47(143): 129–50.

—— (1969). 'The Union of 1707 as an Episode in English Politics', *English Historical Review*, 84(322): 498–527.

—— (1978). *The Union of England and Scotland: A Study in Anglo-Scottish Politics of the Eighteenth Century*. Manchester: Manchester University Press.

Robertson, J. (1985). *The Scottish Enlightenment and the Militia Issue*. Edinburgh: John Donald.

—— (1987). 'Andrew Fletcher's Vision of Union', in Roger A. Mason (ed.), *Scotland and England 1286–1815*. Edinburgh: John Donald, 203–25.

—— (1994). 'Union, State, and Empire', in Lawrence Stone (ed.), *An Imperial State at War: Britain from 1689 to 1815*. London: Routlege, 224–57.

—— (ed.) (1995a). *A Union for Empire: Political Thought and the British Union of 1707*. Cambridge: Cambridge University Press.

—— (1995b). 'An Elusive Sovereignty: The Course of the Union Debate in Scotland 1698–1707', in J. Robertson (ed.), *A Union for Empire: Political Thought and the British Union of 1707*. Cambridge: Cambridge University Press.

—— (ed.) (1997). *Andrew Fletcher: Political Works*. Cambridge: Cambridge University Press.

Rokkan, S., and Urwin, D. (1982). *The Politics of Territorial Identity: Studies in European Regionalism*. London: Sage.

Rose, K. (1983). *King George V*. London: Weidenfeld and Nicolson.

Rose, R. (1982). *Understanding the United Kingdom: The Territorial Dimension in Government*. London: Longman.

—— (1989). *Politics in England: Change and Persistence*, 5th edn. Basingstoke: Macmillan.

Ross, J. (1985). 'Letter to Prof. James Mitchell', in J. Mitchell (2002).

Rossiter, D., Johnston, R. J., and Pattie, C. (1999). *The Boundary Commissions: Redrawing the UK's Map of Parliamentary Constituencies*. Manchester: Manchester University Press.

Saville, R. (1996). *Bank of Scotland: A History 1695–1995*. Edinburgh: Edinburgh University Press.

Scott, A. D. (1952). 'Federal Grants and Resource Allocation', *Journal of Political Economy*, 60: 534–6.

Scott, P. H (1992). *Andrew Fletcher and the Treaty of Union*. Edinburgh: John Donald.

Scott, W. R. (1910–12). *The Constitution and Finance of English, Scottish and Irish Joint-Stock Companies to 1720*. Vol. 1: *The General Development of the Joint-Stock System to 1720*. Vol. 2: *Companies for Foreign Trade, Colonization, Fishing and Mining*. Vol. 3: *Water Supply, Postal, Street-Lighting, Manufacturing, Banking, Finance and Insurance Companies Also Statements Relating to the Crown Finances*. Cambridge: Cambridge University Press.

Scottish Constitutional Convention (1995). *Scotland's Parliament. Scotland's Right.* Edinburgh: Scottish Constitutional Convention.

Sen, A. K. (1981). *Poverty and Famines: An Essay on Entitlement an Deprivation*. Oxford: Clarendon Press.

Senior, D. (1977). 'Hatchet Job on English Regionalism', *Town and Country Planning*, April, 209–11.

Shepherd, R. (1996). *Enoch Powell: A Biography*. London: Hutchinson.

Short, J., and Nicholas, D. J. (1981). *A Study of Money Flows in the Regions of the United Kingdom 1974/75 to 1977/78*. Mimeo. Durham University, Department of Economics for the Department of the Environment.

Smith, T. B. (1957). 'The Union of 1707 as Fundamental Law', *Public Law*, 99–121.

Smout, T. C. (1963). *Scottish Trade on the Eve of the Union 1660–1707*. Edinburgh: Oliver and Boyd.

—— (1964). 'The Anglo-Scottish Union of 1707: 1. The Economic Background', *Economic History Review*, 41(3): 439–67.

—— (1969a). *A History of the Scottish People 1560–1830*. London: Collins.

—— (1969b). 'The Road to Union', in G. Holmes (ed.), *Britain after the Glorious Revolution 1689–1714*. London: Macmillan, 176–96.

—— (1970). *A History of the Scottish People 1560–1830*, 2nd edn. London: Collins.

Speck, W. A. (1970). *Tory & Whig: The Struggle in the Constituencies 1701–1715*. London: Macmillan.

—— (1981). 'Whigs and Tories Dim Their Glories: English Political Parties under the First Two Georges', in J. Cannon (ed.), *The Whig Ascendancy: Colloquies on Hanoverian England*. London: Edward Arnold.

—— (1994). *The Birth of Britain: A New Nation 1700–1710*. Oxford: Blackwell.

Stasavage, D. (2003). *Public Debt and the Birth of the Democratic State*. Cambridge: Cambridge University Press.

Stevenson, D. (1987). 'The Early Covenanters and the Federal Union of Britain', in R. A. Mason (ed.), *Scotland and England 1286–1815*. Edinburgh: John Donald, 163–81.

Stewart, A. T. Q. (1967). *The Ulster Crisis*. London: Faber and Faber.

—— (1977). *The Narrow Ground: Aspects of Ulster, 1609–1969*. London: Faber and Faber.

Stewart, W. (1921). J. *Keir Hardie: A Biography*. London: Keir Hardie Memorial Committee.

Strauss, E. (1951). *Irish Nationalism and British Democracy*. London: Methuen.

Survey on Scottish Attitudes to Devolution and the Government's White Paper (1974). [computer file]. Colchester, Essex: UK Data Archive [distributor]. SN: 369.

Thatcher, M. (1993). *The Downing Street Years*. London: HarperCollins.

—— (1995). *The Path to Power*. London: HarperCollins.

Thomas, W. A. (1986). *The Stock Exchanges of Ireland*. Liverpool: Francis Cairns.

Thornley, D. (1964). *Issac Butt and Home Rule*. London: MacGibbon and Kee.

Times, The (1965). *The Times Guide to the House of Commons 1964*. London: Times Books.

—— (1974). *The Times Guide to the House of Commons October 1974*. London: Times Books.

Trench, A. (ed.) (2004). *Has Devolution Made a Difference? The State of the Nations 2004*. Exeter: Imprint Academic.

Trystan, D., Scully, R., and Wyn Jones, R. (2003). 'Explaining the "Quiet Earthquake": Voting Behaviour in the First Election to the National Assembly for Wales', *Electoral Studies*, 22: 635–50.

Turner, M. J. (2003). *Pitt the Younger: A Life*. London: St Martins Press.

Wald, K. D. (1983). *Crosses on the Ballot: Patterns of British Voter Alignment Since 1885*. Princeton, N.J.: Princeton University Press.

Walker, G. (1988). *Thomas Johnston*. Manchester: Manchester University Press.

Ward, H., and John, P. (1999). 'Targeting Benefits for Electoral Gain: Constituency Marginality and the Distribution of Grants to English Local Authorities', *Political Studies*, 47 (1): 32–52.

Wells, J., and Wills, D. (2000). 'Revolution, Restoration, and Debt Repudiation: The Jacobite Threat to England's Institutions and Economic Growth', *Journal of Economic History*, 60(2): 418–41.

Whatley, C. A. (1989). 'Economic Causes and Consequences of the Union of 1707: A Survey', *Scottish Historical Review*, 68(2): 150–81.

—— (2000). *Scottish Society 1707–1830: Beyond Jacobitism: Towards Industrialisation*. Manchester: Manchester University Press.

—— (2001). *Bought and Sold for English Gold? Explaining the Union of 1707*, 2nd edn. East Linton: Tuckwell Press.

Wilson, H. (1979). *Final Term: The Labour Government 1974–1976*. London: Weidenfeld and Nicolson and Michael Joseph.

Wilson, R. (1985). 'Imperialism in Crisis: The "Irish Dimension" ', in M. Langan and W. Schwarz (ed.), *Crises in the British State 1880–1930*. London: Hutchinson, 151–78.

Wilson, T. (1989). *Ulster: Conflict and Consent*. Oxford: Blackwell.

Woodham-Smith, C. (1962). *The Great Hunger: Ireland 1845–1849*. London: Hamish Hamilton.

Worcester, R. M., and Gosschalk, B. (1977). MORI Labour Party Research Data, August 1974 [computer file]. Colchester, Essex: UK Data Archive [distributor]. SN: 926.

Wyn Jones, R., and Trystan, D. (1999). 'The 1997 Welsh Referendum Vote', in B. Taylor and K. Thomson (eds.), *Scotland and Wales: Nations Again?* Cardiff: University of Wales Press, 65–93.

Young, H. (1990). *One of Us: A Biography of Margaret Thatcher*, 2nd edn. London: Pan.

Young, J. R. (1999). 'The Parliamentary Incorporating Union of 1707: Political Management, Anti-Unionism and Foreign Policy', in T. M. Devine and J. R. Young (eds.), *Eighteenth Century Scotland: New Perspectives*. Edinburgh: Tuckwell Press.

Ziegler, P. (1993). *Wilson: The Authorised Life of Lord Wilson of Rievaulx*. London: Weidenfeld and Nicolson.

INDEX